AF720332

Luxemburger Juristische Studien –
Luxembourg Legal Studies

edited by

Faculty of Law, Economics and Finance
University of Luxembourg

Volume 19

Allison Östlund

Effectiveness versus Procedural Protection

Tensions triggered by the EU law mandate of *ex officio* review

Nomos

The Deutsche Nationalbibliothek lists this publication in the Deutsche Nationalbibliografie; detailed bibliographic data are available on the Internet at http://dnb.d-nb.de

ISBN 978-3-8487-6004-6 (Print)
978-3-7489-0114-3 (ePDF)

British Library Cataloguing-in-Publication Data
A catalogue record for this book is available from the British Library.

ISBN 978-3-8487-6004-6 (Print)
978-3-7489-0114-3 (ePDF)

Library of Congress Cataloging-in-Publication Data
Östlund, Allison
Effectiveness versus Procedural Protection
Tensions triggered by the EU law mandate of *ex officio* review
Allison Östlund
325 pp.
Includes bibliographic references and index.

ISBN 978-3-8487-6004-6 (Print)
978-3-7489-0114-3 (ePDF)

1st Edition 2019
© Nomos Verlagsgesellschaft, Baden-Baden, Germany 2019. Printed and bound in Germany.

This work is subject to copyright. All rights reserved. No part of this publication may be reproduced or transmitted in any form or by any means, electronic or mechanical, including photocopying, recording, or any information storage or retrieval system, without prior permission in writing from the publishers. Under § 54 of the German Copyright Law where copies are made for other than private use a fee is payable to "Verwertungsgesellschaft Wort", Munich.

No responsibility for loss caused to any individual or organization acting on or refraining from action as a result of the material in this publication can be accepted by Nomos or the author.

Preface by Eleftheria Neframi

This insightful book offers a fresh discourse on the question of judicial protection and the role of the national judge in the legal order of the European Union. At a time when the Member States' obligation to ensure independence of the national judges as element of the rule of law is under constant scrutiny, a thorough and comprehensive inquiry into the contribution of the national judge himself to the standard of judicial protection is welcome and opportune.

In a classic top-down approach national procedural rules, such as those limiting *ex officio* review, which are at the heart of the present work, are seen as limits to the effectiveness of EU law. Given that effective implementation of EU law is tantamount to judicial protection, the national judge, while exercising his European mandate, has the obligation to set aside such national procedural rules. However, this book suggests a bottom-up perspective where national procedural rules are more than a limitation to the effectiveness of EU law and aim at the protection of all litigants, beyond the EU law beneficiaries.

Allison Östlund sets out to provide interesting insights into the balancing exercise between effectiveness of EU law and national procedural rules. The tension between substantive judicial protection through limitation of national procedural autonomy and the national procedural protection standards highlights the essence of the judicial function and a progressive constitutionalisation through the procedural approach to fundamental rights protection in the EU.

Through thorough research and careful analysis of selected case law and literature, this book sheds new light on the interweaving and interaction of national and European legal orders. The author's interdisciplinary background enriches the book with clarity, critical spirit, didactical and profound analysis, and sufficient detail to afford the link between technical questions and overarching horizontal fundamental principles.

It has been a great pleasure to work with Allison Östlund and I am proud to introduce a valuable book for scholars, students and practitioners.

Eleftheria Neframi, Professor of European Law, University of Luxembourg

Preface by Ola Zetterquist

These are exciting times to be part of the judicial family, especially if you like your family gatherings to resemble something like a scene out of "My Big Fat Greek Wedding". Lots of different families and cultures are gathered in one (hopefully) happy community. There are those familiar faces that have been with you ever since you were breast-fed national law in legal kindergarten. Then there are the more recent arrivals. EU law is a member of the legal family that national judges operate within. To many national judges, however, EU law seems to be one of those distant relatives seen only on rare occasions and then with an awkward feeling of unfamiliarity that comes from distance and not quite sharing the same language. The longstanding contact with those other not quite so distant relatives, the European Convention on Human Rights and the European Court of Human Rights, has facilitated the reception of the new family member. However, there are still ample opportunities for clashes over the family-dinner table. National judges of today thus find themselves in a rather new setting and may now and then envy previous generations of judges who needed not bother about exotic new family members and their pesky requirements. As in all big families, adaptation and flexibility are required to keep things running smoothly. Applying both national and European law in everyday work is normally a task that national judges handle both diligently and willingly – all in the service of justice as we know the concept since antiquity and our common forebears. However, some recent developments in EU law have given rise to some deep questions on the role of judges and courts. To some judges this is the legal equivalent of the philosophical soul-searching question of "who am I?". This is the background against which this impressive monograph plays out.

The origin of the recent soul-searching is the approach that the Court of Justice of the European Union (CJEU) has taken on national constraints on *ex officio* review posing obstacles to the enforcement of EU law in national litigation. In particular, the CJEU has focused on national rules preventing judges to apply EU law of their own motion – i.e. limiting their possibilities to investigate elements of law or fact which have not been invoked by the litigants. The purpose of this approach is to promote the effective implementation of EU law, and, by consequence, substantive protection of the rights conferred by EU law. Few judges have sincere objections to the idea of substantive legal protection and effective implementation of laws enacted (effectiveness and protection of rights were indeed the very reasons underlying the notion that EU law was to have direct effect[1]). The problematic issue is that the obligation imposed by the CJEU may seem to be at odds with the idea that most judges have of their office. Judges are the objective arbiters who dispense justice, be it national or European, from above the messy stage of the parties to the case. The notion of a "fair trial" by an "impartial tribunal", which is the very essence of the right contained in art. 6 of the European Convention of Human Rights, implies that judges stay above the scene of the parties and do not themselves become actors on it. The principles of judicial passivity and party disposition in civil law cases exist for good reasons. The effective implementation of Union law therefore risks coming at the expense of procedural equal treatment.

To be fair, the CJEU has never told national judges to ditch the notion of procedural equality but rather to strike a balance that ensures both EU law effectiveness and appropriate standards of procedural protection conferred by both national and European law. This is a formidable judicial task, worthy of Dworkin's famous superjudge Hercules. National judges, slightly ill at ease with the new requirements imposed by the European relatives, may take the gloomy view that they are more likely to fail on both counts – still asking themselves who they really are in the legal family-drama – actors or arbiters. On this complicated issue they are now greatly helped by this important contribution on how to navigate the precarious waters between the right to a fair and impartial trial and the obligation to ensure the effective application of substantive EU law. I am proud and honoured to introduce you to this formidable monograph by my friend and colleague Dr. Allison Östlund.

Ola Zetterquist, Associate Professor of European Law at the University of Gothenburg and Judge at the Court of Appeal for Western Sweden

---

1 Pierre Pescatore, "The Doctrine of 'Direct Effect': An Infant Disease of Community Law?", European Law Review [1983] pp. 155-177.

Thank you!

My deepest appreciation and gratitude are directed to Professor Eleftheria Neframi for having supervised the PhD thesis on which this book is based. Since I first started my research, she has guided me in every step of this process and been a great source of inspiration in her own academic endeavors. Her contributions on legal substance have been invaluable, and her persistent encouragement and optimism have invigorated my enthusiasm and confidence in my research. I am also profoundly grateful to Judge Ola Zetterquist of the Court of Appeal for Western Sweden, who remained available to me throughout the project as co-supervisor and shared his perspectives and experiences from combining legal practice with academic work, stimulating my interest in the role of the national judge in Union law.

My gratitude is also directed to Professors Herwig Hofmann and Johan van der Walt of the University of Luxembourg, whose doors were always open to me and who, any time I entered, offered new perspectives and insights into my research topics. I would like to thank them, together with Judge Sacha Prechal of the Court of Justice of the EU and Professor Morten Broberg of the University of Copenhagen, for coming to Luxembourg to share their observations and expertise.

I would also like to thank my advisors along the way, who have taken the time to read my work at various stages and to help me structure my ideas. Professor Arjen Meij of the University of Luxembourg generously offered his time from the early stages of the project, reading numerous drafts and providing valuable insights that were decisive for the direction that my research would take. Pascal Cardonnel of the Court of Justice invited me to investigate a variety of intriguing legal issues, all of which were luxuriously tailored to my own specific research interests and therefore greatly inspired my original research proposal.

I remain indebted to those of my friends and colleagues who took the time to help me finalize my work by reading and commenting on this manuscript. Zheni Zhekova, Catherine Warin, Clelia Lacchi, Andra Giurgiu, Anna Wallerman, Sebastian Wejedal, André Passet and Lotta Rogosik all set aside time to read my drafts in great detail, increasing the quality of my work (of course, all errors remain mine alone). Likewise, Anthi Beka of the Court of Justice and Jonas Hallberg of the Swedish Board of

Trade continuously shared with me their ideas and gave invaluable feedback. In addition, I thank all my friends from Luxembourg and Sweden who encouraged and inspired me along the way.

Last but foremost, I would like to thank my family, particularly my parents Lauren Lissner-Östlund and Stellan Östlund, for their unfailing love and support.

Table of Contents

Abbreviations

Art(s).	Article(s)
ASA	Association Suisse de l'Arbitrage/Swiss Arbitration Association
Behav. Sci. Law	Behavioral Sciences and the Law
Cah. dr. eur.	Cahiers de droit européen
cf.	compare
CFR	Charter of Fundamental Rights of the European Union, also referred to as the Charter
Ch.	Chapter
CJEU	Court of Justice of the European Union, also referred to as the Court of Justice
C.J.Q.	Civil Justice Quarterly
CLR	California Law Review
CMLR	Common Market Law Review
DCFR	Draft Common Frame of Reference
EC	European Community
ECHR	European Convention for the Protection of Human Rights and Fundamental Freedoms
ECJ	European Court of Justice
ECL	European Constitutional Law Review
ECtHR	European Court of Human Rights
ed(s).	editor(s)
edn.	edition
EEC	European Economic Community
EFTA	European Free Trade Association
EJCL	Electronic Journal of Comparative Law
EJPR	European Journal of Political Research
ELJ	European Law Journal
ELR	European Law Reporter
E.L. Rev.	European Law Review
EN	English
ERA	Europäische Rechtsakademie/Academy of European Law
ERPL	European Review of Public Law
ERT	Europarättslig tidskrift
et seq.	and that which follows
EU	European Union, also referred to as Union
Eur. Procurement & Pub. Private Partnership L. Rev.	European Procurement & Public Private Partnership Law Review

Eur. Rev. Pr. L.	European Review of Private Law
f./ff.	folio/next page(s)/paragraph(s)
fn.	footnote
FR	France/French
FT	Förvaltningsrättslig Tidskrift
Hague J Rule Law	Hague Journal on the Rule of Law
Harv. L. Rev.	Harvard Law Review
ibid.	ibidem, mentioned previously
I•CON	International Journal of Constitutional Law
J.D.E.	Journal de droit européen
J. Int'l Arb.	Journal of International Arbitration
JEPP	Journal of European Public Policy
JILP	NYU (New York University) Journal of International Law and Politics
JT	Juridisk Tidskrift
LIEI	Legal Issues of Economic Integration
Loy. L.A. L. Rev.	Loyola of Los Angeles Law Review
MJECL	Maastricht Journal of European and Comparative Law
NGO	Non-governmental organization
no.	number
OJ	Official Journal of the European Union
p(p).	page(s)
para(s).	paragraph(s)
PEJP	Principle of effective judicial protection
QB	Queen's Bench Division
RAND	The Research and Development Corporation
REALaw	Review of European Administrative Law
Rev. Aff. Eur.	Revue des affaires européennes
sic	sic erat scriptum (EN: thus was it written)
TEU	Treaty on European Union
TFEU	Treaty of the Functioning of the European Union
UK	United Kingdom of Great Britain and Northern Ireland
UNCITRAL	United Nations Commission on International Trade Law Model Law on International Commercial Arbitration
US	United States of America
v./vs.	versus
viz.	namely
YEL	Yearbook of European Law

1 Introduction

Procedural idiosyncrasy is not (like national costume or regional cuisine) to be nurtured for its own sake.[2]

The present work deals with the tension between the effectiveness of the law of the European Union (EU or Union law) and national rules of procedure, especially those affecting application of EU law by national courts of their own motion. Constraints on *ex officio* review[3] of law and facts that have not been invoked by the parties aim to ensure litigants' procedural protection[4] through safeguards such as equality of arms and due process of proceedings. This allows litigants to participate actively in all aspects forming part of the ambit of their dispute, as well as protecting them from judge partiality. On the other hand, a judge's resort to *ex officio* review in and of itself grants an element of procedural protection, by ensuring that applicable law is applied irrespective of the parties' litigating capacities. Although the latter consideration is a procedural measure, taken to compensate for procedural imbalances between parties, it is justified by the overall interest in ensuring that the law is applied correctly, so that the beneficiary

2 Judgment of the Court of Appeal (UK) in *Dresser UK Ltd v. Falcongate Ltd* (1992) QB 502 522 H, CA, per Bingham L.J. On legal/procedural formalism, see C. J. Peters, 'Legal Formalism, Procedural Principles, and Judicial Constraint in American Adjudication', in *General Principles of Law – The Role of the Judiciary*, ed. Pineschi, L. (Switzerland: Springer, 2015), 24.

3 The terms "*ex officio* review" and review of a court's "own motion" are used synonymously to describe the power of a court to take into account aspects of a case before it which have not been invoked by the parties to the proceedings; R. Lauwaars, 'The Application of Community Law by National Courts Ex Officio', *Fordham International Law Journal*, 31 (2007), 1161; F. C. de la Torre, 'Le relevé d'office par la juridiction communautaire', *Cah. dr. eur.*, 41 (2005), 395, 398; Le Masson, Jean-Marc, 'La recherche de la vérité dans le procès civil', *Droit et société*, 38 (1998), 21-32, 29.

4 Procedural protection is here used in the meaning described by Jolowicz as forming part the judicature's prerogative of "procedural justice", emphasizing the rule of the court as an arbitrator rather than a truth-seeker; A. J. Jolowicz, 'Substantive and Procedural Justice in Civil Litigation: A Measure of the Role of Civil Litigation', in *De tous horizons. Mélanges Xavier Blanc-Jouvan*, ed. Fauvarque-Cosson, B. (Paris: Société de législation comparée, 2005).

of substantive law can prevail in the litigation; in other words, in the interest of providing substantive protection.[5]

The present work takes its starting point in tensions that arise when this dynamic is elevated to the Union law level, and examines the pressures resulting from the national judge's additional obligations under Union law. To be sure, the interests of procedural protection and legal certainty endorsed by such procedural safeguards do not have national law as their sole source, but also form part of Union law principles safeguarded through the procedural side of the principle of effective judicial protection.[6] In this way, the priority of procedural protection is layered through oftentimes overlapping – but sometimes diverging – concepts of it originating in Union law.[7] Moreover, the priority of correct application of *substantive* law is multiplied in the layering of applicable legislation, also complicating the national courts' mandate to grant substantive protection by correct application of the law, if necessary of their own motion.

The latter priority is encapsulated in the mandate of ensuring the effectiveness of Union law (to be given context-specific definitions throughout this book). The term effectiveness is accordingly used when referring to protection *through* the national judge's correct application in Union law in

---

5 This concept is based on the more theoretically loaded term "substantive justice" as contrasted against procedural justice. For present purposes, the term "substantive protection" indicates a judge's quest for the "truth", a mandate which is opposed to the notion of adversarialism, but which forms part of the rationale of *ex officio* review. On "truth" versus "justice" as dispute resolution objectives, see J. Thibaut and L. Walker, 'A Theory of Procedure', *CLR*, 66 (1978).

6 Art. 47 CFR establishes that: "Everyone whose rights and freedoms guaranteed by the law of the Union are violated has the right to an effective remedy before a tribunal in compliance with the conditions laid down in this Article. Everyone is entitled to a fair and public hearing within reasonable time by an independent and impartial tribunal previously established by law. Everyone shall have the possibility of being advised, defended and represented. Legal aid shall be made available to those who lack sufficient resources in so far as such aid is necessary to ensure effective access to justice." On the various procedural components forming part of the procedural side of effective judicial protection under Union law, see e.g. F. Wilman, *Private Enforcement of EU Law before National Courts: The EU Legislative Framework* (Northampton: Elgar European Law and Practice, 2015), 41ff. Such aspects include e.g. standard of judicial review, individual standing, time-limits, the rights of defense, equality of arms, and the fundamental access to court.

7 As will later be developed, this description of multiple levels of protection does not suffice to cover the level of complexity, as additional layers are added by procedural requirements deriving from *inter alia* the ECHR.

the litigation before him,[8] whereas the more general term substantive protection is used when referring to the wider endeavor to deliver substantively correct judgments.[9]

In the encounter between Union law and national law, this layering adds additional tensions to an already intricate balancing exercise carried out by the national judge. The context of Union law, supplementing the responsibility for substantively correct judgments with the requirement of correct, full and/or effective application of EU law, has given rise to a variety of new questions, and provided new answers to fundamental issues concerning the co-operation between the Member State and the Union judicature.[10] The present work examines how the mission entrusted to Member State courts, forming part of the EU law judiciary, to collaborate with the Court of Justice of the EU in ensuring the application and interpretation of the Treaties,[11] has been carried out through the dialogue of the preliminary reference procedure. On its side, the Court of Justice carries out its mandate of ensuring the uniform application and interpretation of the Treaties (Art. 19(1) TEU), while at the same time stepping into a sphere of law in which the EU institutions lack competence.

The central material of this study is preliminary rulings delivered by the Court of Justice, in response to questions posed by national courts about how to deal with national rules of procedure that were potentially capable of giving rise to obstacles to the effective enforcement of Union law. The selected cases concern the seized judge's application of national procedural law; primarily provisions precluding *ex officio* review in circumstances where the latter is needed in order to correctly apply Union law. In response to such preliminary references, the Court of Justice has expanded on several fundamental principles for the decentralized enforcement of

8 See P. van Cleynenbreugel, 'Effectiveness through fairness? 'Due process' as an institutional precondition for effective decentralized EU competition law enforcement', in *Procedural Fairness in Competition Proceedings*, eds. Nihoul, P. and T. Skoczny (Northhampton: Elward Elgar, 2015), 69.

9 See, e.g. N. H. Andrews, 'The Passive Court and Legal Argument', *C.J.Q.*, 7 (1988), 125-40, 133.

10 CJEU judgment in *Online Games Handels GmbH*, C-685/15, EU:C:2017:452.

11 See Art. 19(1), sub-para. 2 TEU: "Member States shall provide remedies sufficient to ensure effective legal protection in the fields covered by Union law." See also CJEU Opinion *delivered pursuant to Article 218(11) TFEU*, 1/09, EU:C:2011:123, 69 and CJEU judgment in *Associação Sindical dos Juízes Portugueses v. Tribunal de Contas*, C-64/16, EU:C:2018:117, 33: The national courts, in collaboration with the Court of Justice, "fulfil a duty entrusted to them jointly of ensuring that in the interpretation and application of the Treaties the law is observed."

Union law, including but not limited to the doctrine of full effect, the requirements of effectiveness and equivalence and the principle of effective judicial protection. The interpretations of these principles in the relevant case-law on *ex officio* review have given rise to several new questions (and provided new answers) to fundamental issues concerning the encounter between Member State courts and the Union judicature in the contested area of national procedural autonomy.[12]

The examination of the case-law is informed by an approach based on legal theory of court procedure concerning the fundamental role of the judge according to the procedural tradition in which the latter carries out his function.[13] The issue of *ex officio* review encapsulates ideological choices of key interest in the scholarship on legal theory, including but not limited to the preservation of the objective and subjective legitimacy of the court system,[14] the balancing between elements of adversarial and inquisi-

12 See e.g. M. Bobek, 'Why There is no Principle of 'Procedural Autonomy' of the Member States', in *The European Court of Justice and the Autonomy of the Member States*, eds. de Witte, B. and H. Micklitz (Antwerp: Intersentia, 2012), 305-22.

13 Relying particularly on J. Thibaut and L. Walker (1978); J. A. Jolowicz (2005), 'Da mihi factum dabo tibi jus: A Problem of Demarcation in English and French Law', in *On Civil Procedure*, ed. J. A. Jolowicz (Cambridge: Cambridge University Press, 2000); N. H. Andrews (1988), 125-40; L. L. Fuller, 'The Forms and Limits of Adjudication', *Harv. L. Rev.*, 92 (1978), 353-409.

14 A. Arnull, 'Judicial Activism and the European Court of Justice: How Should Academics Respond?', in *Judicial Activism at the European Court of Justice*, eds. de Witte, B., E. Muir and M. Dawson (Edward Elgar Publishing, 2013), 211-32, 109-11; see also S. Drake, 'More Effective Private Enforcement of EU Law Post-Lisbon: Aligning Regulatory Goals and Constitutional Values', in *New Directions in the Effective Enforcement of EU Law and Policy*, eds. Drake S. and M. Smith (Northampton: Edward Elgar Publishing, 2016), 17-20, referring to constitutional values including judicial protection and procedural safeguards: "In a liberal democratic society, regulatory goals may be promoted by public powers on condition that the constitutional values are also respected. Adherence to these values to the requisite degree ensures that the pursuit of the regulatory goals by society is legitimate" (19).

torial adjudication,[15] the norm of judge passivity,[16] and the responsibility vested in the seized judge for safeguarding wider collective interests, beyond the litigants' legal interests.[17] In view of these stakes, the topic of *ex officio* review as Union law mandate is deserving of the in-depth examination presented here. As observed by Storskrubb, reflecting on the ideological implications of Union-level harmonization of civil procedure:[18]

> procedural regulation embodies social distributive functions in society in that it embodies a social agenda of how we wish to resolve our disputes. Thus, despite their ostensibly technical nature, civil procedural rules too enforce a political choice, which does not necessarily converge across the Union[.]

1.1 Research objectives

Two research objectives have guided the structure of this book. The first objective has been to understand the balancing exercise prescribed by the Court of Justice in order to help the national judge prioritize between Union law effectiveness and national procedural safeguards. As described above, the context of *ex officio* review triggers a tension between effective enforcement of Union law (through rules allowing/requiring *ex officio* review) versus procedural protection (through rules protecting against judge partiality by precluding *ex officio* review). This balancing exercise is foreseen by the first research question: *How is the balance struck between substantive protection (through effective application of EU law) and procedural protection (pursuant to national procedural law) in the Court of Justice's case-law on* ex officio *review?*

---

15 Today, such labels are prototypes of adjudication models that do not exist in their pure form. The term inquisitorialism is thus used in its contemporary meaning of antithesis of adversarialism, as employed in H. S. Shin 'Adversarial and Inquisitorial Procedures in Arbitration', *The RAND Journal of Economics*, 29 (1998), 378-405, whereas the present work focuses on the grey zone characterizing Member State traditions, representing hybrids between the two, yet with an expressed emphasis on adversarialism.

16 N. H. Andrews (1988), 125-40; S. Buhai, 'Access to Justice for Unrepresented Litigants: A Comparative Perspective', *Loy. L.A. L. Rev.*, 42 (2008), 979-1020.

17 J. Engström, 'National Courts' Obligation to Apply Community Law Ex Officio – The Court Showing New Respect for Party Autonomy and National Procedural Autonomy?', *REALaw*, 1 (2008), 67-89, 73.

18 E. Storskrubb, *Civil Procedure and EU Law: A Policy Area Uncovered* (Oxford University Press, 2008), 21.

Producing a consolidated answer to this question is a difficult endeavor, especially in view of the casuistic approach taken by the Court, and its frequent choice to ultimately defer to the national judge. It should be clarified from the outset that answering the question as to how the balance is struck will not entail a comprehensive examination of the case-law, but distill conditions and factors of particular significance towards making a prioritization between the goals at issue. The present work thus approaches its research questions selectively and qualitatively, by using examples and tracing trends.[19]

This study also distinguishes between various beneficiaries of effective judicial protection in and of itself. Tensions between the substantive and procedural side of the principle of effective judicial protection have most often been triggered by the prevalence of divergent beneficiaries, each of which have legitimate claims on protection by national courts, yet from different perspectives. As this issue has evolved rapidly, the perspective was widened beyond the context of *ex officio* review, so as to take into account clarifications recently provided by the Court of Justice. The second research objective is thus to place the arisen issues relating to *ex officio* review into a wider context, by examining the Court of Justice's case-law on effective judicial protection. Since Art. 47 CFR[20] contains both prerogatives of substantive and procedural protection,[21] the issue of balancing Union law effectiveness against procedural protection again arises. The second research question accordingly places the case-law on *ex officio* review in its wider context: *How is the balance struck between substantive and procedural protection in the Court of Justice's case-law on effective judicial protection?*

19 Qualitative analysis refers to a method in which the research materials are studied through in-depth text analysis, taking into account language, purpose and context; see e.g. P. Esaiasson, M. Gilljam, H. Oscarsson, L. Wängnerud, *Metodpraktikan. Konsten att studera samhälle individ och marknad.* 2 edn. (Stockholm: Nordstedts Juridik, 2004), 233ff.

20 Charter of Fundamental Rights of the European Union (Consolidated version), OJ C 202, 7/6/2016, 389.

21 On the various procedural components forming part of effective judicial protection under Union law, see e.g. F. Wilman (2015), 41-44.

1.2 Delimitations and structure

A delimitation to court rules concerning *ex officio* review is warranted by the above-described ideological implications for adjudication models.[22] The focus on the role of national judges also entails a delimitation to *ex officio* review in the context of *judicial* proceedings, whereas the procedures of administrative bodies largely fall outside the scope of the study. Although the issue of public authorities' application of EU law of their own motion is a mechanism of enforcement worthy of consideration, it is not as controversial from the perspective of procedural theory and ideology. Likewise, rules relating to the ambit of the proceedings before the EU courts are of comparative interest, alas representing too wide a topic to integrate in this work (aside from occasional references to the Rules of Procedure of the Court of Justice).[23] These delimitations are carried on into Chapters 4-5, where the notion of procedural protection is, as well, approached from the vantage point of judicial protection granted by national courts.

Finally, the notion of "full effect" following the *Simmenthal* ruling[24] is primarily examined in terms of its consequences for national courts' constitutional mandate of review and for the effectiveness of the preliminary reference procedure. For this reason, the tangating matter of state liability[25] is not elaborated.

---

22 There exist other procedural mechanisms whose encounter with EU law trigger some of the same issues, particularly the principle of *res judicata*. However, a narrower focus is chosen to lay the ground for a deeper analysis, reserving discussion on the related line of case-law on *res judicata* to situations in which the issues converge.

23 On this topic, see F. C. de la Torre (2005); A. Meij, 'The Rules of the Game. Party Autonomy in the EU Courts', in *De Regels en het Spel, Opstellen over Recht, Filosofie, Literatuur en Geschiedenis aangeboden aan Tom Eijsbouts*, eds. Reestman, J-H., A. Schrauwen, M. van Montfrans and J.H. Jans (The Hague: Asser, 2011); B. Vesterdorf, 'Le relevé d'office par le juge communautaire' in *Une Communauté de Droit. Festschrift für Gil Carlos Rodríquez Iglesias*, eds. Colneric, N., D. Edward, J.-P. Puissochet and D. Ruiz-Jarabo Colomer (Berlin: Berliner Wissenschafts-Verlag, 2003); F. Clausen, 'Les moyens d'ordre public dans le contentieux relevant de la Cour de justice de l'Union europée ne' (Université Paris 2, 2017); R. Barents, 'EU Procedural Law and Effective Legal Protection', *CMLR*, 51 (2014), 1462.

24 CJEU judgment in *Amministrazione delle finanze dello Stato v. Simmenthal*, 106/77, EU:C:1978:49.

25 CJEU judgment in *Francovich and Bonifaci v. Italy*, joined cases C-6/90 and C-9/90, EU:C:1991:428; CJEU judgment in *Brasserie du Pêcheur v. Bundesrepublik Deutschland and The Queen / Secretary of State for Transport, ex parte Factortame and Others*,

The book is structured in six chapters. Chapter 2, following the present chapter, sets the scene for the context of national procedural autonomy by defining fundamental concepts, including general principles of EU law, that instruct national courts in their dealings with national rules of procedure. The purpose of the chapter is to introduce basic tools and describe their evolution in view of dealing with procedural obstacles (in a wide sense) – particularly the following aspects: national procedural and institutional autonomy as follow from the principle of conferral,[26] the doctrine of "full effect" (the *Simmenthal* mandate[27]), the *Rewe* principles of equivalence and effectiveness,[28] the procedural "rule-of-reason",[29] and the principle of effective judicial protection.

Chapter 2 provides definitions and context for the subsequent chapters, whereas the issue of effectiveness of EU law versus national procedural safeguards is inherent to areas of national procedural and institutional autonomy[30] and therefore transpires throughout this work. Chapter 2 is limited to the general case-law on procedural obstacles to EU law effectiveness, and addresses only at an introductory level the case-law expanded on in Chapters 3-5. Here, central points of contention are explained and observations are made based on the general case-law and its commentary in the scholarship, whereas the research questions are only preliminarily addressed.

Subsequent Chapter 3 starts with an overview of the underlying imperatives governing political choices at the basis of various models of adjudication. A starting point is taken in theory on court procedure, in order to substantiate the discussion about the ideological conflicts at stake in bal-

---

joined cases C-46/93 and C-48/93, EU:C:1996:79; CJEU judgment in *Gerhard Köbler v. Republik Österreich*, C-224/01, EU:C:2003:513.

26 Also referred to as the principle of attributed powers/competences.

27 CJEU judgment in *Amministrazione delle finanze dello Stato v. Simmenthal*, 106/77, EU:C:1978:49.

28 CJEU judgment in *Rewe v. Landwirtschaftskammer für das Saarland*, 33/76, EU:C:1976:188.

29 CJEU judgment in *van Schijndel v. Stichting Pensioenfonds voor Fysiotherapeuten*, joined cases C-430/93 and C-431/93, EU:C:1995:441; CJEU judgment in *Peterbroeck, Van Campenhout & Cie v. Belgian State*, C-312/93, EU:C:1995:437.

30 Procedural autonomy indicates the competence of the Member States to lay down the rules of procedure applicable to EU law matters before national courts and authorities; institutional autonomy indicates the Member States' competence to decide on courts' authority and jurisdiction to deal with matters of EU law; M. Accetto and S. Zleptnig, 'The Principle of Effectiveness: Rethinking Its Role in Community Law', *European Public Law*, 11 (2005), 394-95.

ancing substantive against procedural protection.[31] Chapter 3 next systematizes the Court of Justice's case-law on *ex officio* review, emphasizing the following circumstances of significance to the described balancing exercise: The legal basis for obligations imposed on the referring court, the seized judge's pre-existing power to expand the ambit of the dispute of his own motion, the availability of justifications for national rules restricting *ex officio* review, the consequences of procedural omissions by the beneficiary party, and the importance of the relevant rule in view of the collective benefits of its enforcement or, where relevant, in view of its public policy status. A strand of consumer protection case-law is next reviewed, accounting for the latter's legislative context which places the division of competence on procedural regulation in a distinctive light. The chapter concludes by addressing more generally the first research question,[32] identifying key factors that tilt the balance between effectiveness of EU law and procedural protection.

Chapter 4 employs the notion of *beneficiaries* of Union rules and rights so as to unlock certain particularly problematic issues in the prioritization between Union law effectiveness and individual procedural protection. Emphasis is placed on certain key parameters governing the EU mandate of *ex officio* review, rationalizing choices by recourse to the beneficiaries of effectiveness and effective judicial protection. Explanations linked to expenses for litigation are examined, the "right" to affordable litigation costs is contemplated as forming part of the test of effective judicial protection, account is taken of legal sources bolstering protective prerogatives, and the reasons for and against overlooking procedural omissions by beneficiaries of Union law are reviewed.

Chapter 5 addresses the second research question[33] against this backdrop. A range of instances are contemplated in which there were divergent beneficiaries of a) effective judicial protection on the one hand and effectiveness on the other hand, and b) the substantive versus procedural prerogatives of effective judicial protection in and of itself.[34] It could be objected that the relationship between effectiveness of substantive EU law

31 I.e. between substantive and procedural justice, see A. J. Jolowicz, (2005) or adversarial versus inquisitorial mandates, see H. S. Shin (1998), 378-405.

32 *How is the balance struck between substantive and procedural protection in the case-law on* ex officio *review?*

33 *How is the balance struck between substantive and procedural protection in the Court of Justice's case-law on effective judicial protection?*

34 As contained in the different components of Art. 47 CFR, but also derived from additional sources, including EU secondary law, international and national law.

and effective judicial protection is not inherently characterized by conflict.[35] Chapter 5 nonetheless focuses on situations of divergence, as such cases elucidate the fundamental tension at the heart of the present work. Therefore, a purposive selection of cases has been made, which does not give rise to generalizations but permits an analysis based on examples from the outer flanks.[36] Biases arising from such a selection are avoided by the way in which it is analyzed: not to support a hypothesis of tension, but to understand how such tensions, where present, are resolved.

Chapter 6 concludes by proposing an overall interpretation on factors and circumstances tilting the balance between Union law effectiveness and procedural protection, both with respect to the *ex officio* mandate and to the contemporary outlook of the right to effective judicial protection. The resulting representation of divergent beneficiaries is systematized along the following lines: To the extent that the substantive side of the principle of effective judicial protection is given priority over its procedural side, this will have the effect of limiting the protective scope of the principle to the beneficiaries of EU substantive law.[37] To the extent that the procedural side of the principle of effective judicial protection is prioritized in the case-law, this may be understood as extending its protective scope to any litigant hoping for a proper conduct of proceedings.[38]

---

35 A view based on convergence, rather than opposition, is e.g. taken by H. C.H. Hofmann, 'Effective Judicial Remedies Before the National Courts', in *The EU Charter of Fundamental Rights*, eds. Ward, A., S. Peers, T. Harvey and J. Kenner, (Oxford: Hart Publishing, 2014). See also S. Prechal 'Between Effectiveness, Procedural Autonomy and Judicial Protection', in *Challenges of Law in Life Reality, Liber Amicorum Marko Ilešič*, eds. Arabadjiev, A., M. Pavliha, M. Ilešič, A. Polajnar-Pavčnik and B. Koritnik (Ljublana: Pravna faculteta Univerze v Ljubljani, 2017 a), 399-400: "the inclusion of provisions on judicial protection in secondary law goes hand in glove with the tendency to strengthen the application and enforcement of Union law, the 'substantive effectiveness' of EU law".

36 The analysis does not seek to test a hypothesis or theoretical proposition, but instead examines materials widely in search of patterns and explanatory observations. An overarching theory forming part of the research findings can therefore ultimately only take form during and after carrying out the analysis; C. Hay, *Political Analysis. A Critical Introduction* (Hampshire: Palgrave, 2002), 29-33.

37 Including quasi-substantive rules and rights, i.e. in which effective judicial protection represents the chief objective of substantive legislative measures.

38 The present simplification does not account for relevant additional sources giving substance to the principle of effective judicial protection. Such differentiation will nevertheless be made in Chapters 4-5.

2 Principles and concepts delimiting the field of national procedural autonomy

The present chapter focuses on the legal sphere of national procedural and institutional autonomy, in which the power of Member States to regulate procedural rules governing *inter alia* sanctions,[39] competences, jurisdiction and remedies[40] is influenced by their obligations under EU law. The chapter primarily examines the demands developed in the case-law of the Court of Justice on effective enforcement or implementation[41] of other (mainly

39 The term "sanction" refers to "instruments of legal coercion that, in every Member State, guarantee the respect for the law [...]"; J.M. de Wilmars, 'L'efficacité des différentes techniques nationales de protection juridique contre les violations du droit communautaire par les autorités nationales et les particuliers', *Cah. dr. eur.* (1981), 390ff.

40 The notion of remedies is a multifaceted term, subject to various interpretations in different legal traditions. For the present purposes, remedies are understood as courts' means of enforcement of individual rights – in the EU law context, the mechanisms through which courts can safeguard Union rights through prescribing legal measures or consequences. As defined by the Court of Justice in an early ruling, CJEU judgment in *Jean-E. Humblet v. Belgian State*, 6/60, EU:C:1960:48, pp. 571-72: "it may generally be presumed that a substantive right has as its corollary that it provides the person in whose interest it operates with the means of enforcing it himself by proceedings before the courts". In practice, this entails two elements: firstly, to have standing, and secondly, to be able to obtain something. This follows from Wennerås' definition of remedial rules, allowing individuals legal means to seek their enforcement by governing "the conditions and restrictions, under which individuals are enabled to bring and maintain actions before courts of law"; P. Wennerås, *The Enforcement of EC Environmental Law* (New York: Oxford University Press, 2007), 76-77.

41 Because this book focuses on the judicial side of implementation of EU law, it is appropriate to sometimes use the term "enforcement" interchangeably with implementation, when emphasizing the role of the national judge in implementation through enforcement against one litigating party. The Court of Justice's seminal stance in *van Gend en Loos v. Administratie der Belastingen*, 26/62, EU:C:1963:1 gives a description of the implementation role of courts, that corresponds to the here chosen definition: "The vigilance of individuals concerned to protect their rights amounts to an effective supervision in addition to the supervision entrusted by Articles [258] and [259] to the diligence of the Commission and of the Member States" (p. 13). To be sure, the term "enforcement" is used in a wider sense than the more common practice of referring to sanctions against breaches

substantive) principles of EU law, entailing a balancing exercise between competences of the Member States versus the EU in the contentious field of procedural law.

This chapter is divided into three sections – the first section introducing and defining fundamental concepts, the second discussing the extent to which procedural competence can be said to remain with the Member States, and the third explaining the development of the principle of effectiveness into a quasi-autonomous principle of effective judicial protection.

Section 2.1 defines concepts essential to understanding European requirements on national rules applicable to Union litigation – namely the notions of procedural and institutional autonomy, the distinction between substantive and procedural rules, and the distinction between direct and indirect collision of norms.

Section 2.2 deals with the principle of conferral as foundation for the existence of any "autonomy" in domains of reserved Member State competence.[42] The section examines various potential legal bases for EU competence in the field of procedural law, as well as rules that the Court of Justice has developed to harness the remaining autonomy left to the Member States.

Among such rules are the duty of sincere co-operation, the principles of effectiveness and equivalence, and the requirement of effective judicial protection. Section 2.3 describes the evolution of the principle of effectiveness, on the one hand, and the principle of effective judicial protection, on the other. While there may be legitimacy to limiting procedural autonomy, in order to ensure the effective enforcement of EU law, there is also a rationale for relaxing the requirements on Member States' courts to co-operate, in order to ensure the judicial protection of individuals. National courts consequently have a clear mandate to act as simultaneous protectors of the common Union interest in substantive legal integration and as guardians of individual procedural rights.

---

of Union law, as in e.g. CJEU judgment in *Commission v. Greece (Greek Maize)*, 68/88, EU:C:1989:339.

42 P. van Cleynenbreugel, 'Judge-Made Standards of National Procedure in the Post-Lisbon Constitutional Framework', *E.L. Rev.*, 12 (2012 a).

2.1 Introductory distinctions and definitions of Member State autonomy

From the outset, it is important to define key concepts for the decentralized enforcement of EU law. The definition of national procedural autonomy that will be provided in section 2.1.1 hinges on a few other notions. National procedural autonomy is, to begin with, to be distinguished from the concept of national institutional autonomy (2.1.2). The former indicates the competence of the Member States, within certain limits, to lay down *rules of procedure* applicable to EU law matters before national courts and authorities; the latter indicates the Member States' competence under the same circumstances to decide on courts' *authority and jurisdiction* to deal with matters of EU law.[43]

The scope of national procedural autonomy pertains to the area of procedural law. Yet, it is only impacted by Union law to the extent that its functionality affects the exercise or enforcement of norms of substantive Union law.[44] Section 2.1.3 accordingly treats the relationship between material norms, belonging to "substantive law" on the one hand, and procedural, institutional and remedial rules, belonging to "procedural law" on the other.

2.1.1 Legal foundations of the principle of national procedural autonomy

The principle of national procedural autonomy describes a freedom of choice for Member States in deciding on the procedural conditions involved in the resolution of matters of EU law by their courts and authorities.[45] This is, in turn, based on the assumption that the national procedural framework is "sufficient and adequate for granting the enforcement of EU law and protection of rights conferred on individuals."[46] In the early case-law of the Court of Justice, national procedural autonomy implied that "national legal systems should determine the procedural conditions

43 M. Accetto and S. Zleptnig (2005), 394-97.

44 A. Wallerman, *Om fakultativa regler. En studie av svensk och unionsrättslig reglering av skönsmässigt beslutsfattande i processrättsliga frågor* (Uppsala: Iustus förlag, 2015), 91.

45 D.-U. Galetta, 'The Jurisprudence of the European Court of Justice on the Procedural Autonomy of EU Member States', *Ius Publicum Network Review* (2011), 9.

46 L. M. Ravo, 'The Role of the Principle of Effective Judicial Protection in the EU and its Impact on National Jurisdictions', *Sources of Law and Legal Protection*, Triestine Lecture (2012), 108.

governing actions and remedies intended to grant legal protection of the interests of a person adversely affected by an infringement of EU law".[47] Or, as worded more simply by Advocate General Maduro: "national courts, when they apply Community law, may do so pursuant to their own procedural rules".[48]

Depending on the lens through which we regard it, national procedural autonomy can be deemed an expression of Member States' sovereignty, or a retained competence to be exercised in the decentralized application of EU law, enjoyed insofar as EU procedural rules have not yet been adopted.[49] Based on the possible approaches to defining autonomy, the issue invites a fundamental theoretical query on the nature of the principle. In the latter light (i.e. retained competences), national procedural autonomy can be seen not as emanating from Member States' sovereignty, but rather a principle whose function is subordinate, serving the purpose of ensuring the application of substantive EU law.[50]

Still, in the context of decentralized enforcement of EU law,[51] the exercise of procedural competence belongs to the Member States' side of judicial co-operation between national courts and the Court of Justice in ensuring not only effective enforcement of EU law,[52] but also the safeguarding of common values and a judicial implementation based on mutual

47 CJEU judgment in *Rewe v. Landwirtschaftskammer für das Saarland*, 33/76, EU:C:1976:188. See also L. M. Ravo, (2012), 109.

48 Opinion of Advocate General Maduro in *van der Weerd and Others v. Minister van Landbouw, Natuur en Voedselkwaliteit*, joined cases C-222/05 to C-225/05, EU:C:2007:124, 13.

49 S. Prechal and K. Cath, 'The European Acquis of Civil Procedure: Constitutional Aspects', *Uniform Law Review – Revue de droit uniforme*, 19 (2014), 180.

50 C. Kakouris, 'Do the Member States Possess Judicial Procedural "Autonomy"?', *CMLR*, 34 (1997), 1390. It has further been suggested that procedural autonomy should ultimately be finally as procedural competence of the Member States; W. van Gerven, 'Of Rights, Remedies and Procedures', *CMLR*, 37 (2000), 502; A. Beka, *The Active Role of Courts in Consumer Litigation. Applying EU Law of the National Courts' Own Motion* (Cambridge: Intersentia, 2018), 24-25.

51 See M. Eliantonio, 'The Future of National Procedural Law in Europe: Harmonisation vs. Judge-Made Standards in the Field of Administrative Justice', *EJCL* (2009), 1; M. Dougan, *National Remedies before the Court of Justice: Issues of Harmonisation and Differentiation* (Oxford: Hart, 2004), 1-4; B. Dubey, 'Administration indirecte et federalisme d'execution en Europe', *Cah. dr. eur.*, 39 (2003), 87-134.

52 V. Skouris, 'The Principle of Procedural Autonomy and the Duty of Loyal Cooperation of National Judges under Article 10 EC', in *Tom Bingham and the Transformation of the Law: A Liber Amicorum*, eds. Andenæs, M.T., D. Fairgrieve, B.

trust.[53] This division of labor is foreseen in Art. 19(1) TEU, via the specification introduced through Lisbon that it is the Court of Justice's task to "ensure that in the interpretation and application of the Treaties the law is observed", whereas it is the obligation of the Member States to "provide remedies sufficient to ensure effective legal protection in the fields covered by Union law."[54]

The effectiveness of Union law is, at this decentralized level of enforcement, contingent upon the framework laid down in the national legislation (whereas, by contrast, the provision of substantive Union rights are a matter for primary or secondary Union legislation).[55] This is "based on the assumption that national remedies and procedures were basically sufficient and adequate for granting the enforcement of EU law and the protection of rights conferred upon individuals."[56] As the Court of Justice has emphasized on several occasions, this is the case in the absence of Union legislation explicitly governing Member State procedure.[57] In practice, it is up to the national legislator to provide a framework that makes it possible for the national judge to correctly exercise this mandate. Art. 19(1) TEU is thus an extension of the procedural side of the duty of sincere co-operation, enshrined in Art. 4(3) TEU, to take all necessary measures to ensure

---

Markesinis, E. McKendrick and S. B. A. Rix (Oxford: Oxford University Press, 2009), 494-95; H.-W. Micklitz and B. de Witte, *The European Court of Justice and the Autonomy of the Member States* (Cambridge: Intersentia, 2012), 283.

53 CJEU judgment in *Associação Sindical dos Juízes Portugueses v. Tribunal de Contas*, C-64/16, EU:C:2018:117, 30-32; CJEU judgment in *Slowakische Republik v. Achmea BV*, C-284/16, EU:C:2018:158, 34; CJEU judgment in *Bashar Ibrahim*, joined cases C-297/17, C-318/17, C-319/17 and C-438/17, EU:C:2019:219, 83.

54 Art. 19(1) TEU. On the division of labor, see e.g. E. F. Hinton, 'Strengthening the Effectiveness of Community Law: Direct Effect, Article 5 EC, and the European Court of Justice', *JILP*, 31 (1998), 311; A. M. van den Bossche, 'Private Enforcement, Procedural Autonomy and Article 19(1) TEU: Two's Company, Three's a Crowd', *YEL*, 33 (2014), 46ff.; A. Gerbrandy, 'The Dual Identity of National Judges in the EU and the Implausibility of Uniform and Effective Application of European Law throughout the European Union', *REALaw*, 7 (2014), 38.

55 V. Skouris (2009), 493; M. Claes, *The National Courts' Mandate in the European Constitution* (Oregon: Hart Publishing, 2006), 120-21.

56 L. M. Ravo (2012), 109.

57 CJEU judgment in *Rewe v. Landwirtschaftskammer für das Saarland*, 33/76, EU:C:1976:188, 5; CJEU judgment in *Comet BV v. Produktschap voor Siergewassen*, 45/76, EU:C:1976:191, 13.

that Union objectives and values are promoted by the national judge.[58] Where the applicability or scope of Union rights is in the hands of the national judge, the latter is expected to use the powers available to him to cooperate in the pursuit of Union objectives, if necessary requesting the assistance of the Court of Justice by way of a preliminary reference.[59]

A crucial reason for leaving the procedural conditions of EU law enforcement to the Member States lies in the principle of subsidiarity:[60] competences are to be exercised at the national or regional level, as far as this is sufficient and appropriate.[61] Although the most traditional use of the principle of subsidiarity is in the legislative context,[62] once legislation has been enacted at the Union level, the question arises as to its execution or imple-

---

58 See Neframi, Eleftheria, 'Quelques réflexions sur l'article 19, paragraphe 1, alinéa 2, TUE et l'obligation de l'Etat membre d'assurer la protection juridictionnelle effective', in *La Constitution, l'Europe et le droit, Mélanges en l'honneur de Jean-Claude Masclet*, ed. Boutayeb, C. (Paris: Publications de la Sorbonne, 2013), 806, in which, to this aspect, is added developments of the consequences of Art. 19(1) TEU in relationship to the principle of effectiveness, the principle of procedural autonomy and the duty of loyalty and Art. 47 CFR.

59 CJEU judgment in *Slowakische Republik v. Achmea BV*, C-284/16, EU:C:2018:158, 34-37. See also (anteceding *Achmea*) P. Pescatore, 'Court of Justice of the European Communities. References for preliminary rulings under Article 177 of the EEC Treaty and cooperation between the Court and national courts' (Luxembourg: Office for Official Publications of the European Communities, 1986), 10-13.

60 Art. 5(3) TEU. The principle is applicable in areas where the Members States and the EU share competences and is clarified in Protocol (No 2) of the Treaty on the Functioning of the European Union (Consolidated version), on application of the principles of subsidiarity and proportionality, OJ C 115, 9/5/2008, 206. The latter expressly applies only to preparatory legislative acts; H. C.H. Hofmann, G. Rowe and A. Türk, *Administrative Law and Policy of the European Union* (Oxford: Oxford University Press, 2011), 125-29.

61 See also V. Skouris (2009), 494; M. Accetto and S. Zleptnig (2005), 394; A. Arnull, 'The Principle of Effective Judicial Protection in EU law: An Unruly Horse?', *E.L. Rev.*, 36 (2011), 52; E. F. Hinton (1998), 311-12.

62 European Parliament, 'The Principle of Subsidiarity', Fact Sheets on the European Union – 2017 (10/2016). The subsidiarity test is contained in Art. 5(3) TEU: "the Union shall act only if and in so far as the objectives of the proposed action cannot be sufficiently achieved by the Member States, either at central level or at regional and local level, but can rather, by reason of the scale or effects of the proposed action, be better achieved at Union level", and as Hofmann notes, the test "is not without difficulties in application"; H. C.H. Hofmann (2011), 127. O. Dubos in 'The Origins of the Proceduralisation of EU Law: A Grey Area of European Federalism', *REALaw*, 8 (2015 b) further argues that procedural harmonization would run contrary to the subsidiarity test.

mentation. It has been argued that in many cases it is in fact appropriate that the execution of Union legislation be carried out at Member State level – this is indeed at the core of the principle of decentralized enforcement/implementation of Union law.[63] As a result, as soon as Member State competence of decentralized enforcement exists in reference to a given legislation, it is natural that litigation and other proceedings ensuing from the decentralized implementation of this legislation take place before Member State authorities or courts. In this event, national authorities and courts hold the necessary knowledge, both of the national context for the Union rules at stake, and of the rules of procedure governing their own dealings with matters before them. Therefore, the same way as the principle of subsidiarity instructs decentralized enforcement by Member States, it justifies the exercise of procedural autonomy in the context of Union litigation before national courts.[64]

The principle of procedural autonomy is more frequently, however, derived from the principle of attributed powers, requiring a Treaty basis for any assumption of EU competence.[65] As has been noted by many scholars, there is no general empowerment allowing the Union to lay down procedural rules applicable to Member States' procedures.[66] This means that general and binding procedural harmonization via legislation is precluded, whereas it is possible that procedural rules be laid down for the purpose of particular legislative fields of Union law, as has already been done in many instances.[67] One point of view is that only where Union procedural legislation is absent can national procedural autonomy be said to exist – which would define procedural autonomy as prevailing only residually to sector-specific procedural Union rules.[68] This is one of the most widely accepted interpretations of national procedural autonomy, defined by the Court of Justice in its *Rewe* judgment: In the absence of Union rules governing the

---

63 B. Dubey (2003).

64 On the principle of subsidiarity as basis for Member State competence of decentralized enforcement, see ibid., 97-99. Art. 291 TFEU allows for the adoption of Union acts when measures at the decentralized level are insufficient, while Art. 197 TFEU emphasizes the responsibility of the Member States to ensure the effective implementation of Union law. This is justified by the need for coordination between Member States and uniform conditions for implementation of Union law; A. Beka (2018), 19-20.

65 B. Dubey (2003), 101.

66 Cf. M. Eliantonio (2009), 3; D.-U. (2010), 10; O. Dubos (2015 b), 7.

67 M. Eliantonio (2009), 3; O. Dubos (2015 b), 7.

68 For a critical discussion on the concept of residual or ancillary competence on procedural law, see C. Kakouris (1997), 1396 and E. Storskrubb, (2008), 19.

matter, it is for the domestic legal systems to designate the courts and tribunals having jurisdiction and to lay down procedural rules for safeguarding rights, which individuals derive from Union law.[69] In other words, irrespective of EU competences to regulate aspects of Member State procedures, *de facto* lack of existing Union legislation leaves room for Member States' procedural law to apply.

It has thus far been discussed where national procedural autonomy comes from, but not so much what it is. As indicated above, procedural autonomy gives Member States a freedom or discretion in deciding on the procedural framework, allowing national courts (and administrative authorities[70]) to treat cases involving application of Union law according to the same rules as wholly internal situations. The use of the word "autonomy" is, however, problematic, or taking into account the strict meaning of the term, confusing at best: "the ability to act and make decisions without being controlled by anyone else".[71] Autonomy, on its face, thus indicates the lack of limitations to a freedom or discretion. By contrast, any useful conceptualization of the term national procedural autonomy must, in the EU law context, also take into account its limits.[72] In the face of such limits (which indeed turn out to be rather far-reaching) it has been argued that national procedural autonomy in effect does not exist, or at least does not imply any *de facto* autonomy for the Member States.[73]

---

69 CJEU judgment in *Rewe v. Landwirtschaftskammer für das Saarland*, 33/76, EU:C:1976:188, 5; see also C. Kakouris (1997), 1395-96.

70 CJEU judgment in *Fratelli Costanzo v. Comune di Milano*, 103/88, EU:C:1989:256, 30-31; CJEU judgment in *Ciola*, C-224/97, EU:C:1999:212, 26, 30; CJEU judgment in *Trustees of the BT Pension Scheme*, C-628/15, EU:C:2017:687, 54. See also J.T. Lang, 'The Duties of National Authorities under Community Constitutional Law', *E.L. Rev.*, 23 (1998), 110; M. Accetto and S. Zleptnig (2005), 398; S. Prechal (2017 a), 391.

71 M. Bobek (2012), 320. See also critical discussion in S. Prechal and K. Cath (2014), 180-81; P. van Cleynenbreugel, (2012 a), 91; J-U. Franck, 'Rights, remedies and effective enforcement in air transportation: *Ruijsenaars*. Joined Cases C-145/15 and C-146/15, *K. Ruijssenaars and Others v. Staatssecretaris van Infrastructuur en Milieu*, Judgment of the Court (Eighth Chamber) of 17 March 2016, EU:C:2016:187', *CMLR*, 54 (2017), 1875; A. Wallerman, 'Manoeuvering Procedural Autonomy in Sweden: Is *Materielle Prozessleitung* the Answer?', in *Procedural autonomy: Room for Manoeuvre,* eds. Nylund, A., B. Krans (Intersentia, forthcoming 2019).

72 D.-U. Galetta, *Procedural Autonomy of EU Member States: Paradise Lost? A Study on the "Functionalized Procedural Competence" of EU Member States* (Heidelberg: Springer, 2010).

73 See e.g. M. Bobek (2012); C. Kakouris (1997), 1411.

In line with this, a definition of national procedural autonomy as "an 'autonomous' choice of the means aimed at guaranteeing the effectiveness of EU law" has been proposed.[74] Procedural autonomy thus allows Member States to design procedural law as they wish, but this must be done for the purpose, or at least in the spirit, of ensuring that the said rules do not stand in the way of effective enforcement of Union law. Similarly, the principle of procedural autonomy has been described as indicating that, aside from the basic principles of direct effect and primacy, "the remaining questions must be answered on the basis of national law".[75] The latter has been referred to as "second generation" Union law.[76]

When identifying "first generation" versus "second generation" Union law, it is appropriate to ask whether the legal basis for the exercise of public authority can be traced back to Union or to national legislation. There is a fundamental need to address this question; following a distinct line of reasoning, in cases where the legal basis can be traced back to Union law, national courts are merely "utilized" for the purposes of enforcing Union law within a field of EU competence.[77] That means that they share jurisdiction over the matter with the Court of Justice, and also that certain requirements can be imposed on them for the purpose of guaranteeing the said enforcement.[78]

Ascribing the procedural settings to the decentralized enforcement of Union law thus has two sides: the freedom that it implies and the restrictions by which it is circumscribed.[79] On the one hand, national rules of procedure are applied more or less equally to contexts inside and outside the scope of Union law. If national competence over remedies is taken as

74 D.-U. Galetta (2011), 12, relying on CJEU judgment in *SpA Salgoil v. Italian Ministry of Foreign Trade*, 13/68, EU:C:1968:54; CJEU judgment in *Firma Gebrüder Lück v. Hauptzollamt Köln-Rheinau*, 34/67, EU:C:1968:24.

75 M. Claes (2006), 119ff.

76 The terms were first coined by J.M. de Wilmars (1981), 379; recalled in M. Claes (2006), 119.

77 This has been advanced, for instance, by C. Kakouris (1997), 1391-94. See also A.M. Burley and W. Mattli, 'Europe before the Court: A Political Theory of Legal Integration', *International Organization*, 47 (1993), 41-76; S. Drake (2016), 15; and J. Dederke and D. Naurin, 'Friends of the Court? Why EU governments file observations before the Court of Justice', *EJPR* (2017), 12.

78 C. Kakouris (1997), 1392-93; A. Rosas, 'The National Judge as EU Judge: Opinion 1/09', in *Constitutionalising the EU Judicial System. Essays in Honour of Pernilla Lindh*, eds. Cardonnel, P., A. Rosas and N. Wahl (Oxford: Hart Publishing, 2012), 105-21.

79 A. M. van den Bossche (2014), 55-56.

starting point, then the character of this competence is an ability to decide on the "modalities under which Treaty rights are exercised."[80] Procedural autonomy allows the national judges seized with matters of Union law to proceed more or less "as usual".

On the other hand, national courts must make use of available remedies in an appropriate manner to give effect to Union law. National judges' targeted use of their powers was prescribed in Advocate General Warner's *Rewe* Opinion, a cautious precursor to what would successively become the requirement of "useful effect":[81]

> Where Community law confines itself to forbidding this or that kind of act on the part of a Member State and to saying that private persons are entitled to rely on the prohibition in their national Courts, without prescribing the remedies or procedures available to them for that purpose, there is really no alternative to the application of the remedies and procedures prescribed by national law. [...] I see it as a situation in which Community law and national law operate in combination, the latter taking over where the former leaves off, and working out its consequences.[82]

The possibility of protecting and enforcing Union rights is hence constrained by the conditions of the national procedural law environment, which may in certain cases mean that the said rights cannot always be fully protected. Union law typically lays down substantive obligations of result, whereas the Member States are left at their own devices as to the means used to achieve the end.[83] A national court can very well rely on the Court of Justice for guidance on both substance and procedure, but is left to find its own route when ruling conclusively in the case before it.[84]

---

80 M. Dougan (2004), 18.

81 Opinion of Advocate General Warner in *Rewe v. Landwirtschaftskammer für das Saarland*, 33/76, EU:C:1976:167, 2002. "Useful effect" is for the present purposes used when referring to *"effet utile."* Although the difference is not conceptually clear-cut, where appropriate, the term "full effect(iveness)" is used when referring to *"plein effet"*. See further U. Šadl 'The Role of Effet Utile in Preserving the Continuity and Authority of European Union Law: Evidence from the Citation Web of the Pre-Accession Case Law of the Court of Justice of the EU', *European Journal of Legal Studies*, 8 (2015), 24-25.

82 Opinion of Advocate General Warner in *Rewe v. Landwirtschaftskammer für das Saarland*, 33/76, EU:C:1976:167, 2003.

83 On the obligation of comportment as corollary to obligation of result under the duty of loyalty, see E. Neframi, 'L'État membre au service de l'Union', *Annuaire de droit européen 2004* (2006), 52.

84 On the obligation of result in attaining Union objectives through judicial co-operation with the Court of Justice, see E. Neframi, 'La rôle du juge national dans le

2.1.2 National institutional autonomy

The decentralized enforcement of Union law prescribes that Member States retain a certain freedom in granting jurisdiction and competence to courts and authorities that appropriately empowers them to apply Union law.[85] The freedom that this implies has prompted the observation that institutional autonomy "represents reality", in contrast to procedural autonomy, which "does not exist".[86] The present section accordingly distinguishes between national procedural autonomy and institutional autonomy, both of which the Court touched upon in *Rewe* and *Comet*.[87]

This sphere of national institutional autonomy involves not only the choice of public bodies competent to deal with matters of Union law, but also "how these bodies should be entrusted with the powers to implement Union law requirements".[88] As a consequence, competence for national public bodies (supposedly) cannot be created by EU law (or jurisprudence).[89] The Court of Justice has e.g. held that:[90]

---

cadre du renvoi préjudiciel : une marge d'appréciation?', in *Renvoi préjudiciel et marge d'appréciation du juge national*, ed. E. Neframi (Brussels: Larcier, 2015), 24.

85 Since Member State institutional autonomy has been "largely unaffected by Community law [the division of competences being] irrelevant for the purpose of Union law"; M. Accetto and S. Zleptnig (2005), 394; L. Corrias, *The Passivity of Law. Competence and Constitution in the Court of Justice* (Amsterdam: Springer, 2011), 135.

86 C. Kakouris (1997), 1411.

87 "[I]t is for the national legal order of each Member State to designate the competent courts and to lay down the procedural rules for proceedings designed to ensure the protection of the rights which individuals acquire through the direct effect of Community law." CJEU judgment in *Comet BV v. Produktschap voor Siergewassen*, 45/76, EU:C:1976:191, 13; see, similarly, CJEU judgment in *Rewe v. Landwirtschaftskammer für das Saarland*, 33/76, EU:C:1976:188, 5.

88 M. Klamert, *The Principle of Loyalty in EU Law* (New York: Oxford University Press, 2014), 127.

89 L. Corrias (2011), 135.

90 CJEU judgment in *International Fruit Company*, joined cases 51/71 to 54/71, EU:C:1971:128, 3. See also CJEU judgment in *Deutsche Milchkontor*, joined cases 205 to 215/82, EU:C:1983:233, 17: It is for the Member States "to ensure that Community regulations [...] are implemented within their territory. In so far as Community law, including its general principles, does not include common rules to this effect, the national authorities when implementing Community regulations act in accordance with the procedural and substantive rules of their own national law."

> Although under Article 5 of the Treaty the Member States are obliged to take all appropriate measures, whether general or particular, to ensure fulfillment of the obligations arising out of the Treaty, it is for them to determine which institutions within the national system shall be empowered to adopt the said measures.

Institutional autonomy is not without limits – it prevails only in the absence of Union secondary legislation on the matter (similarly to procedural autonomy). The exercise of EU legislative competence would then have the consequence of pre-empting Member States' competences, why it has been described as *residual*.[91] However, despite its similarities with the *Rewe* formula (discussed in sections 2.2.3.4-5), the difference in legal basis is consequential – the principle of primacy making the lack of procedural harmonization immaterial.

The characterization of institutional autonomy as *subsidiary*, in the sense that Member States are obliged to ensure that national law governing the matter does not create obstacles to the full effectiveness of EU law, is more convincing.[92] The Court of Justice has traditionally maintained as general rule that institutional autonomy should be exercised in a way that does not endanger the uniform application of EU law, meaning that institutional autonomy reigns only insofar as it does not prevent national authorities from e.g. disapplying national law or applying Union law (even without having jurisdiction or power for this choice).[93] Indeed, a crucial implication of the Court of Justice's pre-supposition of national courts' and authorities' power to apply EU law (when necessary to ensure its effectiveness), is that Union law in fact has the capacity to create competences for Member State public bodies.[94]

---

91 O. Dubos (2015 b), 19-20; see e.g. CJEU judgment in *Deutsche Milchkontor*, joined cases 205 to 215/82, EU:C:1983:233, 17.

92 O. Dubos (2015 b), 20.

93 J. M. Davidson, 'The Full Effect of Community Law – An Increasing Encroachment upon National Law and Principles', *REALaw*, 1 (2008), 115-16, in referece to CJEU judgment in *Vereniging Nationaal Overlegorgaan Sociale Werkvoorziening and Others (VNOSW)*, joined cases C-383/06 to C-385/06, EU:C:2008:165. See also L. Corrias (2011), 136.

94 J. M. Davidson (2008), 116: "If an authority is obliged to apply, it is assumed to have such a competence; and if national incompetence does not relieve the authority of the duty to apply, it must have been attributed the power to do so by Community law".

Depending on the national legal context, such matters may fall under the application of rules on either procedure or competence.[95] As will be seen, the Court has in its rulings concerning competences and jurisdiction displayed a proclivity to applying the principle of primacy to obstacles that are, *prima facie*, procedural ("structural primacy").[96] Traditionally, the distinction between primacy and the duty of sincere co-operation as legal basis has instructed the choice between "creating" new competences for national courts or requiring them to act only within their existing discretion.[97] In the wake of the Lisbon Treaties (codifying the obligation to provide remedies against breaches of Union law through the introduction of Art. 19 TEU), there is a new impetus and legal basis for requiring courts to provide remedies in excess of their powers under national legislation.[98]

---

95 S. Prechal and K. Cath (2014) identify the need for a wider term encompassing all areas of decentralized enforcement by national courts: "The terms 'enforcement autonomy' and 'remedial autonomy' are sometimes used as species of 'procedural autonomy'. These terms imply that, unless EU law provides otherwise, the enforcement of EU law, including the enforcement against infringements through sanctions, and the determination of the available remedies, is a matter for the Member States" (181).

96 CJEU judgment in *Kühne & Heitz NV v. Produktschap voor Pluimvee en Eieren*, C-453/00, EU:C:2004:17; CJEU judgment in *Amministrazione dell'Economia e delle Finanze and Agenzia delle entrate v. Fallimento Olimpiclub Srl*, C-2/08, EU:C:2009:506. Even so, not only rules of procedure were here at stake (legal effects of finality etc.), but also the competence to amend or revoke administrative acts, which also triggers matters of institutional autonomy. The requirement of full effectiveness also formed the basis for ensuring that judicial competences were created in order to make available damages for manifest encroachments on Union rights by the last judicial instance: "Application of that principle cannot be compromised by the absence of a competent court"; CJEU judgment in *Gerhard Köbler v. Republik Österreich*, C-224/01, EU:C:2003:513, 44.

97 In case-law on the finality of decisions and rulings, the issue of the seized court's discretion or power under national law has served as dividing line, sometimes dealt with under the principles of equivalence and effectiveness (e.g. CJEU judgment in *Dragoş Constantin Târşia v. Statul român*, C-69/14, EU:C:2015:662, 41) and sometimes under the principle of primacy (e.g. Opinion of Advocate General Léger in *Kühne & Heitz NV v. Produktschap voor Pluimvee en Eieren*, C-453/00, EU:C:2003:350, 66).

98 This use of the full effect approach to institutional obstacles can be traced back to the rise of the principle of effective judicial protection, even before the Lisbon reform; see CJEU judgment in *Unibet (London) Ltd and Unibet (International) Ltd v. Justitiekanslern*, C-432/05, 64-65, where, although the national court was not required to offer self-standing declaratory action, the ground was shaken under the "no-new-remedies-rule".

National institutional autonomy has also been described as *conditional*,[99] in view of the Court's unwillingness to validate procedural safeguards at the cost of effectiveness. Rulings on the revocation of subsidies have provoked the issue of procedural protection through legal certainty, which, together with the principle of legitimate expectations, typically governs the possibility of recovery under national procedural law. The Court of Justice has taken a restrictive stance towards justifications that have relied on fundamental principles of national procedural law, tilting the balance towards effectiveness over legal certainty.[100] Procedural encroachments on the full effectiveness of Union law will be addressed in section 3.2.2.6 (on the topic of inverse vertical litigation) and in section 5.3.4 (in connection to objective justifications).

2.1.3 Procedural, remedial and institutional rules vs. substantive rules

Member States' reserved domain of procedural competence pertains to the adoption, interpretation and application of national procedural and institutional rules. It has been suggested that national norms aimed to "sanction" the respect of EU substantive law in a very broad sense fall within the area of procedural law and are thereby covered by the principle of national procedural autonomy.[101] The term "sanction" should in this sense include "instruments of legal coercion that, in every Member State, guarantee the respect for the law [...]".[102] In other words, we are here looking at rules which provide more general instruments of enforcement, be they:

---

99 J. M. Davidson (2008), 116.

100 Ibid., 118: "the principles of legality and legal certainty under national law may be taken into account, only insofar as they are interpreted restrictively, form part of the Community legal order and their application does not conflict with the full effect of Community law". The requirements follow from CJEU judgment in *Vereniging Nationaal Overlegorgaan Sociale Werkvoorziening and Others (VNOSW)*, joined cases C-383/06 to C-385/06, EU:C:2008:165, 52-53, with reference to CJEU judgment in *Deutsche Milchkontor*, joined cases 205/82 to 215/82, EU:C:1983:233, 30; CJEU judgment in *Flemmer and Others*, joined cases C-80/99, C-81/99 and C-82/99, EU:C:2001:525, 60; CJEU judgment in *Republik Österreich v. Martin Huber*, C-336/00, EU:C:2002:509, 56 and CJEU judgment in *Stichting ROM-projecten v. Staatssecretaris van Economische Zaken*, C-158/06, EU:C:2007:370, 24.

101 D.-U. Galetta (2010), 1-2, in turn drawing on the reasoning of J. M. de Wilmars (1981).

102 J. M. de Wilmars (1981), 390ff.

- Institutional rules – in the sense of giving authority for enforcement by certain bodies;
- Procedural rules – laying down rules governing the procedure of enforcement; or
- Remedial rules – allowing individuals legal means to seek their enforcement by governing "the conditions and restrictions, under which individuals are enabled to bring and maintain actions before courts of law."[103]

Procedural rules of national law therefore, as an overall definition for the present work, "refer to the practical rules according to which a remedy is to be pursued in a court of law."[104]

Whether a given rule is of procedural nature cannot be judged with reference to the typology laid down in national law, since the consequence of that would be that rules with similar functions may be given dissimilar treatment.[105] Therefore, it is necessary to start with a terminological dividing line between substantive and procedural rules that stands as a common Union law standard. According to a common typology, the difference between substantive and procedural/institutional/remedial norms of national law is that the latter have the capacity of creating *indirect* collisions with substantive EU law, whereas the former give rise to *direct* collisions.[106]

Distinctions in the scholarship between substantive and procedural rules are based on whether a rule establishes a right or lays down a tenet that will help resolve the way in which to deal with the protection or enforcement of rights. In e.g. the seminal *Simmenthal* case,[107] two possible collisions of law could for these purposes be discerned. On the one hand, Italian rules requiring veterinary inspections were incompatible with Community rules of free movement – categorized as a direct collision of norms.[108] On the other hand, decisive for the outcome in this case was not

103 P. Wennerås (2007), 76-77.

104 Ibid.

105 D.-U. Galetta (2010), 1; O. Dubos (2015 b), 8; S. Prechal and K. Cath (2014), 181.

106 See also S. Prechal and R. Widdershoven, 'Redefining the Relationship between 'Rewe-effectiveness' and Effective Judicial Protection', *REALaw*, 4 (2011 b), 32-33. This dividing line is similar to the one referred to in the scholarship as primary versus secondary rules – primary rules demanding performance or abstention from certain behavior, while secondary rules ascertaining that performance or abstention can be ensured in practice; see e.g. O. Dubos (2015 b), 8.

107 CJEU judgment in *Simmenthal*, 106/77, EU:C:1978:49.

108 R. Ortlep and M. Verhoeven (2012), 2-3.

only the choice between these two sets of substantive rules, but also norms governing the hierarchy of courts.[109] For this situation, the following definition of indirect collision of norms is more apposite:[110]

> cases in which rules of national law hinder the effect of EU law in the national legal order, although EU law and national law do not provide different, incompatible legal regimes for the same factual situation.

What is then the specific difference between these two situations? In the first case, the two rules are applicable to the same situation, but lead to opposite outcomes. This collision is solved in EU law the same way as in German law, in which centralized law is applied instead of decentralized law to the extent that the two are incompatible[111] – equivalent to the principle of primacy in the EU law context.

In the second case, by contrast, there exists a national rule that could potentially need to be set aside in order to guarantee the right to free movement (i.e. the competence rule for the lower court); however, there is no equivalent centralized (i.e. EU law) rule to replace it with.[112] In line with this, an EU law-friendly resolution of the situation requires no more than that the national obstacle be considered for removal, after balancing its *raison d'être* against the interest of ensuring the right to free movement. This difference in approach justifies the distinction between primacy and loyal co-operation as legal bases for Union law requirements on national procedural law. In the case of primacy, there is an absolute obligation of compliance whereas under the duty of loyal co-operation, what can at most be de-

109 Here, a lack of competence for the seized court to single-handedly (without making prior reference to the constitutional court) set aside national law so as to guarantee the right of free movement. The latter type of obstacle has been paid renewed attention in CJEU judgment in *A v. B and Others*, C-112/13, EU:C:2014:2195 and CJEU judgment in *Global Starnet Ltd v. Ministero dell'Economia e delle Finanze*, C-322/16, EU:C:2017:985.

110 The typology of direct collision of norms corresponds to the notion of "material primacy" as opposed to "structural primacy," the latter corresponding to indirect collisions of norms since procedural rules need to be set aside to allow Union law effectiveness; R. Ortlep and M. Verhoeven (2012), 2. See also M. Claes (2006), 129ff.; C. Lacchi, 'Preliminary References to the Court of Justice of the EU and Effective Judicial Protection: Towards a More Protection-Oriented Approach of Article 267 TFEU' (University of Luxembourg, 2017), 142-43.

111 Art. 31 German Basic Law *[Grundgesetz für die Bundesrepublik Deutschland]* vom 23. Mai 1949 (BGBl. S. 1) stipulates that "*Bundesrecht bricht Landesrecht*" (EN: Federal law overrides state law), a rule with effect only when the collision of law leads to two incompatible outcomes when applied to the same set of facts.

112 R. Ortlep and M. Verhoeven (2012), 2.

manded is that procedural obstacles precluding national judges from taking into consideration and/or applying Union law be overcome,[113] all within the discretion of the national judge carrying out that balancing act.[114]

The thus far presented definitional characteristics are symptomatic, albeit not consistently decisive, for the choice between two instructions for national courts. Irrespective of which path is chosen, both the duty of sincere co-operation and the principle of primacy can bring about constraints for the national judge in his application of rules within the sphere of national procedural autonomy. The forthcoming section will approach the relationship between the respective prerogatives of the EU and the Member States in the field of procedural law, under the influence of the said instructions for national courts.

2.2 The principle of conferral and the duty of sincere co-operation

Restrictions on national procedural autonomy exist only in the context of decentralized implementation of EU law,[115] meaning in the event that Member States are implementing or otherwise enforcing substantive rules of EU law.[116] It is thus necessary to discuss not only the difference between procedural and substantive rules, but also the substantive context in which Member State procedural autonomy can be said to be limited. Within this area, the procedural competence of the Member States becomes restricted as soon as the legal context entails enforcement or implementation of EU law.

---

113 As has been recalled on numerous occasions in reference to interlocutory procedures; see e.g. CJEU judgment in *Aziz Melki and Sélim Abdeli*, joined cases C-188/10 and C-189/10, EU:C:2010:363, 44-45; CJEU judgment in *A v. B and Others*, C-112/13, EU:C:2014:2195, 37-46.

114 See CJEU judgment in *Willy Kempter KG v. Hauptzollamt Hamburg-Jonas*, C-2/06, EU:C:2008:78, 45, as well as the seminal ruling of the CJEU in *Kühne & Heitz NV v. Produktschap voor Pluimvee en Eieren*, C-453/00, EU:C:2004:17, 28, where the Court of Justice accepted the notion of discretion as decisive when the duty of sincere co-operation forms the legal basis for obligations of the national judge, while the Advocate General had emphasized the principle of primacy; Opinion of Advocate General Léger in *Kühne & Heitz NV v. Produktschap voor Pluimvee en Eieren*, C-453/00, EU:C:2003:350, 66.

115 See M. Eliantonio (2009), 1; M. Dougan (2004), 1-4; B. Dubey (2003), 87-134.

116 A. Wallerman (2015), 92.

As clarified in the previous section, procedural constraints on Union law effectiveness are usually not dealt with in the same manner as a collision of substantive norms (the difference of treatment relating to the choice between the principles of primacy and of loyal co-operation).[117] Compared to encroachments upon the principle of primacy of EU law, the Court of Justice has traditionally relaxed its review of national procedural obstacles. Section 2.2.1 discusses this choice of legal basis in the (ostensibly) less invasive principle of sincere co-operation, entailing a balancing exercise rather than an absolute obligation of compliance.

Section 2.2.2 discusses the overarching principles that determine whether a certain competence falls into the category of Union or Member State competence. In this vein, it is necessary to develop the notion of Member State "residual" competence insofar as Union legislation is absent, as well as the reach and legal bases of existing Union legislation on procedural matters.

Following this, a distinct albeit contested interpretation of Union procedural competence is discussed, in which procedural requirements hinge onto substantive Union rules (2.2.3).[118] The section examines the revival of the notion of "implied" Union procedural competence, the gap-filling function of the duty of sincere co-operation, the notion of legal protection of Union rights, the twin principles of equivalence and effectiveness, the balancing exercise between effectiveness of Union law and procedural safeguards, and the obligation of providing effective remedies, invigorated through Art. 19(1) TEU.

2.2.1 Legal basis in the duty of sincere co-operation or primacy

A key tool for choosing principle by which a collision of norms (direct or indirect) is to be resolved, is by distinguishing between substantive and procedural rules of national law.

117 R. Ortlep and M. Verhoeven, 'The Principle of Primacy Versus the Principle of National Procedural Autonomy', *Netherlands Administrative Law Library*, April-June 2012 (2012), 2.

118 Albeit dismissing the prevalence of an "actual implicit EU competence", e.g. Galetta argues that an implied competence in procedural matters exists in an "attenuated form", via the doctrine of full effect; D.-U. Galetta (2010), 9-11.

This dividing line has not always been granted. In the case-law starting with *Simmenthal*,[119] the Court of Justice seemed to derive from the principle of primacy an obligation to set aside national rules of procedural character, rather than basing its ruling on the duty of sincere co-operation.[120] The chosen solution may find its explanation in the singular connection between direct effect and decentralized enforcement by national courts, foreseen already in the foundational ruling in *van Gend en Loos*: The reason for granting direct effect to Community law provisions was to entrust individuals' "legal heritage" to national courts, by soliciting the latter to apply Treaty provisions in the case before them.[121] Therefore, at least as concerns directly effective provisions of (then) Community law, the original mandate of decentralized enforcement had its roots in the principle of primacy. In this view, it was logical that the latter should give rise to "hard" obligations for national judges.[122] The early case-law thus forecasted that the principle of primacy would govern the decentralized enforcement of directly effective Union norms, whereas the duty of sincere co-operation would remain a legal basis for national courts to enforce rules lacking direct effect.

---

119 CJEU judgment in *Simmenthal*, 106/77, EU:C:1978:49; CJEU judgment in *The Queen v. Secretary of State for Transport, ex parte Factortame*, C-213/89, EU:C:1990:257; CJEU judgment in *Francovich and Bonifaci v. Italy*, joined cases C-6/90 and C-9/90, EU:C:1991:428.

120 A choice which has been criticized in the scholarship for over-emphasizing or misusing the function of the principle of primacy; see e.g. S. Prechal (1998), 684-85. Note, however, M. Claes (2006), 126, using the notion of structural supremacy, which demands that competences be used or created to ensure the full effectiveness of Union law (in reference to CJEU judgment in *Simmenthal*, 106/77, EU:C:1978:49 and CJEU judgment in *The Queen v. Secretary of State for Transport, ex parte Factortame*, C-213/89, EU:C:1990:257).

121 CJEU judgment in *van Gend en Loos v. Administratie der Belastingen*, 26/62, EU:C:1963:1, pp. 12-13; see also S. Drake (2016), 20.

122 See particularly CJEU judgment in *van Gend en Loos v. Administratie der Belastingen*, 26/62, EU:C:1963:1, p. 13: "The vigilance of individuals concerned to protect their rights amounts to an effective supervision in addition to the supervision entrusted by Articles 169 and 170 to the diligence of the Commission and the Member States. It follows from the foregoing considerations that, according to the spirit, the general scheme and the wording of the Treaty, Article 12 must be interpreted as producing direct effects and creating individual rights which national courts must protect."

This approach was successively abandoned in favor of a typology where direct collisions[123] or collisions of primary rules[124] would in most instances indicate that the choice of law is to be dictated by the principle of primacy, according to which EU law is given precedent over national conflicting law.[125] By contrast, indirect collisions of law, or collisions of primary with secondary rules, should be resolved in a way that as far as possible ensures the effectiveness of Union law.[126] The principle of primacy therefore in most cases governs collisions of substantive law, whereas the duty of sincere co-operation is used to overcome procedural obstacles to the enforcement of Union law.

This distinction has also given rise to some confusion,[127] as the Court of Justice was not consistent in its choice between the above indicated formulas.[128] Oscillations have been explained as hinging on whether merely substantive provisions were in conflict, or a more complex constellation of substantive and procedural provisions[129] – the latter of which may trigger,

123 As previously noted, pursuant to the terminology of R. Ortlep and M. Verhoeven (2012), 3-4.

124 Under the terminology of O. Dubos (2015 b).

125 Ibid.; R. Ortlep and M. Verhoeven (2012).

126 On the respective consequences of "direct" and "indirect" conflict, see S. Prechal, 'Community Law in National Courts: The Lessons from van Schijndel', *CMLR*, 35 (1998), 685; S. Prechal and R. Widdershoven (2011 b), 32-33.

127 In reference to CJEU judgment in *Simmenthal*, 106/77, EU:C:1978:49 and CJEU judgment in *The Queen v. Secretary of State for Transport, ex parte Factortame*, C-213/89, EU:C:1990:257, this choice has been given the explanation that in national law there was indeed no remedy available – why the *Rewe* line could not be applied since the latter did not require the creation of new remedies in national law; M. Claes (2006), 129-31.

128 S. Prechal (1998), 684-90; M. Claes (2006), 122; S. Prechal and Rob Widdershoven, 'Effectiveness or Effective Judicial Protection: A Poorly Articulated Relationship', in *Today's Multi-layered Legal Order: Current Issues and Perspectives*, ed. T. Baumé (Paris: Zutphen, 2011 a), 283-96. See also R. Ortlep and M. Verhoeven (2012), 6, commenting on CJEU judgment in *Ciola*, C-224/97, EU:C:1999:212 and CJEU judgment in *Ministero dell'Industria, del Commercio e dell'Artigianato v. Lucchini SpA*, C-119/05, EU:C:2007:434, where the Court of Justice relied on the principle of primacy even though the legal force of precedents and the finality of judgments belong to national/institutional autonomy.

129 S. Prechal (1998), 683-90, referring to CJEU judgment in *van Schijndel v. Stichting Pensioenfonds voor Fysiotherapeuten*, joined cases C-430/93 and C-431/93, EU:C:1995:441; CJEU judgment in *SpA Alois Lageder and others v. Amministrazione delle Finanze dello Stato*, joined cases C-31/91 to C-44/91, EU:C:1993:132; CJEU judgment in *Gabriel Alonso-Pérez v. Bundesanstalt für Arbeit*, C-394/93, EU:C:1995:400.

alternatively, the *Simmenthal* mandate, the *Rewe* formula or the principle of effective judicial protection.[130]

In view of what appears to be a re-introduction of the full effect requirement to deal with issues of institutional autonomy and constitutional obstacles (both of which may overlap with procedural law and certainly contain elements of indirect collisions of law), we may expect that the last word on this matter has not been said.[131] The propensity to transfer (back) procedural obstacles within the reach of the principle of primacy has palpable advantages from an enforcement perspective.[132] However, it prompts the constitutional query whether the Court of Justice, in doing so, is acting within its mandate, following the division of competences between the EU and the Member States as described in the forthcoming section. Allowing procedural obstacles to be dealt with under the duty of sincere co-operation is a more conservative solution, insofar as the measure falls under Member States' reserved domains.

2.2.2 The principle of conferral as the sole basis for EU competence

The (supposed) existence of national procedural autonomy is the result of, on the one hand, the limited conferral of procedural competence on the Union, and on the other hand, the limited extent of Union exercise of existing competences to legislate on procedural matters. The present section starts by examining the principle of conferral, discussing the consequences of the proposition that Member State procedural autonomy reigns "in the absence of EU legislation" (2.2.2.1). Since under this dictum, any exercise of powers must stem from a legal basis in the Treaties, various such bases

130 J. Krommendijk, 'Is There Light on the Horizon? The Distinction Between "Rewe Effectiveness" and the Principle of Effective Judicial Protection in Article 47 of the Charter after Orizzonte', *CMLR*, 53 (2016), 1405 at fn. 52.

131 See e.g. CJEU judgment in *Gervais Larsy v. Institut national d'assurances sociales pour travailleurs indépendants*, C-118/00, EU:C:2001:368; CJEU judgment in *Ministero dell'Industria, del Commercio e dell'Artigianato v. Lucchini SpA*, C-119/05, EU:C:2007:434; CJEU judgment in *Winner Wetten GmbH v. Bürgermeisterin der Stadt Bergheim*, C-409/06, EU:C:2010:503; CJEU judgment in *Aziz Melki and Sélim Abdeli*, joined cases C-188/10 and C-189/10, EU:C:2010:363; CJEU judgment in *A v. B and Others*, C-112/13, EU:C:2014:2195, 39-44.

132 The supplementary tool of full effectiveness was, already in CJEU judgment in *Theresa Emmott v. Minister for Social Welfare and the Attorney General*, C-208/90, EU:C:1991:333, 17-21, applied in order to overcome procedural obstacles to which the *Rewe* principles were not opposed.

proposed for Union procedural competences are discussed next, in light of the academic debate (2.2.2.2).

The issue of competence requires taking a step back to regard the constitutional elements of the EU legal structure and the type of legal co-existence between Member States and Union institutions that it requires.[133] In an archetypal federation, the respective exercise of power by centralized and decentralized bodies has to be regulated in order to avoid turf disputes.[134] Constitutional rules are found in federal structures that designate who is in charge of what. The starting point for any discussion on competences must therefore be where such rules can be found and who has the power to adopt and to modify them.[135] Such decision-making is to be found at the federal/centralized level of government, meaning that rules of competence may be found in federal statutes or constitutions and that interpretative authority is given to federal-level courts.[136] In the EU, rules of competence are likewise found at the central, i.e. Union level, of law-making. However, in the EU federal structure, the original granting of competence has been deferred to the Member States, who have in some instances chosen to (and in others not to) confer powers on the Union institutions by providing a Treaty basis.[137]

This principle is found in Art. 5 TEU, stating that "The limits of Union competences are governed by the principle of conferral [...] the Union

133 S. Douglas-Scott, *Constitutional Law of the European Union* (Harlow: Longman, 2002), 192ff. gives a detailed account of the division of powers from the theoretical perspective of federalism.

134 Ibid., 193.

135 On the 'executive federalist' structure of the EU and interrelated typology of legal acts, as a matter of competence in the realm of the EU or the Member States, see H. C.H. Hofmann, 'Legislation, Delegation and Implementation under The Treaty of Lisbon: Typology Meets Reality', *European Law Journal*, 15 (2009) 4, 482-505, 497-99.

136 C. Kakouris (1997), 1391. See also, in reference to the federal structure of the United States, R. Schütze, 'Federalism as Constitutional Pluralism: 'Letter from America'', in *Constitutional Pluralism in the European Union and Beyond*, eds. Avbelj M. and J. Komárek (Portland: Hart Publishing, 2012), 185, describing traditional federalism as States giving up part of their sovereignty to a nation that will nevertheless remain "incomplete". On the structure and order of the EU versus the Member States from a philosophical perspective, see O. Zetterquist, 'Out with the New, in with the Old – Neo-Roman Constitutional Thought and the Enigma of Constitutional Pluralism in the EU', in ibid., 224-29.

137 K. St Clair Bradley, 'Powers and Procedures in the EU Constitution: Legal Bases and the Court', in *The Evolution of EU Law*, eds. Craig, P. and G. de Búrca (Oxford: Oxford University Press, 2011 b), 85-109 (86).

shall act only within the limits of the competences conferred upon it by the Member States in the Treaties to attain the objectives set out therein." The creation of rules concerning the division of competences between the Union and the Member States has already taken place by way of Treaty adoptions and amendments. Any additional competences must equally be granted through new Treaties or Treaty amendments, which requires unanimity among Member States and can therefore be said to remain in the hands of the Member States.[138]

A consequential difference between traditional federalism and European Union federalism is thus that the Union institutions are precluded from centrally transferring competences, i.e. they lack "*kompetenz-kompetenz*"[139] mutually and autonomously.[140] This is still a contested assertion, especially given that the Member States, through the so-called flexibility and harmonization clauses, have permitted the Union legislature to effectively create new competences under particular circumstances.[141] This possibility aside, competences are today exclusively granted through Treaty provisions, ensuring that the fundamental power of transferring competences remains with the Member States.[142] *In theory*, the principle of attributed powers

---

138 Art. 48 TEU provides both for ordinary Treaty revision by unanimous decision and simplified Treaty revision applicable to certain parts of the TFEU – however, under Art. 48(6) TEU, increase of competence through a simplified revision procedure is precluded. See further B. de Witte, 'Treaty Revision Procedures after Lisbon', in *EU Law after Lisbon*, eds. Biondi, A., P. Eeckhout, and S. Ripley (Oxford: Oxford University Press, 2012), 119ff.

139 C. Kakouris (1997), 1391; L. Corrias (2011), xi-xii; T. Tridimas 'Constitutional Review of Member State Action: The Virtues and Vices of an Incomplete Jurisdiction', *I•CON*, 9 (2012), 738.

140 While a Union institution cannot transfer Member State competences to another institution or to itself, this does not mean that they cannot delegate competences internally and check each other.

141 Arts. 114 and 352 TFEU. Concerning the risk that spill-over effects of existing Treaty competences, as well as excessive use of the harmonization and flexibility clauses, jeopardize the principle of conferral, see R. Schütze, *European Constitutional Law* (Cambridge: Cambridge University Press, 2012), 153.

142 Although the Court of Justice and the Supreme Courts of some Member States have opposing views on the authority to interpret the scope of competences; P. Craig, 'The ECJ and *Ultra Vires* Action: A Conceptual Analysis', *CMLR*, 48 (2011); M. Mahlmann, 'The Politics of Constitutional Identity and its Legal Frame – the Ultra Vires Decision of the Federal Constitutional Court', *German Law Journal*, 11 (2010); M. Beyer-Katzenberger, 'Judicial Activism and Judicial Restraint at the Bundesverfassungs-gericht: Was the *Mangold* Judgment of the European Court of Justice an *Ultra Vires* Act?', *ERA Forum*, 11 (2011); C. Lacchi (2017), 106-19.

means that through reading the Treaties, one should be able to conclude whether a given area of competence has been granted the Union, any remaining areas belonging to the residual competence of the Member States.[143] Yet, *in practice*, this is not straightforward.[144]

Having laid this general ground, the pertinent question for the two next sections is the modalities through which the Union legal structure distributes competences that could be used to regulate national procedural law applicable to procedures which have a Union legal basis.

2.2.2.1 "Insofar as no provisions of Community law are relevant..."

If it is accepted that action by Union institutions must be based either on Treaty provisions or implied by/inferred from Treaty objectives,[145] then it is necessary to consider whether existing Treaty provisions can be said to give rise to competence for Union action affecting Member State procedural law. This is what the Court of Justice has undertaken to do on the many occasions in which it has examined – in reference to specific contexts of litigation – the existence or absence of Union rules applicable to national procedural law. Its most frequently cited formulation on national procedural autonomy may be recalled:[146]

---

143 Member State competence is further bolstered by Protocol (No 25) of the Treaty on the Functioning of the European Union (Consolidated version), on the exercise of shared competence, OJ C 115, 9/5/2008, 307, clarifying that "[t]he scope [...] only covers those elements governed by the Union act in question and therefore does not cover the whole area", and by Art. 2(2) TFEU which returns competences back to the Member States once the Union has ceased to exercise them.

144 H. C.H. Hofmann (2009), 497-99 recaps the typology of acts under the Treaties up to and under the Lisbon structure. In the EU system of decentralized implementation, even though Member States still retain technically residual competences, practically whenever there is resort e.g. to Arts. 291 TFEU paired up with a legal basis (for example Art. 114 TFEU), the expression of the residual competences changes from implementation to oversight of the delegation, and therefore can be said to be limited. On vertical and horizontal separation of powers, see E. Neframi, 'Exigence de cohérence et action extérieure de l'Union européenne', *Le Droit, les Institutions et les politiques de l'Union européenne face à l'impératif de cohérence* (Presses Universitaires de Strasbourg, 2009).

145 D.-U. Galetta (2010), 9.

146 CJEU judgment in *Rewe v. Landwirtschaftskammer für das Saarland*, 33/76, EU:C:1976:188, 5; CJEU judgment in *Comet BV v. Produktschap voor Siergewassen*, 45/76, EU:C:1976:191, 13, recalled in e.g. CJEU judgment in *Dragoş Con-*

> [I]n the absence of any relevant Community rules, it is for the national legal order of each Member State to designate the competent courts and to lay down the procedural rules for proceedings designed to ensure the protection of the rights which individuals acquire through the direct effect of Community law[.]

The above account has been attributed various meanings, ranging from lack of Treaty basis for institutional and procedural competences, to lack of secondary Union law providing applicable procedural rules for a particular national litigation context.[147]

The first alternative – lack of Treaty-based procedural competence – is founded on a broad presumption of national powers to "determine remedies and procedural rules".[148] This interpretation means that as Union (primary) law stands today, there is no provision of procedural competence for the Union. Therefore, procedural legislation on the Union side lacks legal basis. Although two Treaty provisions are sometimes invoked as appropriate legal bases for Union procedural competence (viz. the harmonization and flexibility clauses[149]), their use has been ruled out by the Court of Justice for the purpose of general procedural competence.[150]

The alternative reading of the above *Rewe/Comet* dictum[151] suggests that Union primary law bases exist whereas Union secondary law is in many instances lacking.[152] In this line of reasoning, there exist appropriate provisions in the Treaties upon which rules could be established in secondary law, which would be applicable to Member State procedure, when Union rules or rights are at stake. *Comet* and *Rewe* indeed envisaged appropriate

---

stantin Târşia v. Statul român, C-69/14, EU:C:2015:662, 26; CJEU judgment in *Hansruedi Raimund v. Michaela Aigner*, C-425/16, EU:C:2017:776, 40.

147 On lack of Treaty-based competence, see M. Dougan (2004), 14; D.-U. Galetta (2010), 10-11. On the presence of primary law basis but lack of secondary law provisions, see C. Kakouris (1997), 1395-96.

148 M. Dougan (2004), 14.

149 Arts. 114 and 352 TFEU.

150 CJEU judgment in *Firma Gebrüder Lück v. Hauptzollamt Köln-Rheinau*, 34/67, EU:C:1968:24; on the harmonization clause, see CJEU judgment in *Germany v. Parliament and Council (Tobacco advertising case)*, C-376/98, EU:C:2000:544, 83.

151 CJEU judgment in *Hans Just I/S v. Danish Ministry for Fiscal Affairs*, 68/79, EU:C:1980:57, 25; CJEU judgment in *Francovich and Bonifaci v. Italy*, joined cases C-6/90 and C-9/90, EU:C:1991:428, 42; CJEU judgment in *Brasserie du Pêcheur v. Bundesrepublik Deutschland and The Queen/ Secretary of State for Transport, ex parte Factortame and Others*, joined cases C-46/93 and C-48/93, EU:C:1996:79, 83, 90.

152 C. Kakouris (1997), 1395; M. Dougan (2004), 19-20; L. M. Díez-Picazo, 'Towards a Unified Judicial Protection in Europe (?)', *ERPL*, 9 (1997), 975.

Treaty bases for the (then) Community to enact procedural rules applicable to Member State procedure, which the Court proceeded to note had at that time not been done.[153] Views in the literature even go so far as to propose that "the Community is competent to establish its own harmonized system of procedural law by means of secondary law."[154] When applying national procedural law in the context of decentralized enforcement of Union law (when national courts are "utilized" as organs of Union law), national law is only ancillary and provisional.[155] The possibility of deriving an implied competence from existing areas of substantive Union policy was rejected already in the *Lück* judgment of 1968, where the Court maintained that the necessity to ensure substantive Union law cannot give rise to necessary procedural competences.[156] According to this line of argumentation, the limits of competence laid down in the Treaty should strictly preclude Union procedural competence of both explicit and implicit nature.[157]

This said, how do we explain that the Union legislator has, in various areas of secondary Union law, successively enacted legislation with far-reaching implications for national judicial and administrative procedure, while at the same time the Court of Justice has increasingly intervened in matters of procedures, competences and remedies?[158] The *de facto* proceduralization process has been described as a "long standing reality", expressing a manifestation or direction of European federalism.[159] Drawing on these observations, the forthcoming section looks more closely at how this devel-

153 CJEU judgment in *Comet BV v. Produktschap voor Siergewassen*, 45/76, EU:C:1976:191, 14; CJEU judgment in *Rewe v. Landwirtschaftskammer für das Saarland*, 33/76, EU:C:1976:188, 5, referring to the harmonization and flexibility clauses.

154 C. Kakouris (1997), 1395.

155 Ibid., 1396.

156 CJEU judgment in *Firma Gebrüder Lück v. Hauptzollamt Köln-Rheinau*, 34/67, EU:C:1968:24, 2.3.

157 D.-U. Galetta (2010), 11.

158 This is e.g. the case in the area of public procurement. See e.g. Directive 2007/66/EC of the European Parliament and of the Council of 11 December 2007 amending Council Directives 89/665/EEC and 92/13/EEC with regard to improving the effectiveness of review procedures concerning the award of public contracts, OJ L 335, 20/12/2007, 31 and its predecessor Council Directive 89/665/EEC of 21 December 1989 on the coordination of the laws, regulations and administrative provisions relating to the application of review procedures to the award of public supply and public works contracts, OJ L 395, 30/12/1989, 33.

159 O. Dubos (2015 b), 7.

opment has taken place, and which legal bases have been and could be used in its support.

2.2.2.2 Proposed legal bases for EU procedural competence

Under the principle of conferral, any rules applicable to Member State procedure must be paired with a particular legal basis for competence attribution. Appropriate such legal bases can, as the Treaties stand today, mainly be found in sector-specific competence provisions,[160] which are not in themselves sufficient for harmonization of national procedural law.[161] A few openings for procedural measures, under particular conditions supplementing sector-specific competences, are provided in the Treaties; specifically, the harmonization clause (Art. 114 TFEU), the flexibility clause (Art. 352 TFEU), effective implementation as a common interest (Art. 197 TFEU), and judicial co-operation on civil matters (Art. 81 TFEU).[162]

Pursuant to the harmonization clause, approximation of laws can be achieved by way of ordinary legislative procedure as long as the object of the legislation is the "establishing and functioning of the internal market."[163] What is primarily envisioned is to overcome obstacles to the rights of free movement and distortions of the internal market that result from discrepancies between Member States' legislation. Post-Lisbon, the Court of Justice has moderated a case-law which was previously rather generous towards the reach of (now) Art. 114 TFEU. In the enactment of secondary Union legislation which effects national procedural rules, it has become necessary to look particularly at the substantive consequences that disparities in national procedural law can give rise to.[164] A case-by-case examina-

160 M. Dougan (2004), 15; A. Wallerman (2015), 88.

161 D.-U. Galetta (2010), 10.

162 CJEU judgment in *Rewe v. Landwirtschaftskammer für das Saarland*, 33/76, EU:C:1976:188, 5; CJEU judgment in *Comet BV v. Produktschap voor Siergewassen*, 45/76, EU:C:1976:191, 14; O. Dubos (2015 b); M. Dougan (2004), 14; D.-U. Galetta (2010), 10.

163 Art. 114 TFEU.

164 The use of Art. 114 TFEU required that 1) Union legislation must harmonize national laws, not leaving disparities in national legislation; 2) disparities in national legislation must give rise to trade obstacles or distortion of competition and 3) the legislation must be capable of obliterating these obstacles or distortive mechanisms; CJEU judgment in *Germany v. Parliament and Council (Tobacco advertising case)*, C-376/98, EU:C:2000:544; see further H. C.H., 'The International Market in a Context of Deepening Integration – Long on Content and

tion is required, while Art. 114 TFEU cannot be used to harmonize national procedural law across sectors. The Public Procurement Directives are one example of secondary legislation with a clear impact on national procedural rules, adopted on the basis of the harmonization clause.[165] A multitude of other legislative "measures" have been adopted for administrative co-operation on this basis, re-opening the requirement of approximation of laws for more flexible use.[166]

The flexibility clause (Art. 352 TFEU) was also suggested by the Court of Justice in the *Rewe* case as appropriate legal basis for enacting future Union procedural legislation.[167] This provision has been modified in its Lisbon version and no longer needs to be triggered by internal market objectives – it can now be used more widely for "the objectives set out in the Treaties", in the event that the latter do not prescribe necessary competences.[168] In its new wording, the formal procedure for adopting legislation under the flexibility clause is alas more cumbersome,[169] and adopted measures cannot entail harmonization where that would otherwise be ex-

---

Short on Modes of Delivery?', in *Of Courts and Constitutions: Liber Amicorum in Honour Of Nial Fennelly*, eds. Bradley, K., N. Travers, A. Whelan, and N. Fennelly (Oxford: Hart Publishing, 2014 b), 141-54.

165 Council Directive 89/665/EEC of 21 December 1989 on the coordination of the laws, regulations and administrative provisions relating to the application of review procedures to the award of public supply and public works contracts, OJ L 395, 30/12/1989, 33; see also Council Directive 92/13/EEC of 25 February 1992 coordinating the laws, regulations and administrative provisions relating to the application of Community rules on the procurement procedures of entities operating in the water, energy, transport and telecommunications sectors, OJ L 76, 23/3/1992, 14.

166 Based on the requirement of approximation of Member State laws, the use of Art. 114 TFEU to transfer implementing powers from the Member States to EU bodies was the subject of controversy in CJEU judgment in *United Kingdom of Great Britain and Northern Ireland v. Parliament and Council (ENISA)*, C-217/04, EU:C:2006:279; CJEU judgment in *United Kingdom v. Parliament and Council (Smoke flavourings)*, C-66/04, EU:C:2005:743 and CJEU judgment in *United Kingdom v. Parliament and Council (ESMA)*, C-270/12 EU:C:2014:18; with comments in H. C.H. Hofmann (2014 b), 148.

167 CJEU judgment in *Rewe v. Landwirtschaftskammer für das Saarland*, 33/76, EU:C:1976:188, 14.

168 Art. 352 TFEU can be used both as a basis for competences within a policy area where the Union already has some – albeit insufficient – competences for the envisioned legislation, and as a basis for legislative competences outside the areas covered by the Treaties; R. Schütze (2012), 160.

169 Now requiring approval both by the Council and the Parliament, Art. 352(1) TFEU.

cluded by the Treaties. Although procedural harmonization has indeed not been prohibited in the Treaties, today's restrictions on the use of the flexibility clause make it unavailable for transversal procedural harmonization.[170]

Alongside Art. 114 and Art. 352 TFEU, the Treaties provide provisions that, in the absence of EU competence, represent mechanisms of "inverse subsidiarity".[171] Art. 197 TFEU effectuates a new coordinating competence for the purposes of administrative co-operation, which is additional to more specific bases in the Treaties. It is justified by the objective of effective implementation of Union law in Member States, as an essential matter of common interest. While Art. 197(2) TFEU states that "[n]o Member State shall be obliged to avail itself of such support", the provision grants a competence to the EU legislature to resort to regulatory measures in order to help Member States "improve their administrative capacity to implement Union law."[172] Implementation can be seen as broader than enforcement, encompassing "both the executive power to adopt delegated norms as well as the administrative and judicial power to enforce legislation in individual circumstances."[173] Seeing as under Art. 291 TFEU "Member States are responsible for adopting all measures of national law necessary to implement legally binding Union acts", the Treaties endorse the principle of indirect administration,[174] ensuing from the principles of conferral and of

---

170 O. Dubos (2015 b), 23.

171 In the sense of prescribing central coordination when national measures are not sufficient, as the mechanism foreseen in Art. 197 TFEU. See further B. Bertrand, *Le juge de l'Union européenne, juge administratif* (Brussels: Bruylant, 2012), 219, 231.

172 On this matter, see P. Craig, *EU Administrative Law* (New York: Oxford University Press, 2012), 26. A strict interpretation of Art. 197 TFEU should "preclude the possibility for the EU political institutions to adopt measures of harmonization in certain sectors envisaging, together with the harmonization of substantive rules, also instruments of cooperation among national administrations and the EU authorities"; M. Cremona, *Compliance and the Enforcement of EU Law* (Oxford: Oxford University Press, 2012), 56. Yet, it is evident that while Art. 197 TFEU excludes harmonization for administrative implementation, this has not prevented the creation of harmonizing structures supporting the administrative implementation of internal market law. See e.g. P. van Cleynenbreugel, '"Meroni" Circumvented? Article 114 TFEU and EU Regulatory Agencies', *MJECL*, 21 (2014), 87-88.

173 A. Beka (2018), 19.

174 As noted in ibid., fn. 75: Art. 291 TFEU in its French version, under (1) on the implementing powers of the Member States, uses "*mise en œuvre*", whereas, the implementing powers of the Commission under (2) is called "*exécution*".

sincere co-operation.[175] "Essential for the proper functioning of the Union", effective implementation can be functionalized into a "hard" duty when paired with Treaty provisions aimed at the Member States.[176]

Another relevant legal basis in the Treaties is Art. 81 TFEU on judicial co-operation in civil matters having cross-border implications. Similarly to the harmonization clause, rules enacted on this basis must be necessary in order to achieve common market objectives. However, in contrast to the harmonization clause, the provision is aimed specifically at the harmonization of *civil* procedural rules that are applied in cross-border litigation; particularly to allow for judicial co-operation between Member States and to achieve a common standard for cross-border matters such as jurisdiction and choice/conflict of laws.[177] Still, the notion of civil matters is interpreted widely enough to encompass also litigation between individuals and public authorities "where the public authority acts in the exercise of its powers."[178] Art. 81 TFEU thus appears to envisage a wide range of regulative activities, both affecting internal and cross-border litigation – also including proceedings that do not strictly belong to the field of civil litigation, which would allow Art. 81 TFEU to serve as an appropriate legal basis for procedural harmonization within clearly delimited fields.

Looking more closely at the requirement that harmonization measures pursuant to Art. 81 TFEU be necessary for the "functioning of the internal market",[179] the envisioned test is whether disparities between Member State rules in fact have a negative impact upon Union integration. This involves verifying whether legislative disparities would lead business actors to avoid establishment in other Member States for fear of problems caused by the judicial system in which they would need to litigate: Are there any substantive Union rights put at peril or inequality of competition prompted by differences in court protection granted in the different Member

175 I.e. Arts. 5 and 4 TEU.

176 On the importance of Art. 291 TFEU in the wake of its codification in the Lisbon Treaties, see J. Ziller, 'Les concepts d'administration directe, d'administration indirecte et de co-administration et les fondements du droit administratif européen', in *Traité de droit administratif européen*, eds. Auby J.-B. and J. Dutheil de la Rochère (Brussels: Bruylant, 2007), 327-28. On Art. 197 TFEU paired with the duty of sincere co-operation, see E. Neframi, 'Principe de coopération loyale et principe d'attribution dans le cadre de la mise en œuvre du droit de l'Union', *Cah. dr. eur.*, 1 (2016), 221-51.

177 M. Eliantonio (2009), 4.

178 CJEU judgment in *LTU Lufttransportunternehmen GmbH & Co. KG v. Eurocontrol*, 29/76, EU:C:1976:137, 4.

179 Art. 81(2) TFEU.

States? The point of interest is here whether commercial actors' fear in this regard is substantial enough to distort competition within the Union.[180] This connection to the furthering of the internal market is not a Lisbon-era novelty; the Amsterdam Treaty wording also allowed for its use "in so far as necessary" for the functioning of the internal market. However, the change of formulation in the Lisbon Treaties of the market condition to "particularly when necessary" has been taken to represent an alleviation of the internal market condition from requiring this connection to rather emphasizing its importance.[181]

Even though Art. 81 TFEU envisions judicial co-operation on cross-border matters, it lists functions, some of which are relevant in internal litigation contexts equally to cross-border contexts.[182] The wide and rather inexact wording of the post-Lisbon provision has the potential of broadening the scope of Union procedural competence more generally.[183] As has been argued, this can serve as the basis for harmonizing civil procedure applicable equally to internal as to cross-border litigation.[184] Yet, despite its apparently broad reach, there still needs to be a foundation in substantive Union law within a certain area in order to lay the ground for procedural harmonization.[185]

2.2.3 Implications of the duty of sincere co-operation

The above account prompts the overall observation that there is still, after Lisbon, no clear and sufficient EU competence for *transversal* procedural legislation,[186] giving rise to a continued presumption of national competence.[187] The Court of Justice has nevertheless laid down requirements that

180 M. Eliantonio (2009), 5.
181 E. Storskrubb (2008), 45-46.
182 In sub-paras. (e)-(h) we find e.g. effective access to justice, elimination of obstacles to the proper functioning of proceedings, and training of judicial staff – i.e. concerns about ensuring the quality of court proceedings on a more general level.
183 E. Storskrubb (2008), 45.
184 O. Dubos (2015 b), 24.
185 A. Wallerman (2015), 92.
186 D.-U. Galetta (2010), 10.
187 Cf. M. Dougan (2004), 19-20, on procedural rules governing actions for State liability: "[A]s matter of practice, the presumption of national autonomy applies unless and until either the Community legislature or the Court have actively assumed responsibility for specifying the conditions under which an infringement

imply binding obligations for the Member States, with transversal procedural reach.[188] On what does the Court of Justice base its assumption of jurisdiction for laying down such obligations?

The present section deals with an explanation labeled "functionalized competence", primarily based on the Member States' duty of sincere co-operation (Art. 4(3) TEU).[189] A contested interpretation of Union procedural competence is discussed, namely that of implied EU competence within specific areas of law, in the spirit of sincere co-operation (2.2.3.1).[190] Section 2.2.3.2 reconsiders the nexus of direct effect and the duty of sincere co-operation, followed by a reflection in 2.2.3.3 on the initially preferred solution of laying down procedural obligations under the requirement of legal protection or full effect. Next are introduced the conventional limitations to national procedural autonomy (equivalence, 2.2.3.4 and effectiveness, 2.2.3.5). Then, the procedural rule-of-reason is introduced in its capacity to allow the *Rewe* principles to be bypassed, containing in and of itself tools for balancing the substantive interests in effective enforcement of Union law against the protective priorities underlying Member States' rules of procedure 2.2.3.6. Finally, the remedial mandate[191] of national courts is linked to the requirement of effective judicial protection (2.2.3.7).

2.2.3.1 What to do in the meantime: Implied competence?

Prevailing interpretations of the principle of attributed powers indicate that any action of the Union institutions should be based either on explicit Treaty competences, or on implied competences that can be inferred from

of one's Treaty rights will lead to the imposition of liability to make reparation."

188 Viz. the principles of equivalence/effectiveness (CJEU judgment in *Rewe v. Landwirtschaftskammer für das Saarland*, 33/76, EU:C:1976:188; CJEU judgment in *Comet BV v. Produktschap voor Siergewassen*, 45/76, EU:C:1976:191) and effective judicial protection (CJEU judgment in *Johnston*, 222/84, EU:C:1986:206.

189 D.-U. Galetta (2010), 11ff.; O. Dubos (2015 b), 21-22.

190 See D.-U. Galetta (2010), 9-11.

191 The term "remedial mandate" denotes the responsibilities incumbent on national judges both when choosing between available remedies provided by the national legislator (i.e. remedial autonomy), and when stepping in to fill gaps in legal protection where individuals lack avenues for enforcing their Union law-derived rights.

existing substantive Treaty prerogatives.[192] Take for instance sector-specific legislation that features procedural guidelines. Where the purpose of secondary legislation is not to achieve harmonization of procedural law, but rather to attain goals of substantive law, the substantive competence basis could possibly give rise to an "implied" procedural competence to do what is necessary in order to be able to achieve the said substantive goals.[193] Sector-specific legislation has had an important influence on procedural rules both within the line of case-law concerning consumer protection, discussed in Chapter 3-4 below, and in the case-law developing the principle of effective judicial protection, discussed in Chapter 5. These developments are better understood taking into account the effects of such secondary legislation on the division of powers between the EU and the Member States.

In other secondary legislation, the main purpose has been some level of harmonization of procedural standards themselves. For example, the legal basis of the Directive on the burden of proof in discrimination cases was that of social policy, within Union substantive competence.[194] Nevertheless, to realize the policy of eliminating discrimination based on gender, a reversal of the burden of proof was necessary – a procedural obligation incumbent on national courts. This may represent the "discovery" of an implied competence, which has been justified by the need to ensure the effectiveness of substantive Union law.[195]

A differentiation must nevertheless be made between the described "implied" legislative competence and the Court of Justice's guidelines for decentralized enforcement – maintaining that Member States must provide necessary procedural means to uphold substantive Union law is not the same as laying down in secondary law the modalities of such procedural means. Whether or not we refer to the latter as an implied competence,[196] it must be distinguished from the situation in which the Court of Justice prescribes, as Union law prerogatives, restraints on national courts' exer-

---

192 O. Dubos, 'Que reste-t-il de l'autonomie procédurale du juge national ? Histoire de l'attribution d'une compétence au norm de l'effectivité et de l'efficacité du droit de l'Union', in *Renvoi préjudiciel et marge d'appréciation du juge national*, ed. E. Neframi (Brussels: Larcier, 2015 a), 162; D.-U. Galetta (2010).

193 R. Schütze, *European Union Law* (Cambridge: Cambridge University Press, 2015).

194 Council Directive 97/80/EC of 15 December 1997 on the burden of proof in cases of discrimination based on sex, OJ L 14, 20/1/1998; then Art. 2 TEU.

195 O. Dubos (2015 b), 21.

196 Ibid., 21-22.

cise of national procedural competence, in which case legal bases must be found elsewhere than in substantive Union law provisions.

Implied competences do not find support in the foundational tenet of Member States' procedural autonomy, laid down in the *Rewe* and *Comet* rulings. The necessity, in the exercise of national procedural competence, to guarantee the full effect of the substantive Union law provisions at issue, has nevertheless been understood in the scholarship to give rise to a form of implied EU competence "in an attenuated form".[197] Following this reasoning, the starting point for identifying an "attenuated form" of implied competence is the existence of substantive Union provisions, which individuals hope to invoke before national courts. Having established their direct effect, there may be circumstances in which the direct application of substantive provisions of Union law (even when recognized under the principle of primacy as hierarchically superior to national law), may not be enough to ensure their realization or useful effect, i.e. so that they can effectively be relied upon by their intended beneficiaries.[198] In such circumstances, additional action may need to be taken by a seized court. To be sure, Union provisions do not need to have direct effect to require collaboration by national courts (or authorities).[199] Member States are bound by substantive Union law as to the results, whereas the means are left to the Member States. It is this obligation to collaborate towards results defined at the Union level that to some extent restrains Member State discretion in terms of how they construct and apply national procedural law.[200]

The notion of implied Union procedural competence alas makes less sense in the post-Lisbon era. It goes against the spirit of the principle of conferral, which precludes competence exercise that cannot be read from the Treaties. Particularly, the Treaties of Lisbon were intended to obliterate the need for, and thereby also the use of, implied competences by provid-

---

197 D.-U. Galetta (2010), 11.

198 Ibid. See, analogously, CJEU judgment in *Rendon Marín*, C-165/14, EU:C:2016:675, 75; CJEU judgment in *Secretary State for the Home Department v. CS*, C-304/14, EU:C:2016:674, 29-30; CJEU judgment in *Chavez-Vilchez and Others*, C-133/15, EU:C:2017:354, 64, where the "intrinsic connection" between residence rights for third country nationals (Member State competence) and the freedom of movement for Union citizens (Union competence) justified a competence creep of sorts in order to avoid denying citizens genuine enjoyment of the substance of their EU citizenship.

199 F. Snyder explains in 'The Effectiveness of European Community Law: Institutions, Processes, Tools and Techniques', *The Modern Law Review*, 56 (1993), 50, the gap-filling function of the duty of loyalty in the absence of direct effect.

200 D.-U. Galetta (2010), 11.

ing a competence catalogue,[201] through which all competences previously found in the case-law would become explicit.[202] Moreover, Art. 5(2) TEU has, in its new wording, been supplemented with the *e contrario* clarification that "Competences not conferred upon the Union in the Treaties remain with the Member States." The Lisbon Treaties therefore appeared to close any door that would have allowed for procedural competences to be based on substantive internal powers.

Case-law anteceding the Lisbon reform has nevertheless found a work-around, based on the requirement of effective implementation of EU substantive law. Members States have not conferred competences on the EU in a special sphere of exercise of public authority; the power to impose penalties. Yet, in this line of case-law (*Taricco et seq.*), the need to ensure effectiveness carried implications for the premise of national procedural autonomy in judicial proceedings within fields of competence otherwise belonging to the Member States. In the relevant cases, national legislation, including short limitation periods for tax infringements and thus inadequately dissuasive effect against serious tax fraud, was found liable to affect the financial interests of the EU.[203] Although the national legislator in principle remained free to prescribe criminal or administrative penalties for tax fraud, the procedural framework could not be pliant to the point that perpetrators of serious fraud could easily evade criminal accountability.[204]

Members States' obligation to impose effective and dissuasive penalties against infringements of EU law thus had an impact on the legislative and procedural (judicial) autonomy of Members States[205] – even in the event

201 A codified endeavor to make explicit "the jurisprudence of the Court to facilitate the action of the Union [...] in particular when dealing with the external dimension of internal policies and action." Final report of Working Group VII on External Action, 16 December 2002, Convention on the Future of Europe - Conv 459/02 – WGII 17, Brussels, 16/10/02. See further M. Klamert (2014), 143.

202 E.g. Art. 216(1) TFEU codified the doctrine of "implied" external powers, transforming it into a formalized tool to achieve objectives assigned to the EU through the Treaties. By contrast, the Treaties do not include provision for any "internal implied competences"; M. Klamert (2014), 143-44.

203 CJEU judgment in *Taricco and others*, C-105/14, EU:C:2015:555.

204 CJEU judgment in *Luca Menci*, C-524/15, EU:C:2018:197, 19-21; CJEU judgment in *M.A.S.*, C-42/17, EU:C:2017:936, 34-42.

205 CJEU judgment in *Taricco and others*, C-105/14, EU:C:2015:555; CJEU judgment in *Luca Menci*, C-524/15, EU:C:2018:197, 19-21; see further M. Timmerman, 'Balancing Effective Criminal Sanctions with Effective Fundamental Rights Protection in Cases of VAT Fraud: Taricco', *CMLR*, 53 (2016), 779-96.

that they were not implementing EU law in its traditional meaning.[206] Not only did that lead to expanding the field of application of EU law (particularly the Charter),[207] but also to placing authorities' and courts' freedom to apply national standards of procedural protection under scrutiny against EU law standards, including both effectiveness under the Treaties as above described and fundamental rights protection under the Charter.[208]

Pursuant to this revived doctrine of implied competences (based on an obligation of enforcement), substantive Union law provisions were still not alone a sufficient basis for prescribing procedural law obligations. Procedural obligations hinging on substantive rules, rights or objectives may take different legal forms, where a distinction should be maintained between legal bases for enacting constricted Union legislation with secondary procedural ramifications as earlier described,[209] versus Member States' ancillary responsibility for implementation – which, under Art 197(1) TFEU, is a "common interest" that cannot autonomously give rise to Member State obligations unless paired with other Treaty provisions, e.g. Arts. 291 TFEU and 4(3) TEU.[210] The duty of sincere co-operation, enshrined in Art. 4(3) TEU, also steps in for the latter purpose of consolidat-

206 CJEU judgment in *Åklagaren v. Hans Åkerberg Fransson*, C-617/10, EU:C:2013:105, 46, 48; see further E. Hancox, 'Meaning of Implementing EU Law under Article 51 (1) of the Charter: Åkerberg Fransson', *CMLR*, 50 (2013), 1420-21; S. Prechal, 'The Court of Justice and Effective Judicial Protection: What Has the Charter Changed?', in *Fundamental Rights in International and European Law*, eds. Paulussen, C., T. Takácz, V. Lazić and B. van Rompuy (The Hague: Springer, 2016), 146ff.

207 CJEU judgment in *Eugenia Florescu v. Casa Județeană de Pensii Sibiu*, C-258/14, EU:C:2017:448, 48; CJEU judgment in *Luca Menci*, C-524/15, EU:C:2018:197, 19-24.

208 CJEU judgment in *Luca Menci*, C-524/15, EU:C:2018:197, 25ff. Implied competences are, however, not exercised without nuance – see e.g. CJEU judgment in *M.A.S.*, C-42/17, EU:C:2017:936, where the referring court was left some discretion to comply with the principles of legality and non-retroactivity in criminal proceedings, as laid down in national law (59-62).

209 I.e. sector-specific substantive competence areas in the Treaties and Arts. 81 and 114 TFEU.

210 Which was inherent in CJEU judgment in *Åklagaren v. Hans Åkerberg Fransson*, C-617/10, EU:C:2013:105, 25-27 and CJEU judgment in *Taricco and others*, C-105/14, EU:C:2015:555, 36-39, linking Member States' sanction regimes to substantive Union objectives rather than to harmonization.

ing procedural obligations based on a duty to effectively enforce/implement Union objectives in primary and/or secondary law.[211]

2.2.3.2 The duty of sincere co-operation to fill the shoes of direct effect

The duty of sincere co-operation is not unique to EU law, having its origin in a traditional principle of public international law; namely the duty of harmonious interpretation of national law with international Treaty obligations.[212] The latter principle requires that national courts, in the face of inconsistencies between national law and international treaties, interpret national law in a way that is consistent with their Treaty obligations.[213] The rationale for the principle of harmonious interpretation is that national courts can base their reasoning on a presumption that the national law, which they are applying, has been brought (by the legislator) into conformity with their state's international obligations.[214] Therefore, presumably, any legislative gaps or uncertainties, giving rise to alternatives for the judiciary, should be handled in a manner that allows compliance with international law obligations.[215]

Under Union law, the duty of sincere co-operation[216] accordingly requires that domestic law be interpreted in a manner that allows the delivery of a ruling in compliance with Union law. In some circumstances, na-

---

211 In CJEU judgment in *Åklagaren v. Hans Åkerberg Fransson*, C-617/10, EU:C:2013:105, 25-27; CJEU judgment in *Taricco and others*, C-105/14, EU:C:2015:555, 36-39 and CJEU judgment in *Massimo Orsi*, C-217/15, EU:C:2017:264, 16, the substantive objective in Art. 325 TFEU was paired with the duty of sincere co-operation, construed in binding terms as an obligation to enforce secondary Union law (Council Directive 2006/112/EC of 28 November 2006 on the common system of value added tax, OJ L 347, 11/12/2006, 1).

212 Also referred to as the principle of good faith; see e.g. H. G. Schermers and D. Waelbroeck, *Judicial Protection in the European Union*, 6 edn. (The Hague: Kluwer Law International, 2001), § 205-8; J. H. Jans, R. de Lange, S. Prechal, and R. J. G. M. Widdershoven, *Europeanisation of Public Law* (Groningen: Europa Law Publishing, 2007), 51, 99.

213 A. Rosas, E. Levits, and Y. Bot, eds., *La Cour de Justice et la Construction de l'Europe : Analyses et Perspectives de Soixante Ans de Jurisprudence* (The Hague: Asser Press, 2013), 601.

214 See e.g. CJEU judgment in *Pfeiffer and Others*, joined cases C-397/01 to C-403/01, EU:C:2004:584, 112.

215 U. Bernitz and A. Kjellgren, *Europarättens grunder* (Vällingby: Norstedts juridik AB, 2007), 71.

216 Here used synonymously with the duty/principle of loyalty.

tional courts are required to set aside national law to give effect to Union law – this would be the case where national law collides with directly effective provisions of Union law. There are, however, other circumstances in which the Union provisions at stake lack direct effect – in which case the principle of loyalty has the function of filling this gap by requiring a national court to nonetheless give an interpretation of national law that is consistent with Union law obligations.[217]

The difference between these two obligations (of interpreting national law in a Union-friendly manner versus of setting aside national law or interpreting it *contra legem*[218]) is most easily approached from the point of view of direct effect as a dividing line. The direct effect of a provision would require its application by national courts, as a matter of primacy, no matter the content of national law.[219] In the absence of direct effect, the Court of Justice has increasingly been confronted with the question of what type of demands can be placed on national courts and authorities to nevertheless ensure effectiveness of Union law. Although traditionally, the case-law has predominantly focused on the criteria for direct effect[220] and aspects of its protective scope,[221] it has become increasingly clear that the force of direct effect cannot be all-encompassing and that voids need to be properly dealt with.[222] Therefore, and perhaps logically, we have seen a transformation of the duty of sincere co-operation from normative statement to general principle of law, with the capacity of bringing about obligations for the Member States.[223]

This capacity has been described as a gap-filling function.[224] There are situations in which direct effect is absent (either because a provision lacks direct effect or because it cannot be applied in e.g. horizontal relation-

217 F. Snyder (1993), 42-43.

218 I.e. construing a law in a manner contrary to its express wording.

219 CJEU judgment in *Costa v. E.N.E.L.*, 6/64, EU:C:1964:66; CJEU judgment in *van Gend en Loos v. Administratie der Belastingen*, 26/62, EU:C:1963:1.

220 CJEU judgment in van *Gend en Loos v. Administratie der Belastingen*, 26/62, EU:C:1963:1.

221 See e.g. CJEU judgment in *Unilever Italia SpA v. Central Food SpA*, C-443/98, EU:C:2000:496; CJEU judgment in *CIA Security International SA v. Signalson SA and Securitel SPRL*, C-194/94, EU:C:1996:172; CJEU judgment in *Union royale belge des sociétés de football association and Others v. Bosman and Others*, C-415/93, EU:C:1995:463.

222 S. Prechal, 'Does Direct Effect Still Matter?', *CMLR*, 37 (2000), 1067-69.

223 E. F. Hinton (1998), 319-21, F. Snyder (1993), 50-53.

224 V. Skouris (2009), 494; E. F. Hinton (1998), 321ff.; S. Drake (2016), 22-23.

ships[225]) and situations in which direct effect is "rendered ineffective by Member State action or inaction."[226] Consequently, individuals' role in safeguarding the effectiveness of Union law is left in the hands of Member State public bodies who gain exclusive control over ensuring Union law effectiveness.[227] It is here that the duty of sincere co-operation steps in to ascertain that Member State authorities and courts take this responsibility seriously and do not act in bad faith to jeopardize the effectiveness of Union law.[228] This is the key rationale for garbing Member States with a more general duty of sincere co-operation; namely as a counterweight against this vulnerability.[229]

The location outside the reach of direct effect alas brings with it certain limitations. The duty of sincere co-operation can only require national courts and authorities to carry out their obligations to the extent that they are garbed with powers to do so. Therefore, the duty of sincere co-operation does not, in principle, require a national judge to take measures that he is not mandated to take, such as interpreting national law against its wording, and it cannot form the basis for the imposition of new remedies.[230]

---

225 CJEU judgment in *Marshall v. Southampton and South-West Hampshire Area Health Authority (Marshall I)*, 152/84, EU:C:1986:84, 48; CJEU judgment in *Faccini Dori v. Recreb*, C-91/92, EU:C:1994:292, 20.

226 E. F. Hinton (1998), 321.

227 See, on private enforcement by individuals: M. Dougan, 'Who Exactly Benefits from the Treaties? The Murky Interaction Between Union and National Competence over the Capacity to Enforce EU Law', *Cambridge Yearbook of European Legal Studies*, 12 (2012), 92-96; F. Wilman (2015); S. Drake, (2016), 15ff.

228 In this vein, the cumulative means of ensuring effectiveness of Union law – through direct effect, consistent interpretation, the availability of damages for breach of EU law, and the harmonizing potential of the doctrine of full effect – have been described as both bolstering private enforcement to the benefit of individual actors, and filling "a political function of social control"; F. Snyder (1993), 46.

229 E. F. Hinton (1998), 321.

230 CJEU judgment in *Impact v. Minister for Agriculture and Food and Others*, C-268/06, EU:C:2008:223, 100; CJEU judgment in *Maribel Dominguez v. Centre informatique du Centre Ouest Atlantique and Préfet de la région Centre*, C-282/10, EU:C:2012:33, 25; CJEU judgment in *Association de médiation sociale v. Union locale des syndicats CGT and Others (AMS)*, C-176/12, EU:C:2014:2, 39; CJEU judgment in *Dansk industri*, C-441/14, EU:C:2016:278, 32; CJEU judgment in *Criminal proceedings against Maria Pupino*, C-105/03, EU:C:2005:386. See, by comparison, CJEU judgment in *Vereniging Nationaal Overlegorgaan Sociale Werkvoorziening and Others (VNOSW)*, joined cases C-383/06 to C-385/06, EU:C:2008:165, 40.

Having thus laid down the main limitations of the duty of sincere co-operation, we take a closer look at what can actually be demanded in its name. The content of this duty follows already from the wording of Art. 4(3) TEU:

> Pursuant to the principle of sincere cooperation, the Union and the Member States shall, in full mutual respect, assist each other in carrying out tasks which flow from the Treaties.
>
> The Member States shall take any appropriate measure, general or particular, to ensure fulfillment of the obligations arising out of the Treaties or resulting from the acts of the institutions of the Union.
>
> The Member States shall facilitate the achievement of the Union's tasks and refrain from any measure which could jeopardise the attainment of the Union's objectives.

Art. 4(3) TEU draws a picture of far-reaching obligations for Member States, including for the national judge. These aspects have been referred to as "positive obligations" entailed by the duty of sincere co-operation.[231] They have been broken down into specific responsibilities for national courts and authorities, but also, as originally intended, for Member States in their interaction with each other and the EU institutions.[232]

The "negative obligation" enshrined in the principle of sincere co-operation is also spelled out explicitly in the TEU: "The Member States shall [...] refrain from any measure which could jeopardize the attainment of the Union's objectives."[233] This negative side of the duty of sincere co-operation takes the more traditional form of the international law principle of good faith. In the EU context, this *inter alia* entails, on the legislative side, abstention from adopting legislation that runs contrary to the Treaties, and on the judiciary side, abstention from enforcing e.g. agreements and obligations that infringe EU law.[234]

231 P. van Cleynenbreugel (2012 b); M. Klamert (2014), 10.

232 H. G. Schermers and D. Waelbroeck (2001), §§ 207-12; E. F. Hinton (1998), 319-21; D. Simon, 'Les fondements de l'autonomie du droit communautaire', *Droit international et droit communautaire. Perspectives actuelles* (2000), 242-44.

233 Art. 4(3)(3) TEU.

234 See e.g. CJEU judgment in *Cullet v. Leclerc*, C-231/83, EU:C:1985:29, 20; CJEU judgment in *Eco Swiss China Time Ltd v. Benetton International NV*, C-126/97, EU:C:1999:269; CJEU judgment in *Silvia Georgiana Câmpean*, C-200/14, EU:C:2016:494, 42-44, 71; CJEU judgment in *Dansk industri*, C-441/14, EU:C:2016:278, 27-35.

With regards to obligations incumbent on national courts, the Court of Justice has clarified several steps of co-operation with the Art. 267-procedure in which national courts may be required to defy higher court authorities as well as the legislator. First of all, national courts are required to overcome obstacles to making preliminary references, in order to pose a question to the Court of Justice, even if this requires them to disregard previous national jurisprudence or procedural obstacles of any variety (negative obligation).[235] Secondly, obstacles put in place by the legislator hindering the national judge from doing so have been considered contrary to the "very essence"[236] of EU law, implying a positive duty incumbent on the national legislator to take measures in order to furnish the national judge with necessary powers to make preliminary references to the Court of Justice at his widest possible discretion (below referred to as the "*Rheinmühlen* mandate").[237] Finally, once having received a judgment from the Court of Justice, national courts are required to abide by it, if necessary in defiance of earlier jurisprudence or of the hierarchy between courts (positive obligation).[238]

It is useful to use as illustration a child who is autonomous when walking alone to school, but whose autonomy is limited by the positive obligation of actually arriving. This agreement on autonomy may be "functional-

---

235 CJEU judgment in *Georgi Ivanov Elchinov v. Natsionalna zdravnoosiguritelna kasa*, C-173/09, EU:C:2010:581; CJEU judgment in *Cartesio Oktató és Szolgáltató bt*, C-210/06, EU:C:2008:723.

236 CJEU judgment in *Puligienica Facility Esco SpA (PFE) v. Airgest SpA*, C-689/13, EU:C:2016:199, 41; CJEU judgment in *A v. B and Others*, C-112/13, EU:C:2014:2195, 37.

237 CJEU judgment in *Mecanarte-Metalurgica da Lagoa v. Alfandega do Porto*, C-348/89, EU:C:1991:278, 44; CJEU judgment in *Cartesio Oktató és Szolgáltató bt*, C-210/06, EU:C:2008:723, 88; CJEU judgment in *Aziz Melki and Sélim Abdeli*, joined cases C-188/10 and C-189/10, EU:C:2010:363, 41; CJEU judgment in *Georgi Ivanov Elchinov v. Natsionalna zdravnoosiguritelna kasa*, C-173/09, EU:C:2010:581, 35.

238 CJEU judgment in *Georgi Ivanov Elchinov v. Natsionalna zdravnoosiguritelna kasa*, C-173/09, EU:C:2010:581, 30; CJEU judgment in *Puligienica Facility Esco SpA (PFE) v. Airgest SpA*, C-689/13, EU:C:2016:199, 38; CJEU judgment in *A v. B and Others*, C-112/13, EU:C:2014:2195, 46 (the latter applying to the disregard of interlocutory procedures preceding preliminary references). The duty of sincere co-operation also emphasizes the obligation incumbent on the Union and its institutions to co-operate loyally with the Member States and to give assistance to them in carrying out their tasks, e.g. by the Court of Justice assisting Member State courts by responding to preliminary references; H. G. Schermers and D. Waelbroeck (2001), § 211.

ized",[239] so as to include a variety of other practical aspects, as long as their connection, or rationale, is the facilitation of arriving safely to school. In the EU law conceptualization, this positive obligation would correspond to the duty of sincere co-operation in reaching the decided goal. The Court of Justice has stated that the obligation "does not restrict the powers of the competent national courts to apply, from among the various procedures available under national law, those which are appropriate for the purpose of protecting the individual rights conferred by community law."[240] Yet, the autonomy is limited in the sense that the chosen means must be appropriate in order to protect individual (directly effective) rights – an obligation of result.[241]

By laying down minimum requirements on such means, in effect the Court of Justice is assuming that Member States responsibly "endow [...] themselves with the proper instruments to sanction the respect for EU law."[242] Member States' procedural competence is thus "conditional" upon the obligation of ensuring the useful effect of individual rights granted under Union law. Galetta has described this as an "implicit EU competence on procedural matters in the attenuated form, which leads [...] to a 'functionalized' procedural competence."[243] Member States "retain a procedural competence that remains in a 'subservient function' in relation to their obligation to guarantee the effectiveness of EU substantive law."[244] Yet, it is not a mechanism of primacy requiring national rules to be set aside, but rather that they be balanced, as far as possible, against the interests of protecting Union rights.[245]

239 As previously discussed, the terminology has been advanced by D.-U. Galetta (2010), 13.

240 CJEU judgment in *Firma Gebrüder Lück v. Hauptzollamt Köln-Rheinau*, 34/67, EU:C:1968:24.

241 On the mandate of the national judge in the functioning of the preliminary reference procedure, and particularly his obligation of result towards attaining Union law objectives through judicial co-operation with the Court of Justice, see E. Neframi (2015), 24; E. Neframi (2006), 52.

242 D.-U. Galetta (2010), 13.

243 Ibid.

244 Ibid. On the subject of this subservience/recipient of Union obligations (the legislator or national courts), see e.g. D. Simon (2000), 243 and S. Prechal, *Directives in EC Law. 2 edn* (New York: Oxford University Press, 2005), 318-20.

245 E. Neframi, 'La force intégrative du statut de l'Etat membre sur la fonction juridictionnelle', in *Le statut d'Etat membre de l'Union européenne*, ed. Potvin-Solis, L. (Brussels: Bruylant, 2018), 349-50.

2.2.3.3 From consistent interpretation to legal protection of individual rights

How, then, is the step taken from the duty of sincere co-operation, with its inherent limitations as above described, to curtailing Member State procedural autonomy? Let us approach this question by isolating the implications of the duty of sincere co-operation for the judiciary, as opposed to the legislator. If national legislation makes it impossible for individuals to rely on rights protected by Union law, then it is up to the judiciary to remedy this encroachment.[246] It has, however, long been recognized that horizontal litigation represents a situation in which national courts cannot be categorically expected to enforce centralized rules against other individuals, contrary to the expressed will or instruction of the national legislator. The example of horizontal litigation illustrates the difficulties that arise when consistent interpretation is insufficient to ensure legal protection of Union rights, whereas legislative review is beyond the limits of the seized court's jurisdiction.

The responsibility of courts for individuals' breaches of each other's rights is not a controversy exclusive to EU law. According to the State Action Doctrine, founded by the US Supreme Court in the civil rights era,[247] the moment a State court instance endorses behavior by individual parties that runs contrary to federal constitutional rights of due process, a violation is taking place in the courtroom; the judge is himself at fault by not taking measures against the offender. Therefore, lack of individual accountability for complying with centralized (federal) norms does not shield the decentralized court from an obligation to safeguard the same centralized norms in the context of litigation between individuals.

In the EU law context, this rationale is at the core of legal protection of individual rights. The case-law on directives' lack of horizontal effects illustrates how a legal gap was filled by expanding the reach of the duty of sincere co-operation in view of protecting individual Union law beneficiaries. In its initial case-law, the Court of Justice had established that individuals cannot rely on a directive against private parties, since directives cannot create obligations for individuals, being binding only "in relation to each

246 S. Prechal (2005), 319.

247 US Supreme Court judgment in *Shelley v. Kraemer*, 334 U.S. 1, 68 S. Ct. 836, 92 L. Ed. 1161 (1948). See also US Supreme Court judgment in *Burton v. Wilmington Parking Authority*, 365 U.S. 715, 81 S. Ct. 856, 6 L. Ed. 2 d 45 (1961).

Member State to which it is addressed" (the "*Marshall* dictum").[248] The Court of Justice instead indicated two other manners in which individuals could vindicate their rights under Union law against other individual parties without relying on their direct effect; first, through damages under the State liability doctrine, and secondly through national courts' duty of consistent interpretation.[249]

The Court of Justice successively recognized that in order to induce compliance with far-reaching obligations contained in directives, the duty of consistent interpretation had to be construed in a way that would sufficiently bind Member State courts and authorities so as to ensure their enforcement.[250] This implies that the Court of Justice may in fact have wished to relax earlier case-law in order not to leave individuals in a precarious legal position as soon as they faced infringements imputable to individuals rather than state parties. Yet, instead of reversing the *Marshall* dictum, the Court of Justice proceeded to prescribe other means and methods for national courts to comply with the duty of consistent interpretation.[251]

The case-law successively expanded the potential of horizontal effects of directives, clarifying how the duty of sincere co-operation and the requirement of full effect/legal protection interact to cover a variety of situations outside the reach of direct effect,[252] ostensibly blurring the boundary be-

---

248 CJEU judgment in *Faccini Dori v. Recreb*, C-91/92, EU:C:1994:292, 2, 24; CJEU judgment in *Marshall v. Southampton and South-West Hampshire Area Health Authority (Marshall I)*, 152/84, EU:C:1986:84, 48, see e.g. M. Burley and W. Mattli (1993), 61. The notion of state organs has for this purpose successively been expanded: CJEU judgment in *Elaine Farrell*, C-413/15, EU:C:2017:745, 26-29.

249 CJEU judgment in *Faccini Dori v. Recreb*, C-91/92, EU:C:1994:292, 26-27. See further F. Snyder (1993), 41-44, on the gaps left after the identification of direct effect, and the role of damages and consistent interpretation as secondary means of ensuring effectiveness.

250 This matter is discussed in D. Leczykiewicz, 'Effectiveness of EU Law before National Courts: Direct Effect, Effective Judicial Protection, and Member State Liability', in *Oxford Handbook of European Union Law*, eds. Arnull A. and D. Chalmers (Oxford: Oxford University Press, 2015), under title V.; G. de Búrca, 'The Legal Effects of Directives: Policy, Rules and Exceptions', *ELR*, 34 (2009).

251 CJEU judgment in *Marleasing v. Comercial Internacional de Alimentación*, C-106/89, EU:C:1990:395, 13.

252 CJEU judgment in *Pfeiffer and Others*, joined cases C-397/01 to C-403/01, EU:C:2004:584, 111; reiterated in CJEU judgment in *Seda Kücükdeveci v. Swedex GmbH & Co. KG*, C-555/07, EU:C:2010:21, 45 and CJEU judgment in *Dansk industri*, C-441/14, EU:C:2016:278, 29.

tween consistent interpretation and legislative review.[253] The gap-filling function of the duty of sincere co-operation indicates a subsidiary relationship with full effect, capable of compelling a judge to set aside national law as a matter of legal protection/full effectiveness (even in the absence of direct effect), under the rationale that the method of consistent interpretation was not adequate for this purpose.[254]

To close the circle, it is useful to return to the scholarly account of "functionalization" of the duty of sincere co-operation to serve the useful effect of Union directives and particularly their beneficiaries.[255] The duty of sincere co-operation first merely required an interpretation consistent with "the *objective* which [the Directive] pursues,"[256] but has nonetheless evolved into a duty to provide legal protection in order to ensure the full effectiveness of Union law.[257] Once national courts are dealing with rules which, as applied in a case before them, are capable of encroaching upon individual rights, the requirement of legal protection may be used to compel national courts to ensure that the violation does not give rise to legal losses for individuals. This means carrying out consistent interpretation of national law in order to give priority to a reading that complies with Union law; and, where this is not sufficient, setting aside conflicting national legislation.[258] The complementarity between the prescribed measures shows how the duty of sincere co-operation has been functionalized to compel national courts to take measures in excess of their competence

---

253 D. Leczykiewicz (2015), 13: "the scope of application of national provisions should be restricted by applying them only insofar as they are compatible with the Directive concerned."

254 CJEU judgment in *Dansk industri*, C-441/14, EU:C:2016:278, 16, 35; see also CJEU judgment in *Seda Kücükdeveci v. Swedex GmbH & Co. KG*, C-555/07, EU:C:2010:21, 51, with further commentary on both cases in U. Šadl and S. Mair, 'Mutual Disempowerment: Case C-441/14 Dansk Industri, acting on behalf of Ajos A/S v Estate of Karsten Eigil Rasmussen and Case no. 15/2014 Dansk Industri (DI) acting for Ajos A/S v. The estate left by A', *ECL*, 13 (2017), 347-68.

255 D.-U. Galetta (2010), 13.

256 CJEU judgment in *Von Colson and Kamann v. Land Nordrhein-Westfalen*, 14/83, EU:C:1984:153,15.

257 CJEU judgment in *Marleasing v. Comercial Internacional de Alimentación*, C-106/89, EU:C:1990:395, 9; CJEU judgment in *Dansk industri*, C-441/14, EU:C:2016:278, 35. See further, F. Snyder (1993), 42-43.

258 Or (a third option which is not here dealt with) in the event of violations in the past, to grant damages to individuals who have suffered from breaches of Union law; V. Skouris (2009), 497-500.

under national law, a requirement which the original duty of sincere co-operation had not comprised.[259]

The forthcoming sections deal with two additional requirements that the duty of sincere co-operation has given rise to – namely the principles of equivalence and effectiveness – which have equally undergone transformations through interpretations in the case-law, hinging on the courts' powers and obligations under national law. The principle of effectiveness has been interpreted as requiring, in various instances, minimum/adequate,[260] or conditioned effectiveness,[261] during the different phases of its development.[262] The principle of equivalence has, in turn, been clarified in terms of the appropriate national comparator,[263] and the procedural rule-of-reason has been held to be equally applicable to the principle of equivalence.[264]

2.2.3.4 The principle of *Rewe*-equivalence

In its well-known *Rewe* dictum, the Court of Justice held that, on the basis of the duty of sincere co-operation, procedural conditions governing an ac-

259 The "full effect" tool was substituted for the *Rewe* formula in CJEU judgment in *Theresa Emmott v. Minister for Social Welfare and the Attorney General*, C-208/90, EU:C:1991:333, for no other apparent reason than needing a "sharper" tool to overcome procedural obstacles (16-17).

260 Corresponding to the respective notions of "impossible in practice" as orignally introduced in CJEU judgment in *Rewe v. Landwirtschaftskammer für das Saarland*, 33/76, EU:C:1976:188, 5, versus "excessively difficult"; see further A. P. Komninos, 'New Prospects for Private Enforcement of EC Competition Law: Courage v. Crehan and the Community Right to Damages', *CMLR*, 39 (2002), 465; W. van Gerven (2000), 501-36.

261 Including the procedural rule-of-reason introduced through CJEU judgment in *van Schijndel v. Stichting Pensioenfonds voor Fysiotherapeuten*, joined cases C-430/93 and C-431/93, EU:C:1995:441.

262 For a more detailed account, see M. Dougan, 'The Vicissitudes of Life at the Coalface: Remedies and Procedures for Enforcing Union Law before the National Courts', in *The Evolution of EU Law*, eds. Craig, P. and G. de Búrca (New York: Oxford University Press, 2011 a), 405-38.

263 CJEU judgment *in Abdelhafid Bensada Benallal v. État belge*, C-161/15, EU:C:2016:175; CJEU judgment in *Silvia Georgiana Câmpean*, C-200/14, EU:C:2016:494; CJEU judgment in *Evelyn Danqua v. Minister for Justice and Equality*, C-429/15, EU:C:2016:789.

264 P. Craig and G. de Búrca, (2011 b), 239; CJEU judgment in *Levez v. Jennings Ltd*, C-326/96, EU:C:1998:577, 44.

tion founded on EU law "may not be less favorable than those relating to similar actions of a domestic nature."[265] For the first time, the pre-existing Union principle of non-discrimination was given a procedural guise.[266] This principle of equivalence requires national courts to compare the procedural conditions governing two litigation contexts: on the one hand, Union-based litigation and on the other, purely domestic claims.[267] The purpose is to ascertain whether the "procedural feasibility" of the claims in each regime would lead to more or less favorable outcomes.[268] This comparison brings about a few problems.

First of all, the reference to "similar actions" immediately poses the same difficulty, as does the principle of non-discrimination in substantive Union law – namely finding a national claim or legal action that corresponds to the contested Union law-based claim.[269] Comparison is allowed "where the purpose and cause of action are similar."[270] However, there are an increasing number of litigation types in which a claim can only be based on Union law; a "purely domestic" national claim does not exist.[271] This "missing comparator"[272] problem places situations outside the reach of the principle of equivalence, unless one were to proceed to a high enough level of abstraction to find a "similar" domestic action. The Court has opted for a narrow view on the principle of equivalence by rejecting national

265 CJEU judgment in *Rewe v. Landwirtschaftskammer für das Saarland*, 33/76, EU:C:1976:188, 6.

266 D.-U. Galetta (2010), 24; see particularly subsequent CJEU judgment in *Direcţia Generală Regională a Finanţelor Publice Braşov v. Vasile Toma*, C-205/15, EU:C:2016:499.

267 CJEU judgment in *Palmisani v. INPS*, C-261/95, EU:C:1997:351, 34-38; CJEU judgment in *Levez v. Jennings Ltd*, C-326/96, EU:C:1998:577, 43; CJEU judgment in *EOS KSI Slovensko*, C-448/17, EU:C:2018:745, 38-40.

268 M. Bobek (2012), 314ff.

269 J. H. Jans, R. de Lange, S. Prechal, and R. J. G. M. Widdershoven (2007), 46ff.

270 CJEU judgment in *ET Agrokonsulting-04-Velko Stoyanov v. Izpalnitelen direktor na Darzhaven fond «Zemedelie» - Razplashtatelna agentsia*, C-93/12, EU:C:2013:432, 39. For a strict application of the criteria of similar type of action, see CJEU judgment in *ÖBB Personenverkehr*, C-417/13, EU:C:2015:38, 70-75 and CJEU judgment in *Dragoş Constantin Târşia v. Statul român*, C-69/14, EU:C:2015:662, 34.

271 See e.g. CJEU judgment in *Evelyn Danqua v. Minister for Justice and Equality*, C-429/15, EU:C:2016:789, 32-35.

272 M. Bobek (2012), 313-15; S. Prechal (2017 a), 394.

causes of actions displaying all too great differences.[273] The problem of identifying the relevant comparator has also surfaced in connection with the issue of *ex officio* review, triggering the difficulty of comparing Union with national public policy.[274]

Secondly, comparisons of similar purposes and causes of action require the Court of Justice to examine and even interpret *national* law – which is at odds with its mandate to exclusively deal with application, interpretation and validity of *Union* law.[275] Interpretation and application of national law is reserved for the national judge,[276] why the equivalence assessment risks perturbing the division of labor between the Court of Justice and the national courts. The Court of Justice is bound to base its reasoning exclusively on the (sometimes limited) description of information exposed in the preliminary reference.[277] The Court's lack of information and understanding makes it difficult to proceed, remaining strictly within its jurisdiction, with an examination of the role and function of the procedural rule in its particular national context.[278] The exercise of surreptitiously interpreting national law to decide on its compatibility with Union law also makes the content of the preliminary rulings less generic and therefore also less valuable as guidance for other Member States.[279]

---

273 CJEU judgment in *Dragoş Constantin Târşia v. Statul român*, C-69/14, EU:C:2015:662; CJEU judgment in *Orizzonte Salute*, C-61/14, EU:C:2015:655; CJEU judgment in *Silvia Georgiana Câmpean*, C-200/14, EU:C:2016:494, 52-55.

274 CJEU judgment in *Dirk Frederik Asbeek Brusse*, C-488/11, EU:C:2013:341, 44; CJEU judgment in *Froukje Faber*, C-497/13, EU:C:2015:357, 56-57; CJEU judgment in *Abdelhafid Bensada Benallal v. État belge*, C-161/15, EU:C:2016:175; see also the analogous discussion on effective judicial protection in CJEU judgment in *Banco Primus SA v. Jesús Gutiérrez García*, C-421/14, EU:C:2017:60, 42.

275 Art. 267 TFEU; see further A. Meij (2011), 266.

276 CJEU judgment in *Da Costa en Schaake NV, Jacob Meijer NV, Hoechst-Holland NV v. Netherlands Inland Revenue Administration*, joined cases 28/62 to 39/62 EU:C:1963:6, pp. 31, 38; CJEU judgment in *Virginie Pontin v. T-Comalux SA*, C-63/08, EU:C:2009:666; CJEU judgment in *Littlewoods Retail Ltd and Others v. Her Majesty's Commissioners of Revenue and Customs*, C-591/10, EU:C:2012:478, 31; CJEU judgment in *ET Agrokonsulting-04-Velko Stoyanov v. Izpalnitelen direktor na Darzhaven fond «Zemedelie» - Razplashtatelna agentsia*, C-93/12, EU:C:2013:432.

277 CJEU judgment in *Atanas Ognyanov (I)*, C-614/14, EU:C:2016:514,18-21.

278 M. Bobek (2012), 315, see CJEU judgment in *EOS KSI Slovensko*, C-448/17, EU:C:2018:745, 40.

279 This matter has been highlighted by M. Bobek (2012), 312-15; see also, on this matter, D.-U. Galetta (2010), 24-25.

Thirdly, there is a problem of inverse discrimination brought about by the requirement that Union law-based claims be given *at least as favorable* treatment as claims based on national law. The problems arising from this situation are not immediately apparent unless approached from the viewpoint of procedural equality.[280] As soon as Union law-based claims are given more favorable treatment, a litigant relying on national law will find himself in a less favorable situation compared to if he were basing his claims on Union law.[281] In *A v. B*, the Court was asked whether the principle of equivalence could be used to decline to make a preliminary reference, by giving Union-law based claims the same treatment (via an interlocutory constitutional review procedure) as constitutionality challenges, including under the ECHR.[282] The Court of Justice rejected this notion, recalling that the principle of equivalence could not be relied upon in order to avoid the duty of making a preliminary reference to the Court of Justice,[283] with the outcome of prescribing more favorable procedural treatment for Union law-based claims than for other claims.

Finally, the legal basis of the *Rewe* principles has been reconsidered. Post-Lisbon, we have seen the principle of effective judicial protection increasing in importance and sometimes substituting the duty of sincere cooperation as basis for obligations in the sphere of procedural autonomy.[284] Although the principles of equivalence and effectiveness do not appear to

---

280 For a similar reasoning on such "spillover" effects in the procedural context, see M. Dougan (2012), 79.

281 P. Craig and G. de Búrca, *EU Law: Text, Cases, and Materials*, 5 edn. (New York: Oxford University Press, 2011 a), 240; A. Wallerman (2015), 103; M. Dougan, 'In Defence of Mangold?', in *A Constitutional Order of States?*, eds. Arnull, A., C. Barnard, M. Dougan, and E. Spaventa (Cornwall: Hart Publishing, 2011 b), 242; T. Heukels, 'Joined Cases C-430/93 and C-431/93, van Schijndel and van Veen v. Stichting Pensioenfonds voor Fysiotherapeuten; and Case C-312/93, Peterbroeck, van Campenhout & Cie SCS v. Belgian State, Both Judgments of the Court of 14 December 1995 (Full Court)', *CMLR*, 33 (1996), 349.

282 CJEU judgment in *A v. B and Others*, C-112/13, EU:C:2014:2195, 24-26; see further D. Düsterhaus, 'Procedural Primacy and Effective Judicial Protection – A Trilogue. Case C-112/13 A v. B and Others, EU:C:2014:2195', *MJECL*, 23 (2016), 317-31.

283 CJEU judgment in *A v. B and Others*, C-112/13, EU:C:2014:2195, 45.

284 See e.g. CJEU judgment in *Impact v. Minister for Agriculture and Food and Others*, C-268/06, EU:C:2008:223, 48-55; CJEU judgment in *Deutsche Energiehandels- und Beratungsgesellschaft mbH v. Bundesrepublik Deutschland (DEB)*, C-279/09, EU:C:2010:811, 59-63.

be declining in importance or use,[285] the principle of equivalence has, as part of the *Rewe* formula, been sorted directly under the wider umbrella of effective judicial protection (which must be understood as requiring non-discriminatory access to court).[286]

Under the auspices of the equivalence test, a fundamental rights approach was accordingly applied by the Court of Justice in the *Toma* ruling.[287] The case concerned rules on court fees discriminating between public bodies and private litigants. The Court of Justice's reasoning, prompted by the Charter provisions evoked by the referring court, singled out the principle of equality before the law (Art. 20 CFR) as umbrella concept under which certain components of Art. 47 may be ordered:[288]

> The Court has already stated that Article 47 of the Charter includes, as a component of the principle of effective judicial protection, the principle of equality of arms or procedural equality [...] the latter principle constitutes a specific expression of the general principle of equality before the law found in Article 20 of the Charter[.]

Although the Court of Justice ultimately found no violation of the principle of equivalence,[289] it remains to be seen whether, in the future, coupling the right to equality before the law with the right to effective judicial protection will be capable of bolstering also the principle of equivalence.

2.2.3.5 The principle of *Rewe*-effectiveness

The principle of equivalence has, conceivably due to the earlier discussed criticisms,[290] taken a secondary role to the second tier of the *Rewe* doctrine;

---

285 CJEU judgment in *Dragoş Constantin Târşia v. Statul român*, C-69/14, EU:C:2015:662; CJEU judgment in *Direcţia Generală Regională a Finanţelor Publice Braşov v. Vasile Toma*, C-205/15, EU:C:2016:499; CJEU judgment in *Evelyn Danqua v. Minister for Justice and Equality*, C-429/15, EU:C:2016:789; CJEU judgment in *EOS KSI Slovensko*, C-448/17, EU:C:2018:745.

286 Opinion of Advocate General Jääskinen in *Orizzonte Salute*, C-61/14, EU:C:2015:307, 24; commented by J. Krommendijk (2016), 1398-1400.

287 CJEU judgment in *Direcţia Generală Regională a Finanţelor Publice Braşov v. Vasile Toma*, C-205/15, EU:C:2016:499.

288 Ibid., 36; cf., with respect to equivalent protection between EU Member States, CJEU judgment in *Bashar Ibrahim*, joined cases C-297/17, C-318/17, C-319/17 and C-438/17, EU:C:2019:219, 66.

289 CJEU judgment in *Direcţia Generală Regională a Finanţelor Publice Braşov v. Vasile Toma*, C-205/15, EU:C:2016:499, 57.

290 M. Bobek (2012), 315; F. Wilman (2015), 31; S. Prechal (1998), 687.

the principle of effectiveness.[291] In the *Rewe* and *Comet* rulings, the Court of Justice clarified that, even when the principle of equivalence was complied with,[292] national procedural regimes could be contrary to Union law (once again due to the duty of sincere co-operation) "if the conditions [...] made it impossible in practice to exercise the rights which the national courts are obliged to protect."[293] Initially, the principle of effectiveness was assumed only to apply to directly effective Treaty provisions and provisions of secondary law attributed direct effect.[294] Later, it became clear that the scope of the principle of effectiveness had to be widened: Irrespective of the absence or presence of direct effect in a given case, it needed to be ensured that national courts and authorities not undermine the "effect or the effectiveness" of Union law in general.[295]

Similarly to the duty of sincere co-operation, *Rewe*-effectiveness has been broken down into two sides: on the one hand, an exclusionary side which prevents Member States from relying on national procedural law to justify violating substantive Union law, and on the other hand, a creationist side, with the potential of requiring national judges to take positive steps to ensure the effectiveness of substantive Union law.[296] The exclusionary side of the principle allows national courts to apply national procedural rules only insofar as they do not "jeopardize either the scope or the effectiveness" of Union rules.[297] In this way, national rules are described as "subservient"

291 A. Wallerman (2015), 101; M. Bobek (2012), 315; J. H. Jans, R. de Lange, S. Prechal, and R. J. G. M. Widdershoven (2007), 43ff.

292 The requirements of equivalence and effectiveness are in other words cumulative; see e.g. Opinion of Advocate General Szpunar in *Silvia Georgiana Câmpean*, C-200/14, EU:C:2016:99, 37.

293 CJEU judgment in *Rewe v. Landwirtschaftskammer für das Saarland*, 33/76, EU:C:1976:188, 5; CJEU judgment in *Comet BV v. Produktschap voor Siergewassen*, 45/76, EU:C:1976:191, 13.

294 CJEU judgment in *Marshall v. Southampton and South-West Hampshire Area Health Authority (Marshall II)*, C-271/91, EU:C:1993:335, 21-24.

295 A. Ward, 'Effective Sanctions in EC Law: A Moving Boundary in the Division of Competence', *ELJ*, 1 (1995), 214.

296 M. Klamert (2014), 128-31; S. Prechal and R. Widdershoven (2011 a), 289-90; A. F. M. Brenninkmeijer, 'The Influence of Court of Justice Case Law on the Procedural Law of the Member States', in *Administrative Law Application and Enforcement of Community Law in the Netherlands*, eds. Vervaele, J. A. E. and K.-A. Andrean-Gellert (Deventer-Boston: Kluwer Law and Taxation Publ., 1994), 111ff. See also, on the positive side of the principle of effectiveness, P. van Cleynenbreugel, 'The Confusing Constitutional Status of Positive Procedural Obligations in EU Law', *REALaw*, 5 (2012 b), 93ff.

297 CJEU judgment in *Adidas AG*, C-223/98, EU:C:1999:500, 25.

and "ancillary" to Union law by the way in which they are to be set aside as soon as they pose obstacles to its effective implementation.[298] The setting aside of national procedural rules is thus the basic instrument that the principle of effectiveness places in the hands of the national judge.[299]

On the creationist side of the principle of *Rewe*-effectiveness, we find an obligation to ensure that remedies and sanctions guaranteeing the effectiveness of Union law are in place. It has already been shown that the Court of Justice did have some difficulties reconciling the limits of the duty of sincere co-operation, namely in that it only intervenes in a national judge's choice between such options that are *intra vires*, minded to ensure the effectiveness of Union law provisions lacking direct effect.[300] Normally, the duty of sincere co-operation would intervene on the exclusionary side of the principle of effectiveness (so that interpretations of national law that jeopardize Union law may be avoided).

With the elaboration of sub-categories of certain obligations included under the umbrella of sincere co-operation, further consequences have sequentially ensued. As a result of "functionalization" of the duty of sincere co-operation,[301] national courts must in practice consider all existing possibilities of interpretation available to them in order to find a solution, within their powers, to deliver a judgment that ensures the effectiveness of Union law.[302] As already seen, the Court has required that the national judge not only interpret provisions at stake in the national proceedings, but also consider all applicable national law in order to ascertain whether

---

298 M. Klamert (2014), 128.

299 This obligation was implicit in the early CJEU judgments in *Rewe v. Landwirtschaftskammer für das Saarland*, 33/76, EU:C:1976:188 and *Comet BV v. Produktschap voor Siergewassen*, 45/76, EU:C:1976:191, while it became explicit later, at the same time as its outer limits were clarified, in CJEU judgments *Peterbroeck, Van Campenhout & Cie v. Belgian State*, C-312/93, EU:C:1995:437; *van Schijndel v. Stichting Pensioenfonds voor Fysiotherapeuten*, joined cases C-430/93 and C-431/93, EU:C:1995:441 and *Heemskerk BV and Firma Schaap v. Productschap Vee en Vlees*, C-455/06, EU:C:2008:650.

300 CJEU judgment in *Marshall v. Southampton and South-West Hampshire Area Health Authority (Marshall II)*, C-271/91, EU:C:1993:335; CJEU judgment in *Marleasing v. Comercial Internacional de Alimentación*, C-106/89, EU:C:1990:395; CJEU judgment in *Pfeiffer and Others*, joined cases C-397/01 to C-403/01, EU:C:2004:584.

301 D.-U. Galetta (2010), 13.

302 CJEU judgment in *Centrosteel Srl v. Adipol GmbH*, EU:C:2000:402, 16-17; CJEU judgment in *Pfeiffer and Others*, joined cases C-397/01 to C-403/01, EU:C:2004:584, 113-15; CJEU judgment in *Dansk industri*, C-441/14, EU:C:2016:278, 33.

there exists a way out in order to deliver a "Union-law-friendly" interpretation.[303] What had originally taken the form of an exclusionary choice (to abstain from certain options when presented with a *smorgasbord* of several) has turned into an obligation to actively search for additional interpretational options until (ideally) a "Union-friendly" option is found and added to the *smorgasbord*. Once placed inside the range of available options, the national judge can easily make the (negative) choice, under the duty of sincere co-operation, to exclude all options that were originally on the table. Nevertheless, the national judge is here asked to make the positive choice of creating for himself new options that have not necessarily been triggered by the litigation.[304]

This development, from initially leaving the matter of remedies at the discretion of the national judge, to ultimately introducing positive obligations (including the creation of new remedies), has sometimes been held in mind in the scholarship, when referring to the transformation (in the mid-1980's) from a first stage of cautionary self-restraint to a second stage of judicial interventionism.[305] The boundaries between these phases are not clear-cut, and there have also been inconsistencies within the phases as to when the national judge was allowed a wide margin of discretion in the sphere of national procedural autonomy, versus when the judge had to set

303 CJEU judgment in *Marleasing v. Comercial Internacional de Alimentación*, C-106/89, EU:C:1990:395, 7,13; CJEU judgment in *Pfeiffer and Others*, joined cases C-397/01 to C-403/01, EU:C:2004:584, 118-19.

304 On negative obligations for judges transforming into positive obligations for Member State legislators, see P. van Cleynenbreugel (2012 b), 88-90. This issue has been clarified to the effect that while the duty of sincere co-operation precludes the national legislator from adopting provisions incompatible with EU law, the seized court must check whether the said legislation runs contrary to the principle of effectiveness and accordingly take measures to ensure compliance (CJEU judgment in *Silvia Georgiana Câmpean*, C-200/14, EU:C:2016:494, 71).

305 On this "core narrative", see M. Dougan (2011 a), 408ff. The term "judicial interventionism" is here used, in favor of the politically charged term "judicial activism", to denote a radical approach to national procedural law. The latter term, as defined by Arnull, has a wider scope, comprising the delivery of rulings that enter into the prerogatives of the legislator, as well as "'result-oriented judging'. This means deciding a case in order to further some policy or other objective of the judge." A. Arnull (2013), 217-18; referring to K. D. Kmiec, 'The Origin and Current Meanings of "Judicial Activism"', *CLR*, 92 (2004). On the interaction between political and legal prerogatives guiding the preliminary reference procedure, and the embedded factors inducive towards judicial interventionism, see J. Dederke and D. Naurin (2017), 2.

aside national procedural law in the spirit of ensuring the effectiveness of Union law.[306] The Court of Justice's directions following from this second era have been described as difficult to understand and at times unpredictable,[307] particularly in reference to the contrast between rather broad requirements of full effectiveness in some cases[308] *vis-à-vis* the emphasis on procedural autonomy in others.[309]

Accordingly, in the mid-1990's, there was yet another change in the Court of Justice's dealings with the sphere of national procedural autonomy: First of all, the case-law has been interpreted as waning interventionism on the side of the Court of Justice.[310] Secondly, it has clarified some of the earlier ambiguities concerning the assessment to be made by the national judge (and the level of discretion implied thereby), by introducing the possibility of justifying encroachments upon the principle of effectiveness.[311]

2.2.3.6 Assessing procedural obstacles in light of their role and function

The tradition of objective justifications for limiting Union law effectiveness has a relatively long history, the Court having early on foreseen the need for a balancing exercise to nuance the prerogatives of enforcing Union law (also with respect to procedural obstacles).[312] In *Emmott*, Advo-

---

306 M. Dougan (2004), 30; M. Dougan (2011 a), 426; S. Prechal (1998), 689.

307 S. Prechal (1998), 689-90.

308 I.e. cases based on the *Simmenthal* requirement of full effectiveness, but which may more readily be resolved via the *Rewe* formula; S. Prechal (1998), 689-90.

309 CJEU judgment in *Gabriel Alonso-Pérez v. Bundesanstalt für Arbeit*, C-394/93, EU:C:1995:400; CJEU judgment in *SpA Alois Lageder and others v. Amministrazione delle Finanze dello Stato*, joined cases C-31/91 to C-44/91, EU:C:1993:132.

310 M. Dougan (2011 a), 417-19; M. Dougan (2004), 29; A. Ward (1995), 211ff.

311 M. Dougan (2004), 34; S. Prechal (1998), 690.

312 Already in CJEU judgment in *Rewe v. Landwirtschaftskammer für das Saarland*, 33/76, EU:C:1976:188, 5 and CJEU judgment in *Comet BV v. Produktschap voor Siergewassen*, 45/76, EU:C:1976:191, 18, was the Court of Justice's deference to national procedural autonomy based on recognition of the fact that limitation periods are put in place to ensure legal certainty and proper conduct of the proceeding.

cate General Mischo had recognized that national time-limits may pose obstacles for individuals hoping to vindicate Union law-derived rights:[313]

> The laying down of such time-limits with regard to actions of a fiscal nature is an application of the fundamental principle of legal certainty protecting both the tax-payer and the administration concerned.

Such considerations would soon crystallize into a standard method for the Court of Justice to approach procedural obstacles, within the purview of the *Rewe* formula:[314]

> Over time, the approach of the Court on procedural autonomy has yielded from an abstract test to a stronger insistence on the effectiveness principle, which had a deeper and deeper influence on national procedural remedies: on some occasions by requiring the importance of the EU right to be weighted against the scope and purpose of the national rule.

Whereas in the early case-law, such considerations were implicit in the Court's general reasoning about the system of protection offered by national procedural law,[315] the post-1995 case-law became more explicit about the concrete function and use of such considerations.[316]

A standard method was set out in this third stage, referred to as an era of judicial "retreat",[317] with the delivery of the twin rulings in *van Schijndel*[318] and *Peterbroeck.*[319] In both cases, the issue was whether national courts were obliged to raise matters of Union law of their own motion. The pursuit of effectiveness would undoubtedly be furthered by the requirement on national courts to raise matters of Union law *ex officio.*[320] Yet, procedural rules precluding *ex officio* review (or laying down limits on circumstances when this is allowed) are put in place for imperative reasons of le-

---

313 Opinion of Advocate General Mischo in *Theresa Emmott v. Minister for Social Welfare and the Attorney General*, C-208/90, EU:C:1991:164, 17; see, more recently, CJEU judgment in *Hampshire County Council v. C.E. and N.E.*, joined cases C-325/18 PPU and C-375/18 PPU, EU:C:2018:739, 77.

314 L. M. Ravo (2012), 109.

315 Ibid., 109-10; M. Dougan (2004), 31; S. Prechal (1998), 691.

316 M. Dougan (2004), 29.

317 Ibid.

318 CJEU judgment in *van Schijndel v. Stichting Pensioenfonds voor Fysiotherapeuten*, joined cases C-430/93 and C-431/93, EU:C:1995:441.

319 CJEU judgment in *Peterbroeck, Van Campenhout & Cie v. Belgian State*, C-312/93, EU:C:1995:437.

320 J. H. Jans, R. de Lange, S. Prechal, and R. J. G. M. Widdershoven (2007), 308.

gal certainty, potentially rendering them inappropriate to subvert.[321] Therefore, it is logical for national judges, when encountering such rules containing tensions *vis-à-vis* the effectiveness of Union law, to balance the formers' function and necessity against the latter's demands.

The Court of Justice accordingly provided concrete guidelines to evaluate the factors involved in national courts' balancing of national procedural rules against Union law effectiveness. The Court's responses had, in the earlier case-law, varied from abstract references to the duty to comply with the principles of effectiveness and equivalence, to a more concrete direction to set aside particular procedural rules that were found to violate the said principles. In the *van Schijndel* and *Peterbroeck* rulings, the Court of Justice allowed national courts discretion in determining the matter of compliance, whereas it also introduced a formula for carrying out this assessment, taking several factors into account.[322]

These factors were, at the time, summarized by legal scholars along the following lines: First of all, the "principles or aims underlying these rules must, as such, be compatible with the Community legal order."[323] Second, the rule must be attributed certain fundamental value, in the sense of forming "part of the legal heritage common to the Member States."[324] The test left to the national judge was understood to go beyond assessing the abstract importance of the national procedural rule in itself. It rather came down to weighing, *in casu*, the procedural purposes it serves against the costs brought about by its strict application. The test was later boiled down to the following three questions:[325]

---

321 As argued by S. Prechal and N. Shelkoplyas ('National Procedures, Public Policy and EC Law. From van Schijndel to Eco Swiss and Beyond', *Eur. Rev. Pr. L.*, 5 (2004), 593), national rules of procedure, that are on the one hand contrary to the principles of effectiveness or equivalence, but on the other hand justified by fundamental procedural considerations and put in place for particular and legitimate reasons, "should not be dismissed for the simple reason that they seriously hamper the application of Community law provisions." See also A. M. van den Bossche (2014), 52.

322 CJEU judgment in *van Schijndel v. Stichting Pensioenfonds voor Fysiotherapeuten*, joined cases C-430/93 and C-431/93, EU:C:1995:441, 19-21; CJEU judgment in *Peterbroeck, Van Campenhout & Cie v. Belgian State*, C-312/93, EU:C:1995:437, 14.

323 S. Prechal (1998), 690; see also C. Kakouris (1997), 1404.

324 S. Prechal (1998), 691; in reference to CJEU judgment in *van Schijndel v. Stichting Pensioenfonds voor Fysiotherapeuten*, joined cases C-430/93 and C-431/93, EU:C:1995:441, 21.

325 M. Dougan (2004), 30.

> (i) whether the exercise of the [Union] right is indeed adversely affected by the operation of the national provision;
>
> (ii) if so, whether the national provision pursues a legitimate policy objective; and
>
> (iii) if so, whether the national provision pursues that policy objective in a legitimate manner, consistent with the margin of discretion left to the Member State by [Union] law.

This assessment as to whether the appropriateness and necessity of the national rule outweighs its costs in the form of Union law effectiveness resembles a test of proportionality[326] – working not so much to protect a right as to balance procedural autonomy against a Union law-based minimum procedural standard.[327]

Having instituted the procedural rule-of-reason, the extent of discretion granted the national judge remained to be determined. If the rule-of-reason had the benefit of helping national judges choose, its waters would become muddled by the way in which the Court of Justice from time to time carried out also this assessment *for* the national judge. As the Court of Justice can respond (in the place of the national judge) to the question of whether the principles of effectiveness and equivalence have been complied with, it should equally be able to assess (for the national judge) whether the national rule at stake appears to be justified by its role and purpose in the national legal system. Yet, the Court of Justice neither has the knowledge nor the jurisdiction to rule on the application or interpretation of national law,[328] whereas by carrying out the rule-of-reason test, it is doing just that. An approach that was intended to help national courts make a judgment call has instead resulted in the Court of Justice increasingly scrutinizing individual procedural provisions of national law in greater detail than was earlier called for by the principles of effectiveness and equivalence.[329] Criticisms have additionally been raised that judg-

326 E.g. P. Wennerås (2007), 88-90, draws parallels with the proportionality requirement for derogating from substantive Union law pursuant to the doctrine of "mandatory requirements".

327 In this balancing act, it has been argued that rather exceptional circumstances are needed for placing stricter requirements on national procedural rules in the context of Union law litigation; S. Prechal and N. Shelkoplyas (2004), 593.

328 CJEU judgment in *Da Costa en Schaake NV, Jacob Meijer NV, Hoechst-Holland NV v. Netherlands Inland Revenue Administration*, joined cases 28/62 to 39/62 EU:C:1963:6, pp. 31, 38; CJEU judgment in *Karl Schwarz*, C-321/07, EU:C:2009:104, 49.

329 S. Prechal (1998), 691.

ments based on the rule-of-reason are inherently casuistic and therefore cannot have general reach, lack value as precedent,[330] and risk hampering uniformity and predictability.[331]

The rule-of-reason has moreover been deemed redundant since most procedural rules are put in place for a good reason; accordingly, they can also normally be justified.[332] Against this, the counterargument has been advanced that, what was new with the *van Schijndel/Peterbroeck* formula was not the necessity in itself of carrying out this balancing test, but the instruction, aimed at national judges, not to take for granted that procedural rules hampering Union law effectiveness are legitimate and necessary. Instead, the test was to be understood as encouraging national judges to take a critical stance on national procedural law. Dealing in a careful and critical manner with their intended role and function, as well as their effects *in casu*, should ensure that national rules of procedure would not by default be considered justified.[333] In this perspective, the rule-of-reason has been held to represent increased interventionism rather than, as is sometimes purported, deference.[334]

The idea of weighing the advantages of a given solution in a Member State against its costs for Union law effectiveness gives credence to a method where each side of the balance is attributed a certain value. Thus understood, it would complicate the task of the national judge: Not only would the *national* procedural rule need to be weighed (in importance) but also, ostensibly, the adversary *Union* interest. Wennerås has in this vein wondered whether the Court of Justice may intend to "scrutinize national procedural laws with different intensity, depending on the aim and importance of the Community right the exercise of which is being restricted by national procedural law" (albeit recognizing that such an interpretation

330 S. Prechal and N. Shelkoplyas (2004), 593; S. Prechal (1998); J. Engström (2008), 71.

331 I.e. based on an argumentation similar to the criticisms against the national comparator test, discussed in connection with the equivalence principle. See also V. Couronne, 'L'autonomie procédurale des États membres de l'Union européenne à l'épreuve du temps', *Cah. dr. eur.*, 46 (2010), 301-2; S. Drake (2016), 26.

332 S. Prechal (1998), 692.

333 The examination requires a rigorous analysis so that rules which "might well be justified *in principle*, having regard to their particular objectives and their overall procedural environment, may yet infringe the principle of effectiveness *in practice* for reasons specific to the given claimant's situation." M. Dougan (2004), 31-32.

334 Ibid., see also P. Wennerås (2007), 88-90.

does not follow directly from *van Schijndel/Peterbroeck*).[335] The hypothesis finds some support in the case-law of the late 1990's when the Court of Justice used the notion of public policy[336] to identify fields of Union law requiring a heightened level of procedural protection[337] – yet, it has since been clarified that the prospective public policy status of a Union rule is not intended to form part of the rule-of-reason test.[338]

The recent case of *M.A.S.* contains an analogous reasoning to justify derogation from the obligation of effective enforcement of EU law, particularly emphasizing the importance of the legality and non-retroactivity requirements in criminal law traditions common to the Member States.[339] The issue of statutory limitations for VAT fraud belongs to a grey zone of procedural law which is not yet harmonized,[340] and the *M.A.S.* case itself belongs to a recent line of case-law with novel procedural implications. Even assuming that a new form of enforcement competence has crystallized, a procedural proportionality test of kinds is equally applicable there – whereas emphasis is placed not only on a procedural safeguard's role and

335 On the one hand, "nothing [in *Peterbroeck*] suggests that the balancing formula places any relevance on the right in question. The balancing to be conducted by national courts amounts to weighing the restrictive impact of the procedural rule in question against any legitimate functions or purposes it promotes." On the other hand, Wennerås takes note of certain policy areas and interests that carry special weight and therefore might "influenc[e] the level of intensity of the ECJ's review of national procedural laws." Ibid., 89-90.

336 The notion of public policy is here used in the meaning proposed by Professor Roel de Lange: "norms that are so fundamental for the legal order that they have to be respected, regardless of procedural obstacles." In other words, the present use does not refer to its wider concept, i.e. to limit fundamental rights under e.g. the European Convention on Human Rights and Fundamental Freedoms (ECHR), as amended by Protocols Nos. 11 and 14, 4 November 1950, ETS 5 or to justify restrictions of the fundamental economic freedoms; see R. de Lange, 'The European Public Order, Constitutional Principles and Fundamental Rights', *Erasmus Law Review*, 1 (2007), 8-9.

337 I.e. consumer protection and competition law; see e.g. Opinion of Advocate General Saggio in *Océano Grupo Editorial and Salvat Editores*, joined cases C-240/98 to C-244/98, EU:C:1999:620, 25-26; CJEU judgment in *Eco Swiss China Time Ltd v. Benetton International NV*, C-126/97, EU:C:1999:269, 37-41.

338 Rather, the Court of Justice has dealt with rules of public policy status at the stage of examining whether national procedural law complies with the principle of equivalence; CJEU judgment in *Eco Swiss China Time Ltd v. Benetton International NV*, C-126/97, EU:C:1999:269 and CJEU judgment in *Abdelhafid Bensada Benallal*, C-161/15, EU:C:2016:175, 31-35.

339 CJEU judgment in *M.A.S.*, C-42/17, EU:C:2017:936, 51-53.

340 Ibid., 44.

function in the national legal system, but also on its relative weight as fundamental right within the EU.[341] In this respect, it has more in common with the derogation test under the principle of full effectiveness (see section 3.2.2.6), than the procedural rule-of-reason.

The last of the three stages of case-law coincides with the reinforcement of yet another general principle of Union law: that of effective judicial protection. Despite the interconnection between the principles of effectiveness and effective judicial protection, their avenues for justification must be differentiated. The procedural rule-of-reason does not service encroachments on effective judicial protection, as the latter forms part of EU fundamental rights law, providing its own toolset for justification of derogations (developed in section 5.3).[342]

2.2.3.7 Linking the remedial mandate to effective judicial protection

The described spider-net of Union-based requirements on national courts – sometimes founded on full effect, sometimes on sincere co-operation, sometimes requiring new remedies, sometimes deferring to the national procedural framework, etc. – has been described as naturally confusing, considering the opacity of the issues of competence and role division in the area of procedural law.[343] It was accordingly welcomed that the Lisbon Treaties introduced, if not a new legal basis, then at least a codified clarification of the role of national judges.[344] Art. 19(1) TEU states that "Member States shall provide remedies sufficient to ensure effective legal protection in the fields covered by Union law", an addition that was intended to ensure that the complementarity between the national courts' and the Court of Justice's supervision managed to deliver a "complete system of legal remedies".[345]

---

341 Ibid., 51-59.

342 Opinion of Advocate General Jääskinen in *Orizzonte Salute*, C-61/14, EU:C:2015:307, 33-36.

343 S. Drake (2016), 13.

344 Ibid., 28.

345 CJEU judgment in *Inuit Tapiriit Kanatami*, C-283/11 P, EU:C:2013:625, 92, referring in particular to the review of the legality of Union legislation to be carried out by the Court of Justice and the national courts. On the function of Art. 19(1) TEU, see more recently CJEU judgment in *Associação Sindical dos Juízes Portugueses v. Tribunal de Contas*, C-64/16, EU:C:2018:117, 32; CJEU judg-

Art. 19(1) TEU has been ascribed the "potential to provide the CJEU at the very least with a legitimate legal basis for its existing system of remedies which would in turn grant the national courts a stronger mandate for engaging in their enforcement role."[346] As professed by the European Parliament:[347]

> Community law remains a dead letter if it is not properly applied in the Member States, including by national judges, who are therefore the keystone of the European Union judicial system and who play a central and indispensable role in the establishment of a single European legal order.

The implications of the new Art. 19 TEU venture further still than this potential normative force. In its function as legal basis, Art. 19(1) has been proposed to supplement the *Rewe* principles, and to require courts to carry out judicial review even beyond what followed from case-law on the principle of effective judicial protection.[348] The dual codification of national judges' "remedial mandate"[349] in Art. 19(1) TEU and the principle of effective judicial protection in Art. 47 CFR to some extent solved the prob-

---

ment in *Carlos Escribano Vindel v. Ministerio de Justicia*, C-49/18, EU:C:2019:106, 62.

346 S. Drake (2016), 28.

347 European Parliament resolution of 9 July 2008 on the role of the national judge in the European judicial system (2007/2027(INI)), OJ C 294 E, 3/12/2009, 27, point 2: EU law.

348 Opinion of Advocate General Mazak in *Banca Antoniana Popolare Veneta*, C-427/10, EU:C:2011:595; Opinion of Advocate General Jääskinen in *Bundeswettbewerbsbehörde v. Donau Chemie AG and Others*, C-536/11, EU:C:2013:67; Opinion of Advocate General Wahl in *Macinský and Macinská*, C-482/12, EU:C:2013:765, 67 at fn. 26; Opinion of Advocate General Wathelet in *Test Claimants (III) in the Franked Investment Income Group Litigation*, C-362/12, EU:C:2013:538.

349 Member States are, similarly to procedural autonomy, said to enjoy remedial autonomy, in their choice of sanctions and remedies under national procedural law. It is "first and foremost for the national legal order to provide appropriate remedies" – because decentralized enforcement is in the hands of national courts which are bound by the national legal framework, and because Union law does not provide for separate remedies to sanction breaches of Union law; M. Claes (2006), 144. The notion of "remedial mandate" is in the present work used to denote the responsibilities incumbent on national judges both when choosing between available remedies provided by the national legislator, and when stepping in to fill gaps in legal protection where individuals lack avenues for enforcing their Union law-derived rights. The notion of remedial mandate thus hinges onto the notion of remedies and the context of remedial autonomy (as earlier defined).

lem of basing positive obligations on the principle of effectiveness: When exclusively founded on the duty of sincere co-operation, obligations thus entailed will (in principle) be restricted by what a national judge can do *within* his powers under national law. When the principle of effectiveness is paired with the duty to provide legal protection (as a quasi-independent legal Treaty basis), the prospective reach for positive obligations becomes wider.[350]

Increasingly referred to in recent case-law,[351] Article 19(1) TEU may therefore give fuel to imposing positive obligations on Member States, particularly in order to require new remedies and expand the powers of national courts.[352] In this last function, it supplements Art. 47 CFR, as well as sharpening the duty of sincere co-operation.[353] It has even been proposed that Art. 19(1) could reasonably replace the duty of sincere co-operation as legal basis for the *Rewe* principles, which would strengthen them but also

---

350 On the one hand, *Unibet* maintains Art. 4(3) TEU as legal basis also for the principle of effective judicial protection, yet nonetheless paves the road for an obligation, in exceptional cases, to create new remedies; CJEU judgment in *Unibet (London) Ltd and Unibet (International) Ltd v. Justitiekanslern*, C-432/05, EU:C:2007:163 with comments in A. Arnull (2011), 54. On the other hand, the Member-State side of the principle of effective judicial protection enshrined in Art. 19(1) TEU and Art. 47 CFR has been proposed as an independent legal basis for the creation of new remedies; P. van Cleynenbreugel (2012 b), 94; see also V. Roeben, 'Judicial Protection as the Meta-Norm in the EU Judicial Architecture', *Hague J Rule Law* (2019), https://doi.org/10.1007/s40803-019-00085-3, 10-11.

351 CJEU judgment in *Texdata Software GmbH*, C-418/11, EU:C:2013:588, 78; CJEU judgment in *Liivimaa Lihaveis MTÜ v. Eesti-Läti programmi 2007-2013 Seirekomitee*, C-562/12, EU:C:2014:2229, 68; CJEU judgment in *ClientEarth v. The Secretary of State for the Environment, Food and Rural Affairs*, C-404/13, EU:C:2014:2382, 52; CJEU judgment in *Lesoochranárske zoskupenie VLK (II)*, C-243/15, EU:C:2016:838, 50; CJEU judgment in *Associação Sindical dos Juízes Portugueses v. Tribunal de Contas*, C-64/16, EU:C:2018:117, 32; CJEU judgment in *Slowakische Republik v. Achmea BV*, C-284/16, EU:C:2018:158, 50-55.

352 J. Krommendijk (2016), 1405.

353 S. Drake (2016), 29-30. As noted, the duty of sincere co-operation cannot, in principle, require the introduction of new remedies nor require interpretations *contra legem*; CJEU judgment in *Association de médiation sociale v. Union locale des syndicats CGT and Others (AMS)*, C-176/12, EU:C:2014:2, 39; CJEU judgment in *Dansk industri*, C-441/14, EU:C:2016:278, 32.

grant them a greater measure of legitimacy and legality in the form of a less constrained legal basis.[354]

It was, *inter alia*, in light of the Charter's alignment with the Treaties[355] and potential coupling with Art. 19(1) TEU, that the Lisbon reform showed promise to strengthen the principle of effective judicial protection. Initially, some uncertainty prevailed as to whether Art. 19(1) TEU requires "only" the provision of effective remedies and *legal* (as opposed to *judicial*) protection. It has nevertheless been clarified that the system of mutual trust charges Member States with ascertaining that matters of EU law are dealt with by their judicial systems, which are governed by the rule of law and thus assumed to fully meet the requirements of Art. 47 CFR.[356] The forthcoming sections will trace the emergence of a sharper and at the same time more nuanced principle of effective judicial protection, in comparison to its closest sibling, the principle of effectiveness.

2.3 Progressive influence of the principle of effective judicial protection

Increased reliance on the principle of effective judicial protection brought about further demands (but also further confusion) concerning the contemporary meaning of the principle of effectiveness.[357] Although effective judicial protection is also concerned with courts' protection of Union rights, it adds a distinct perspective to their effective exercise – namely the *quality* of protection ensured by courts acting as Union bodies of enforcement. The principle of effectiveness has in other words been formally reinforced through the requirement of effective judicial protection,[358] so that

354 S. Drake (2016) 30; cf. H. C.H. Hofmann (2014 a), on the constraint placed on Art. 47 CFR by Art. 52(2) CFR, to the effect that Art. 47 CFR must be interpreted "under the conditions and within the limits" defined by the Treaties.

355 Pursuant to Art. 6(1) TEU, "The Union recognises the rights, freedoms and principles set out in the Charter of Fundamental Rights of 7 December 2000, as adapted on 12 December 2007, which shall have the same legal value as the Treaties."

356 CJEU judgment in *Associação Sindical dos Juízes Portugueses v. Tribunal de Contas*, C-64/16, EU:C:2018:117, 29-37, CJEU judgment in *Slowakische Republik v. Achmea BV*, C-284/16, EU:C:2018:158, 34; see comments by V. Roeben (2019), 9-11.

357 K. Lenaerts, I. Maselis, and K. Gutman, *EU Procedural Law* (New York: Oxford University Press, 2014), 110. See also A. Arnull (2011).

358 S. Prechal and N. Shelkoplyas (2004), 591; S. Prechal (2016), 145.

individuals gain effective access to judicial venues for enforcement of their rights under Union law.

The present section maps its evolution, from requiring various levels of effectiveness in order to safeguard the rule of EU law, to the duty to provide judicial protection of individuals litigating before Member State courts (2.3.1). This includes the requirement of access to courts (2.3.2), particular requirements imposed on national courts (once seized) to ensure the quality of protection (2.3.3) and the creation of new remedies in the name of effective judicial protection (2.3.4). A discussion ensues on the altered constitutional status of the principle of effective judicial protection in the wake of the Lisbon Treaties (2.3.5). The origins of the principle of effectiveness are there schematically compared to the principle of effective judicial protection, whereas their respective avenues for justification will only be addressed in a preliminary manner, to be further distinguished in Chapter 5.

2.3.1 Evolution of the principle of effective judicial protection

The case-law on procedural autonomy has, since its founding in the 1970's, gone through several transformations in terms of how far-reaching obligations the duty of sincere co-operation is understood to bring about. Although designations and delimitations of these time-periods have been criticized for not heeding the nuances of each period to sufficiently characterize them as "restrained" or "interventionist",[359] such chronological categories are useful for systematization.

The developments have been divided into three phases: first a period of "severe judicial restraint", in which Member State procedural autonomy was, on balance, given priority over considerations of effectiveness; next a period of "judicial interventionism" in the mid-1980's to mid-1990's, prescribing a higher level of intervention in the procedural autonomy of the Member States; and thirdly, in the mid-1990's and onwards, a period of "retreat" characterized by a case-by-case approach of justification and proportionality.[360]

To clarify the structure of the forthcoming sections, the table below elucidates how the (approximate) chronology of the doctrine of effective judi-

---

359 M. Dougan (2011 a), 407-8.

360 See, on this "core narrative", M. Dougan (2011 a), 412-13; M. Dougan (2004), 29ff.; F. Wilman (2015), 32.

cial protection corresponds to the phases described in this "core narrative" on national procedural autonomy:

Chronology	Core narrative	Effective judicial protection
1970 - mid-1980	*First phase*: Judicial restraint	(-)
Mid-1980 - mid-1990	*Second phase*: Judicial interventionism	Enjoyment of rights cannot be effective unless protected by courts (2.3.2).
Mid-1990 - 2000	*Third phase*: Retreat/rule-of-reason	Continued: Enjoyment of rights cannot be effective unless protected by courts (2.3.2).
Early 2000	(-)	Mere access is not enough: Requirements on the judiciary (2.3.3).
2007 - 2013	(-)	The creation of new remedies to ensure *de facto* judicial protection (2.3.4).
2013 - present	(-)	New legal bases give rise to distinctive levels of protection (section 2.3.5 and Chapter 5).

2.3.2 Enjoyment of rights cannot be effective unless protected by courts

Although judicial protection by courts has come to the foreground since the Lisbon codification, the requirement dates to early case-law of the Court of Justice. The tenets of primacy and direct effect, laid down in *Costa v. Enel* and *van Gend en Loos*,[361] presupposed that once individuals are in a position to rely on Community law rights, the national judicial system will provide the framework for litigating, and remedies sufficient to ensure their protection.[362] In this way, the notion of legal protection forms part of the constitutional framework of Union law, with an intrinsic connection to its original cornerstones.[363]

361 CJEU judgment in *Costa v. E.N.E.L.*, 6/64, EU:C:1964:66, pp. 593-94 (primacy); CJEU judgment in *van Gend en Loos v. Administratie der Belastingen*, 26/62, EU:C:1963:1, p. 13 (direct effect).

362 M. Burley and W. Mattli (1993), 60-62; L.M. Ravo (2012), 107ff.

363 See M. Dougan (2011 a), 409. For a similar take on CJEU judgment in *Costa v. E.N.E.L.*, 6/64, EU:C:1964:66, regarding the inter-embeddedness of the doctrine of primacy and autonomy in national judges' decentralized enforcement, see D. Simon (2000), 323-38, 247-48.

The first explicit reference to effective judicial protection was made much later, in the 1984 judgment in *Von Colson*, requiring that remedies against gender discrimination be "real and effective" in the form of sanctions by which individuals can avail themselves before courts.[364] The principle of equal treatment laid down in Union secondary law was to be upheld by effective sanctions, requiring Member States to provide direct and immediate court protection by adopting "measures which are sufficiently effective to achieve the objective of the directive and to ensure that those measures may in fact be relied on before the national courts by the persons concerned."[365]

Effective judicial protection was promoted to general principle of EU law in the case of *Johnston*, which expressly referred to a "right" to effective judicial remedies, allowing beneficiaries of Community law to "pursue their claims by judicial process" (referred to as judicial control).[366] The Court recognized that the protection provided through EU secondary law[367] was in its turn based on the protection foreseen by Arts. 6 and 13 ECHR. Therefore, the national court was not only dealing with a directive, but also with a general principle of law in the light of which the former had to be interpreted.[368] As per *Johnston*, the status of the principle of effective judicial protection indicated that it would apply even without the existence of a codified rule in secondary legislation.[369]

Any uncertainties as to whether such an interpretation was correct came to be obviated by the *Heylens* case,[370] where the invoked substantive provision was a fundamental Treaty right, whilst there was no codified right of access to court contained in the Treaty at the time. The Court of Justice ruled that the claimants were, nonetheless, entitled to this under the general principle of effective judicial protection derived from the constitutional

364 CJEU judgment in *Von Colson and Kamann v. Land Nordrhein-Westfalen*, 14/83, EU:C:1984:153, 22-23; see further M. Klamert (2014), 79-83.

365 CJEU judgment in *Von Colson and Kamann v. Land Nordrhein-Westfalen*, 14/83, EU:C:1984:153, 18.

366 CJEU judgment in *Johnston*, 222/84, EU:C:1986:206, 17-18; see further A. Arnull, 'The Beat Goes On', *E.L. Rev.*, 12 (1987); A. F. M. Brenninkmeijer (1994), 113ff.; A. Arnull (2011), 52-53.

367 Art. 6 Council Directive 76/207/EEC of 9 February 1976 on the implementation of the principle of equal treatment for men and women as regards access to employment, vocational training and promotion, and working conditions, OJ L 39, 14/2/1976, 40.

368 CJEU judgment in *Johnston*, 222/84, EU:C:1986:206, 18-19.

369 See further S. Prechal and R. Widdershoven (2011 a), 286; A. Arnull (2011), 53.

370 CJEU judgment in *Heylens*, 222/86, EU:C:1987:442.

traditions of the Member States and from the ECHR.[371] It would subsequently be clarified that the right to effective judicial protection extended to all areas of primary and secondary law.[372] This scope of the principle served the protection of individuals in all Union litigation, be they litigating before Union courts or Member State courts acting as Union organs.[373]

The 1991 *Emmott* ruling marked a peak before "judicial retreat".[374] Although the case concerned access to court,[375] the requirement of full effect was elected in order to prevent the national court from permitting the State to rely on national time-limits, where the invoked Community legislation had not been properly transposed.[376] The principle of judicial protection was not mentioned, whereas the requirement of full effect was applied in a subsidiary manner, discarding the *Rewe* test – on account of its insufficiency – for a sharper tool.

Emmott has been considered one of the more interventionist rulings in terms of impact on national procedural autonomy.[377] Its far-reaching implications led the Court to subsequently state that, as long as the principles of effectiveness and equivalence are respected, Member States may indeed resist overdue claims for repayment based on a directive that had not yet been transposed (i.e. subverting its findings in *Emmott*).[378] In *Fantask*, the Court of Justice did not refer to a right to effective judicial protection, which may perhaps have been fitting since the case equally concerned individuals' access to courts. This coincided with a shift in the case-law in the mid-1990's in the direction of deference.[379] We may ask whether the notion of effective judicial protection was avoided in favor of the *Rewe* princi-

371 Ibid., 14.

372 CJEU judgment in *Kraus*, C-19/92, EU:C:1993:125, 40 (freedom of establishment); CJEU judgment in *MRAX*, C-459/99, EU:C:2002:461, 101 (right of residence for third country nationals); CJEU judgment in *Borrell*, C-104/91, EU:C:1992:202 (freedom of establishment and freedom to provide services).

373 See e.g. S. Prechal and R. Widdershoven (2011 a), 287.

374 CJEU judgment in *Theresa Emmott v. Minister for Social Welfare and the Attorney General*, C-208/90, EU:C:1991:333.

375 Time-barring of claims preventing litigants from invoking Union law in litigation against a Ministry (defendant).

376 CJEU judgment in *Theresa Emmott v. Minister for Social Welfare and the Attorney General*, C-208/90, EU:C:1991:333, 16-17.

377 A. Arnull (2011), 53.

378 CJEU judgment in *Fantask and Others v. Industriministeriet*, C-188/95, EU:C:1997:580, 42-52.

379 Ostensibly, in *Fantask* to reverse an all too "interventionist" approach to unimplemented directives; A. Arnull (2011), 53.

ples, so as to emphasize Member State autonomy in this spirit of restraint.[380]

2.3.3 Mere access is not enough: Requirements on the judiciary

The rulings in *Johnston* and *Heylens* had already clarified that for the protection of Union rights to be considered effective, individuals must be able to turn to national courts to vindicate them.[381] Once access to courts had been ensured, this case-law did not disclose what was required for the protection granted by a court to be considered effective in itself. This would alter in the 2000's when the Court of Justice "moved beyond the mere problem of 'access to justice' and expressed views on how national procedure should be regulated"[382]: The time was ripe to lay down what can be expected of decisions delivered by national courts in order to deem judicial protection secured. Access to a court is redundant if the seized court does not have the necessary powers to grant appropriate procedural protection under national law. The Court of Justice, in a series of cases, laid down requirements that can all be said to ascertain a certain quality and scope of the review to be carried out by national courts.

First of all, the Court of Justice referred to its own earlier definition of courts/tribunals within the meaning of Art. 267 TFEU, clarifying which judicial bodies are capable of making a preliminary reference to the Court of Justice.[383] These requirements are also to be utilized when ascertaining whether an individual has been granted effective judicial protection, and

380 Cf. e.g. CJEU judgment in *van Schijndel v. Stichting Pensioenfonds voor Fysiotherapeuten*, joined cases C-430/93 and C-431/93, EU:C:1995:441; CJEU judgment in *Peterbroeck, Van Campenhout & Cie v. Belgian State*, C-312/93, EU:C:1995:437, in which equally any reference to effective judicial protection was absent.

381 CJEU judgment in *Heylens*, 222/86, EU:C:1987:442; CJEU judgment in *Johnston*, 222/84, EU:C:1986:206.

382 P. van Cleynenbreugel (2012 b), 92, referring to CJEU judgment in *Boxus and Others*, joined cases C-128/09 to C-131/09, C-134/09 and C-135/09, EU:C:2011:667.

383 Namely, whether such a body has compulsory jurisdiction, whether its procedures are *inter partes*, whether it applies rules of law, and whether it is independent and impartial; CJEU judgment in *Graham J. Wilson v. Ordre des avocats du barreau de Luxembourg*, C-506/04, EU:C:2006:587, 48. See also CJEU judgment in *Vaassen-Goebbels v. Beambtenfonds voor het Mijnbedrijf*, 61/65, EU:C:1966:39; CJEU judgment in *Pardini v. Ministero del commercio con l'estero*, 338/85, EU:C:1988:194; CJEU judgment in *Pretore di Salò v. X*, 14/86, EU:C:1987:275;

whether a Member State has fulfilled its obligation under Art. 19(1) TEU to provide effective legal remedies in the fields covered by EU law.[384]

Secondly, courts must be independent and impartial, requirements corresponding to those of Art. 6 ECHR, as interpreted by the ECtHR.[385] Concerning *independence*, the Court of Justice has emphasized the protection of the court body against "external intervention or pressure liable to jeopardize the independent judgment of its members".[386] The independence of judges entrusted to ensure compliance with EU law was later explicitly linked to "the very essence of the rule of law" and therefore also activated Art. 19(1) TEU.[387] Concerning judicial *impartiality*, the Court of Justice has underlined litigants' equality of arms; particularly the interests of the parties, on the one hand, and the absence of interests in the outcome of the case by the national court, on the other.[388] The equality of arms between litigants has been maintained as an integral component of effective judicial protection, whereas it has recently triggered an additional legal basis in Art. 20 CFR by linking the notion of procedural equality to the general principle of equality before the law.[389]

CJEU judgment in *François De Coster v. Collège des bourgmestre et échevins de Watermael-Boitsfort*, C-17/00, EU:C:2001:651.

384 This connection between Art. 267 TFEU and Art. 19(1) TEU was developed in CJEU judgment in *Associação Sindical dos Juízes Portugueses v. Tribunal de Contas*, C-64/16, EU:C:2018:117, 38-41 and CJEU judgment in *Slowakische Republik v. Achmea BV*, C-284/16, EU:C:2018:158; see J. Hallberg and A. Östlund, 'Början på slutet för skiljeförfaranden i internationella investeringsskyddsavtal? EU-domstolens avgörande i *Achmea*', *JT*, 4 (2017/2018), 841.

385 CJEU judgment in *Graham J. Wilson v. Ordre des avocats du barreau de Luxembourg*, C-506/04, EU:C:2006:587, 48-49 with comments in H. C.H. Hofmann, (2014 a). See also CJEU judgment in *TDC A/S v. Erhvervsstyrelsen*, C-222/13, EU:C:2014:2265, 30-32; CJEU judgment in *Ramón Margarit Panicello*, C-503/15, EU:C:2017:126, 37-38; CJEU judgment in *Online Games Handels GmbH*, C-685/15, EU:C:2017:452, 60-62; CJEU judgment in *Soufiane El Hassani*, C-403/16, EU:C:2017:960, 40; CJEU judgment in *Associação Sindical dos Juízes Portugueses v. Tribunal de Contas*, C-64/16, EU:C:2018:117, 35-44.

386 CJEU judgment in *Graham J. Wilson v. Ordre des avocats du barreau de Luxembourg*, C-506/04, EU:C:2006:587, 49; see more recently CJEU judgment in *Carlos Escribano Vindel v. Ministerio de Justicia*, C-49/18, EU:C:2019:106, 66.

387 CJEU judgment in *Associação Sindical dos Juízes Portugueses v. Tribunal de Contas*, C-64/16, EU:C:2018:117, 36-41; see V. Roeben (2019), 10-11.

388 CJEU judgment in *Graham J. Wilson v. Ordre des avocats du barreau de Luxembourg*, C-506/04, EU:C:2006:587, 52-58.

389 CJEU judgment in *Direcţia Generală Regională a Finanţelor Publice Braşov v. Vasile Toma*, C-205/15, EU:C:2016:499, 35-36; cf. CJEU judgment in *Bashar*

It has also been established, in reference to case-law of the ECtHR, that under circumstances casting doubt on a lower instance's impartiality to the point that it cannot be considered a *de facto* court, the appeal instance has to be capable of carrying out review in both fact and law.[390] It should not only be *possible* to apply for review by an organ designated by a Member State as a court or tribunal, but such bodies must also, in order to comply with the principle of effective judicial protection a) fulfill the criteria of a court or tribunal within the meaning of the ECHR, and b) be competent to review the matter of Union law that the affected party wishes to have examined – even if this entails review of the case both in fact and in law.[391]

In the same spirit, the Court of Justice has named various other ways in which national obstacles render litigation before national courts too cumbersome: by rules concerning burden of proof,[392] by requirements on the provision of legal aid,[393] by demanding that pre-trial procedures and out-of-court settlements not precondition or preclude subsequent access to court,[394] and by requiring that decisions delivered by national authorities include their reasons, in order for the affected individual to be able to de-

---

Ibrahim, joined cases C-297/17, C-318/17, C-319/17 and C-438/17, EU:C:2019:219, 66. Art. 20 CFR states that "Everyone is equal before the law."

390 CJEU judgment in *Graham J. Wilson v. Ordre des avocats du barreau de Luxembourg*, C-506/04, EU:C:2006:587, 61-62. See further H. C.H. Hofmann (2014 a), especially on the requirements of the ECHR (fn. 183): ECtHR judgment in *Engel and Others v. Netherlands, application no.* 5100/71; 5101/71; 5102/71; 5354/72; 5370/72; ECtHR judgment in *Société Stenuit v. France, application* no. 11598/85; ECtHR judgment in *Janosevic v. Sweden Case*, application no. 34619/97; ECtHR judgment in *Jussila v. Finland*, application no. 73053/01; ECtHR judgment in *Menarini v. Italy*, application no. 43509/08.

391 CJEU judgment in *Europese Gemeenschap v. Otis NV and Others*, C-199/11, EU:C:2012:684, 49; CJEU judgment in *Berlioz Investment Fund SA*, C-682/15, EU:C:2017:373, 53-59. These requirements do not give access to a certain level in the court hierarchy; CJEU judgment in *Brahim Samba Diouf v. Ministre du Travail, de l'Emploi et de l'Immigration*, C-69/10, EU:C:2011:524, 69; cf. CJEU judgment in *Moussa Sacko*, C-348/15, EU:C:2017:591, 40-49, pinioning the scope of review so as not to entail an unlimited right to be heard.

392 CJEU judgment in *Enderby v. Frenchay Health Authority and Secretary of State for Health*, C-127/92, EU:C:1993:859, 13-19; CJEU judgment in *Specialarbejderforbundet i Danmark v. Dansk Industri (Royal Copenhagen)*, C-400/93 EU:C:1995:155. Neither case explicitly relies on effective judicial protection, yet this is inherent in the reasoning of the judgments, cf. *Royal Copenhagen* (26).

393 CJEU judgment in *Deutsche Energiehandels- und Beratungsgesellschaft mbH v. Bundesrepublik Deutschland (DEB)*, C-279/09, EU:C:2010:811; CJEU judgment in *Vladimir Peftiev*, C-314/13, EU:C:2014:1645.

394 CJEU judgment in *Alassini and Others*, C-317/08, EU:C:2010:146.

fend his case before a court.[395] These requirements bore implications not only for individuals' fundamental access to national courts, but also for their possibilities of litigating *successfully*. In so doing, the Court of Justice expanded the notion of effective judicial protection so as not only to enable an individual to litigate on Union rights, but to have his case dealt with in a way that fulfilled the quality criteria laid down by the ECtHR.[396]

The introduced requirements had the view of ensuring that individuals could effectively rely on EU law provisions before national courts. The challenge is here to identify what sets these requirements aside from those which would otherwise fall under the notion of effectiveness. The types of quality controls introduced included e.g. evidential rules, rules concerning standing, and rules on competences of seized courts, impacting obstacles that in earlier case-law may have been interpreted as capable of making the exercise of Union rights "virtually impossible or excessively difficult".[397] However, the point of interest at hand is *judicial* proceedings, whereas the principle of effectiveness required that means be provided for individuals to effectively have their Union law rights guaranteed, whether by public authorities or in the context of court proceedings.[398]

Effective judicial protection thus *sharpened* the principle of effectiveness in the sense that access to court was considered necessary in order to ensure the effectiveness of Union law.[399] This is partly explained by the fact that up until 2009, the principle of effective judicial protection had not yet been equipped with an autonomous Treaty basis. Even though it was recognized as a general principle of EU law (and, from 2000, codified in the Charter), Member States' duties stemming from it traditionally had to be traced back to Treaty obligations.[400]

---

395 CJEU judgment in *Mellor*, C-75/08, EU:C:2009:279.

396 CJEU judgment in *Deutsche Energiehandels- und Beratungsgesellschaft mbH v. Bundesrepublik Deutschland (DEB)*, C-279/09, EU:C:2010:811, 30-31; CJEU judgment in *Claude Chartry v. État belge*, C-457/09, EU:C:2011:101, 25; CJEU judgment in *KME Germany and Others v. Commission*, C-272/09 P, EU:C:2011:810, 92-94; CJEU judgment in *Chalkor v. Commission*, C-386/10 P, EU:C:2011:815, 51-54; see further H. C.H. Hofmann (2014 a).

397 See e.g. CJEU judgment in *Fantask and Others v. Industriministeriet*, C-188/95, EU:C:1997:580, 47-48.

398 CJEU judgment in *Trustees of the BT Pension Scheme*, C-628/15, EU:C:2017:687, 54-59 (together with the requirement of full effectiveness).

399 J. H. Jans, R. de Lange, S. Prechal, and R. J. G. M. Widdershoven (2007), 50-51; S. Prechal and N. Shelkoplyas (2004), 591.

400 In the context of national procedural autonomy, the relevant Treaty bases were substantive provisions paired with the duty of sincere co-operation. In this light,

2.3.4 The creation of new remedies to ensure *de facto* judicial protection

In earlier case-law concerning national procedural autonomy, the Court had vowed that the duty of loyal co-operation (on which the principles of effectiveness and equivalence are founded), should not require the creation of new remedies under national law.[401] The case-law of 2007 and onwards nevertheless clarified a point to which earlier rulings had only alluded – namely national judges' obligation, under certain circumstances, to provide remedies previously unavailable to them. Under the principle of remedial autonomy, the *use* of a remedy is the responsibility of the national judge, whereas by implication the responsibility for the *existence* of a remedy is incumbent on the national legislator.[402]

The case-law discussed in the present section spelled out what had already been indicated in *Factortame* and *Francovich*[403] – namely, that if remedies necessary to ensure the principle of effectiveness were not available under national law,[404] then the seized court must not only set the latter aside, but also take positive measures to provide adequate and appropriate remedies (prompting an ancillary legislative obligation to create such remedies for future use). In *Francovich*, the Court had found that in order to ensure individuals full protection of Union rights, national courts must be able to grant damages for breaches of EU law.[405] The "no new remedy-rule" would, in *Unibet*, be sustained as long as there were other, even indirect, remedies available to individuals suffering legal losses due to incom-

---

it was logical for requirements on access to courts to be founded on the principle of effectiveness.

401 As the principle of loyal co-operation requires Member State organs to do what is possible, within the constraints of their existing powers, to ensure the correct implementation of Union law; CJEU judgment in *Rewe v. Landwirtschaftskammer für das Saarland*, 33/76, EU:C:1976:188, 5; CJEU judgment in *Comet BV v. Produktschap voor Siergewassen*, 45/76, EU:C:1976:191, 16; CJEU judgment in *The Queen v. Secretary of State for Transport, ex parte Factortame*, C-213/89, EU:C:1990:257, 19-23; CJEU judgment in *Rewe-Handelsgesellschaft Nord mbH and Rewe-Markt Steffen v. Hauptzollamt Kiel*, 158/80, EU:C:1981:163.

402 On remedial autonomy, see S. Prechal and K. Cath (2014), 180-81; M. Claes (2006), 144; J-U. Franck (2017), 1875.

403 CJEU judgment in *The Queen v. Secretary of State for Transport, ex parte Factortame*, C-213/89, EU:C:1990:257; CJEU judgment in *Francovich and Bonifaci v. Italy*, joined cases C-6/90 and C-9/90, EU:C:1991:428.

404 In these cases, interim relief and action for damages.

405 CJEU judgment in *Francovich and Bonifaci v. Italy*, joined cases C-6/90 and C-9/90, EU:C:1991:428.

patibility between Union and Member State law.[406] An individual seeking to establish an infringement of his Union law rights, should however under no circumstances have to subject himself to personal legal risks by violating national law in order to be able to seize a national judge.[407]

The no new remedy-rule has undergone additional modifications in the post-Lisbon era, especially as interpreted in several Opinions[408] in light of the codification of the duty to provide effective remedies.[409] Advocate General Wathelet has underscored the importance of legal certainty in litigants' choice between existing remedies.[410] Remedies provided under national law must be assessed autonomously in terms of their capacity to provide judicial protection:[411]

> If [...] a Member State makes a number of legal remedies available to individuals, the second subparagraph of Article 19(1) TEU requires that each of those remedies ensure effective legal protection, and a legal remedy cannot offer 'effective' protection unless the conditions in accordance with which it may be used and achieve a positive outcome are known in advance.

The above reasoning is in line with the *Unibet* dictum insofar that the evaluation of sought remedies must account for the existence of other remedies under national law. Yet, Art. 19(1) TEU provides a sharper tool of evaluation: Remedies must – following Wathelet's position – both individually and in interface with each other ensure effective judicial protection.

---

406 CJEU judgment in *Unibet (London) Ltd and Unibet (International) Ltd v. Justitiekanslern*, C-432/05, EU:C:2007:163, 47-50, 64.

407 Ibid.

408 See e.g. Advocate General Mazák in his Opinion in *Banca Antoniana Popolare Veneta*, C-427/10, EU:C:2011:595 and Opinion of Advocate General Jääskinen in *Bundeswettbewerbsbehörde v. Donau Chemie AG and Others*, C-536/11, EU:C:2013:67, especially 66-70.

409 Art. 19(1) TEU.

410 On the retroactive barring of claims due to modifications in time limitations, see Opinion of Advocate General Wathelet in *Test Claimants (III) in the Franked Investment Income Group Litigation*, C-362/12, EU:C:2013:538, 76.

411 Opinion of Advocate General Wathelet in *Test Claimants (III) in the Franked Investment Income Group Litigation*, C-362/12, EU:C:2013:538, 48-50: "As soon as taxpayers choose one of the national legal remedies available [...] or have recourse to the only national legal remedy available, they must come under the protection offered by the general principles of EU law. [...] The fact that the litigants could have chosen another cause of action, fully consistent with the principles of equivalence and effectiveness, is irrelevant in that regard."

A distinct line of case-law has sought to ensure that third parties not be excluded from judicial protection in national litigation.[412] In its initial case-law on standing in environmental proceedings, the Court of Justice linked rights of participation to rules granting access to review in secondary EU law and non-Treaty instruments, without mentioning the general principle of effective judicial protection.[413] In the event that fundamental access to court was barred due to restrictive rules on standing, the Court of Justice required that national courts make the review procedure available insofar as e.g. the Aarhus Convention so required, which included allowing environmental organizations standing to bring claims before national courts.[414] While not overtly requiring the creation of new remedies, in effect a cause of action was made available to new groups of litigants.[415] In *Boxus*, national courts were compelled to create procedures making it possible to review national legislation pursuant to challenges against projects falling within the scope of the Aarhus Convention.[416] Although the relevant standing rights were initially based solely on secondary law, the principle of effective judicial protection was evoked to require national courts to grant collective bodies standing in EU environmental law cases.[417] In particular, the use of Art. 19(1) TEU, paired with

412 Opinion of Advocate General Jääskinen in *Bundeswettbewerbsbehörde v. Donau Chemie AG and Others*, C-536/11, EU:C:2013:67, 66-70; CJEU judgment in *Djurgården-Lilla Värtans Miljöskyddsförening v. Stockholms kommun genom dess marknämnd*, C-263/08, EU:C:2009:631, 39, 52; CJEU judgment in *ClientEarth v. The Secretary of State for the Environment, Food and Rural Affairs*, C-404/13, EU:C:2014:2382.

413 CJEU judgment in *Djurgården-Lilla Värtans Miljöskyddsförening v. Stockholms kommun genom dess marknämnd*, C-263/08, EU:C:2009:631; CJEU judgment in *Bund für Umwelt und Naturschutz Deutschland, Landesverband Nordrhein-Westfalen (Trianel)*, C-115/09, EU:C:2011:289.

414 CJEU judgment in *Bund für Umwelt und Naturschutz Deutschland, Landesverband Nordrhein-Westfalen (Trianel)*, C-115/09, EU:C:2011:289.

415 Ibid., 50; see also CJEU judgment in *Lesoochranárske zoskupenie VLK (Brown Bear)*, C-240/09, EU:C:2011:125, 52, commented by M. Eliantonio in 'Case C-240/09, Lesoochranárske zoskupenie VLK v. Ministerstvo životného prostredia Slovenskej republiky, Judgment of the Court of Justice (Grand Chamber) of 8 March 2011', *CMLR*, 49 (2012), 767-91.

416 CJEU judgment in *Boxus and Others*, joined cases C-128/09 to C-131/09, C-134/09 and C-135/09, EU:C:2011:667, 57; see comments by P. van Cleynenbreugel (2012 b), 93ff.; L.M. Ravo (2012), 116ff.

417 CJEU judgment in *Lesoochranárske zoskupenie VLK (Brown Bear)*, C-240/09, EU:C:2011:125; CJEU judgment in *Lesoochranárske zoskupenie VLK (II)*, C-243/15, EU:C:2016:838, 54-62; see also CJEU judgment in *ClientEarth*, C-404/13, EU:C:2014:2382, 52.

Art. 47 CFR, provided legal bases for requiring a "wide access to justice", including for third party associations, in the form of adequate and effective remedies and a fair hearing before a tribunal.[418]

Pairing the principle of effective judicial protection with Art. 19(1) TEU thus consolidated a language of positive obligations to make available previously inaccessible remedies in the sphere of national procedural autonomy. Even though the Court of Justice earlier expected national courts to overcome obstacles to the effectiveness of Union law by merely setting aside national procedural obstacles, room has been created for indicating *what* the national legislators should put in the place of the disapplied national rules.[419] The *Rewe* formula, precluding national procedural law from posing unacceptable obstacles to the application of Union law, had been formulated negatively and therefore – at least in principle – had limited capacity to activate positive obligations. By contrast, the principle of effective judicial protection "works as a standard entailing positive (procedural) obligations and which could give rise to new remedies and national powers."[420] The principal addressee of the requirement of effective judicial protection is thus the seized court, whereas such calls on national courts will have to be supported also by the addressees of Art. 19(1) TEU – national legislators.[421]

---

418 CJEU judgment in *Lesoochranárske zoskupenie VLK (II)*, C-243/15, EU:C:2016:838, 54-62. Consumer case-law has nonetheless taken an increasingly restrictive stance on standing for consumer associations: CJEU judgment in *Pohotovosť s.r.o. v. Miroslav Vašuta (II)*, C-470/12, EU:C:2014:101; CJEU judgment in *EOS KSI Slovensko*, C-448/17, EU:C:2018:745; CJEU judgment in *Asociación de Consumidores Independientes de Castilla y León*, C-413/12, EU:C:2013:800, 50; CJEU judgment in *Jorge Sales Sinués v. Caixabank*, joined cases C-381/14 and 385/14, EU:C:2016:252; see comments by C. Warin, 'Individual Rights and Collective Interests in EU Law: Three Approaches to a Still Volatile Relationship', *CMLR*, 56 (2019), 478-80.

419 On the "narrow" version of direct effect, requiring a replacement norm, see S. Prechal, 'Direct effect, indirect effect, supremacy and the evolving constitution of the European Union', in *The Fundamentals of EU Law Revisited: Assessing the Impact of the Constitutional Debate*, ed. Barnard, C. (New York: Oxford University Press, 2007), 44-45.

420 J. Krommendijk (2016), 1405, W. van Gerven (2000), 534.

421 On the division of responsibilities between judiciary and legislative instances, see earlier work in D. Simon (2000), 247.

2.3.5 Convergence of effectiveness and effective judicial protection

Up until the Lisbon Treaties, the foundation for the principle of effective judicial protection, as interpreted in the case-law, was incorporated in Union law through both the common constitutional traditions of the Member States and through Art. 6 ECHR, to which all Member States were and are contracting parties. As a constitutional principle, and as an International Treaty Law tenet binding on the contracting parties, it should be complied with by the Union and by its Member States when they carry out their obligations under Union law. It has appeared, since the 1980's, in a variety of secondary law instruments.[422]

In the post-Lisbon era, the legal basis of the principle became easier to discern. Art. 47 CFR had already codified (for the purposes of Union law) the contents of the principle, including detailed obligations inspired by the requirements of Art. 6 ECHR:

> Everyone whose rights and freedoms guaranteed by the law of the Union are violated has the right to an effective remedy before a tribunal in compliance with the conditions laid down in this Article.
>
> Everyone is entitled to a fair and public hearing within reasonable time by an independent and impartial tribunal previously established by law. Everyone shall have the possibility of being advised, defended and represented.
>
> Legal aid shall be made available to those who lack sufficient resources in so far as such aid is necessary to ensure effective access to justice.

The principle was strengthened not only by the CFR's elevated legal status post-Lisbon, but also by Art. 19(1) TEU, laying down the remedial mandate incumbent on national legislators: "Member States shall provide

422 E.g. Council Directive 89/665/EEC of 21 December 1989 on the coordination of the laws, regulations and administrative provisions relating to the application of review procedures to the award of public supply and public works contracts, OJ L 395, 30/12/1989, 33; Directive 2002/21/EC of the European Parliament and of the Council of 7 March 2002 on a common regulatory framework for electronic communications networks and services, OJ L 108, 24/4/2002, 33; Directive 2004/38/EC of the European Parliament and of the Council of 29 April 2004 on the right of citizens of the Union and their family members to move and reside freely within the territory of the Member States amending Regulation (EEC) 1612/68 and repealing Directives 64/221/EEC, 68/360/EEC, 72/194/EEC, 73/148/EEC, 75/34/EEC, 75/35/EEC, 90/364/EEC, 90/365/EEC and 93/96/EEC, OJ L 229, 29/6/2004, 35; Council Directive 2005/85/EC of 1 December 2005 on minimum standards on procedures in Member States for granting and withdrawing refugee status, OJ L 326, 13/12/2005, 13.

remedies sufficient to ensure the effective legal protection in the fields covered by Union law."[423] Such remedies are today understood to correspond to the requirements enumerated in Art. 47 CFR.[424]

The ascent of the principle of effective judicial protection has brought with it a closer scrutiny of national procedural law than did the previous *Rewe*-criteria. It has not entirely replaced the principles of effectiveness and equivalence;[425] yet, as pointed out in the scholarship, it is not always clear when *Rewe*-effectiveness is considered a sufficient level of protection and when the more severe *Johnston* test is to be applied.[426] Effective judicial protection has been held by some to encompass or embody the principle of effectiveness,[427] by others to be specific and autonomous from the principle of effectiveness,[428] and by yet others to contain a potential discord *vis-à-vis* effectiveness.[429]

Coming back to the matter of positive and negative standards, the effectiveness principle required that national courts take measures to ensure that vindication of Union rights not be rendered "virtually impossible or excessively difficult"[430](usually considered a negative standard). By contrast, the principle of effective judicial protection paves the way for posi-

423 Art. 19(1) TEU.

424 CJEU judgment in *Associação Sindical dos Juízes Portugueses v. Tribunal de Contas*, C-64/16, EU:C:2018:117, 29-37; CJEU judgment in *Carlos Escribano Vindel v. Ministerio de Justicia*, C-49/18, EU:C:2019:106, 62, as anticipated by S. Prechal and R. Widdershoven (2011 b), 37. Note, however, that Art. 19(1) TEU pertains to judicial *and* administrative bodies, as opposed to the principle of effective judicial protection.

425 J. Krommendijk (2016), 1402, has observed that even though CJEU judgment in *Deutsche Energiehandels- und Beratungsgesellschaft mbH v. Bundesrepublik Deutschland (DEB)*, C-279/09, EU:C:2010:811 indicated a decline in importance of the *Rewe* formula, CJEU judgment in *Orizzonte Salute*, C-61/14, EU:C:2015:655 shows that "*Rewe* is not "dead"". See more recently CJEU judgment in *EOS KSI Slovensko*, C-448/17, EU:C:2018:745; CJEU judgment in *Nikolay Kantarev v. Balgarska Narodna Banka*, C-571/16, EU:C:2018:807, 118ff.

426 S. Prechal and R. Widdershoven (2011 a), 289; J. Krommendijk (2016), 1402ff.

427 M. Accetto and S. Zleptnig (2005), 388; J. H. Jans, R. de Lange, S. Prechal, and R. J. G. M. Widdershoven (2007), 51.

428 See e.g. S. Prechal and R. Widdershoven (2011 b), 31; A. Arnull (2011), 68.

429 M. Safjan and D. Düsterhaus, 'A Union of Effective Judicial Protection: Addressing a Multi-level Challenge through the Lens of Article 47 CFREU', *YEL*, (2014), 2-3.

430 CJEU judgment in *Francovich and Bonifaci v. Italy*, joined cases C-6/90 and C-9/90, EU:C:1991:428, 43; CJEU judgment in *Peterbroeck, Van Campenhout & Cie v. Belgian State*, C-312/93, EU:C:1995:437, 12; CJEU judgment in *Fantask and Others v. Industriministeriet*, C-188/95, EU:C:1997:580, 47.

tive obligations in the creation of new remedies,[431] even though it can also entail negative obligations such as setting aside national procedural rules.[432]

The reinforced legal status of the principle of effective judicial protection may accordingly bridge the competence gap represented by the absence of Union procedural standards. As a result of primary law codification of the principle of effective judicial protection, it cannot as easily be argued that procedural rules are absent in Union law as soon as there exists no applicable secondary law procedural framework:[433]

> national courts are directly obliged to carry out this review as a matter of EU law. Since 'effective judicial protection' constitutes a directly valid extension of EU law itself, the scope of national procedural autonomy, a principle applied in the *absence* of EU law on the matter, is limited.

Incorporation in EU primary law of the right to effective judicial protection did not end the saga. As will be seen in Chapter 5, requirements on court proceedings have been paired with multiple other legal bases, standards, and values above and beyond Art. 47 CFR: viz. effective remedies/ legal protection (Art. 19(1) TEU), the rule of law (Art. 2 TEU) and equality before the law (Art. 20 CFR).[434]

This fundamental shift has also brought about a potential change in possibilities for justification of rules that would otherwise have to be set aside under the duty of sincere co-operation. We have seen how the *van Schijndel* formula introduced a proportionality test of kinds, according to which some procedural obstacles were deemed necessary for the proper conduct of the national proceedings, seen in their case-specific litigation context.[435] Similarly, national procedural or institutional rules that encroach on ef-

---

431 S. Prechal and R. Widdershoven (2011 b), 40-41.

432 CJEU judgment in *The Queen v. Secretary of State for Transport, ex parte Factortame*, C-213/89, EU:C:1990:257, 21-23.

433 P. van Cleynenbreugel (2012 b), 91.

434 E.g. CJEU judgment in *Direcţia Generală Regională a Finanţelor Publice Braşov v. Vasile Toma*, C-205/15, EU:C:2016:49; CJEU judgment in *Associação Sindical dos Juízes Portugueses*, C-64/16, EU:C:2018:1179; CJEU judgment in *Slowakische Republik v. Achmea BV*, C-284/16, EU:C:2018:158; CJEU judgment in *Carlos Escribano Vindel v. Ministerio de Justicia*, C-49/18, EU:C:2019:106; CJEU judgment in *Bashar Ibrahim*, joined cases C-297/17, C-318/17, C-319/17 and C-438/17, EU:C:2019:219, 66. These developments will be considered in Chapter 5.

435 CJEU judgment in *van Schijndel v. Stichting Pensioenfonds voor Fysiotherapeuten*, joined cases C-430/93 and C-431/93, EU:C:1995:441; CJEU judgment in *Peterbroeck, Van Campenhout & Cie v. Belgian State*, C-312/93, EU:C:1995:437.

fective judicial protection can be justified insofar as they correspond to objectives of general interest not involving disproportionate and intolerable interferences with the substance of the right.[436]

> where the principle of effective judicial protection was applied, the Court appeared to be more committed to grant effectiveness of the right of the individual to judicial protection as such, rather than linking its reasoning to the effectiveness of EU law. In such cases, the application of the principle was linked to a fundamental right and implied a balance between competing interests.[437]

This balancing act is more complex than the rule-of-reason, not the least because it entails weighing effective judicial protection as a self-standing value against other procedural safeguards such as legal certainty – many of which form part of what can be described as Member State-specific guarantees for effective judicial protection of *any* litigating individual. It is, from this perspective, intuitive that justifications under the fundamental rights approach would, in practice, prove capable of shortcutting procedural protection – in contrast to the *van Schijndel* formula which, by design and purpose, bolstered procedural protection under national law.

The principle of effectiveness does not, in this perspective, fit quite snugly under the umbrella of effective judicial protection, nor is the effectiveness of Union rules in all cases furthered by compliance with the principle of effective judicial protection.[438] Several instances of this are found in the case-law explored in Chapters 3-4, whereas available justifications under *inter alia* the fundamental rights approach and their consequences for individual procedural protection will be addressed in Chapter 5.

2.4 Interim conclusions

The evolution described in the present chapter concerned principles governing the decentralized enforcement carried out by national courts when fulfilling their mission as Union judges. The duty of sincere co-operation early on surpassed the principle of primacy as basis for requiring Member States to set aside *procedural* rules containing obstacles to the enforcement of Union law. Particularly the twin requirements of effectiveness and equivalence formed a basis for constraints on national courts' exercise of

---

436 CJEU judgment in *Alassini and Others*, C-317/08, EU:C:2010:146.

437 L. M. Ravo (2012), 118.

438 J. Krommendijk (2016), 1417; S. Prechal (2017 a), 403.

(the supposed) procedural autonomy of the EU Member States. The principle of primacy with its requirement of "full effect" has, however, regained relevance in the sphere of national institutional autonomy.[439]

In the context of decentralized enforcement, the degree of effectiveness of EU law is, generally, dependent on the bounty of national rules of court procedure: "substantial provisions are likely to be ineffective in the absence of an adequate procedural mechanism aimed at ensuring their application."[440] The tools provided by the Court of Justice have had as primary priority to support the effective enforcement of Union law, which is not surprising in view of the overall task of the Court of Justice to "ensure that in the interpretation and application of the Treaties the law is observed."[441]

Although tools favoring effectiveness are numerous,[442] this does not mean that effectiveness of EU law automatically trumps procedural protection. The Court of Justice has specifically devised formulas to allow the national judge to carry out a balancing exercise between effectiveness and procedural protection through e.g. legal certainty. Examples of this are the rule-of-reason, the balancing exercise prescribed for the requirement of full effect, and the proportionality test used under the fundamental rights approach and the "implied procedural competence" doctrine.[443]

These moderating formulas – joined to the effectiveness requirement in its various guises – instruct a seized court on how to exercise any remaining discretion within the areas of national procedural and institutional autonomy, and help strike a balance between procedural protection under national law and the effectiveness of Union law. Still, such proportionality measures cannot be taken to be inherently deferential, but may equally be understood as encouragement for national judges to take a critical stance on national procedural rules, and not by default consider them justified in view of their function to ensure the proper conduct of proceedings.[444] In

439 On the distinct context of constitutional review, see M. Bossuyt and W. Verrijdt, 'The Full Effect of EU Law and of Constitutional Review in Belgium and France after the Melki Judgment', *ECL*, 7 (2011).

440 A. Adinolfi, 'The "Procedural Autonomy" of Member States and the Constraints Stemming from the ECJ's Case Law: Is Judicial Activism Still Necessary?', in *The European Court of Justice and the Autonomy of the Member States*, eds. Micklitz H.-W. and B. de Witte (Cambridge: Intersentia, 2012), 292.

441 Art. 19(1) TEU.

442 E.g. the duty of sincere co-operation, consistent interpretation, *Rewe*-effectiveness, full effectiveness, *effet utile,* etc; see distinctions in U. Šadl (2015), 24ff.

443 CJEU judgment in *M.A.S.*, C-42/17, EU:C:2017:936.

444 See M. Dougan (2004), 31-32; P. Wennerås (2007), 88-90.

this perspective, even the *van Schijndel* formula (on its face, the most deferential) may in fact be regarded as a tool of effectiveness of EU law.

The protection of individuals seeking enforcement of EU law was also – at least formally – bolstered through the right to effective judicial protection, initially entailing access to courts, and subsequently requirements of judicial independence, equality of arms etc. Art. 19(1) TEU, requiring effective remedies to be provided in the fields covered by EU law, has increasingly been joined to Art. 47 CFR, laying down a right to effective judicial protection. These principles embody both the priorities of effectiveness and procedural protection by courts, deriving legal authority from sources beyond EU law. Yet, the protection of substantive rules of EU law is not always the same as the protection of procedural rights of individuals[445] – in fact, as will be seen in Chapters 4-5, individual procedural rights may in instances be at odds with the effective enforcement of EU law. The forthcoming chapter examines how the tools so far introduced – especially the *Rewe* formula, the requirement of full effect and the principle of effective judicial protection – have been interpreted by the Court of Justice in response to preliminary references concerning national constraints on *ex officio* review.

445 O. Dubos (2015 b), 21.

3 Balancing effectiveness against procedural protection through *ex officio* review

The present chapter addresses whether national courts are at liberty, or even obliged, to apply EU law of their own motion; that is, where the relevant EU law provisions have not been invoked by either party in the national proceedings. The terms "*ex officio* review" and review of a court's "own motion" are used synonymously to describe the power of a court to take into account aspects of a case before it which have not been invoked by the parties to the proceedings.[446] This may entail *inter alia* the judge's reliance on applicable law that has not been invoked for resolving the litigation before him (*jura novit curia*), as well as the investigation of factual circumstances not put forward by the parties, insofar as their consideration is necessary to apply other legal provisions than those invoked.[447] It is the latter measure that gives rise to difficulties of legal certainty, and is therefore often precluded under national law. Moreover, the prevalence of new facts implicated in the exercise of applying non-invoked law frequently gives rise to a tension between national law and EU law. The present work therefore places emphasis on the latter meaning, viz. "all action that a court can be required to take and which make[s] it go outside the ambit of the proceedings as set by the parties."[448]

Ex officio review has various functions in national legal orders, ranging from individual procedural interests of the parties in predictable and unbiased procedural treatment, to the safeguarding of collective interests in upholding rules of public policy. However, in the Union law context, the key function of intervening in national judges' review of their own motion is to ensure the effective implementation of Union law and the effective judicial protection of the beneficiary of rights derived from Union law, both of which are served by the national court's introduction *ex officio* of Union law into litigation before it. Emphasis will accordingly be placed on the

446 R. Lauwaars (2007), 1161; F. C. de la Torre (2005), 398; J.-M. Le Masson (1998), 29.

447 J.-M. Le Masson (1998), 29. The present definition addresses the functions of *ex officio* review that are most central to this work, although, depending on the legal system, *ex officio* measures may be more varied than above described.

448 J. Engström (2008), 67.

Court of Justice's considerations when dealing with such situations, which have necessitated it to strike a balance between safeguarding Union rights, on the one hand, and upholding procedural rights under national law, on the other. The present chapter will systematize the case-law delivered by the Court of Justice concerning national rules governing *ex officio* review, in an attempt to identify the direction of historical and contemporary legal developments.

Before embarking on the case-law, however, a contextualization is provided in the form of an overview and introduction of the most important legal concepts related to *ex officio* review, in order to describe issues of principle theoretical importance at stake in the choice between intervention and passivity on the side of the judge (3.1). These introductory pages will thus deal with the principle of party disposition or party control, its rapport with the principal objective of court litigation, the tension between judge passivity and the overriding interest in truth-finding, and the necessity of judge impartiality and equality of arms for ensuring a fair trial. Particularly, the challenges to the principle of procedural equality posed by the practical reality of imbalances in the quality of legal representation will be discussed (3.1.1). Next will be addressed purposefully left legal gaps in parties' litigation and the extent to which courts can reasonably leave these gaps unfilled (3.1.2). Subsequently, distinct issues will be dealt with, which serve as dividing lines for when *ex officio* intervention may be called for, namely variations within the ordinary court system (3.1.3-3.1.4) and the distinction between introducing law versus facts *ex officio* (3.1.5). The section will be concluded by an assessment of whether effective judicial protection is best served by a national court's initiative or lack of initiative to carry out examinations of its own motion, based on the requirements of Art. 6 ECHR, particularly from the perspective of equality of arms between litigants (3.1.6).

The subsequent case-law review (3.2) focuses on preliminary rulings delivered by the Court of Justice that either dealt with, or had significant implications for, national procedural rules governing courts' powers of *ex officio* review. Section 3.2.1 examines the consequences of the more general case-law for the development of the requirement of "full effect", including its implications in the form of a mandate for national courts to apply EU law and if necessary make preliminary references of its own motion.

Section 3.2.2 discusses, beyond an abstract mandate of *ex officio* review, the introduction of a concrete obligation of *ex officio* review for national judges, including the balancing act to be carried out between the interests in substantive enforcement of EU law and the justifications for adhering to strict and preclusive national rules of procedure.

Section 3.2.3 distills an approach to national public policy exceptions allowing *ex officio* review when general rules of procedure would otherwise preclude it. Exceptions under national law for public policy rules have the potential of emphasizing the public interest in ensuring a correct outcome in the relevant proceedings, at the possible expense of strict adherence to an ideology of adversarialism. The section will demonstrate that although the Court of Justice has been favorably inclined to allowing such derogations for the purposes of ensuring effective enforcement of Union law as a matter of national public policy, it does not go so far as to compel the automatic introduction of Union law as a matter of Union public policy.

Finally, section 3.2.4 examines an area where a lesser measure of deference is demonstrated by the Court of Justice, namely in consumer litigation within the scope of applicability of EU directives put in place to protect consumers in a financially and procedurally vulnerable position. The Court of Justice's increased level of interventionism is explained by two elements: First, it is justified with reference back to the courts' mandate of protecting the procedurally weaker litigant, which has its foundations in conceptual choices of procedural policy. Secondly, it is justified by the circumstance that the EU consumer legislative framework has to a great degree harmonized procedural law aspects of consumer litigation, including regulating *ex officio* review through the sanction of nullity and voidness.

3.1 *Ex officio* review as method for courts to safeguard public and private interests

Limits on *ex officio* review are tightly connected to the presumption which is held in most of the EU Member States, namely that the judge "knows the law" and has a freedom of maneuver in determining the legal significance or categorizations that can be deduced from the circumstances and facts put forward by the parties (*jura novit curia*).[449] Governed by such a presumption, a judge, who chooses to apply rules that have not been introduced in the parties' argumentation, will normally not be going outside the ambit of the proceedings unless the examination of these rules also requires the judge to examine factual circumstances that have not been in-

449 F. C. de la Torre (2005), 398.

voked by the parties.[450] By contrast, if the application of rules that have not been invoked by the parties requires the judge to investigate additional facts and circumstances, he is venturing outside the ambit of the proceedings as defined by the parties.[451]

The reasons for, and against, going outside the ambit of the proceedings can be summarized in the following way. On the one hand, there is a responsibility for a seized court to ensure that a materially sound judgment may be delivered irrespective of the capacities and actions of the litigants or their legal counsel: "an erroneous position should not be accepted as good law simply because counsel have passed it by in silence and have not sought to challenge it."[452] The essence of this argument is that the court should primarily serve the function of securing "the public interest in receiving the best doctrine", even at the expense of the litigants' prerogative to direct the content and ambit of their litigation.[453]

On the other hand, such actions should not override the litigants' right to a fair hearing. Significant support for the passive judge was put forwards by Lon Fuller in "The Forms and Limits of Adjudication".[454] In this seminal work, Fuller paints a picture of a judge who abstains from *ex officio* review so as to allow the parties (e.g. through legal counsel) to set the legal and factual framework. The reasons for the judge to subordinate himself to the parties' wishes are, in Fuller's view: the empowerment of the parties through enhancement of their experience of meaningful participation in the proceedings, the importance of predictability for ensuring the proceedings' integrity, and the perception of impartiality of the seized body.[455]

The argument of passivity, convincing as it may be, should be supplied with justification as to why it is that parties' participation must be safe-

450 R. Lauwaars (2007), 1161.

451 J. Engström (2008), 67.

452 Judgment of the Court of Appeal (UK) in *Goldsmith v. Sperrings*, (1977) 2 All E.R. 557, 572 A-B.

453 N. H. Andrews (1988), 130.

454 L. L. Fuller, 'The Forms and Limits of Adjudication', *Harv. L. Rev.*, 92 (1978).

455 Ibid., 388-91. As held by J. Chipman Gray in *The Nature and Sources of the Law* (Macmillan, 1921), 114-15: "A judge of an organized body is a man appointed by that body to determine duties and the corresponding rights upon the application of persons claiming those rights. It is the fact that such application must be made to him, which distinguishes a judge from an administrative officer. The essence of a judge's office is that he shall be impartial, that he is to sit apart, is not to interfere voluntarily in affairs ... but is to determine cases which are presented to him." The extract referred to *ex officio* initiation of proceedings but is illustrative also for *ex officio* consideration of legal and/or factual claims.

guarded. Various supplementary justifications have been put forward: First of all, the principle of party disposition[456] is a prerequisite for ensuring a "fair hearing", including through maintaining judge impartiality.[457] The dispositive principle would not allow the court to deal with matters not raised by the parties, since, by doing so, the new matters introduced in the litigation would help one party prevail in the litigation, thus depriving the other party of drawing benefit from his superior litigation conduct. Also, how can it be ruled out, once the judge is allowed to introduce elements in the litigation not raised by the parties, that this is done in a biased manner, by introducing elements to help one party whilst abstaining from introducing elements that would possibly help the other party? In response, it has been pointed out that a judge's quest for the "truth" or endeavor to safeguard the public interest beyond the interests of the parties is not necessarily at odds with the right to a fair hearing. Should the judge find that pertinent aspects could be, but have not been, raised by the parties to the proceedings, he must take care that these considerations are not born out of a desire to benefit one party at the expense of the other. Having ascertained that the need for introducing new elements in the litigation is legitimate in this sense, nothing prevents the judge from doing so in a transparent manner that gives both parties the opportunity to comment and, if necessary, dispute the judge's analysis.[458]

Secondly, an experience of participation will increase parties' willingness to accept the outcome, i.e. the ruling, as just, even if it has not been in

456 On the principle of party disposition, here used synonymously with the dispositive principle and the principle of party control/autonomy, see Advocate General Trstenjak in *Pénzügyi Lízing*, C-137/08, EU:C:2010:401, 110: "it is for the parties to take the initiative, under which the parties are responsible for submitting all relevant facts on which the court must then base its decision." Or, as explained by S. Prechal and N. Shelkoplyas (2004), 595: "According to the principle of parties' freedom of disposition, in civil proceedings the initiative as to the extent and manner in which the parties should proceed lies in their hands. They determine the issues to be ruled on by the court and it is up to them, in principle, to choose the cause of action or defence, as well as the remedy they are seeking. The court will intervene only in very exceptional circumstances, for instance in order to protect certain individual rights where the protection is a matter of public interest. For Community law, the parties' freedom of disposition implies that Community law is not to be applied when the parties – intentionally or by negligence – do not rely on Community law provisions." See also F. C. de la Torre (2005), 398 and A. Meij, (2011), 261-62.

457 N. H. Andrews (1988), 127.

458 Ibid., 133.

their favor.[459] This observation has been made based on quantitative studies of the effects of participation through the granting of legal representation as such,[460] but the argument can easily be made that, if parties' experiences of litigation improve through legal representation, then the empowerment of these representatives should even further empower their clients. This second point has not been as often addressed in the scholarship on *ex officio* review.[461] The argument can readily be made, though, that the intervention *ex officio* by a judge will not in itself decrease parties' participation in the litigation – it will, if anything, prompt them to extend their argumentation, and thereby their participation, not only to debate with their counter-parties, but also with the seized judge. So, once again, the proposition that any *ex officio* intervention should entail the opportunity for parties to comment thereupon would be an appropriate solution, which on a practical level would not compromise nor reduce party participation in the proceedings.

Thirdly, the adversarial procedure, of which the principle of party disposition forms an indispensable component, ensures that the judge is given knowledge of the "truth" in its fullest possible detail. A judge can be expected to know the applicable law; this does not mean though, that he can construct and test all the possible arguments available as to how to interpret the law and how to apply it to the facts, without the help of the parties. The driving force behind the litigation, under this approach, is the incentive for parties to self-servingly put forward all available lines of argumentation to convince the judge. Only through such incentive is the judge furnished with the maximum amount of information that allows him to take all relevant aspects into account when ascertaining the "truth".[462] In response to this third justification, it has however been underlined that the opportunity for the parties to comment on any elements introduced *ex offi-*

459 A. Lind and T. Tyler, *The Social Psychology of Procedural Justice* (New York: Plenum Press, 1988); M. Boccaccini, J. Boothby, and S. Brodsky, 'Development and Effects of Client Trust in Criminal Defense Attorneys: Preliminary Examination of the Congruence Model of Trust Development', *Behav. Sci. Law,* 22 (2004).

460 R. Sandefur, 'The Impact of Counsel: An Analysis of Empirical Evidence', *Seattle Journal for Social Justice,* 9 (2010); R. Sandefur, 'Effects of Representation on Trial and Hearing Outcomes in Two Common Law Countries', *International Sociological Association,* (2005).

461 See, however, J. A. Jolowicz (2005), 562.

462 Ibid., 558.

cio will provide the judge with more material on which to base his judgment than he would have had access to, had he not intervened.[463]

In sum, the two positions do not necessarily need to exclude each other. A middle ground between the positions in favor of, on the one hand, full-fledged adversarialism and, on the other hand, ensuring public interest in substantively "correct" rulings, can be found in the principle of due notice: In order for *ex officio* review to be carried out in a way that does not bring with it factual lacunas or procedural disadvantages/injustices, the judge must ensure that parties are not "taken by surprise" by the judges' actions. Therefore, the judge must allow parties to comment on legal or factual considerations introduced by a court of its own motion.[464] Indeed, it is this particular conduct that has been prescribed by the ECtHR in order for a judge to intervene *ex officio* without encroaching upon the right to a fair trial under Art. 6 ECHR.[465]

3.1.1 The "poor client" dilemma – *ex officio* review for the protection of the procedurally weaker litigant

Having looked at the most basic motives for and counter-arguments against judge passivism, we can examine the self-standing arguments in favor of judge intervention. The most fundamental paradox of the ideology of adversarial procedure is that, in the spirit of equality of arms between parties, it presupposes that the parties fight with equal arms to begin with. If a judge were to abstain entirely from intervening in the litigation before him, he should ideally be assured that the respective parties are equipped to bring to the table sufficient legal and factual elements to allow him to make a correct decision.

The equipment referred to is represented by the legal expertise and resources of the parties or their' counsel, which brings with it the self-evident problem that better litigation is costlier. The mechanism is the same as in traditional warfare: In the end, it is not the righteousness of the cause

---

463 Ibid., 558-59.

464 N. H. Andrews (1988), 131; N. H. Andrews, *English Civil Procedure: Fundamentals of the New Civil Justice System* (Oxford: Oxford University Press, 2003), 87.

465 ECtHR judgment in *Clinique des Acacias et autres v. France*, applications no. 65399/01, 65406/01, 65405/01 and 65407/01, 39; ECtHR judgment in *Prikyan and Angelova v. Bulgaria*, application no. 44624/98, 42; see also CJEU judgment in *Gesellschaft für Abfallentsorgungs-Technik GmbH (GAT) v. Österreichische Autobahnen und Schnellstraßen AG*, C-315/01, EU:C:2003:360, 49.

that will win you the battle, but your arms supply, which is in turn decided by your purchasing power to procure arms as well as your capacity to make friends who will sell you arms. Or, to bring the imagery back into the courtroom: On the one hand, one may be tempted to abstain from prosecuting an impoverished man who stole bread to feed his family. On the other hand, if you desist prosecution because he is vulnerable, you create problems of equality before the law unless you provide criminal amnesty for all poor.[466]

Adversarial ideals of procedure thus require that parties (or their counsel) have the knowledge and diligence to furnish the judge with whatever information he needs in order to make an informed decision.[467] As discussed in the above, granting the parties control over the litigation will guarantee that the court is provided with all necessary factual and legal aspects that could affect its argumentation, thereby ensuring that the judge need not carry out investigation on his own. Therefore, such a procedure will only be "fair" if also the parties have equal arms to begin with.[468]

This they often do not have in practice: The assumption of equal footing between litigants has little to do with the reality of civil litigation, in which the quality of parties' litigation may be dependent on their respective capacity to pay for their legal representation.[469] Nor in administrative proceedings can it be assumed that the individual party has the resources at hand to litigate against a public body on equal terms, measured by the skills and knowledge of the legal counsel. With this in mind, it is important to ask what the implications are for the tasks of the court. On the one hand, it is clear that the principle of equality of arms, as enshrined in the

---

466 On the risk of over-compensating for the precarious position of the weaker party, see N. H. Andrews (2003), 112. The dilemma was contained already in Exodus: "Do not deny justice to your poor people in their lawsuits [...] Do not show favoritism to a poor man in his lawsuit"; Holy Bible, Exodus 23.3 and 23.6: Laws of Justice and Mercy, *New International Version*, Biblica (2011 version). See also Holy Bible, Deuteronomy 1:17, *New International Version*, Biblica (2011 version): "Do not show partiality in judging; hear both small and great alike."

467 P. Westberg, *Civilrättskipning* (Stockholm: Norstedts juridik, 2013), 159; A. Robberstad, *Mellom tvekamp og inkvisisjon: straffeprosessens grunnstruktur belyst ved fornærmedes stilling* (Oslo: Universitetsforlaget, 1998), 17.

468 This variant of procedural fairness is referred to by Andrews as "equity" since it is concerned with relationship between the litigants' lawyers and the legal system in terms of "fair play" in practice. N. H. Andrews (2003), 128ff.

469 Intersights, 'Right to a fair trial under the European Convention on Human Rights (Article 6)', in *Intersights Manual for Lawyers*, (London, 2009), 21; N. H. Andrews (2003), 111.

right to a fair trial, does not require litigants to have access to legal representation of equal quality (or, for that matter, cost): "The cost of litigation and an imbalance in the financial resources available to one party with the other is not, in civil cases at least, a ground for concluding that the less well-off party is deprived of a fair trial."[470]

On the other hand, in the event that the legal strategies of one of the litigating parties is deficient to the degree that it gives rise to lacunas capable of changing the substantive outcome of the case, the principle of adversarialism has bitten its own tail. Why? Because the principle of party control is founded on the idea of the judge remaining passive so as to give room for parties' counsel to build as substantial and complete a picture of the case as possible. Yet, the resulting idea of passivity, having become a restricting rule for the judge, will – unless somehow loosened – prohibit him from filling any lacunas left by the parties. If in the end a party does not successfully argue the case, this will give rise to a legal gap, which a rigidly adversarial procedure will not allow the judge do remedy. Hence, from the point of view of equality of arms; if the judge treats the parties equally, under the requirement of equality of arms, the resulting lacunas will in the worst scenario be produced as the result of one party's lack of knowledge and the other party's well-informed wishes to leave the void unfilled. The judge's passivity will in this case unfortunately work only to the benefit of the stronger party who is aware of the lacuna but does not wish to bring it to anyone else's attention.

Having thus discussed the disadvantages of judge passivity, the unavoidable question pertains to the implications of making a break from it in order to ensure procedural "equity", as compared to formal "equality" in treatment. Procedural equity does not require strict equality in the sense of symmetry in the treatment of parties; rather it attempts to achieve "fair play" by also compensating for the conditions under which the litigation takes place, requiring e.g. proportionate responses to procedural errors. In this way it is a form of more "flexible" procedural equality.[471] The most intuitive solution in this spirit is to garb the court with a responsibility, or at least a mandate, to step in to carry out its own legal investigation. Such a mandate would allow the court to fill any gaps arising out of the parties' litigation choices, be they made by strategy, necessity or inadvertence. But, and this is where the difficulty arises, what circumstances should trigger

470 Judgment of the Court of Appeal (UK) in *Official receiver v. Stern*, (2000) 1 WLR 2230, per Sir Richard Scott, 44; cited in N. H. Andrews (2003), 112.

471 On procedural equity as compared to equality, see N. H. Andrews (2003), 128ff.

such expanded powers for the court, and in which interests should such investigation be carried out?

To deal with this question, we would have to consider that gaps in legal argumentation may arise in a variety of circumstances. In a first category, we find (unintentional) legal gaps due to *defective legal argumentation*.[472] In some types of proceedings, parties are not represented by lawyers at all, but represent themselves. This is e.g. the case in Swedish administrative proceedings in which self-representation is most often deemed to be sufficient due to the "simplicity" of the framework of applicable rules.[473] In these cases, the potential inefficiency of self-representation may be compensated by the court, which is not only empowered to, but also obliged to, look out for the interests of the procedurally weaker party.[474] If a party is not represented at all, the judge should not place too heavy a burden on him for making solid legal arguments.[475]

Secondly, in the event that parties are represented not by private lawyers but by state lawyers under a legal aid program, the complaint is sometimes made that the quality of the representation is lacking.[476] This situation has much in common with the example of non-public lawyers that are paid by financially weak parties – formally the party is granted representation, but in practice the representation may have been more efficient were it not for

---

472 J. A. Jolowicz (2005), 554-55.

473 Preparatory works for Swedish New Law on Legal Aid [*Ny rättshjälpslag*] regeringens proposition 1996/97:9, 117. See further D. Kleist and S. Wejedal, 'Tala är silver, tiga är guld. Om muntlig förhandling i förvaltningsmål, särskilt i skattemål', *FT*, 4 (2013), 359-60; S. Wejedal, 'Rätten till biträde – Om biträdeskostnaders hantering vid svenska domstolar' (University of Gothenburg, 2017), 920.

474 Preparatory works for Swedish New Law on Legal Aid [*Ny rättshjälpslag*], Regeringens proposition 1996/97:9, 117. Generally, in administrative proceedings, the court is given a more active role than in civil proceedings; J. Engström (2008), 73.

475 U. von Essen, *Processramen i förvaltningsmål: ändring av talan och anslutande frågor* (Stockholm: Norstedts juridik, 2009), 62, 119. This is particularly the case where vulnerable litigants are represented by a legal guardian: The court is required to take their interests into account even if it requires investigation beyond the ambit of the proceedings; S. Wejedal and A. Östlund, *Advokatens roll. Om ändamålsenlig rollfördelning i mål om tvångsvård av barn* (Stockholm: Santérus, 2016).

476 Quality deficits being due to the working-conditions and pay scheme for the appointed public lawyers; S. E. Mounts, 'Public Defender Programs, Professional Responsibility, and Competent Representation', *Wisconsin Law Review*, (1982), 474-75, 482-83.

the party's lacking capacity to pay. This difficulty is colorfully illustrated in the context of consumer protection litigation.[477] In addition to the weaker party's lacking capacity to pay for quality representation, there are other perils, which are not exclusive to, but certainly aggravated, in litigation between commercial and private parties:

- The disproportionate cost of litigation as compared to succumbing to the claims of the commercial party;[478]
- The risk of taking on the counter-party's legal fees;[479]
- The increased risk of knowledge deficits when it comes to rights granted under non-national legislation such as EU consumer protection legislation.[480]

The generally described problems with weak litigation are exacerbated by the level of difficulty entailed in the existence of multiple layers of applicable law, of which "procedurally weak" litigating parties cannot be expected to be aware.[481] In these circumstances, there is reason to suggest that a court may need to compensate for this lack by carrying out its own investigation to ensure effective judicial protection of the weaker party.[482] This is especially the case as a heavy responsibility is incumbent on the national judge when acting as a Union judge to safeguard Union rights of individuals.[483]

---

477 Where the Court of Justice (as will be discussed below) has elucidated the need for the seized court to step in to fill oversights made by the weaker litigating party to ensure the effective judicial protection of the latter. See e.g. CJEU judgment in *Océano Grupo Editorial and Salvat Editores*, joined cases C-240/98 to C-244/98, EU:C:2000:346, 25-27.

478 Ibid., 22. See further M. Tulibacka, 'Proceduralisation of EU Consumer Law and its Impact on European Consumers', *REALaw*, 8 (2015), 60.

479 N. H. Andrews (2003), 112; M. Tulibacka (2015), 57.

480 CJEU judgment in *Océano Grupo Editorial and Salvat Editores*, joined cases C-240/98 to C-244/98, EU:C:2000:346, 26.

481 J. Engström (2008), 81; A. Beka (2018), 125. See e.g. CJEU judgment in *Cofidis SA v. Jean-Louis Fredout*, C-473/00, EU:C:2002:705, 33; CJEU judgment in *BBVA SA v. Pedro Peñalva López*, C-8/14, EU:C:2015:731, 40.

482 J. Engström (2008), 73.

483 A. Gerbrandy (2014), 37, 42; R. Plender, 'The Role of National Judges in Implementing Uniform Rules of Jurisdiction and Choice of Law in the European Union', in *A Constitutional Order of States? Essays in EU Law in Honour of Alan Dashwood*, eds. Arnull, A., C. Barnard, M. Dougan and E. Spaventa (Cornwall: Hart Publishing, 2011), 421.

Yet, the mandate for the court to do so is not as clear as in instances of self-representation,[484] due to the arbitrariness involved in determining whether a given representation is wanting: Is it the perceived skills of the lawyer that should determine the level of intervention required, or is it his pay-check? And in the case of the state-appointed lawyer, it cannot be assumed that because he is state-appointed he would be unable to litigate skillfully... The list of questions can perhaps be made longer, but the above is sufficient to identify a discretion and thereby a potential for arbitrariness: Having given the court such a mandate, is there not a risk that a court over-compensates for procedural "weakness" to an extent that the judge's own impartiality can be doubted?[485] A way to solve this is to create a legal procedural rule of general applicability, as to where to draw the line – which we will hopefully find in any legal system which allows, albeit preconditions, *ex officio* review. When looking at specific procedural rules which specify which type of *ex officio* interventions are allowed, and following which conduct, we keep in mind that the purpose of such rules is to give a solution that is generally applicable (and thereby does not show favoritism) in order to balance the interest of procedural equality or equity against the interest in ensuring substantive justice.

3.1.2 The "savvy lawyer" dilemma – safeguarding mandatory law in the public interest

Above, situations in which a court may be expected to step in to fill unintentional gaps due to deficient legal argumentation were dealt with. The present section deals with the situation in which the legal gap is not the result of litigation lapses, but rather an informed choice not to bring certain elements or arguments to the table. The main reason not to invoke a legal or factual element is because it is viewed as non-beneficial to the case. The prerogative for judge intervention then only arises if also the opposing counsel chooses not to invoke the same aspect, whereas the judge finds the aspect pertinent. Here, the choice of intervention will not be based on any motive to serve or protect either party – rather, it would be the choice of non-intervention that would act to the material benefit of the parties.

484 And "best interests" representation.

485 On the risk of over-compensating for the precarious position of the weaker party, see N. H. Andrews (2003), 112.

In the scholarship, it has been pointed out that if parties agree on which aspects to litigate and which aspects to leave outside of the litigation, it would be unreasonable for the judge to expand the scope of the litigation by second-guessing them on this point: "If a party is content that a point of law that would operate in his favor should be disregarded or if both parties wish to proceed on the assumption that the law is to a certain effect, it seems unreasonable – and contrary to the dispositive principle – that they should be prevented from doing so."[486] To the extent that such second-guessing would be beneficial to one party and not to the other, it would give rise to inequality and a perception of partiality on the side of the court, if the judge were to proceed to promote the interests of one side of the litigation without being requested by the parties to consider those interests.

This may be true for factual components of the litigation, which parties choose to (or not to) put before the judge. Yet, when it comes to legal aspects, it is clearly less reasonable to let the parties agree on the interpretation – and even less, the content – of the law.[487] On the one hand, it is arguably not reasonable for parties to be able to force a judge to give an unmerited decision contrary to the public interest.[488] For example, in litigation concerning anti-competitive agreements or arrangements falling within the category of unlawful state aid, there are incentives for parties on both sides to ask that the judge disregard the unlawfulness of the agreement or transaction at the center of the litigation.[489] It is in view of the public, rather than the private, interest at stake in such proceedings that anti-competitive agreements are garbed with nullity and are therefore unenforceable – in order specifically to ensure that courts refuse to enforce such agreements irrespective of the wishes of the parties.[490] On the other hand, it is inherent to non-mandatory law that parties can derogate from it through private contract, and therefore they should also be respected by the court in their wishes to do so. Against this background, it is logical that

---

486 J. A. Jolowicz (2005), 554.

487 Particularly if they propose an incorrect reading of it; ibid.

488 J. Engström (2008), 73.

489 As was the case in e.g. CJEU judgment in *Ministero dell'Industria, del Commercio e dell'Artigianato v. Lucchini SpA*, C-119/05, EU:C:2007:434.

490 In this perspective, it is logical that the Court of Justice has indicated that Union provisions of mandatory character should in some circumstances be applied *ex officio*: CJEU judgment *in Eco Swiss China Time Ltd v. Benetton International NV*, C-126/97, EU:C:1999:269. See further J. H. Jans, R. de Lange, S. Prechal, and R. J. G. M. Widdershoven (2007), 310-11.

for example in the UK, a judge is *allowed* but not *obliged* to follow the wishes of the parties.[491] This permits the judge to assess whether the parties' wishes can be respected without this taking place at the public expense.

It is against this background that the distinction between mandatory and non-mandatory law becomes central in determining whether courts can allow parties to purposefully circumscribe the ambit of the proceedings by choosing what to include and what not to include in their litigation. However, it is also at this point where the choice of a national judge to carry out *ex officio* review is not done in the interest of safeguarding the procedural rights of the litigants but rather in the interest of safeguarding public policy.[492] From this perspective, *ex officio* review cannot be justified by the need to ensure procedural protection (as neither party is beneficiary of the rights being safeguarded through *ex officio* review), and must instead be justified by the effective enforcement of mandatory rules, i.e. more closely related to the principle of effectiveness.

3.1.3 The objective of the proceedings – truth-seeking or dispute resolution?

The extent to which parties are given control over the proceedings, and by consequence, the courts' powers and/or duties to review matters of law or fact that have not been raised by the litigants, goes back to the core function of judicial proceedings, namely the role of the judge and the responsibility of the parties for determining the ambit of the proceedings. These aspects are, in their turn, contingent upon both the character of the proceedings and the legal traditions prevailing in a given state:[493] most particularly in their overall objective of either seeking the "truth" or resolving a dispute.[494]

On an overall level, the truth-seeking mandate imposes itself with greater force in higher courts, in view of their responsibility for delivering precedents, whereas in lower courts the dispute-resolving function is em-

491 J. A. Jolowicz (2005), 555.

492 On this distinction, see e.g. J. H. Jans, R. de Lange, S. Prechal, and R. J. G. M. Widdershoven (2007), 313.

493 J. Engström, 'Effektivt rättsskydd i förvirring - Nationell process- och sanktionsrätt i ljuset av C-253/00 Muñoz', *ERT*, 1 (2003), 72, 81.

494 On the dichotomy between "truth" versus "justice" as dispute resolution objectives, see e.g. J. Thibaut and L. Walker (1978).

phasized, with varying force between legal traditions.[495] The difficulty with lower courts is the following: If we can accept that justice in lower courts is only a service offered to private litigants, we must presume that there is no public function for lower courts in terms of creating precedents. Spigelman would, contrary to this, argue that civil courts do serve public functions beyond the resolution of private disputes:[496]

> A court is not simply a publicly funded dispute resolution centre. The enforcement of legal rights and obligations, the articulation and development of the law, the resolution of private disputes by public affirmation of who is in the right and who is in the wrong, the denunciation of conduct by a public process with public outcomes – these are all public sources served by courts, even in the resolution of private disputes. An economist might call them "externalities". They constitute collectively, a core function of government.

This idea of the public function of courts was given considerable attention already in the 1970's by Abram Chayes,[497] who compared the traditional functions of civil litigation (namely the resolution of private disputes) to what courts actually did in modern adjudication of the time.[498] Chayes noted that certain traits of litigation, particularly the isolation of legal effects for the litigating parties, had become less pertinent with time and therefore called for a re-thinking of the procedural principles founded on these elements. Chayes accordingly observed an evolution in the actual substance of litigation towards increasingly addressing public concerns,

---

495 In UK civil proceedings, for example, truth-seeking is supposedly "so obviously part of the court's role that it does not need to be stated expressly." UK case-law on *ex officio* review has, nevertheless, taken a critical stance, emphasizing the role of the court as rather a "state-based dispute resolution system." J. A. Jolowicz (2005), 563.

496 J. Spigelman, 'Judicial Accountability and Performance Indicators', *C.J.Q.*, 21 (2002), 26; see also N. H. Andrews (1988), 125-26.

497 A. Chayes (in 'The Role of the Judge in Public Law Litigation', *Harv. L. Rev.*, 89 (1976), see particularly 1310ff.) used the term "public law litigation" to describe litigation with a public interest vested in its outcome. The notion of "civil courts" there pertained to the US notion of civil litigation, which is wider than the continental definition and included what I here refer to as both civil and administrative proceedings.

498 Similar observations have been made concerning the public law features of civil litigation. On "mixed" disputes, see e.g. J. Thibaut and L. Walker (1978), 560ff.; on public investment in civil justice, see N.H. Andrews, 'Nurturing Civil Justice', in *Festschrift für Rolf Sturner zum 70. Geburtstag. 2. Teilband*, eds. Bruns, A., C. Kern, J. Münch, A. Piekenbrock, A. Stadler and D. Tsikrikas (Tübingen: Mohr Siebeck, 2013), 1395ff.

through e.g. class action, affected third parties (including victims), and other external (even regulatory) interests in the outcome of civil suits. When the public (or members thereof) are affected by the outcome of litigation, they most often do not benefit from direct representation in the proceedings – the task therefore falling on the seized judge, as far as possible, to ensure the public interest.[499] This can be done by way of *ex officio* review in fact or law, which however comes at the risks mentioned in the above.

An alternative option, which mitigates these risks, is for the judge to require, in order to proceed, that new parties or intervenients be heard – including through the appointment of guardians *ad litem*,[500] *amici curiae*,[501] various technical expert witnesses[502] and even "class" representatives who would be informed of their option of entering the proceedings by public notice.[503] Having done as much, though, the court has indeed stepped outside the sphere of party control. And whilst this allows him to generate legally "sound" judgments, the nuisance that arises from such measures is that the judge can thereby bind the parties on the one hand, and future judges through creating precedents on the other (through *ratio decidendi*). If not, the option remains to use *obiter dicta* for the purposes of discussing issues, which cannot have legal effects on the parties. Or, vice versa, if the "externalities" cannot be included in the judgment, but the judgment gives rise to a decision which may not become precedence due to the limitations imposed by the dispositions of the parties, it would be possible to abstain from reporting the case in order to signal its lack of precedence.[504]

499 A. Chayes (1976), 1282-83.

500 Circumstances for appointing guardians *ad litem* are explained in e.g. P. Mohr, 'Report of the Working Group on the Allocation of Decision Making', *Fordham Law Review*, 64 (1996), 1327-28.

501 N. H. Andrews (1988), 136.

502 For a more critical stance, see H. S. Shin (1998), 402-3.

503 A. Chayes (1976), 1311-12.

504 All these options have been discussed in favorable terms in N. H. Andrews (1988), 135-38.

3.1.4 The type of court proceedings – greater need for intervention in vertical litigation?

The "type" of proceedings refers to the dividing lines between civil proceedings, criminal proceedings and administrative proceedings.[505] The advantages and disadvantages associated with judicial passivism in civil procedure have been at the fore of the academic debate,[506] whereas the specific conditions for *ex officio* review in administrative proceedings have gained less attention in the European law scholarship.[507]

To begin with, how closely the below descriptions reflect existing procedural law depends on the legal system we are looking at, and the way in which the role of the court is defined therein. The courts' mandate may, on the one hand, be regarded as consisting of protecting the interests of the parties, particularly their procedural interests. This tradition is termed *recours subjectif* and implies an emphasis on e.g. ensuring the litigants' rights. On the other hand, the court's fundamental mandate may lie in the enforcement of substantive law and the realization of the public policy objectives underlying these rules, in which case we are rather looking at what is termed *recours objectif*.[508] The tradition of *recours objectif* will endorse *ex officio* review more readily than the tradition of *recours subjectif*,[509] although different views on these matters prevail in different EU Member

505 For the purposes of this work, the term civil proceedings is used in the meaning of litigation between private parties, be they natural or legal persons. The term criminal proceedings is used to describe proceedings through which state authorities enforce substantive penal law through criminal sanctions. The term administrative proceedings is used in the meaning of proceedings between natural or legal persons on the one hand and public authorities on the other hand, concerning non-contractual rights or obligations under public law *not* belonging to the fields of criminal or tort law, whether litigation takes place before civil or administrative courts. This definition deviates from an equally common meaning of the term, namely procedures under the regulatory framework for the administration and functioning of public bodies.

506 A. Wallerman, 'Towards an EU Law Doctrine on the Exercise of Discretion in National Courts? The Member States' Self-Imposed Limits on National Procedural Autonomy', *CMLR*, 53 (2016), 339; J. Engström (2003), 167; A. Beka (2018), 77ff., 360-61; S. Whittaker, 'Who Determines What Civil Courts Decide? Private Rights, Public policy and EU Law', *Oxford Legal Research Paper Series*, 46 (2012), 1.

507 See however R. Lauwaars (2007); J. Engström (2008), 71ff.

508 J. H. Jans, R. de Lange, S. Prechal, and R. J. G. M. Widdershoven (2007), 313.

509 S. Prechal (1998), 706; J. Engström (2008), 74-75.

States, the most palpable dividing line being that between common law and continental law.[510]

On a general level, it can be noted that throughout the legal systems of the EU, civil litigation is governed by the idea of *recours subjectif*, whereas the approaches are more divergent when it comes to the aim of administrative proceedings.[511] Administrative proceedings are somewhat less problematic, due to the lesser need for judicial passivism in this setting. After all, a civil court intervening for the benefit of one party in a civil dispute is at greater peril of producing a perception of court bias, whereas an administrative court intervening for the benefit of an individual party in proceedings against a public authority may be perceived as having legitimate purposes for doing so. These are considerations that fit well into the rule-of-reason introduced by the Court of Justice, in which the advantages, in the form of e.g. safeguarding substantive rights, may be balanced against the underlying reasons for courts being precluded from examining the same substantive rights in the event that they have not been invoked by the parties.[512] Nonetheless, the relevance of also studying the context of administrative proceedings should not be dismissed, particularly since the interest in protecting an individual litigating against the authorities has not been recognized by the Court of Justice as warranting special treatment,[513] in the same way that for example a consumer has when litigating against a commercial contracting party.[514]

Administrative proceedings are vertical insofar that the parties are constituted by, on the one hand, a public authority and, on the other hand, one or several individual parties. The proceedings may, however, have horizontal elements, e.g. in the situation that there is a tension of interests between several individual parties whose legal interactions with the public

---

510 F. C. de la Torre (2005), 398.

511 S. Whittaker (2012); S. Prechal (1998), 706; J. Engström (2008), 74.

512 CJEU judgment in *Peterbroeck, Van Campenhout & Cie v. Belgian State*, C-312/93, EU:C:1995:437; CJEU judgment in *van Schijndel v. Stichting Pensioenfonds voor Fysiotherapeuten*, joined cases C-430/93 and C-431/93, EU:C:1995:441.

513 See e.g. CJEU judgment in *van der Weerd and Others v. Minister van Landbouw, Natuur en Voedselkwaliteit*, joined cases C-222/05 to C-225/05, EU:C:2007:318.

514 J. Engström (2008), 81-82; CJEU judgment in *Océano Grupo Editorial and Salvat Editores*, joined cases C-240/98 to C-244/98, EU:C:2000:346; CJEU judgment in *Cofidis SA v. Jean-Louis Fredout*, C-473/00, EU:C:2002:705; CJEU judgment in *Rampion and Godard*, C-429/05, EU:C:2007:575.

authority are at stake.[515] In administrative proceedings, there is a central responsibility for the court to take an active role, since often rules and values of importance not only to the parties, but also to the public, are at stake.[516]

Administrative courts may also bear the responsibility of protecting the party who is most often at a procedural disadvantage, namely an individual litigating against a public authority with greater resources at its disposal to defend its case.[517] In this situation, it is the vertical relationship between the parties, as such, which would justify *ex officio* measures by the seized court. The same may be said of criminal proceedings, which are also vertical in character; prosecutors often have greater resources at their disposal than defendants. In both instances (administrative and criminal proceedings), rendered judgments will be expected to reflect an objectively justified interpretation of the law, irrespective of the capabilities of the parties to present their case. What is here described is administrative and criminal courts' responsibility for "the search for the truth."[518]

In civil proceedings, by contrast, the relationship between the parties is typically horizontal insofar that an individual party is litigating against another individual – irrespective of whether the parties have different capacities and legal resources. The proceedings' framework of grounds, circumstances and evidence in turn constitute what is commonly referred to as the ambit of the procedure or the limits of the dispute.[519] The justifications of these standards lie specifically in the private nature of the rights at stake: As the rights are of individual nature, the litigating parties should be free to dispose over their legal exaction of these rights. Although allowing for party disposition runs the risk of producing substantively deficient judgments, this potential forfeiture may be justified by recourse to the contractual freedom of the parties (and the absence of public stakes in the outcome).[520] In civil proceedings, therefore, the principles of party autonomy

515 E.g. in public procurement cases; on this topic, see E. Sandin, 'Åberopsbörda i mål om offentlig upphandling? Två steg framåt, ett steg bakåt', *JT*, 10 (2009), 925.

516 If the court is charged with taking budgetary or environmental considerations into account, it may be that the principle of party disposition will need to give way to such considerations of public policy character (e.g. in public procurement procedures or infrastructure authorizations requiring impact assessments).

517 J. Engström (2008), 73.

518 Ibid.

519 S. Prechal and N. Shelkoplyas (2004), 595.

520 J. Engström (2008), 73.

and judge passivity are of greater importance and together define the principle of party disposition.[521]

This tenet comes with the caveat that also civil proceedings may have elements of collective or third-party imbedded interests, in so-called "public law litigation".[522] The presence of such interests can, in instances, justify deviation from the principle of party disposition for reasons of safeguarding public policy, also in the context of private litigation.

Having examined the differences in priorities between vertical and horizontal litigation, we turn finally to a civil litigation context in which the priority of "playing according to the rulebook" clearly trumps the priority of delivering substantively correct awards; namely, arbitration proceedings. One of the traditional justifications for the principle of party disposition is its capacity to persuade parties to seek justice in court rather than extra-judicially.[523]

In Jolowicz's reasoning, this subjective experience is particularly important for the losing party, whose perception of justice having been done cannot rely on substantive application of the law (which in the end did not turn out in his favor). Instead, his main consolation will be the experience of procedural justice:[524]

> In less law-abiding societies than we are now accustomed to, if the parties to a dispute are to be persuaded to submit to the jurisdiction of the court rather than resort to self-help, each of them must be satisfied that he will have a full and fair opportunity to present his own case and to challenge his opponent before an independent and impartial umpire or referee.

If this reasoning is dated with regard to today's civil litigation (indeed, in the interest of procedural economy, out-of-court settlements are often considered favorable), here lies one motive that, in any event, attracts parties to settle their disputes through arbitration rather than through court litigation. This is one main reason for the more forceful application of the principle of party disposition in the arbitration context. By contrast, if it is not the search for an objective "truth" that justifies moderation of the principle of party disposition before ordinary courts, it may at least be the deliv-

---

521 S. Prechal and N. Shelkoplyas (2004), 595. See also CJEU judgment in *Rampion and Godard*, C-429/05, EU:C:2007:575, 51-56.

522 A. Chayes (1976), 1282-83.

523 J. A. Jolowicz (2005), 562.

524 Ibid.

ery of useful and correct precedents; increasingly so with higher levels of appeal:[525]

> [E]ven if Fuller's paradigm of passive adjudication mirrored English arbitration, there is a vital difference between arbitrators and senior judges. The higher civil courts, unlike arbitrators, have a responsibility to preserve and improve the quality of the doctrine which they seek to apply. Surely, they should be able to escape the shackles of counsel's arguments.

By comparison, arbitration proceedings follow a different logic, a chief reason for this being the incentive in the principle of party disposition towards making arbitration litigation more attractive to disputing parties.

3.1.5 Even if the court knows the law, how can it know the facts?

There remains one legal concept to help disentangle some of the intricacies in the Court of Justice's case-law on *ex officio* review, namely the difference between a court introducing elements of law versus elements of fact in the litigation before it.

The introduction of elements of law is uncontroversial in continental law traditions that are guided by the principle of *jura novit curia* (the court knows the law).[526] The fundamental assumption is here that the seized court has access to all limbs of applicable law, and needs only factual information from the litigating parties, to which he will proceed to apply relevant applicable law: *da mihi factum dabo tibi jus* (give me the fact, I give you the right).[527] As a result of this, the choice of applicable legal rule should be for the judge, not the parties. The rule of *jura novit curia* is not as familiar in the common law, which is assumed to place greater responsibility on the parties not only to present facts, but also to assemble pleadings

---

525 N. H. Andrews (1988), 132.

526 F. A. Mann, 'Fusion of the Legal Professions?', *Law Quarterly Review*, 93 (1977), 369ff.; S. Buhai (2008). Specifically, 13 of the "old" Member States apply the principle: Germany, Austria, Belgium, Denmark, Spain, Finland, France, Greece, Italy, Luxembourg, the Netherlands, Portugal and Sweden; see F. C. de la Torre (2005), 398; E. Werlauff, *Common European Procedural law. European Law requirements imposed on national administration of Justice* (Gylling: DJOF Publishing Copenhagen 1999); A. Wallerman (2019); Ch. 3.3.

527 T. Ereciński, 'When Must National Judges Raise European Law Issues on Their Own Motion?', *ERA Forum* (Springer, 2011), 526; H. Schebsta, 'Does the National Court Know European Law? A Note on *Ex officio* Application after *Asturcom*', *Eur. Rev. Pr. L.*, 4 (2010), 848.

consisting in argumentation on how to apply legal rules to the invoked facts.[528]

In practice, though, neither the distinction between law and fact nor the distinction between common law and continental law is as clear-cut as above portrayed. Starting with the UK, the plaintiff was historically expected to present not only facts in connection with his claim, but also the rule of law on which the court should base its judgment to find in his favor. This obligation was abandoned through procedural reform in 1875, at which point there was no formal requirement of stating the legal basis for a claim. Therefore, the UK version of a cause of action is no more than "a factual situation the existence of which entitles one person to obtain from the court a remedy against another person."[529] Yet, legal counsel not being precluded from specifying legal grounds, and the pre-reform spirit still living on, the common approach is to state a cause of action including both fact and applicable law, hoping that the judge will accept the merits of the pursued argumentation. However, as a result of no legal basis being required, counsel is not bound by his choice: "So long as the facts are before the court, the court may and should draw upon any rule of law that appears to it to be applicable whether either party has formally placed reliance on that rule or not."[530] Therefore, the construction that we have before us clearly corresponds to what we in continental law refer to as the principle of *jura novit curia.*

The French law equivalent of cause of action is *cause de la demande*, whose content is filled, clearly, with arguments of law and, less clearly, with some element of factual allegations. This combination appears in three alternative formulas:[531]

1. The *cause de la demande* is constituted by the legal claim: "the rule of law or the legal category that is invoked."

528 F. A. Mann (1977), 369; Opinion of Advocate General Jacobs in *van Schijndel v. Stichting Pensioenfonds voor Fysiotherapeuten*, joined cases C-430/93 and C-431/93, EU:C:1995:185, 33.

529 Judgment of the Court of Appeal (UK) in *Letang v. Cooper*, (1965) 1 Q.B. 232, per Diplock L.J., 242-43; cited in J. A. Jolowicz (2000), 81.

530 The court should "consider and deal with the legal result of pleaded fact, though the particular legal result alleged is not stated in the pleadings"; Judgment of the Court of Appeal (UK) in *Lever Bros Ltd. v. Bell*, [1931] 1 K.B. 557, per Scrutton L.J., 583; referred to in J. A. Jolowicz (2000), 82.

531 J. A. Jolowicz (2000), 82.

2. It is constituted by the "facts which support the claim *as placed in their legal category.*"
3. It is constituted by the "*circonstances de fait invoquées en vue d'établir le droit subjectif par lequel se traduit juridiquement la prétention soumise au juge.*"[532]

The first category, in other words, considers the cause to be solely constituted by its legal basis, which would then place an exclusive responsibility on the parties to direct the court by selecting the relevant and applicable law to be applied.[533]

Views two and three have similarities, yet the second includes only facts supporting a specific legal claim as identified by the party, which requires the existence of a legal claim put forward by a party. The third one, by contrast, takes as point of departure the claim made by the party, but the content of the cause of action is identified by the circumstance that certain facts have been invoked, whether or not in the end they serve the envisioned legal basis. Motulsky has described this as "*un complexe de faits*" which does not include, in the notion of cause of action, the legal qualification of invoked facts.[534] By implication, such qualification would be left to the seized judge, and even factual elements lacking support in a legal basis could be considered as forming part of the cause of action as long as, in theory, the judge could pair it with an appropriate legal basis. The justification for this is that the courts remain masters of the law and cannot be precluded from granting parties their rights only because of incorrect legal classifications.[535]

532 Ibid., citing H. Motulsky, G. Cornu, J. Foyer, B. Goldman, and F. Fouchard, *Ecrits* (Paris: Dalloz, 1973), 103. [EN: "the factual circumstances invoked in order to establish the subjective right to which the claim submitted to the judge is legally translated."]

533 This interpretation of the French *cause de la demande* is not followed by French courts; J. A. Jolowicz (2000), 83.

534 [English: a constellation of facts]; H. Motulsky, G. Cornu, J. Foyer, B. Goldman, and F. Fouchard (1973), 103-7. The *Cour de Cassation* has specified that the obligation refers to the proper qualification of facts and does not apply to the raising *ex officio* of legal grounds, the latter remaining a faculty; Judgment of the Cour de Cassation (FR), Assemblée plénière, in *Pourvoi N° 06-11343*, Bull. civ. 2007, N° 10, 21 décembre 2007. See further in L. Cadiet, J. Normand, S. Amrani Mekki, *Théorie générale du procès* (Presses universitaires de France, 2013), 757ff.

535 J. A. Jolowicz (2000), 83.

It is the latter interpretation that corresponds to what can be designated a *cause de la demande* in contemporary French procedural practice, and in the French procedural code as it stands today.[536] By implication, the court is liberated from the legal arguments put forward by the parties and can use the invoked facts to grant a remedy on a separate legal basis – which once again translates to the principle of *jura novit curia.*

The above is not intended to reflect the common law versus continental law traditions across Europe, but rather to illustrate that the distinction between law and fact in parties' pleadings is important both in continental law systems governed by *jura novit curia*, and in the common-law construction of the cause of action and its implications for the judge's margin of maneuver.

If we accept that the distinction is important, we also need to consider the modalities of making such distinctions in practice. The main difficulty in maintaining party control over the facts and court control over the law is that the practical maneuvers taken by the parties in the pre-trial stage will lead to the constructions of the facts circumscribing the scope of applicable law. To understand the implications of this proposition, we follow the illustration made by Raymond Martin[537] of how a cause of action is born: Litigation may start with a fact or series of facts that have prompted an individual to seek counsel from a lawyer. The lawyer will proceed to discuss, with the client, possible legal solutions or courses of action, and in assessing them he will legally conceptualize the facts in order to pre-empt the categorization or assessment made by the presumptive judge. In so doing, lawyer and client will identify factual elements as respectively favorable/unfavorable and relevant/irrelevant, and finally make a selection of facts to present to the judge in support of their legal claim. The judge will then be free in his application of the law, but constrained by the circumstance that the factual elements only form the foundation for deciding on

536 See e.g. Art. 12 of the French New Code of Civil Procedure [*Nouveau Code de Procédure Civile, version consolidée au 1 octobre 2016*] according to which "le juge tranche le litige conformément aux règles de droit qui lui sont applicables. Il doit donner ou restituer leur exacte qualification aux faits et actes litigieux sans s'arrêter à la dénomination que les parties en auraient proposée." This was specified at the level of cassation "Il peut relever d'office les moyens de pur droit quel que soit le fondement juridique invoqué par les parties"; see further J. A. Jolowicz (2000), 83.

537 M. Raymond Martin, 'La crise du contradictoire entre juge et avocat', *La Gazette du Palais,* tome 1 (1978).

certain rules of law, while remaining insufficient to decide on others that the parties have not brought to the court's attention.[538]

This dividing line between facts and law sometimes poses terminological problems in the reading of the Court of Justice's case-law on *ex officio* review.[539] National law may not preclude a national court from *applying* Union law *ex officio* – the problem lies in the circumstance that the national court does not have the factual elements before it to form the basis of considering Union law-based claims. The distinction between law and legal claims may pose the same problem, depending on the relevant delimitation of the ambit of the proceedings. As we will see below, this is sometimes what the Court of Justice has referred to when maintaining that Union law should be applied *ex officio* only to the extent that the national court has the powers to do so under national law, or where this can be done without abandoning fundamental procedural principles.[540]

Before venturing into this case-law, however, a few words will be said about requirements on national courts' *ex officio* review pursuant to the ECHR and the case-law of the European Court of Human Rights.

3.1.6 *Ex officio* review – in the service or disservice of the right to a fair trial under the ECHR?

It has above become clear that intervention *ex officio* by a court has the capacity of ensuring that rights granted to individuals are reinforced through procedural protection in order so the beneficiary of a right can effectively vindicate it before the court. *Ex officio* review can thus remedy existing imbalances between parties in order to place them on the same procedural footing (referred to in the above as procedural "equity"[541]).

At first glance, this translates into a matter of effective judicial protection of the relevant beneficiary. At the same time, allowing *ex officio* review has the capacity of introducing elements of bias or favoritism. As the principle of effective judicial protection (under Union law and Member States'

538 Ibid., discussed in J. A. Jolowicz (2000), 91-92.

539 As highlighted in the Opinion of Advocate General Cruz Villalón in *Société Landsbanki Islands HF*, C-85/12, EU:C:2013:352, 72-73, where details of foreign law were subject to submission of evidence, as were the facts.

540 See e.g. Opinion of Advocate General Jacobs in *van Schijndel v. Stichting Pensioenfonds voor Fysiotherapeuten*, joined cases C-430/93 and C-431/93, EU:C:1995:185, 33.

541 N. H. Andrews (2003), 128ff.

law alike) is closely linked to the right to a fair trial under Art. 6 ECHR, the potential of jeopardizing judge impartiality indicates that *ex officio* review may in some instances hamper effective judicial protection. It is accordingly appropriate to briefly examine the link between *ex officio* review and the requirement of effective judicial protection: Should *ex officio* review be perceived as a tool to be used in the service of judicial protection, or is it rather by refraining from *ex officio* review that the right to a fair trial is best ensured?

This question is approached drawing on the requirements placed on court proceedings, in order to qualify as a fair trial under Art. 6(1) of the ECHR, which stipulates:

> In determination of his civil rights and obligations or of any criminal charge against him, everyone is entitled to a fair and public hearing within reasonable time by an independent and impartial tribunal established by law.

The fundamental requirement under this provision is the right of access to court, a right which is not mentioned explicitly in Art. 6 but which is considered to form an inherent part of the provision.[542] The ECtHR has specified that this guarantee should be understood as pertaining to *effective* access to court,[543] comprising, in order for the right not to be "illusory", the right to institute legal proceedings,[544] and (at least under certain circumstances) access to legal aid for parties that cannot afford legal assistance[545] – i.e. a prerogative to protect vulnerable litigants.

The guarantee in Art. 6(1) that the hearing be "fair" also brings with it certain sub-requirements, including the right to participate effectively in the hearing and the right to equality of arms. While the right to participate effectively was held to follow from the "very notion of an adversarial pro-

542 See e.g. the French version of the Art. 6(1), which explicitly specifies "*à ce que sa cause soit entendue*" [EN: to have his case/cause heard]. The right of access to court was developed in the ECtHR judgment in *Golder v. the United Kingdom*, application no. 4451/70.

543 Ibid., 26-36. That the right of access was to be "effective" was implicit in the judgment, see comments in D. Harris, M. O'Boyle, E. Bates, and C. Buckley, *Harris, O'Boyle & Warbrick: Law of the European Convention on Human Rights* (Oxford: Oxford University Press, 2009), 236ff.

544 ECtHR judgment in *Burdov v. Russia*, application no. 59498/00, 34, where the court denounced ancillary procedural obstacles making access to court "illusory".

545 ECtHR judgment in *Airey v. Ireland*, application no. 6289/73, 26; ECtHR judgment in *Steel and Morris v. the United Kingdom*, application no. 6/70, 61.

cedure"[546] the principle of equality of arms substantiates the fundamental elements of adversarialism and thereby endorses what was ultimately distilled as a right to an adversarial procedure as the governing principle for civil and criminal proceedings alike.[547] On a practical level, the principle of equality of arms requires that each party "be given a reasonable opportunity to present his case under conditions that do not place him at a substantial disadvantage *vis-à-vis* his opponent."[548]

This idea embodies what was referred to in the above as procedural "equity", offering some level of recompense for the weaker party.[549] In its case-law on the right to an independent and impartial court, the ECtHR placed great emphasis not only on the arguments presented by the counter-party, but also on Opinions of Advocate Generals and other officers to the court, especially when such opinions in effect translated into *de facto* opposition to the path pursued by the applicant. When advisors to the court exhibited alliance with the opposing party, this was considered to give rise to an "appearance" of partiality, or a "feeling of inequality," ultimately casting a shadow of doubt on the court's independence.[550] Unless they were paired with adversarial safeguards, such allegiances were considered capable of undermining the appearance, to the public, of the proper administration of justice.[551]

546 ECtHR judgment in *Stanford v. United Kingdom*, application no. 16757/90, 26.

547 The limitation of the article's applicability to "civil rights and obligations" does not mean that all administrative and public law legal relationships fall outside its scope. With time, an increasing number of public law claims have been considered to trigger civil rights and obligations as well. The ECtHR has taken an inclusive stance in interpreting the scope of the article, and clarified that the ECHR is to be interpreted dynamically, in the light of its contemporary circumstances: ECtHR judgment in *Eskelinen and Others v. Finland*, application no. 63235/00, 69; ECtHR judgment in *Ferrazzini v. Italy*, application no. 44759/98, 27. A dynamic interpretation for the purposes of the scope of the notion "civil rights and obligations" includes public and administrative litigation to the extent that the "outcome is decisive for private rights and obligations – the latter including a wide variety of administrative law procedures with primarily economic consequences for individuals." See further D. Harris, M. O'Boyle, E. Bates, and C. Buckley (2009), 218ff.

548 ECtHR judgment in *Kress v. France* application no. 39594/98, 72.

549 Albeit not requiring absolute equality in the *de facto* expenses for legal representation; ECtHR judgment in *Steel and Morris v. the United Kingdom*, application no. 4451/70.

550 D. Harris, M. O'Boyle, E. Bates, and C. buckley (2009), 252.

551 ECtHR judgment in *Borgers v. Belgium*, application no. 12005/86.

The image of independence and impartiality was given weight irrespective of whether there were *de facto* elements of partiality to the detriment of the actual case of the individual litigant.[552] Already evaluations through prisms of public perception could give rise to "aggravated" breaches of the right to an adversarial procedure.[553] As to particular adversarial safeguards, the ECtHR mainly emphasized the "opportunity for the parties [...] to have knowledge of and comment on all evidence adduced or observations filed with a view to influencing the Court's decision."[554] This included an obligation for the seized court to draw the existence of such evidence to the attention of all parties.[555] It is this principle of due notice, under the umbrella of the right to an adversarial procedure, that offers the most guidance as to the appropriate practice of *ex officio* review.[556]

Overall, the ECtHR's doctrine on right to equality of arms and to an adversarial procedure appears to be preoccupied with the facilitation, of the courts' own motion, of access to evidence and observations of all intervenients.[557] But also review in law or fact of courts' own motion has been dealt with by the ECtHR as a matter of adversarial procedure. In a case concerning *ex officio* review, *X & Co. Ltd v. Germany*,[558] the European Commission for Human Rights[559] uncritically endorsed its use not only as a facultative tool, but even as an obligation, in accord with the continental tradition and in disregard of the common law tradition.[560] In this remark-

---

552 D. Harris, M. O'Boyle, E. Bates, and C. buckley (2009), 252.

553 ECtHR judgment in *Vermeulen v. Belgium*, application no. 19075/91, 34: "The breach in question was aggravated by the avocat général's participation in the court's deliberations, albeit only in an advisory capacity. The deliberations afforded the avocat général, if only to outward appearances, an additional opportunity to bolster his submissions in private, without fear of contradiction".

554 Ibid., 33.

555 ECtHR judgment in *Göç v. Turkey*, application no. 36590/97.

556 Setting aside the right to due notice equally violates the right to an adversarial procedure irrespective of whether, *in casu*, any prejudice for the injured party can be shown.

557 D. Harris, M. O'Boyle, E. Bates, and C. Buckley (2009), 254-55; R. C. A. White and C. Ovey, *Jacobs, White & Ovey: The European Convention on Human Rights*, 5 edn. (Oxford: Oxford University Press, 2010), 261ff.

558 Order of the European Commission for Human Righs *X. & Co. Ltd. V. the Federal Republic of Germany*, application no. 3147/67.

559 Hearing the application to the ECtHR at first instance (a procedure abolished in 1998 through Protocol 11 to the European Convention for the Protection of Human Rights and Fundamental Freedoms, Restructuring the Control Machinery Established Thereby, 11 May 1994, ETS 155).

560 See comments in F. A. Mann (1977).

able case, a German court had based its judgment on a legal ground that had not been invoked or mentioned by the litigating parties. The seized court did not give the parties opportunity to submit observations on this ground, triggering one party to bring proceedings before the ECtHR for infringement of Art. 6(1) ECHR.

The Commission was not sympathetic to the argument of the claimant, a UK company, that the German court, in declining to invite oral submissions on the introduced point of law, violated the principle of adversarial procedure. The Commission instead relied on the principle of *jura novit curia* as a generally recognized principle of law (which, of course, German courts observe whereas the applicants came from a legal tradition if not devoid of then at least suspicious towards such a principle[561]). The application was rejected as "manifestly ill-founded" since "the practice of the German courts whereby the parties are not necessarily invited to make oral submissions on all points of law which may appear significant to the courts does not constitute an infringement of the principle of "fair hearing" within the meaning of this provision."[562] The present case demonstrates that, while vowing to safeguard adversarialism as a component of the right to a fair trial, the ECtHR may accept a watered-down version of it, endorsing the continental tradition of *jura novit curia*, while denying parties to submit observations on the application and interpretation of the law chosen by the seized court.

In subsequent case-law of the ECtHR, the seized court's introduction of aspects of law or fact *ex officio* has not in itself been considered an encroachment on adversarial procedure; however, in so doing, the seized court should not take the party by surprise. The ECtHR has emphasized the opportunity to take into account and submit observations based on any elements introduced into the proceedings by the court,[563] in the same way as the adversarial procedure requires that the counter-party's submis-

561 In the UK, the court should "consider and deal with the legal result of pleaded fact, though the particular legal result alleged is not stated in the pleadings"; Judgment of the Court of Appeal (UK) in *Lever Bros Ltd. v. Bell*, [1931] 1 K.B. 557, per Scrutton L.J., 583; referred to in J. A. Jolowicz (2000), 82.

562 Order of the European Commission for Human Righs *X. & Co. Ltd. V. the Federal Republic of Germany*, application no. 3147/67, under "The Law".

563 ECtHR judgment in *Bulut v. Austria*, application no. 17358/90, 50; ECtHR judgment in *Clinique des Acacias et autres v. France*, applications no. 65399/01, 65406/01, 65405/01 and 65407/01, 39; ECtHR judgment in *Prikyan and Angelova v. Bulgaria*, application no. 44624/98, 42; ECtHR judgment in *Bulut v. Austria*, application no. 17358/90, 50. See also ECtHR judgment in *Avotiņš v. Latvia*, ap-

sions of evidence or observations should be subject to due notice before delivering a judgment in the case, as described above.[564] However, the requirement of due notice is not absolute, taking into account that the legal requalification of parties' claims have not been considered to constitute such intervention that must give rise to suspension of the proceedings in order for parties to have the opportunity to submit observations in response.[565] Finally, with regard to the principle of *jura novit curia*, the ECtHR has not recognized the law as subject to party disposition; in other words, the parties cannot dispose over the seized court's interpretation or application of the law as such.[566]

In view of all of this, it appears that in the case-law of the ECtHR, the practice of *ex officio* review is not regarded as a threat to equality of arms or court impartiality, as long as it is exercised with caution and subject to the requirement of due notice.[567] Although the language of the ECHR would appear to easily lend itself to a theoretical argumentation in favor of safeguarding the dispositive principle in the spirit of adversarialism, the case-law on *ex officio* review does not stress its perils for the public perception of court partiality. Nor has the ECtHR, on the other hand, consistently pro-

---

plication no. 17502/07, 98, where enforcement of foreign judgments under Council Regulation (EC) No 44/2001 of 22 December 2000 on jurisdiction and the recognition and enforcement of judgments in civil and commercial matters (Brussels I Regulation), OJ L 012, 16/01/2001, was considered contrary to Art. 6(1) ECHR if enforcement was carried out "without the unsuccessful party having been afforded any opportunity of effectively asserting a complaint as to the unfairness of the proceedings leading to that judgment, either in the State of origin or in the State addressed."

564 This applies equally when the seized court rules *ex officio* on matters of admissibility, legality of a contested act and, most importantly for present purposes, the substitution of grounds. ECtHR judgment in *Clinique des Acacias et autres v. France*, applications no. 65399/01, 65406/01, 65405/01 and 65407/01, 40-43. See, however, ECtHR judgment in *Andret et autres v. France*, application no. 1956/02.

565 P. Gilliaux, *Droit(s) européen(s) à un procès équitable* (Brussels: Bruylant, 2012), 607.

566 Similarly, the General Court has found that although the parties have the right, in the spirit of adversarial procedure, to present arguments as to its correct interpretation, the seized court has been recognized as having a right to propose its own interpretation of the law even without warning the parties in advance of its chosen legal path: Judgment of the Court of First Instance in *Commission of the European Communities v. Anton Pieter Roodhuijzen*, T-58/80 P, EU:T:2009:385, 36.

567 See further R. Ergec and J. Velu, *Convention européenne des droits de l'homme* (Brussels: Bruylant, 2014), 506, § 474.

moted or prescribed the tool of *ex officio* review by aligning it with other procedural rights under Art. 6(1) ECHR.[568]

3.2 An EU law mandate of *ex officio* review for national courts

Initial terminological issues having been addressed, the question remains what may bring these technicalities to the attention of the Court of Justice of the EU. Courts' powers to engage in *ex officio* review are oftentimes, and for a variety of purposes, limited by national procedural rules by reference to the "passive role [a court] should normally observe" or the domestic organization of judicial remedies.[569] As described in the above, a judge's initiative to deviate from the matters put before him may create procedural disadvantages for one of the parties, that risk reducing legal certainty. On the other hand, *ex officio* review may be justified by individual or collective interests whose preservation the litigating parties cannot be relied on to promote.

Among such individual and collective interests, we find rules and rights derived from EU law, whose introduction *ex officio* in national litigation comes with the same general advantages and disadvantages as above described. One may easily anticipate the Treaty's prohibitions on state aid and anti-competitive practices being purposefully disregarded by litigating parties for the simple reason that they are beneficial to neither of them.[570] In such circumstances, a national judge can be expected, under the duty of loyalty, to introduce matters that the parties may have wished to evade. In this example, the effectiveness of EU law in fact does not promote the legal interests or the judicial protection of such parties, who rather benefit from national rules that are contrary to EU law. Instead, protection is granted in favor of abstract interests justifying the relevant rules of EU law, even without the presence of any beneficiary in the given litigation.[571]

There is also the example that a party who could benefit from rights under EU law is not aware of these rights and therefore fails to invoke the

568 See e.g. ECtHR judgment in *Avotiņš v. Latvia*, application no. 17502/07, Joint concurring opinion of Judges Lemmens and Briede, 3.

569 CJEU judgment in *van Schijndel v. Stichting Pensioenfonds voor Fysiotherapeuten*, joined cases C-430/93 and C-431/93, EU:C:1995:441, 22; J. Engström (2008), 67.

570 By avoiding their introduction into a given dispute, the parties would evade the enforcement of EU law, assuming that national procedural law barred the judge from introducing these rules himself (the "savvy lawyer" dilemma).

571 Se e.g. M. Dougan (2012), 95-100.

necessary elements (facts and/or legal claims), with the potential result that the national court applies national legislation that is incompatible with the relevant EU legislation.[572] The aims enshrined in the relevant EU legislation will not be achieved if the national court is also barred from applying them of its own motion.[573] Against this background, requiring national courts to apply EU law of their own motion would be "extremely practical", in terms of empowering national courts to guarantee the full effect and uniform application of EU law.[574] These are some of the considerations that have brought the *ex officio* powers of national judges to the attention of the Court of Justice of the EU.

The case-law of the Court of Justice on *ex officio* review by national judges, delivered by way of preliminary rulings, comes from a variety of fields of law – *inter alia* civil disputes,[575] administrative proceedings,[576] review of arbitration awards,[577] and summary enforcement proceedings.[578] The matter of *ex officio* review has been dealt with both explicitly and implicitly, and has sometimes been hidden behind or intertwined with other matters such as procedural obstacles to making preliminary references to the Court of Justice,[579] the effects of *res judicata*,[580] and the primacy of EU law.[581]

---

572 The "poor client" dilemma, as previously described.

573 J. Engström (2008), 68.

574 J. H. Jans, R. de Lange, S. Prechal, and R. J. G. M. Widdershoven (2007), 308.

575 E.g. CJEU judgment in *van Schijndel v. Stichting Pensioenfonds voor Fysiotherapeuten*, joined cases C-430/93 and C-431/93, EU:C:1995:441; CJEU judgment in *Océano Grupo Editorial and Salvat Editores*, joined cases C-240/98 to C-244/98, EU:C:2000:346.

576 CJEU judgment in *Peterbroeck, Van Campenhout & Cie v. Belgian State*, C-312/93, EU:C:1995:437; CJEU judgment in *van der Weerd and Others v. Minister van Landbouw, Natuur en Voedselkwaliteit*, joined cases C-222/05 to C-225/05, EU:C:2007:318.

577 CJEU judgment in *Eco Swiss China Time Ltd v. Benetton International NV*, C-126/97, EU:C:1999:269; CJEU judgment in *Elisa María Mostaza Claro v. Centro Móvil Milenium SL*, C-168/05, EU:C:2006:675.

578 CJEU judgment in *Asturcom Telecomunicaciones SL v. Cristina Rodríguez Nogueira*, C-40/08, EU:C:2009:615.

579 CJEU judgment in *Peterbroeck, Van Campenhout & Cie v. Belgian State*, C-312/93, EU:C:1995:437.

580 CJEU judgment in *Eco Swiss China Time Ltd v. Benetton International NV*, C-126/97, EU:C:1999:269; CJEU judgment in *Asturcom Telecomunicaciones SL v. Cristina Rodríguez Nogueira*, C-40/08, EU:C:2009:615.

581 Opinion of Advocate General Darmon in *Verholen and Others v. Sociale Verzekeringsbank Amsterdam*, joined cases C-87/90, C-88/90 and C-89/90, EU:C:1991:223.

The case-law will be divided into four categories. There is, firstly, an early line of case-law in which the key questions concerned individuals' access to the preliminary reference procedure via their national judge and the connection between, on the one hand, the principle of primacy of Union law and, on the other hand, the power or obligation of national judges to make a reference to the Court of Justice under Art. 267 TFEU (3.2.1).[582] In *Simmenthal* and *Rheinmühlen*, the power of the national judge to review matters of EU law *ex officio* was asserted in the bypassing by the Court of Justice, relying on the principle of full effect.[583] The first line of case-law culminated in two cases, *Goderbauer*[584] and *Verholen*,[585] in which the Court of Justice maintained the principles indicated *obiter dictum* in *Rheinmühlen*[586] and *Simmenthal*,[587] while temporarily endorsing the full effect of Union law as legal basis for the power or obligation of *ex officio* consideration of EU law.

In a second line of case-law (3.2.2), starting with *van Schijndel*[588] and *Peterbroeck*,[589] the Court of Justice tackled the obligation of *ex officio* review head-on, this matter having been included explicitly in the questions posed by the referring courts. In these cases, the presence of any obligation to review matters of EU law *ex officio* was to be understood as deriving from the

582 CJEU judgment in *Rheinmühlen Düsseldorf v. Einfuhr- und Vorratsstelle für Getreide und Futtermittel*, 166/73, EU:C:1974:3; CJEU judgment in *Amministrazione delle finanze dello Stato v. Simmenthal*, 106/77, EU:C:1978:49.

583 "Full effect(iveness)" is for the present purposes used when referring to "*plein effet*"; U. Šadl (2015), 24-25.

584 CJEU judgment in *Ferdinand M.J.J. Duijnstee v. Lodewijk Goderbauer*, 288/82, EU:C:1983:326.

585 CJEU judgment in *Verholen and Others v. Sociale Verzekeringsbank Amsterdam*, joined cases C-87/90, C-88/90 and C-89/90, EU:C:1991:314.

586 CJEU judgment in *Rheinmühlen Düsseldorf v. Einfuhr- und Vorratsstelle für Getreide und Futtermittel*, 166/73, EU:C:1974:3.

587 CJEU judgment in *Amministrazione delle finanze dello Stato v. Simmenthal*, 106/77, EU:C:1978:49.

588 CJEU judgment in *van Schijndel v. Stichting Pensioenfonds voor Fysiotherapeuten*, joined cases C-430/93 and C-431/93, EU:C:1995:441. See particularly S. Prechal (1998); S. Prechal and N. Shelkoplyas (2004); T. Tridimas, *The General Principles of EU Law* (2006), 463ff.; A. Wallerman (2016), 347ff.

589 CJEU judgment in *Peterbroeck, Van Campenhout & Cie v. Belgian State*, C-312/93, EU:C:1995:437. See particularly T. Tridimas (2006), 461ff.; A. Arnull (2011), 62 and Y. Houyet, 'L'application d'office du droit de l'Union européenne par les juges nationaux', *J.D.E.*, 3 (2010), 71.

requirements of *Rewe*-effectiveness and equivalence, rather than from the primacy of EU law.[590]

After this phase, the complexities and difficulties arising from the principles laid down in *van Schijndel* gave rise to a third line of case-law in which the mandate of *ex officio* review was coupled with the prevalence of public policy rules contained in national law (3.2.3).

Finally, a fourth line of case-law dealt specifically with the special conditions characteristic for consumer litigation and the necessity to provide protection for vulnerable litigants who have substantive EU law on their side (3.2.4).

3.2.1 *Ex officio* review comes within the radar of the Court of Justice

The path towards granting national judges an EU mandate of *ex officio* review can be traced back to the Court of Justice's seminal case-law on the constitutional relationship between the national and the Union legal orders. This path requires us to first revisit the *Simmenthal* and *Rheinmühlen* cases[591] which, while laying the foundation for a profound change of perspective on the central role of lower-level courts in the enforcement of Union law, opened a side door to an obligation of *ex officio* review on a somewhat equivocal legal basis. The present section will deal with the implications of these cases insofar as they are relevant to understanding the origins (and legal bases) of what we may today refer to as a Union law mandate of *ex officio* review.

Section 3.2.1.1 will demonstrate the severity with which the Court of Justice regarded the presence of procedural obstacles precluding national judges from making preliminary references to the Court of Justice (referred to as the "*Rheinmühlen* mandate"). This matter would subsequently resonate throughout the case-law as one of the most important demarcations for acceptable versus non-acceptable obstacles to Union law effectiveness.[592] Section 3.2.1.2 will propose that the powers of constitutional review granted national judges could, at the time, be understood as includ-

590 S. Prechal (1998), 683ff.

591 CJEU judgment in *Amministrazione delle finanze dello Stato v. Simmenthal*, 106/77, EU:C:1978:49; CJEU judgment in *Rheinmühlen Düsseldorf v. Einfuhr- und Vorratsstelle für Getreide und Futtermittel*, 166/73, EU:C:1974:3.

592 See e.g. CJEU judgment in *Peterbroeck, Van Campenhout & Cie v. Belgian State*, C-312/93, EU:C:1995:437, 13.

ing also *ex officio* constitutional review of national law in terms of its compliance with Union law (below labeled the "constitutional mandate").[593]

Section 3.2.1.3 will examine the implications of the prior *obiter dictum* findings regarding *ex officio* review in situations where the matter was operative in the litigation before the referring judge. The examined case-law confirms the existence of a Union law-based mandate of *ex officio* review, already hinted in *Simmenthal* and *Rheinmühlen*, while at the same time indicating the Court of Justice's unwillingness to use the language of duty or obligation unless specifically called for by a given context.[594]

Finally, section 3.2.1.4 will discuss the implications of the first line of case-law, including the importance of defining the type of obstacle contained in national law or practice, in order to determine the legal basis on which to require setting aside national law.[595]

3.2.1.1 Empowering national courts to co-operate with the Court of Justice to ensure the full effectiveness of Union law

The Court of Justice's case-law on *ex officio* review has often referred to the case *Rheinmühlen*,[596] delivered in 1974, despite that the questions posed by the national court in that case concerned the obligation of national courts to make references to the Court of Justice under Art. 267 TFEU, and therefore actually had little to do with *ex officio* review.[597]

---

593 On constitutional obstacles in national law preventing the exercise of the constitutional mandate, see O. Zetterquist (2012), 355-57.

594 E.g. by the binding language of the Convention of 27 September 1968 on jurisdiction and the enforcement of judgments in civil and commercial matters (Brussels Convention), OJ L 299, 31/12/1972, 32, as was applicable in the *Goderbauer* case discussed below; CJEU judgment in *Ferdinand M.J.J. Duijnstee v. Lodewijk Goderbauer*, 288/82, EU:C:1983:326, 14.

595 Case-law, in which the constitutional and *Rheinmühlen* mandates were later developed, falls outside the scope of the present section, insofar as it does not provide guidance on the use of *ex officio* review as a tool for ensuring the enforcement or full effect of EU law. Wider legal developments will instead be discussed in Chapter 5.

596 CJEU judgment in *Rheinmühlen Düsseldorf v. Einfuhr- und Vorratsstelle für Getreide und Futtermittel*, 166/73, EU:C:1974:3; discussed in e.g. C. Kakouris (1997), 1402; S. Prechal and R. Widdershoven (2011 a), 284.

597 CJEU judgment in *Rheinmühlen Düsseldorf v. Einfuhr- und Vorratsstelle für Getreide und Futtermittel*, 166/73, EU:C:1974:3, 3-4.

The Court of Justice was seized to rule on the right of a lower court to make a preliminary reference in defiance of the *ratio decidendi* of a superior court. The Court of Justice stated that national courts could not be deprived of the possibility to refer matters of interpretation of EU law. The Court was in the present ruling less concerned with the rights of litigants to have Union law rights safeguarded by the national court in the proceedings before it, and more with the rights of national judges to pose questions concerning the validity or interpretation of Community law provisions.[598] Recalling the purpose of the preliminary reference procedure of ensuring the uniform application of Community law throughout the Member States, the Court emphasized that the latter would not be possible without the co-operation of the national judges – whose assistance would, in turn, not be possible if their powers to make a preliminary reference were circumscribed by national institutional rules. The Court of Justice therefore insisted that ordinary courts at all levels be garbed with the power, if necessary of their own motion,[599] to make a preliminary reference.

The legal basis for this judgment was (now) Art. 267 TFEU, which *allows* national judges to make a preliminary reference, and in the cases of courts of last instance, *obliges* them to do so.[600] By implication, the powers granted national courts of lower instance through the Treaties gave rise to an obligation for the legislator not to deprive them of this competence by placing constitutional or procedural obstacles in their way.

The subsequent *Simmenthal* ruling[601] had commonalities with *Rheinmühlen* in terms of its concern for (lacking) powers of lower national

---

598 Ibid., 4.

599 Ibid., 3.

600 Equally applicable to constitutional courts and highest ordinary courts. The dividing line is whether a remedy is available against its decision, irrespective of whether any appeal was made in the national proceedings; see CJEU judgment in *Lucio Cesare Aquino v. Belgische Staat*, C-3/16, EU:C:2017:209, 36-38; CJEU judgment in *Global Starnet Ltd v. Ministero dell'Economia e delle Finanze*, C-322/16, EU:C:2017:985, 21-26.

601 CJEU judgment in *Amministrazione delle finanze dello Stato v. Simmenthal*, 106/77, EU:C:1978:49. On the constitutional mandate (*Simmenthal*), see further J. L. da Cruz Vilaça, 'Le principe de l'effet utile du droit de l'Union dans la jurisprudence de la Cour', in *The Court of Justice and the Construction of Europe: Analyses and Perspectives on Sixty Years of Case-Law* (The Hague: Asser press, 2013), 279-306; M. Bossuyt and W. Verrijdt (2011); J. M. Davidson (2008). On the notion of "*Simmenthal*-effectiveness", see M. Bobek (2012); S. Prechal (1998), 687.

courts *vis-à-vis* courts of last instance.[602] Yet, while using the language of full effect and uniform application of Community law, the *Simmenthal* ruling approached the underlying problem of constitutional constraints imposed by court hierarchies from a different perspective:[603]

> [A]ny provision of a national legal system and any legislative, administrative or judicial practice which might impair the effectiveness of Community law by withholding from the national court having jurisdiction to apply such law the power to do everything necessary at the moment of its application to set aside national legislative provisions which might prevent Community rules from having full force and effect are incompatible with those requirements which are the very essence of Community law.

In *Simmenthal*, the foremost concern was for the litigants to have their rights under Union law safeguarded. In this way, the matter of effectiveness of the application of Union law in the national litigation context was at the fore, whereas the effectiveness of the functioning of the Art. 267-procedure was given secondary consideration.[604]

The mandate of national courts to review the constitutionality of national law in light of its compatibility with Union law (if necessary of their own motion[605] and irrespective of whether or not they are garbed with such powers under national law) has widely been labeled the "*Simmenthal* mandate".[606] The mandate can be broken down into two elements:

1. The power of national courts to directly apply provisions of Union law against the wording of national law (in the foreground in *Simmenthal*).[607] This would be the mandate of constitutional review in the

602 Italian legislation required that lower courts pose questions of constitutionality of national primary law to the Constitutional court, a procedure that would have denied the seized court of lower instance to make a preliminary reference to the Court of Justice; CJEU judgment in *Amministrazione delle finanze dello Stato v. Simmenthal*, 106/77, EU:C:1978:49.

603 Ibid., 14, 22.

604 See ibid., 19-20.

605 CJEU judgment in *Amministrazione delle finanze dello Stato v. Simmenthal*, 106/77, EU:C:1978:49, 24: a national court "is under a duty to give full effect to those provisions, *if necessary refusing of its own motion* to apply any conflicting provision of national legislation" (here emphasized).

606 M. Bossuyt and W. Verrijdt (2011); M. Claes (2006), 69-117; D. Piquani, 'The Role of National Courts in Issues of Compliance', in *Compliance and the Enforcement of EU Law*, ed. M. Cremona (Oxford: Oxford University Press, 2012), 135-38.

607 CJEU judgment in *Amministrazione delle finanze dello Stato v. Simmenthal*, 106/77, EU:C:1978:49, 17-28.

form of a power to review (and if necessary set aside) national law in light of its compatibility with Union law, having as its legal basis the principle of primacy pursuant to *Costa v. Enel.*[608] The present work refers to this mandate as the "constitutional mandate".

2. The power/duty of national courts to make a preliminary reference whenever deemed necessary.[609] The interest at stake here is not the effective enforcement of Union law provisions *in casu*, but rather the effectiveness of the procedure itself, requiring national judges to have uninhibited access, following the Treaty, to the Court of Justice for consultation on matters of interpretation and validity of EU law. Deviating from standard terminology, the present work refers to this power of national courts as the "*Rheinmühlen* mandate".

In its findings in *Simmenthal*, the Court of Justice relied on both of these mandates in order to lay down the principle of full effect of Union law.[610] This doctrine actually empowers national courts rather than constraining them in the sense of allowing them to be free or unhindered to carry out their tasks under Union law (be they obligations to apply substantive Union law or to enter into necessary dialogue with the Court of Justice through the Art. 267-procedure) – which is why the label "mandate" is more appropriate than duty or obligation.

On the other hand, the *Simmenthal* ruling brings about twofold constraints on the national legislature. First, the legislature is precluded from subsequent statutory measures undermining directly effective substantive EU law provisions. Secondly, it is precluded from putting in place obstacles for the national courts having the effect of making the preliminary reference procedure unavailable. The latter aspect is appositely illustrated in the reasoning put forward by the Commission in *Rheinmühlen*:[611]

> the national legislature could to a large extent render inoperative [...] Article 177 by enacting provisions which would limit its effect. Such a limitation on

608 Ibid., 17; CJEU judgment in *Costa v. E.N.E.L.*, 6/64, EU:C:1964:66.

609 Which was in the foreground in CJEU judgment in *Rheinmühlen Düsseldorf v. Einfuhr- und Vorratsstelle für Getreide und Futtermittel*, 166/73, EU:C:1974:3 whereas it was auxiliary in CJEU judgment in *Amministrazione delle finanze dello Stato v. Simmenthal*, 106/77, EU:C:1978:49, 19-20.

610 Which can be attributed the legal basis of either primacy (in reference to the constitutional mandate) or procedural effectiveness (in reference to the *Rheinmühlen* mandate).

611 CJEU judgment in *Rheinmühlen Düsseldorf v. Einfuhr- und Vorratsstelle für Getreide und Futtermittel*, 166/73, EU:C:1974:3, II.1.

> the useful effect of Article 177 by the national legislature would infringe the EEC Treaty and would lead to the initiation of procedure under Articles 169 et seq. of the EEC Treaty. In the same way it is impossible to limit the power of referring a case for a preliminary ruling by invoking the binding nature of judgments of superior courts, which in practice would exclude the power to submit cases to the Court.

The constitutional mandate and the *Rheinmühlen* mandate thus constrain the national legislator, while in some cases (lower courts) *empowering* the national judge and in other cases (highest instance) *binding* the national judge.[612] For instance, the ruling in *A v. B* deemed obligatory interlocutory procedures for constitutional review to be contrary to Art. 267 TFEU insofar that they not only prevented courts of highest instance to carry out their duty to make a preliminary reference, but also had the ancillary effect of preventing lower courts from exercising their power to do so.[613]

3.2.1.2 An embryonic power of *ex officio* review

The Court of Justice in both *Rheinmühlen* and *Simmenthal* ventured into the issue of *ex officio* review by the national courts. Having provided the general context of these cases, it is easier to make sense of what the Court of Justice envisaged through its mention of *ex officio* review.

In *Rheinmühlen*, the Court of Justice stated that national courts have the "power and, where appropriate, [...] the obligation to refer a case for a preliminary ruling, as soon as the judge perceives either *of his own motion* or at the request of the parties that the litigation depends on a point referred to in [now 267 TFEU]."[614] Regarded against the backdrop of what has been discussed above under the label of the "*Rheinmühlen* mandate", it is clear that the present allusion to *ex officio* review would have the implication that national judges shall not be precluded by the legislature from making

---

612 CJEU judgment in *Global Starnet Ltd v. Ministero dell'Economia e delle Finanze*, C-322/16, EU:C:2017:985, 21-26.

613 CJEU judgment in *A v. B and Others*, C-112/13, EU:C:2014:2195, 46. See also Opinion of Advocate General Wathelet in *Puligienica Facility Esco SpA (PFE) v. Airgest SpA*, C-689/13, EU:C:2015:263, 29, where legislation preventing a sub-plenary composition of a court ruling in final instance from making a preliminary reference to the Court of Justice had the capacity of placing litigation outside of the Court of Justice's purview.

614 CJEU judgment in *Rheinmühlen Düsseldorf v. Einfuhr- und Vorratsstelle für Getreide und Futtermittel*, 166/73, EU:C:1974:3, 3 (here emphasized).

a preliminary reference, even in the event that the parties have not brought the need for a preliminary reference to the judges' attention through invoking EU law provisions.[615] This opens the door for discretion or empowerment of the national judge, without (yet) suggesting the existence of any *obligation* of *ex officio* review.[616]

In *Simmenthal*, the Court of Justice equally alluded to *ex officio* review: "a national court [...] is under a duty to give full effect to those provisions, *if necessary refusing of its own motion* to apply any conflicting provision of national legislation."[617] The language revealed that *ex officio* review may, in the typology proposed above, also form part of the constitutional mandate of reviewing national legislation in the light of its compatibility with EU law. However, as noted later by Advocate General Jacobs in his review of *Rheinmühlen* and *Simmenthal*, this does not amount to an automatic obligation of *ex officio* review for the national judge; only a requirement of access for individuals.[618]

The *Rheinmühlen* mandate was, in its turn, interpreted as rather laying down that the national court's power to make a preliminary reference must not face obstacles from the legislature, including in the form of making a preliminary reference conditional upon a party invoking Union law,

615 This is true insofar as a preliminary reference is *necessary* to rule on the case for which the court was seized. The Court of Justice need not be hypothetically consulted on inadmissible pleas, placing EU law outside the ambit of the national proceedings; see CJEU judgment in *Lucio Cesare Aquino v. Belgische Staat*, C-3/16, EU:C:2017:209, 44-46.

616 The reference to "power" versus "obligation" in the above quote indicated no more than that the obligation to make a preliminary reference based on *ex officio* grounds or findings was compulsory only for courts of highest instance, Art. 267(3) TFEU: "Where any such question is raised in a case pending before a court or tribunal of a Member State against whose decisions there is no judicial remedy under national law, that court or tribunal *shall* bring the matter before the Court" (here emphasized).

617 CJEU judgment in *Amministrazione delle finanze dello Stato v. Simmenthal*, 106/77, EU:C:1978:49 (here emphasized).

618 Opinion of Advocate General Jacobs in *Peterbroeck, Van Campenhout & Cie v. Belgian State*, C-312/93, EU:C:1995:437, 43: "Those cases show, therefore, that it must always be possible for an individual to bring a claim before a national court and to require the national court to protect his Community rights. They do not suggest that it must in all circumstances be open to the national court, as a matter of Community law, to raise of its own motion issues which the parties have failed to raise."

an interpretation that would recurrently (if not consistently[619]) be confirmed.[620]

> the formulation adopted in *Rheinmühlen* makes it clear that the terms of Article 177 [now Art. 267 TFEU], referring in both the second and the third paragraphs to cases where a question of Community law 'is raised' before a national court, do not limit the scope of Article 177 to cases where the question is raised by a party. The case-law establishes that Article 177 applies also where the national court 'perceives of its own motion' that a question of Community law may be relevant.[621]

Neither in *Rheinmühlen* nor in *Simmenthal* had the national court in fact asked the Court of Justice about their duties or powers to apply EU law *ex officio* – not surprisingly as in both cases, the relevant aspects of Union law already formed part of the substance of the dispute at issue in the main proceedings. As already indicated, any reference to the obligation to *ex officio* review was *obiter dictum*. The two cases nevertheless gave a hint as to how the matter may be dealt with once it came before a national judge, including its legal basis in the principle of primacy under the constitutional mandate, or the principle of effectiveness (of the Art. 267-procedure) under the *Rheinmühlen* mandate. The subsequent case-law would reveal which elements of these *obiter dictum* findings and their implications would form part of the Court of Justice's operational precedence.

3.2.1.3 Power or obligation of *ex officio* review for national courts?

If the *Simmenthal* and *Rheinmühlen* rulings but alluded to an EU mandate of *ex officio* review for national judges, this would be concretized in the

---

619 Cf. CJEU judgment in *Lucio Cesare Aquino v. Belgische Staat,* C-3/16, EU:C:2017:209.

620 CJEU judgment in *Willy Kempter KG v. Hauptzollamt Hamburg-Jonas*, C-2/06, EU:C:2008:78, 41; CJEU judgment in *Cartesio Oktató és Szolgáltató bt*, C-210/06, EU:C:2008:723, 90; CJEU judgment in *Patrick Kelly v. National University of Ireland*, C-104/10, EU:C:2011:506, 62; CJEU judgment in *Consiglio nazionale dei geologi and Autorità garante della concorrenza e del mercato*, C-136/12, EU:C:2013:489, 28.

621 Opinion of Advocate General Jacobs in *Peterbroeck, Van Campenhout & Cie v. Belgian State*, C-312/93, EU:C:1995:437, 44.

1980's and 1990's. The cases *Goderbauer*[622] and *Verholen*[623] dealt explicitly with *ex officio* review as part of the *ratio decidendi*, the Court of Justice having been asked to give guidance on this matter by national courts otherwise precluded by national law from examining Union law of their own motion. The issue of appropriate legal basis was not resolved in a conclusive way through these cases, although it can be derived from them that the choice of legal basis would be context-variable. The cases nevertheless provide answers as to whether *ex officio* review of national law in the light of the latter's compatibility with Union law should be understood as a *power* granted the national judge or a *duty* incumbent on him because of his obligations as EU judge.

In the case *Goderbauer*,[624] the Court of Justice was asked whether the rules on jurisdiction of the Brussels Convention of 1968[625] were to be applied *ex officio*. According to the Convention, Contracting States were required to examine and if necessary declare of their own motion that they had no jurisdiction.[626] As in *Simmenthal*, the Court of Justice dealt with this as a matter of primacy, underlining that the Brussels Convention "must override national provisions which are incompatible with it."[627] The Court of Justice accordingly asserted the obligation of a national court to examine its jurisdiction *ex officio*, despite being precluded by national law from doing so. Key, however, in this reasoning was the existence of a binding treaty obligation governing the jurisdiction test.[628] The ruling

622 CJEU judgment in *Ferdinand M.J.J. Duijnstee v. Lodewijk Goderbauer*, 288/82, EU:C:1983:326; see comments in e.g. S. Whittaker (2012), 28.

623 CJEU judgment in *Verholen and Others v. Sociale Verzekeringsbank Amsterdam*, joined cases C-87/90, C-88/90 and C-89/90, EU:C:1991:314; see comments by T. Heukels (1996), 346-47; A. Ó. Caoimh, 'Issues of EU Law Raised by National Courts of their Own Motion', in *Constitutionalising the EU Judicial System: Essays in Honour of Pernilla Lindh*, eds. Cardonnel, P., A. Rosas and N. Wahl (Oxford: Hart Publishing, 2012), 125-26; A. Beka (2018), 51-52.

624 CJEU judgment in *Ferdinand M.J.J. Duijnstee v. Lodewijk Goderbauer*, 288/82, EU:C:1983:326.

625 Convention of 27 September 1968 on jurisdiction and the enforcement of judgments in civil and commercial matters (Brussels Convention), OJ L 299, 31/12/1972, 32.

626 Art. 19 of the Brussels Convention.

627 CJEU judgment in *Ferdinand M.J.J. Duijnstee v. Lodewijk Goderbauer*, 288/82, EU:C:1983:326, 14.

628 S. Whittaker (2012), 28.

therefore lacked implications beyond the reach of EU instruments expressly regulating the matter of *ex officio* review.[629]

In *Verholen*, the Court was asked to rule on the issue of *ex officio* review by national courts; but this time without reference to e.g. international treaty instruments expressly governing the matter.[630] The ground was thus laid for a first ruling of general scope.

Advocate General Darmon had dealt with the question via the principle of primacy.[631] This approach was, according to Prechal, symptomatic for a terminological misconception prevailing since *Simmenthal*, namely that procedural rules must be set aside as a matter of primacy, when they stand in the way of the possibility to rely on directly effective provisions of EU law. [632] The Opinion had also veered beyond the question posed by the national court, as to whether national courts were *precluded* from engaging in *ex officio* review, venturing into the prevalence of a *duty* to do so:[633]

> A national court [...] is under a duty to give full effect to those provisions by refusing of its own motion to apply any provision of national law which is incompatible with a Community rule having direct effect; it is also required of its own motion to interpret the provisions of its domestic law as far as possible in the light of the wording and the purpose of the Community provision, even if the latter does not have direct effect[.]

The Court of Justice chose another road. The principle of primacy was not retained as legal basis – although the Court of Justice did not discard this

---

629 *Goderbauer* stands unmodified; see CJEU judgment in *Gesellschaft für Antriebstechnik mbH & Co. KG*, C-4/03, EU:C:2006:457, 22-24. However, if a national court assumes jurisdiction because the defendant enters an appearance without contesting jurisdiction, the seized court is not obliged to verify of its own motion whether the latter intended to tacitly accept jurisdiction under the Brussels Convention or similarly worded instruments; CJEU judgment in *Česká podnikatelská pojišťovna as, Vienna Insurance Group v. Michal Bilas*, C-111/09, EU:C:2010:290, 32.

630 CJEU judgment in *Verholen and Others v. Sociale Verzekeringsbank Amsterdam*, joined cases C-87/90, C-88/90 and C-89/90, EU:C:1991:314.

631 Opinion of Advocate General Darmon in *Verholen and Others v. Sociale Verzekeringsbank Amsterdam*, joined cases C-87/90, C-88/90 and C-89/90, EU:C:1991:223, 19.

632 S. Prechal (1998), 683, fn. 11.

633 Opinion of Advocate General Darmon in *Verholen and Others v. Sociale Verzekeringsbank Amsterdam*, joined cases C-87/90, C-88/90 and C-89/90, EU:C:1991:223, 54.

interpretation either.[634] On the matter of power versus duty, the Court of Justice referred back to *Rheinmühlen*, reminding that if a national court has the power and sometimes even an obligation to make a preliminary reference to the Court of Justice, this presupposes that the national court must also be able to decide (of its own motion) whether to apply or disapply the relevant national provisions in the light of EU law.[635] The ruling clarifies that national courts are *not barred* by EU law from examining of their own motion the compatibility of provisions of national law with the applicable directive, yet without discussing the possible prevalence of any such *duty*[636] – i.e. a choice of deference to the national procedural autonomy of the Member States.[637]

The question of duty, embarked on by the Advocate General, had thus been dodged for the moment – the Union law *ex officio* mandate was to be regarded by default as a power, unless an obligation could be traced back to a binding legal basis.[638] The language of duty versus obligation would nevertheless resurface as an important dividing line in subsequent case-law on *ex officio* review.

3.2.1.4 Legal bases for the constitutional and *Rheinmühlen* mandates

The present section has traced the mandate of *ex officio* review back to two seminal cases, both using the language of "full effect". While the *Simmenthal* and *Rheinmühlen* cases were in fact not primarily concerned with *ex officio* review by national judges, but rather with the constitutional (lack of) powers of lower courts, they proved to be an indication of how the matter of *ex officio* review would be treated in the future, when operative *in casu*. In the above, three aspects have been emphasized, all addressed in the scholarship as forming part of the "*Simmenthal* mandate":

1. The cases' common element of dealing with constitutional limitations of powers of lower courts, bringing with them procedural/institutional

634 CJEU judgment in *Verholen and Others v. Sociale Verzekeringsbank Amsterdam*, joined cases C-87/90, C-88/90 and C-89/90, EU:C:1991:314.

635 Ibid., 12-13.

636 Ibid., 15-16.

637 J. Engström (2008), 75.

638 Such as in CJEU judgment in *Ferdinand M.J.J. Duijnstee v. Lodewijk Goderbauer*, 288/82, EU:C:1983 and CJEU judgment in *Gesellschaft für Antriebstechnik mbH & Co. KG*, C-4/03, EU:C:2006:457.

obstacles to making a preliminary reference to the Court of Justice when so required by EU (then EC) law, consequently forming the foundation for a power of *ex officio* review to the extent necessary to overcome obstacles to making a preliminary reference.

The *Rheinmühlen* mandate flowing from the duty to give "full effect" to Community law in this way brought about obligations for the legislator to ensure that national legislation did not stand in the way of the effectiveness of the preliminary reference procedure by blocking the national judge from making a reference. The *Rheinmühlen* mandate was later developed in a series of cases which granted national courts the "widest discretion" in referring matters to the Court of Justice, irrespective of national legal rules or court decisions standing in the way of such a reference.[639] The power of *ex officio* review was here implicit in the national court's liberty to disregard the legislator in order to make a preliminary reference,[640] whether or not such a preliminary reference was prompted by Union law-based legal claims made by the parties.[641] This "widest discretion" doctrine was sustained up until the 2017 ruling in *Aquino* where the obligation to make a preliminary reference ultimately hinged on the Union law-based claim being admissible before the court of last instance.[642] Higher courts are moreover permitted to

---

639 CJEU judgment in *Mecanarte-Metalurgica da Lagoa v. Alfandega do Porto*, C-348/89, EU:C:1991:278, 44-48; CJEU judgment in *Palmisani v. INPS*, C-261/95, EU:C:1997:351, 20; CJEU judgment in *Aziz Melki and Sélim Abdeli*, joined cases C-188/10 and C-189/10, EU:C:2010:363, 41; CJEU judgment in *Georgi Ivanov Elchinov v. Natsionalna zdravnoosiguritelna kasa*, C-173/09, EU:C:2010:581, 26; CJEU Opinion *delivered pursuant to Article 218(11) TFEU*, 1/09, EU:C:2011:123, 83; CJEU judgment in *Puligienica Facility Esco SpA (PFE) v. Airgest SpA*, C-689/13, EU:C:2016:199, 32; CJEU judgment in *Global Starnet Ltd v. Ministero dell'Economia e delle Finanze*, C-322/16, EU:C:2017:985, 21-25.

640 In CJEU judgment in *Cartesio Oktató és Szolgáltató bt*, C-210/06, EU:C:2008:723, 96, review by higher courts was not itself precluded, whereas the decision by the appeal instance may not be binding on the lower court. See further A. Wallerman, 'Överklagande av beslut att begära förhandsavgörande: Några reflektioner med anledning av EFTA-domstolens avgörande i Irish Bank', *ERT*, 2 (2013), 312ff.; M. Bobek, 'Cartesio – Appeals Against an Order to Refer under Article 234 (2) EC Treaty Revisited', *C.J.Q.*, 29 (2010).

641 CJEU judgment in *Willy Kempter KG v. Hauptzollamt Hamburg-Jonas*, C-2/06, EU:C:2008:78; CJEU judgment in *Patrick Kelly v. National University of Ireland*, C-104/10, EU:C:2011:506; CJEU judgment in *Consiglio nazionale dei geologi and Autorità garante della concorrenza e del mercato*, C-136/12, EU:C:2013:489, 28.

642 CJEU judgment in *Lucio Cesare Aquino v. Belgische Staat*, C-3/16, EU:C:2017:209.

invite the seized lower court to reconsider its originally posed question, including amending it or withdrawing it.[643]

2. The aspect that the *Simmenthal* ruling is most famous for, namely the constitutional mandate that it grants ordinary courts at all levels in the national court hierarchy, bringing with it a power to carry out, if necessary *ex officio*, constitutional review of national legislation in view of its compatibility with Union law.[644]
   The constitutional mandate relied on the principle of primacy to similarly grant national judges a power to review the compatibility of national law with the Member State's obligations under Union law, once again of its own motion and, if necessary, by disregarding decisions by higher court instances and obstacles in national legislation.[645]
3. The concept that is sometimes referred to in the scholarship as "*Simmenthal*-effectiveness"[646] with its legal basis in the principle of primacy and its purpose of giving effect to substantive Union law provisions.
   This legal basis was ultimately not preserved at the end of the first line of case-law for the purposes of *ex officio* review, and would consequently be abandoned in favor of the *Rewe* formula, in which the matter of institutional and constitutional obstacles such as those at stake in *Simmenthal*, *Rheinmühlen* and *Verholen* would come to be regarded as obstacles of procedural rather than substantive character.

In retrospect, it was logical to deduce from the obligation to give "full effect" to directly effective provisions of EU law, an emulated obligation to set aside national provisions contrary thereto.[647] In the *Simmenthal* case, constitutional obstacles prevented EU law from enjoying full effect, so the

---

643 CJEU judgment in *Cartesio Oktató és Szolgáltató bt*, C-210/06, EU:C:2008:723, 96. A decision by a higher court can in any event not "take away from those courts the discretion to refer to the Court questions of interpretation of the point of European Union law concerned by such legal rulings", particularly when the lower court "considers that a higher court's legal ruling could lead it to give a judgment contrary to European Union law"; CJEU judgment in *Georgi Ivanov Elchinov v. Natsionalna zdravnoosiguritelna kasa*, C-173/09, EU:C:2010:581, 27.

644 D. Piquani (2012), 135-36; M. Claes, 'Constitutionalizing Europe at its Source: The 'European Clauses' in the National Constitutions: Evolution and Typology', *YEL*, 24 (2005).

645 CJEU judgment in *Aziz Melki and Sélim Abdeli*, joined cases C-188/10 and C-189/10, EU:C:2010:363, 43.

646 See e.g. M. Bobek (2012).

647 S. Prechal (1998), 684.

situation is neither simply a matter of hierarchy of substantive norms, nor an indirect collision between substantive and procedural rules. Nevertheless, since the constitutional clash in *Simmenthal* had its basis in a judge-made rule of procedure, it has been argued that the *Simmenthal* judgment is not coherent with earlier case-law in treating the arisen questions in terms of primacy; rather, they should have been tested against the principles of effectiveness and equivalence.[648]

Inconsistencies between the approaches taken in *Simmenthal*, based on giving precedence to directly effective provisions of EU law,[649] and in *Rewe* and *Comet*, in which the principles of effectiveness and equivalence were introduced,[650] gave rise to criticisms in the academic debate as well as to some confusion in subsequent rulings.[651] Clarification would be provided in the second line of case-law that obstacles of *procedural* nature were required to comply with the principles of effectiveness and equivalence, whereas encroachments of *substantive* nature were normally to be set aside under the principle of primacy.[652] As a result, the matter of *ex officio* review would come to be placed within the context of national procedural autonomy rather than constitutional choices between applicable systems of legal rules.

Forceful as the full effect doctrine may be (in terms of ensuring the effectiveness of the Art. 267-procedure or in terms of empowering national courts to review the compatibility of national law with Union law), its restraining force is on the legislator whereas its implications for the national judge do not go further than granting it a power to carry out its task of acting as a decentralized judge of Union law. In fact, the Court of Justice would later clarify that the *Rheinmühlen* mandate at most granted the seized court a power to disregard practical or procedural obstacles towards

---

648 Ibid., 685-86; CJEU judgment in *Rewe v. Landwirtschaftskammer für das Saarland*, 33/76, EU:C:1976:188; CJEU judgment in *Comet BV v. Produktschap voor Siergewassen*, 45/76, EU:C:1976:191.

649 CJEU judgment in *Amministrazione delle finanze dello Stato v. Simmenthal*, 106/77, EU:C:1978:49, 17-24.

650 CJEU judgment in *Rewe v. Landwirtschaftskammer für das Saarland*, 33/76, EU:C:1976:188, 5; CJEU judgment in *Comet BV v. Produktschap voor Siergewassen*, 45/76, EU:C:1976:191, 13.

651 See discussion in S. Prechal (1998), 689.

652 S. Prechal (1998), 689; referring to CJEU judgment in *van Schijndel v. Stichting Pensioenfonds voor Fysiotherapeuten*, joined cases C-430/93 and C-431/93, EU:C:1995:441; CJEU judgment in *Peterbroeck, Van Campenhout & Cie v. Belgian State*, C-312/93, EU:C:1995:437.

making a preliminary reference if deemed necessary. However, for lower courts, this mandate cannot be transformed into an *obligation*.[653]

When asked to apply the *Rheinmühlen* dictum to the matter of *ex officio* review, the Court of Justice responded by affirming a *power* of *ex officio* review – while declining to clarify whether there was a coupled *obligation* incumbent on the national judge.[654] Four years later, these matters again came to the fore in the twin cases of *Peterbroeck* and *van Schijndel*,[655] in which the Court of Justice surprised legal commentators by reaching opposite outcomes in the respective cases, despite their striking similarities.[656] These two cases require in-depth examination to understand their justifications and implications.

3.2.2 Transformation from power into conditional obligation

If the first line of case-law left any doubt as to the legal basis for the mandate of *ex officio* review, its second line would demonstrate a lasting shift towards the *Rewe* doctrine. The present section begins by considering the seminal case of *Peterbroeck*[657] which, together with *van Schijndel*,[658] would found a Union law *ex officio* mandate for national judges (3.2.2.1).

The previous section also indicated that the circumstances of each case could give rise to either an obligation or a power for national courts. In the present, second, line of case-law, the matter of power versus obligation would be developed into what has been described as a new doctrine on discretion of national courts (3.2.2.2).[659]

---

653 CJEU judgment in *Seda Kücükdeveci v. Swedex GmbH & Co. KG*, C-555/07, EU:C:2010:21, 54-55.

654 CJEU judgment in *Verholen and Others v. Sociale Verzekeringsbank Amsterdam*, joined cases C-87/90, C-88/90 and C-89/90, EU:C:1991:314.

655 CJEU judgment in *van Schijndel v. Stichting Pensioenfonds voor Fysiotherapeuten*, joined cases C-430/93 and C-431/93, EU:C:1995:441; CJEU judgment in *Peterbroeck, Van Campenhout & Cie v. Belgian State*, C-312/93, EU:C:1995:437.

656 J. Engström (2008), 76; G. de Búrca, 'National Procedural Rules and Remedies: The Changing Approach of the Court of Justice', in *Remedies for Breach of EC Law*, eds. Lonbay, J. and A. Biondi (John Wiley & Sons, 1997), 37-46.

657 CJEU judgment in *Peterbroeck, Van Campenhout & Cie v. Belgian State*, C-312/93, EU:C:1995:437.

658 CJEU judgment in *van Schijndel v. Stichting Pensioenfonds voor Fysiotherapeuten*, joined cases C-430/93 and C-431/93, EU:C:1995:441.

659 A. Wallerman (2016), 354ff.

The Court of Justice also introduced a new factor in assessing compliance with the *Rewe* criteria; namely the presence of national procedural principles capable of justifying encroachments on Union law effectiveness. The possibility of justification allowed national courts to weigh the interests of the litigating parties against each other – for the present purposes by balancing the effectiveness of EU law for the benefit of one litigating party against procedural safeguards restricting the use of *ex officio* review. The Court of Justice's approach when deciding on the existence of an *obligation* of *ex officio* review turned out to be dependent on multiple factors, to be balanced against each other on a case-by-case basis. Section 3.2.2.3 will consider the consequences of determining the obligation of *ex officio* review casuistically. On the one hand, this solution leaves national legislators some autonomy and national judges a margin of discretion. On the other hand, the uniformity in the implementation and interpretation of EU law is hampered by inconsistent precedents.

The incompatible outcomes in *van Schijndel* and *Peterbroeck* have been explained by their respective procedural settings (civil versus administrative/higher court versus lower court).[660] The divergent missions of court instances described in section 3.1 above, on a sliding scale between "truth-seeking" and dispute resolution, serve as background for such reasoning.[661] Section 3.2.2.4 will nevertheless reject the notion that the substantive field of law must determine the Union law obligation of *ex officio* review. Instead, preserving the *Rheinmühlen* mandate translated into a requirement of review by a judicial instance. It will be suggested that the latter concern is of chief explanatory force.

A factor that was not spelled out in the second line of case-law, yet alluded to in subsequent references to the *van Schijndel* and *Peterbroeck* cases, was whether national courts are called upon to remedy procedural omissions by claimants/beneficiaries of EU law.[662] The orthodox response

660 J. Engström (2008), 77; M. Hoskins, 'Tilting the Balance, Supremacy and National Procedural Rules', *E.L. Rev.*, 21 (1996), 365-77; A. Ward, *Judicial Review and the Rights of Private Parties in EC Law* (Oxford University Press, 2000), 50ff.

661 Based on the dichotomy described by J. A. Jolowicz (2005). See also, on "truth" versus "justice" as dispute resolution objectives, J. Thibaut and L. Walker (1978).

662 E.g. in Opinion of Advocate General Maduro in *van der Weerd and Others v. Minister van Landbouw, Natuur en Voedselkwaliteit*, joined cases C-222/05 to C-225/05, EU:C:2007:124, 30; CJEU judgment in *Asturcom Telecomunicaciones SL v. Cristina Rodríguez Nogueira*, C-40/08, EU:C:2009:615, 47; CJEU judgment in *Willy Kempter KG v. Hauptzollamt Hamburg-Jonas*, C-2/06, EU:C:2008:78.

(namely that national courts are *not* of their own motion obliged to remedy litigation lapses) makes sense in terms of legal coherence ("use it or lose it").[663] It will nonetheless be demonstrated that this solution cannot be consistently derived from the Court of Justice's case-law (3.2.2.5).

Finally, section 3.2.2.6 addresses a reverse situation where EU law is enforced by the public *against* individual litigants. The impetus of *ex officio* review in this circumstance accordingly serves the public litigant, which is normally dealt with pursuant to a test similar to the *Rewe* test. It will, however, be demonstrated that the possibilities to justify derogations are in this case-law (pertaining to national institutional autonomy) more limited as compared to the procedural rule-of-reason.

3.2.2.1 Obligation of *ex officio* review under *Peterbroeck*

The reference for a preliminary ruling in *Peterbroeck*[664] for the first time explicitly posed the question whether Union law obliged national courts to consider substantive Union law provisions that had not been invoked by the beneficiary party. Under Belgian law, pleas that had not been raised during the administrative stage of the proceedings could only be brought by the applicant within a certain time frame.[665] Since a new plea based on violation of the freedom of establishment had been introduced after this time-limit, the seized court, recognizing that the rule could potentially stand in the way of an effective exercise of rights under EU law, stayed the proceedings in order to request a preliminary ruling.[666]

---

663 For a wider discussion the dictum of *ius vigilantibus scriptum est*, see P. J. Wattel, 'National Procedural Autonomy and Effectiveness of EC Law: Challenge the Charge, File for Restitution, Sue for Damages?', *LIEI*, 35 (2008), 109-32.

664 CJEU judgment in *Peterbroeck, Van Campenhout & Cie v. Belgian State*, C-312/93, EU:C:1995:437. Commentary by T. Tridimas (2006), 461ff.; A. Arnull (2011), 62; Y. Houyet (2010), 71; T. Heukels (1996), 340ff.; M. Eliantonio, 'The Application of EC Law *Ex Officio* – Some News from the Italian Administrative Courts', *REALaw*, 1 (2008), 101-11.

665 Arts. 278, 279 and 282 of the Belgian Income Tax Code [*Code des Impôts sur les Revenues*] CIR de 1992.

666 The reference included the question as to whether "a national court hearing a dispute concerning Community law must set aside a provision of national law which it considers makes the power of the national court to apply Community law which it is bound to safeguard subject to the making of an express application by the plaintiff in the dispute [...]"; CJEU judgment in *Peterbroeck, Van Campenhout & Cie v. Belgian State*, C-312/93, EU:C:1995:437, 10.

The Court of Justice relied on the *Rewe*-effectiveness principle,[667] emphasizing that the *Cour d'Appel* was in effect the first court within the meaning of Art. 267 TFEU to hear the case.[668] Since the relevant time-bar started running already at the time of the submission of the contested decision to the *Cour d'Appel*, the time-limit had expired by the time of the hearing before that court. Therefore, the seized court was "denied the possibility of considering the question of compatibility", as were any other courts in subsequent appeals concerning the same case – in contradiction with the constitutional mandate laid down in *Simmenthal*.[669] The judgment in *Peterbroeck* was firm in its implications for the national judge: National rules precluding *ex officio* review may not have the effect of placing relevant Union law provisions entirely outside the ambit of the proceedings before a "court or tribunal",[670] thereby also placing these matters outside the reach of the preliminary reference procedure.[671] The ruling can be compared to the more detailed reasoning of Advocate General Jacobs, who had favored the opposite outcome while aligning with the *van Schijndel* judgment (discussed below). The Opinion also relied on the principle of *Rewe*-effectiveness,[672] while not objecting to the fact that the time-limit was susceptible to expiration before the date of the hearing.[673]

667 Ibid., 14ff.

668 Ibid., 17.

669 Ibid., 18-19; CJEU judgment in *Amministrazione delle finanze dello Stato v. Simmenthal*, 106/77, EU:C:1978:49, 17-28.

670 Within the meaning of Art. 267 TFEU as defined in CJEU judgment in *Pierre Corbiau v. Administration des contributions*, C-24/92, EU:C:1993:118, 15-17.

671 CJEU judgment in *Peterbroeck, Van Campenhout & Cie v. Belgian State*, C-312/93, EU:C:1995:437, 13, 17.

672 Opinion of Advocate General Jacobs in *Peterbroeck, Van Campenhout & Cie v. Belgian State*, C-312/93, EU:C:1994:184, 30: The length of the 60-day limit was deemed reasonable already by analogy to the time-limit for actions for annulment of Union acts, which, similarly to the Belgian legislation, precludes the introduction of new pleas after a time-limit of two months: then Art. 42(2), now Art. 127(2) Rules of Procedure of the Court of Justice of 25 September 2012, OJ L 265, 29/9/2012, as amended on 18 June 2013, OJ L 173, 26/6/2013, 65.

673 Instead, the Advocate General underlined that the applicant was granted additional time between his appeal and the Director's submission of the case-file to the *Cour d'Appel*, as the period started running from the date of the lodging of a certified copy of the contested decision; Opinion of Advocate General Jacobs in *Peterbroeck, Van Campenhout & Cie v. Belgian State*, C-312/93, EU:C:1994:184, 32.

Four premises prompted the Court of Justice to find (in disagreement with the Advocate General) that the principle of effectiveness was not complied with:[674]

1. The *Cour d'Appel* was the first seized body with the power to make a preliminary reference to the Court of Justice. For this reason, the rule precluding the court from raising EU law provisions also precluded it from making a preliminary reference. The ruling thus endorsed the *Rheinmühlen* mandate,[675] by confirming that national procedural law may not stand in the way of a national court exercising of its own motion its right to make a preliminary reference to the Court of Justice.
2. The second premise was that a 60-day time limit may expire (and had expired) by the date of the hearing. As has been pointed out in the scholarship, this argument is difficult to reconcile with the Rules of Procedure of the Court of Justice, according to which new pleas in law are generally precluded after the expiration of a similar two-month time-limit for appeals.[676] This was also the course taken by Advocate General Jacobs, who argued that the Court of Justice should teach as it practices.[677] The applicants in the national proceedings were in any event not barred from raising relevant points of EU law before a court or tribunal within the meaning of Art. 267 TFEU; on the contrary, their plea based on EU law would have been dealt with by the *Cour d'Appel* if it had been raised in a timely manner. This reasoning was implicit also in the Opinion, which underscored far-reaching possibilities for the applicant to raise matters of EU law at all administrative phases as well as in the first two months of the judicial stage of the proceedings.[678]

---

674 See further T. Tridimas (2006), 462; T. Heukels (1996), 343-44.

675 CJEU judgment in *Rheinmühlen Düsseldorf v. Einfuhr- und Vorratsstelle für Getreide und Futtermittel*, 166/73, EU:C:1974:3, 3-4.

676 T. Tridimas (2006), 462; then Art. 42(2), now Art. 127(2) Rules of Procedure of the Court of Justice of 25 September 2012, OJ L 265, 29/9/2012, as amended on 18 June 2013, OJ L 173, 26/6/2013, 65.

677 Opinion of Advocate General Jacobs in *Peterbroeck, Van Campenhout & Cie v. Belgian State*, C-312/93, EU:C:1994:184, 30-31. On the ambit of the proceedings before the EU courts, see F. C. de la Torre (2005); A. Meij (2011); B. Vesterdorf (2003); F. Clausen (2017).

678 Opinion of Advocate General Jacobs in *Peterbroeck, Van Campenhout & Cie v. Belgian State*, C-312/93, EU:C:1994:184, 32.

3. The third premise was that the time-limit also barred higher courts in Belgium from ruling *ex officio* on matters raised in an untimely manner,[679] which should be understood as indicating that not only was the first seized court prevented from exercising its *Rheinmühlen* mandate, but also higher courts. This perspective had been left unaddressed by the Advocate General.[680]
4. The fourth premise was that the relevant Belgian rules could not be justified by reasons of legal certainty or the proper conduct of proceedings, which the Court of Justice asserted without elaboration or explanation.[681] The Advocate General had not discussed this aspect in length, but did recall that reasonable time-limits for bringing actions had previously been accepted by the Court of Justice, e.g. for purposes of legal certainty[682] – a reasoning that the Court of Justice tacitly endorsed by coining the procedural rule-of-reason.[683]

The overall concern of the first three premises was the connection between judicial protection and the *Rheinmühlen* mandate, in order to deal with new pleas that were time-barred as a result of both procedural omissions by the beneficiary party and of strict time-limits under national procedural law. The ruling provides a precursor for the later developed doctrine of

679 T. Tridimas (2006), 462.

680 Instead, he made an analogy between the exception to this rule provided in the Belgian legislation concerning the force of *res judicata* and the case-law of the Court of Justice, equally providing such an exception. The Advocate General's reasoning in this regard should be taken to mean that the time-barring is more easily justified when taking into account the possibility of exceptional deviation from it; Opinion of Advocate General Jacobs in *Peterbroeck, Van Campenhout & Cie v. Belgian State*, C-312/93, EU:C:1994:184, 22-24.

681 T. Tridimas (2006), 462; CJEU judgment in *Peterbroeck, Van Campenhout & Cie v. Belgian State*, C-312/93, EU:C:1995:437, 20.

682 As would later be reaffirmed by the Court, time-limits normally fall within the area of Member State procedural autonomy insofar as they are not governed explicitly by secondary law nor function in a way that runs contrary to the principles of effectiveness or equivalence; see e.g. CJEU judgment in *Joan Cuadrench Moré v. Koninklijke Luchtvaart Maatschappij NV*, C-139/11, EU:C:2012:741, 25-33.

683 Opinion of Advocate General Jacobs in *Peterbroeck, Van Campenhout & Cie v. Belgian State*, C-312/93, EU:C:1994:184, 34, 29; referring to CJEU judgment in *Theresa Emmott v. Minister for Social Welfare and the Attorney General*, C-208/90, EU:C:1991:333.

"widest discretion",[684] developed for the purposes of *ex officio* review in *Kempter* and *Aquino*.[685] The Court's approach to the *Rheinmühlen* mandate indicates that, albeit formally based on the principles of effectiveness and equivalence, *Peterbroeck* ultimately turned on the underlying issue of judicial protection through access to court. As is familiar, the firmness of the *Peterbroeck* ruling was alas muddled by the delivery of *van Schijndel* on the same day, which would later be recognized as the standard formula for national constraints on *ex officio* review, whereas *Peterbroeck* would be dismissed as an exception.

3.2.2.2 Discretion under national law triggering Union obligation of *ex officio* review

In a second seminal case on *ex officio* review, *van Schijndel*,[686] Dutch procedural rules (in contrast to the Belgian ones discussed in connection with *Peterbroeck*) allowed new pleas to be made for the first time before the court of last instance under the condition that the new claims constituted pleas of law and did not require it to inquire into new facts or circumstances that had not been relied on before the lower courts. The same requirement applied to the consideration of legal grounds of the court's own motion: The judge was at liberty to supplement legal grounds only to the extent that this did not entail supplementing the facts or circumstances re-

684 CJEU judgment in *Mecanarte-Metalurgica da Lagoa v. Alfandega do Porto*, C-348/89, EU:C:1991:278, 44-48; CJEU judgment in *Palmisani v. INPS*, C-261/95, EU:C:1997:351, 20; CJEU judgment in *Cartesio Oktató és Szolgáltató bt*, C-210/06, EU:C:2008:723, 88; CJEU judgment in *Aziz Melki and Sélim Abdeli*, joined cases C-188/10 and C-189/10, EU:C:2010:363, 41; CJEU judgment in *Georgi Ivanov Elchinov v. Natsionalna zdravnoosiguritelna kasa*, C-173/09, EU:C:2010:581, 26; CJEU Opinion *delivered pursuant* to *Article 218(11) TFEU*, 1/09, EU:C:2011:123, 83; CJEU judgment in *Puligienica Facility Esco SpA (PFE) v. Airgest SpA*, C-689/13, EU:C:2016:199, 32; CJEU judgment in *Global Starnet Ltd v. Ministero dell'Economia e delle Finanze*, C-322/16, EU:C:2017:985, 21-25.

685 CJEU judgment in *Willy Kempter KG v. Hauptzollamt Hamburg-Jonas*, C-2/06, EU:C:2008:78, 41; and CJEU judgment in *Lucio Cesare Aquino v. Belgische Staat*, C-3/16, EU:C:2017:209.

686 CJEU judgment in *van Schijndel v. Stichting Pensioenfonds voor Fysiotherapeuten*, joined cases C-430/93 and C-431/93, EU:C:1995:441. See particularly S. Prechal (1998); S. Prechal and N. Shelkoplyas (2004); T. Tridimas (2006), 463ff.; A. Wallerman (2016), 347ff.; T. Heukels (1996); Y. Houyet (2010), 69-76.

lied on by the parties.[687] The *Hoge Raad*, positing that considering the invoked Treaty provisions would require it to transgress these restrictions, asked the Court of Justice whether EU law required it to apply the relevant Treaty articles of its own motion even "if in so doing the court would have to abandon the passive role which it should normally observe".[688]

The Court's response has been consolidated into the following three-tier formula by legal commentators (more simply translated into *must* = *must*, *may* = *must*, *may not* = *must not*)[689] and upheld by the Court of Justice in subsequent case-law:[690]

1. *Where there exists an obligation to consider matters of national law on an* ex officio *basis, the same obligation applies to matters of EU law (must = must).*
   The first tier follows already from the principle of equivalence.
2. *Where national procedural law leaves the national court a choice in the matter, this gives rise to an obligation of* ex officio *review in order to safeguard rights of individuals derived from EU law (may = must).*
   The obligation to apply EU law *ex officio* thus extends only insofar as national procedural rules allow national judges a choice in the matter.[691] Here we see a deviation from the Opinion of the Advocate General, who had suggested that the obligation to apply EU law could only be derived from an existing *obligation* to apply national law *ex officio*, a reasoning that aligns with the equivalence principle.[692] The Court of

687 According to the principle of *jura novit curia*, Art. 48 of the Netherlands Code of Civil Procedure.

688 CJEU judgment in *van Schijndel v. Stichting Pensioenfonds voor Fysiotherapeuten*, joined cases C-430/93 and C-431/93, EU:C:1995:441, 12.

689 S. Prechal (1998), 697-98; A. Wallerman (2015), 118-20; A. Wallerman (2016), 347-48; K. Lenaerts, I. Maselis, and K. Gutman (2014), § 4.40. The formula is to be differentiated from the situation in which *Union* law leaves Member States a regulatory choice, giving the legislator a margin of discretion that is *not* affected by the *van Schijndel* formula; cf. CJEU judgment in *K. Ruijsenaars*, joined cases C-145/15 and 146/15, EU:C:2016:187 (*may* according to Union law = *must not* in national law).

690 Starting with CJEU judgment in *Aannemersbedrijf P.K. Kraaijeveld BV e.a. v. Gedeputeerde Staten van Zuid-Holland*, C-72/95, EU:C:1996:404, confirming the *van Schijndel* dictum as the rule and *Peterbroeck* as the exception.

691 CJEU judgment in *van Schijndel v. Stichting Pensioenfonds voor Fysiotherapeuten*, joined cases C-430/93 and C-431/93, EU:C:1995:441, 14.

692 Although it was not mentioned as such by name in Opinion of Advocate General Jacobs in *van Schijndel v. Stichting Pensioenfonds voor Fysiotherapeuten*, joined cases C-430/93 and C-431/93, EU:C:1995:185, 38.

Justice went further than the Advocate General, deriving an obligation to apply EU law *ex officio* already from the *power/discretion* to apply national law *ex officio*. In other words: If national law *allows* a judge to apply equivalent rules of his own motion, then he is under a corresponding *duty* to apply binding rules of EU law.[693]

That national judges' EU law mandate hinges on existing powers or discretion finds support in case-law outside the context of *ex officio* review, yet within the field of procedural law. Case-law on the finality of judgments and decisions is particularly instructive. In *Kühne*, the duty of sincere co-operation could only be used to require the re-opening of final decisions in the presence of competence granted the seized court.[694] The case *Pizzarotti*[695] relied on the *Rewe* formula to require that national judges make use of existing powers to supplement a final decision to render it in compliance with Union law.[696]

3. *Where the national court has no power to review matters of national law of its own motion, there is no corresponding obligation to review matters of EU law of its own motion (may not = must not).*

The third tier of the *van Schijndel* formula can be derived *e contrario* from the premise of the second tier: If the legislator has left the courts

693 CJEU judgment in *van Schijndel v. Stichting Pensioenfonds voor Fysiotherapeuten*, joined cases C-430/93 and C-431/93, EU:C:1995:441, 14.

694 CJEU judgment in *Kühne & Heitz NV v. Produktschap voor Pluimvee en Eieren*, C-453/00, EU:C:2004:17, 28; commented by T. Corthaut, *EU Ordre Public* (Croydon: Kluwer Law International, 2012), 241ff.; M. Dougan, (2011 a), 433-34; V. Skouris (2009); P. Wennerås (2007), 99-100; M. Klamert (2014), 132; L. Coutron, 'Cour de Justice, 13 janvier 2004, Kühne & Heitz NV/Productschap voor Pluimvee en Eieren', in *Rev. Aff. Eur.*, 13 (2003-2004) 3, 417-34.

695 CJEU judgment in *Impresa Pizzarotti & C. Spa v. Comune di Bari and Others*, C-213/13, EU:C:2014:2067. See commentary in G. Gattinara and F. Picod, 'L'autorité de la chose jugée après l'arrêt Pizzarotti', *Rev. Aff. Eur.*, 3 (2014); V. Couronne, 'La compétence procédurale des Etats-membres de l'Union européenne', (Université Paris 1 Panthéon Sorbonne, 2015), 482; J. Kitsos, 'Public Procurement – Meaning of 'Public Works Contract' – Scope of the Principle of '*Res Judicata*'', *Eur. Procurement & Pub. Private Partnership L. Rev.*, 10 (2015), 207; S. Smith, 'Impresa Pizzarotti v. Comune di Bari (Case C-213/13): Is a Contract for the Leasing of a Building which has not yet been Built a Works Contract, and must a National Court Revisit a Ruling which has led to a Situation which is Incompatible with EU Procurement Legislation?', *Public Procurement Law Review*, (2014), 171-75; D. Simon, 'Autorité de chose jugée des décisions juridictionnelles nationales', *Europe*, 10 (2016).

696 CJEU judgment in *Impresa Pizzarotti & C. Spa v. Comune di Bari and Others*, C-213/13, EU:C:2014:2067, 56, 62.

no power of *ex officio* review, then there is no discretion available for functionalization to promote EU law effectiveness.

This premise has – albeit not quite consistently[697] – been upheld in subsequent case-law. In *Târşia*, a court had considered itself precluded from re-opening a final decision in *civil* proceedings, although under national law such possibility was foreseen for the re-opening of *administrative* decisions having become final through a ruling by an administrative court. The Court of Justice did not require the discretion granted administrative courts to be extended to civil courts; only that claims based on Union law be given the same treatment as claims based on national law (principle of equivalence).[698]

Discretion under national law as dividing line represents two things. First, as argued by Wallerman, it functionalizes any margin of discretion left national judges by the legislator in order for the former to be able to make case-by-case assessments. While this may promote the effectiveness and uniform application of EU law, it may come at the cost of procedural protection of litigants, since this margin of discretion might have allowed national courts to "cater for the needs of individual cases and ultimately promote procedural fairness".[699] Secondly, the Union mandate triggered by judicial discretion may be evaded by national legislators, who need only enact mandatory rules – as opposed to facultative ones – to remove any such margin of discretion that is susceptible to functionalization.[700] This is facilitated by the third tier in *van Schijndel*, under which the Court of Justice drew the line at compulsory national rules prohibiting *ex officio* review, which the seized court was not required to disregard.

Particularly the third tier therefore produces unanticipated consequences, insofar that the margin of discretion is transferred from national courts to the national legislator (who retains a choice between enacting facultative or mandatory procedural rules).[701] On the other hand, it may represent a deliberate deference to national legislators' fundamental design

697 The absence of competence under national law did not prevent the Court of Justice from requiring that national authorities take measures beyond their powers in e.g. CJEU judgment in *Vereniging Nationaal Overlegorgaan Sociale Werkvoorziening and Others (VNOSW)*, joined cases C-383/06 to C-385/06, EU:C:2008:165, 49-53, discussed further in section 3.2.2.6.

698 CJEU judgment in *Dragoş Constantin Târşia v. Statul român*, C-69/14, EU:C:2015:662, 34-35.

699 A. Wallerman (2016), 355.

700 Ibid, 356.

701 Ibid.

of their procedural system. In *van Schijndel*, the Court of Justice accounted for the purpose of the limitation placed on civil courts; that they are only entitled to raise points of law that fall within the subject-matter of the dispute and obliged to base themselves "on the facts put before it."[702] The Court deemed this limitation justified by the principle of party disposition in civil proceedings, and the necessity to limit *ex officio* review to exceptional situations in which intervention is carried out in the public interest.

These consequences are of import to the first research question, namely how to strike a balance between Union law effectiveness (through the judge's reliance on applicable Union law) and procedural protection (enshrined in the principle of judge passivity). In the *van Schijndel* ruling, a precedent was set that endorsed procedural protection as a legitimate priority, albeit requiring it to be sanctioned by mandatory procedural rules in order to override the priority of safeguarding substantive Union law.[703] The justification test, to be developed in the forthcoming section, "expresses the idea that the protection of EU law rights does not take precedence over all other interests that procedural and remedial rules are set to achieve, but that the interest in enforcing EU law rights must be balanced against other deserving interests".[704] Such flexibility allows the national legislator, depending on each legal tradition, to express its priorities between substantive versus procedural protection through statutory technicalities.

3.2.2.3 Rule-of-reason for weighing procedural protection against effectiveness

The *van Schijndel* ruling (together with *Peterbroeck*) introduced the procedural rule-of-reason, which would ultimately become a cornerstone in the Court of Justice's dealings with obstacles to EU law contained in national

---

702 CJEU judgment in *van Schijndel v. Stichting Pensioenfonds voor Fysiotherapeuten*, joined cases C-430/93 and C-431/93, EU:C:1995:441, 20.

703 This precedent applies to the general procedural case-law, while the third, deferential tier, was not consistently upheld in the consumer protection case-law concerning *ex officio* review of consumer-to-business contracts, as will be seen below.

704 J. Engström, 'The Principle of Effective Judicial Protection after the Lisbon Treaty. Reflection in the Light of Case C-279/09 DEB Deutsche Energiehandels- und Beratungsgesellschaft mbH', *REALaw*, 4 (2011), 62.

procedural rules.[705] The Court clarified that rules essential to protect the functioning of the administration of justice, including the principle of party autonomy, may be relied on to justify provisions otherwise contrary to the principle of *Rewe*-effectiveness – thus expanding the possibilities of justification of procedural obstacles beyond the traditional limits of the effectiveness and equivalence principles: [706]

> each case which raises the question whether a national procedural provision renders application of Community law impossible or excessively difficult must be analyzed by reference to the role of that provision in the procedure, its progress and its special features, viewed as a whole.

Although this approach represents an auspicious sensitivity to the procedural settings governing actions of the national judge, it has not escaped criticism. As discussed in 2.2.3.6 above, the rule-of-reason can be perceived as either intrusive or deferential, depending on who is entrusted to ascertain whether procedural obstacles to the application of EU law are objectively justified. If left entirely at their discretion, the rule-of-reason will indeed allow national courts to promote other interests than the full effect of EU law, e.g. legal certainty and the proper conduct of proceedings (as would be seen in later case-law on *ex officio* review, as well as in other contexts such as the finality of judgments).[707] In a separate line of case-law pertaining to national institutional autonomy, the Court of Justice nevertheless clarified that not any justifications could be accepted.[708]

Still, it is not difficult to concede that a casuistic approach, necessitated by the quest for objective justifications, is capable of altering the mandate of the Court of Justice.[709] Following this perspective, case-by-case assess-

705 E.g. recalled in CJEU judgment in *Asturcom Telecomunicaciones SL v. Cristina Rodríguez Nogueira*, C-40/08, EU:C:2009:615, 39; CJEU judgment in *Banco Español de Crédito SA v. Joaquín Calderón Camino*, C-618/10, EU:C:2012:349, 49; CJEU judgment in *Banif Plus Bank Zrt v. Csaba Csipai*, C-472/11, EU:C:2013:88, 33.

706 CJEU judgment in *van Schijndel v. Stichting Pensioenfonds voor Fysiotherapeuten*, joined cases C-430/93 and C-431/93, EU:C:1995:441, 19; CJEU judgment in *Peterbroeck, Van Campenhout & Cie v. Belgian State*, C-312/93, EU:C:1995:437, 14; see J. Engström (2011), 62.

707 See e.g. CJEU judgment in *Willy Kempter KG v. Hauptzollamt Hamburg-Jonas*, C-2/06, EU:C:2008:78, 37.

708 CJEU judgment in *Stichting ROM-projecten v. Staatssecretaris van Economische Zaken*, C-158/06, EU:C:2007:370, 24; CJEU judgment in *Deutsche Milchkontor*, joined cases 205 to 215/82, EU:C:1983:233; CJEU judgment in *Flemmer and Others*, joined cases C-80/99, C-81/99 and C-82/99, EU:C:2001:525, 60; CJEU judgment in *Republik Österreich v. Martin Huber*, C-336/00, EU:C:2002:509, 56.

709 S. Prechal (1998), 697-98.

ments of the Court of Justice might actually mean "re-evaluating [...] policy choices made by the national legislator".[710] When the Court of Justice responds to its own invitation, by undertaking an examination of the possibilities for objective justification, this opens up a potential for judicial policymaking in a field in which EU competence is highly contested, viz. Member State procedural law.

Finally, the casuistic approach means that the case-law of the Court of Justice may itself appear inconsistent when similar legal questions are given divergent solutions.[711] The greater the discord between cases, the less weight a judgment may carry as legal precedent, as the outcome of a given case is explained by circumstances specific to it. This problem was inherent already in the *Peterbroeck* and *van Schijndel* rulings which, despite being foundational for a new line of jurisprudence, appeared to contradict each other. The forthcoming section will outline possible reasons for this ostensible inconsistency, accounting for factual and contextual differences.

3.2.2.4 Reconciling *Peterbroeck* and *van Schijndel*

A central issue that remained unresolved in the second line of case-law was the reconciliation of the Court's respective findings in *van Schijndel* and *Peterbroeck*. The surprising differences in outcome were enabled by the rule-of-reason, which – as described above – turns what would otherwise represent an inconsistency into casuistic case-law, whose implications can only be discovered by reference to the underlying factors in each case.

One such underlying factor that was early on contemplated as potential motive for the *van Schijndel-Peterbroeck* "contradiction" was the difference between civil and administrative proceedings. In the *van Schijndel* judgment, the Court of Justice had emphasized the particular importance of the principle of party disposition in the context of civil proceedings "concerning rights and obligations freely entered into by the parties".[712] The principle of party disposition imposes itself with particular force in proceedings between private parties whereas the prerogatives of judge inter-

710 J. Engström (2008), 71.

711 E. Werlauff (1999), 58, in reference to CJEU judgment in *Peterbroeck, Van Campenhout & Cie v. Belgian State*, C-312/93, EU:C:1995:437. See also S. Prechal and N. Shelkoplyas (2004), 593; S. Prechal (1998); J. Engström (2008), 71.

712 CJEU judgment in *van Schijndel v. Stichting Pensioenfonds voor Fysiotherapeuten*, joined cases C-430/93 and C-431/93, EU:C:1995:441, 21; see comments by J. Engström (2008), 77; A. Ó. Caoimh (2012), 126.

vention resonate more clearly in administrative proceedings (which was the context of the *Peterbroeck* reference).[713]

Yet, the factual setting of the *van Schijndel* case posed a problem to this rationale.[714] The key issue in the national proceedings leading up to the reference was the state-enforced imposition of membership in a public pension scheme. Emphasizing that the proceedings concerned legal rights and obligations "freely entered into" by individuals was misleading, considering that the applicant parties were in fact seeking to preserve a negative right *not* to subscribe to the compulsory occupational pension scheme. As the national proceedings were not of genuine civil law character, the explanatory value of the *form* of the proceedings is here negligible.[715] That an administrative-civil law divide lay behind the differences between the judgments in *van Schijndel* and *Peterbroeck* has accordingly been dismissed in the legal commentary,[716] not the least by reason of the Court of Justice's later clarification that the *Peterbroeck* judgment was distinguished by "circumstances peculiar to the dispute".[717]

If we rule out the civil versus administrative proceedings divide as key parameter, the *Peterbroeck* ruling still clearly emphasized the distinction between higher versus lower courts. This has prompted inquiries whether ensuring legal certainty to a greater degree requires judge passivity in higher

713 S. Prechal and N. Shelkoplyas (2004), 595; J. Engström (2008), 73.

714 J. Engström (2008), 77 f.

715 A proceeding of this kind may readily be characterized as *de facto* administrative since the main reason for appeal before a civil court in the Netherlands appears to be that the provision of occupational pension plans was outsourced to private entities; see Opinion of Advocate General Jacobs in *van Schijndel v. Stichting Pensioenfonds voor Fysiotherapeuten*, joined cases C-430/93 and C-431/93, EU:C:1995:185, 64. They were civil proceedings merely by label but not in substance; A. Wallerman (2015), 143, fn. 634.

716 J. Engström (2008), 77; A. Wallerman (2015), 103-4.

717 CJEU judgment in *van der Weerd and Others v. Minister van Landbouw, Natuur en Voedselkwaliteit*, joined cases C-222/05 to C-225/05, EU:C:2007:318, 40; comments in J. H. Jans and A. T. Marseille, 'Joined Cases C-222-225/05, van der Weerd and others v. Minister van Landbouw, Natuur en Voedselkwaliteit, Judgment of the Court (Fourth Chamber) of 7 June 2007, [2007] ECR I-14233', *CMLR* 234 (2009); X. Groussot, 'Spirit, Are You There? Reinforced Judicial Dialogue and the Preliminary Ruling Procedure', *Eric Stein Working Papers*, (2008), 8ff. See also CJEU judgment in *Eco Swiss China Time Ltd v. Benetton International NV*, C-126/97, EU:C:1999:269, which further supports this point.

than in lower courts,[718] and what importance, in terms of ensuring effective judicial protection, should be placed on the judicial versus administrative stages of appeal (taking into consideration that administrative stages do not grant access to the preliminary reference procedure).[719]

Procedural rules barring new claims before higher court instances are commonplace in the Member States[720] (and also figure in the Court of Justice's rules of procedure[721]). The objective of such rules are, *inter alia*, to ensure that all elements of a case be given due consideration in each judicial instance, and may therefore be justified by the need to promote effective judicial protection. Barring new claims before higher instances is intended to represent a safeguard protecting both claimants and defendants by compelling them to litigate separately on new factual or legal claims, exhausting all available instances. In practice, however, placing a claim outside the ambit of the proceedings is not a guarantee that it can be relitigated,[722] why such rules are often perceived as hurdles – rather than protective measures – by litigants wishing to introduce new claims. It is also from this perspective that bars on new legal claims are at times treated by the Court of Justice as procedural obstacles, to be justified e.g. by the procedural rule-of-reason.

The additional premise in *Peterbroeck* that the time-limit also barred higher courts from ruling on claims raised in an untimely manner, meant that not only were the applicants deprived of access to a court instance that could consider their claims based on EU law, but also deprived of such reconsideration by a higher instance, which would in effect prevent all courts in the chain of appeal from exercising their *Rheinmühlen* man-

---

718 I.e. whether it is reasonable to conclude that courts of lower instance should comply with the *Peterbroeck* rationale whereas higher courts with the less intrusive *van Schijndel* rationale.

719 J. Engström (2008), 77-78.

720 On the ambit of Swedish administrative proceedings, see U. von Essen (2009), 189-90; cf. P. O. Ekelöf and H. Edelstam, *Rättegång: Första häftet* (Stockholm: Norstedts Juridik, 2002), 134. For a comparative account of the ambit of proceedings in higher instances in the Member States, see F. C. de la Torre (2005), 399, with references in fn. 2.

721 See e.g. Arts. 169-70 of the Rules of Procedure of the Court of Justice of 25 September 2012, OJ L 265, 29/9/2012, as amended on 18 June 2013, OJ L 173, 26/6/2013, 65.

722 Insofar as the "new" claim is covered by the preclusive effect of *res judicata* or *litis pendens* of the initial proceedings (depending on whether they have been concluded or are pending).

date.[723] The Court of Justice, in *Peterbroeck* as well as in subsequent case-law, thus accepted the premise that higher courts may not expand the ambit of the proceedings by hearing new pleas or considering new elements in law or fact.[724] The Court of Justice was concerned rather with the effectiveness of the preliminary reference procedure – referring back to *Rheinmühlen* – than the avenues of appeal for the effective exercise of rights under EU law.[725] The priority behind the Court's reasoning was thus access to a "court or tribunal" so as to activate the preliminary reference procedure.[726]

That the judicial character (and not the stage) of appeal was decisive finds support in subsequent case-law.[727] There is no right to bring claims based on EU law at certain levels of appeal[728] – access to court requires ad-

723 T. Tridimas (2006), 462.

724 Which is also in line with the finding in CJEU judgment in *van Schijndel v. Stichting Pensioenfonds voor Fysiotherapeuten*, joined cases C-430/93 and C-431/93, EU:C:1995:441, 22, where a court of last instance could not be compelled to do the same, and CJEU judgment in *Lucio Cesare Aquino v. Belgische Staat*, C-3/16, EU:C:2017:209, where the obligation to make a preliminary reference hinged on the appeal being admissible before the court of last instance.

725 CJEU judgment in *Peterbroeck, Van Campenhout & Cie v. Belgian State*, C-312/93, EU:C:1995:437, 12-13, 17; see also CJEU judgment in *Georgi Ivanov Elchinov v. Natsionalna zdravnoosiguritelna kasa*, C-173/09, EU:C:2010:581, 27 and CJEU judgment in *Diageo Brands BV v. Simiramida-04 EOOD*, C-681/13, EU:C:2015:471.

726 CJEU judgment in *Peterbroeck, Van Campenhout & Cie v. Belgian State*, C-312/93, EU:C:1995:437, 21.

727 CJEU judgment in *Eco Swiss China Time Ltd v. Benetton International NV*, C-126/97, EU:C:1999:269; CJEU judgment in *Alassini and Others*, C-317/08, EU:C:2010:146, 62-67; see J. H. Jans, R. de Lange, S. Prechal, and R. J. G. M. Widdershoven (2007), 310-11. Analogy between *Eco Swiss* and *Peterbroeck* is sound, save one aspect. In the *Eco Swiss* case, the Dutch rules of procedure made it impossible to introduce claims based on EU law for the first time before a judicial instance reviewing an arbitration award. In the *Peterbroeck* case their introduction was not excluded – merely subject to a deadline, which leaves little room for objection, based on its length and similarity to the Court of Justice's own rules on time-barring of claims. The *Peterbroeck* case is haunted by a misunderstanding, namely that the time-barring of claims started running already at the delivery of the administrative decision subject to challenge, rather than at the time when the judicial instance was first seized on appeal and served by the challenged authority.

728 Cf. CJEU judgment in *Diageo Brands BV v. Simiramida-04 EOOD*, C-681/13, EU:C:2015:471, 65, in which the Court of Justice, referring to CJEU judgment in *Georgi Ivanov Elchinov v. Natsionalna zdravnoosiguritelna kasa*, C-173/09,

mission to one instance forming part of the judiciary.[729] Of crucial importance is, therefore, the provision of access to a *judicial* stage of appeal, due to the preliminary reference procedure being reserved for judicial bodies – a requirement that the Court of Justice has since emphasized as forming part of the right to effective judicial protection.[730]

Despite the Court's indication already in *Rheinmühlen*, that courts' access to the preliminary reference procedure is independent of party initiative,[731] the pitch was different in *Peterbroeck* as compared to *Rheinmühlen* – giving rise to one more ambiguity which has since been revisited by the Court of Justice. In the *Rheinmühlen* line of case-law, the Court of Justice clarified that lower courts must have a formal power, unhindered by the legislator or higher court instances, to make a preliminary reference.[732] In the *Peterbroeck* line, national lower courts were globally empowered to do so, whereas a procedural omission on the side of the applicant potentially prevented higher instances from exercising the mandate.[733] The national

---

EU:C:2010:581, 27, expressed the power of a court to make a preliminary reference in the language of a "right" for the beneficiary party to have a preliminary reference put to the Court of Justice. Taking into consideration other language versions of the present judgment, the finding above appears to be be an anomaly – although courts of highest instance certainly have an obligation to make preliminary references, Art. 267 TFEU does not constitute a sanctioned remedy or a right for individual litigants; A. Meij (2011), 263ff.; M. Broberg, 'National Courts of Last Instance Failing to Make a Preliminary Reference: The (Possible) Consequences Flowing Therefrom', *European Public Law*, 22 (2016), 243-56.

729 See e.g. CJEU judgment in *Edwards and Pallikaropoulos*, C-260/11, EU:C:2013:221, 47; CJEU judgment in *Sanchez Morcillo and Abril García (I)*, C-169/14, EU:C:2014:2099, 36; CJEU judgment in *Banco Primus SA v. Jesús Gutiérrez García*, C-421/14, EU:C:2017:60, 48.

730 CJEU judgment in *Alassini and Others*, C-317/08, EU:C:2010:146, 62-67; CJEU judgment in *Slowakische Republik v. Achmea BV*, C-284/16, EU:C:2018:158.

731 Explicitly confirmed later in CJEU judgment in *Willy Kempter KG v. Hauptzollamt Hamburg-Jonas*, C-2/06, EU:C:2008:78; CJEU judgment in *Cartesio Oktató és Szolgáltató bt*, C-210/06, EU:C:2008:723; CJEU judgment in *Patrick Kelly v. National University of Ireland*, C-104/10, EU:C:2011:506; CJEU judgment in *Consiglio nazionale dei geologi and Autorità garante della concorrenza e del mercato*, C-136/12, EU:C:2013:489, 28.

732 CJEU judgment in *Cartesio Oktató és Szolgáltató bt*, C-210/06, EU:C:2008:723; *Diageo Brands BV v. Simiramida-04 EOOD*, C-681/13, EU:C:2015:471, 65; referring to CJEU judgment in *Georgi Ivanov Elchinov v. Natsionalna zdravnoosiguritelna kasa*, C-173/09, EU:C:2010:581, 27.

733 CJEU judgment in *Peterbroeck, Van Campenhout & Cie v. Belgian State*, C-312/93, EU:C:1995:437; cf. CJEU judgment in *Lucio Cesare Aquino v. Belgische Staat*, C-3/16, EU:C:2017:209.

court's power to make a preliminary reference is in this way intertwined with the question of the beneficiary's initiative to bring claims in a timely manner before an appropriate instance. The next section develops the latter aspect by examining the connection between party omission for introducing claims and court responsibility for *ex officio* review.

3.2.2.5 Use it or lose it: Litigants' procedural omissions

It has above been suggested that the Court wished to maintain a difference between the situation in which the applicants had clearly missed their chance to introduce claims based on EU law, versus situations where the applicants were given but one narrow shot at submitting their claims before a court or tribunal within the meaning of Art. 267 TFEU. *Van Schijndel* could accordingly be taken to indicate that the principle of effectiveness does not go so far as to require an appeals court to remedy negligence of a party to invoke his rights under EU law before a lower court, whereas it can be expected to remedy procedural obstacles to *access* to court (*Peterbroeck*). Alas, the cases' factual circumstances do not lend support to this conclusion, given that in *Peterbroeck* the national judge was also in the presence of a procedural omission by the applicant parties, which the judge was nonetheless expected to remedy.

Overlooked opportunities to bring claims thus lacks explanatory force concerning the respectively different outcomes in *van Schijndel* and *Peterbroeck*.[734] The task of ascertaining whether a preliminary reference is necessary primarily falls on the seized judge and is supposed to be independent of any party initiative.[735] The rationale of party negligence vs. diligence has nonetheless occasionally been revived in cases concerning *ex officio* re-

734 By contrast, recourse to aspects of party diligence or omission has seen a renaissance in the consumer protection case-law: CJEU judgment in *Asturcom Telecomunicaciones SL v. Cristina Rodríguez Nogueira*, C-40/08, EU:C:2009:615, 47; CJEU judgment in *Monika Kušionová v. SMART Capital a.s.*, C-34/13, EU:C:2014:2189, 56.

735 CJEU judgment in *Willy Kempter KG v. Hauptzollamt Hamburg-Jonas*, C-2/06, EU:C:2008:78; CJEU judgment in *Cartesio Oktató és Szolgáltató bt*, C-210/06, EU:C:2008:723; CJEU judgment in *Patrick Kelly v. National University of Ireland*, C-104/10, EU:C:2011:506; CJEU judgment in *Consiglio nazionale dei geologi and Autorità garante della concorrenza e del mercato*, C-136/12, EU:C:2013:489, 28.

view.[736] For instance, the reasoning was employed in the Opinions in *Benallal*[737] and *Finanmadrid*,[738] whereas the parameters instructing the balance to be struck were not developed in detail.[739] The ruling in *Aquino* further clarified that where claims based on EU-law are entirely outside the ambit of the proceedings in last instance, a preliminary reference may be deemed unnecessary by the national court since the Court of Justice's subsequent answer – pertaining to an inadmissible claim – would ultimately not be taken into account in the national proceedings.[740]

Case-law on the finality of judgments and decisions provides further guidance, in instances of overlap with the issue of *ex officio* review. A detour will therefore be taken via rulings in which the criteria for re-opening administrative acts had implications for obligations incumbent on the beneficiary of Union law (who had been "wronged" by a prior final decision contrary to EU law).

The seminal ruling in *Kühne* laid down criteria for requiring the re-opening of final administrative acts, one of which was that the original decision was "based on a misinterpretation of Community law which was adopted without a question being referred to the Court for a preliminary ruling."[741] This represented a division of responsibility between errors of the national court (in not making a reference when so required) versus potential errors of the Court of Justice in the (hypothetical) event that the latter had been seized by the national court in the context of the initial proceedings and through its response contributed to the misinterpretation. The above citation contained an embedded element of importance to the

736 E.g. in CJEU judgment in *Asturcom Telecomunicaciones SL v. Cristina Rodríguez Nogueira*, C-40/08, EU:C:2009:615. As expressed by T. Corthaut (2012), 216, referring to the Court of Justice's overall stance on *ex officio* review: "The rule of thumb in respect of national procedural rights for enforcing EU law still is 'use it or lose it'". See further P. J. Wattel (2008), 111 f.

737 Opinion of Advocate General Mengozzi in *Abdelhafid Bensada Benallal v. État belge*, C-161/15, EU:C:2016:3, 42; S. Cazet, 'Relevé d'office', *Europe 2016*, Mai Comm. nº 5 (2016), 13-14.

738 Opinion of Advocate General Szpunar in *Finanmadrid EFC SA v. Jesús Vicente Albán Zambrano and Others*, C-49/14, EU:C:2015:746, 43.

739 The link between omission and litigants' access to the preliminary reference procedure was also addressed in CJEU judgment in *Diageo Brands BV v. Simiramida-04 EOOD*, C-681/13, EU:C:2015:471, 65.

740 CJEU judgment in *Lucio Cesare Aquino v. Belgische Staat*, C-3/16, EU:C:2017:209, 41-45.

741 CJEU judgment in *Kühne & Heitz NV v. Produktschap voor Pluimvee en Eieren*, C-453/00, EU:C:2004:17, 28.

issue of *ex officio* review; namely the extent to which the initially seized court's power or obligation to make a preliminary reference hinges on the litigating parties' choice (or mistake) not to invoke EU law or not to request that a preliminary reference be made. The remainder of the present section will focus on the responsibilities of the applicant in the prior proceedings as dealt with under this criterion.

The referring court in the *Kempter* case had been interested in knowing whether the said *Kühne* criterion (absence of preliminary reference to the Court of Justice) required the individual concerned to have relied on EU law in the first round of proceedings, so as to trigger the seized court to submit a preliminary reference.[742] In principle, such an approach would not at the time have been foreign to the Court of Justice, which in its case-law on *ex officio* review, under the dictum of *ius vigilantibus scriptum est* (colloquially: "use it or lose it"[743]), had not by default required a court to compensate for procedural lapses by the parties (as long as they had at least had a genuine opportunity to raise the point of EU law before a court instance).[744]

Yet, what makes the "use it or lose it" dictum unsatisfactory to transfer from the *ex officio* review to the *res judicata* context is that at the time of a first set of proceedings, it may neither have been obvious to the seized court, nor to the applicants, that EU law was activated by the circumstances of the case, since the later (correct) decision by the Court of Justice would not have been delivered at the time of the omission.[745] It is therefore a relevant query whether individual litigants should bear the consequences of failing to identify applicable EU law provisions.[746] Advocate General Bot and the Court agreed that the criterion should not be taken to imply that the individual must have invoked EU law at any particular instance before the national courts.[747] Rather, it is a national court's respon-

742 CJEU judgment in *Willy Kempter KG v. Hauptzollamt Hamburg-Jonas*, C-2/06, EU:C:2008:78, 21.

743 P. J. Wattel (2008), 111.

744 S. Prechal and N. Shelkoplyas (2004), 598-99; CJEU judgment in *Asturcom Telecomunicaciones SL v. Cristina Rodríguez Nogueira*, C-40/08, EU:C:2009:615, 47.

745 P. J. Wattel (2008), 109-10; A. Östlund and J. Hallberg, 'Kan nya EU-domar läggas till grund för förnyad prövning av slutgiltiga internationella skiljedomar?', *JT*, 3 (2018/19), 675.

746 CJEU judgment in *Willy Kempter KG v. Hauptzollamt Hamburg-Jonas*, C-2/06, EU:C:2008:78, 23.

747 Ibid., 42-43; Opinion of Advocate General Bot in *Willy Kempter KG v. Hauptzollamt Hamburg-Jonas*, C-2/06, EU:C:2007:245, 96.

sibility to ascertain of its own motion whether a preliminary reference is necessary in the case before it:[748]

> it is sufficient if either the point of Community law the interpretation of which proved to be incorrect in light of a subsequent judgment by the Court was considered by the national court ruling at final instance or it could have been raised by the latter of its own motion.[749]

Accordingly, as soon as a preliminary reference was incumbent on the seized court (for whichever of these two reasons), the relevant *Kühne* criterion would be met in instances where a reference had not been made.[750] The unfortunate applicant whose judiciary failed to do so cannot be expected to be a step ahead of his judge: "to recognize such an exigency for the plaintiff would result in shaping an exception to the obligation for the national court to make a preliminary [reference]."[751] In practice, this means that it would be necessary for the national court to examine not only whether an obligation of *ex officio* review exists under national law, but also whether it is prescribed by the Court of Justice. If so, the *Kühne* criterion would be met even if the applicant had not raised his claims based on EU-law in a timely manner or as otherwise foreseen by national law.[752]

The described case-law thus moderated the dictum of *ius vigilantibus scriptum est* by downplaying the vigilance of litigants, while emphasizing the obligations of the later seized court to compensate for the first court's inactivity or error.[753] The case-law on *res judicata* thus aligns with the case-law on *ex officio* review by making the re-opening conditional on the question as to whether, in the first round of proceedings, there would hypothetically have been an obligation to examine Union law *ex officio*, in the event that Union law had not there been invoked. The fourth line of case-law on consumer-to-business litigation, addressed in section 3.2.4, would further nuance this dictum, accounting and compensating for con-

748 Ibid., 99; referring back to CJEU judgment in *CILFIT v. Ministero della Sanità*, 283/81, EU:C:1982:335, 10-11.

749 CJEU judgment in *Willy Kempter KG v. Hauptzollamt Hamburg-Jonas*, C-2/06, EU:C:2008:78, 44.

750 See also T. Corthaut (2012), 242.

751 X. Groussot and T. Minssen, 'Res Judicata in the Court of Justice Case-Law: Balancing Legal Certainty with Legality', *ECL*, 3 (2007), 404.

752 T. Corthaut (2012), 242. In the wake of CJEU judgment in *Lucio Cesare Aquino v. Belgische Staat*, C-3/16, EU:C:2017:209, such an obligation can nevertheless be expected to arise less frequently.

753 CJEU judgment in *Willy Kempter KG v. Hauptzollamt Hamburg-Jonas*, C-2/06, EU:C:2008:78.

sumers' litigation disadvantages. For instance, the Union law mandate of *ex officio* review was even taken to mean that the ambit of the second round of proceedings could be expanded to include also factual aspects that in the first round of proceedings would have prompted an obligation of *ex officio* review to the benefit of a consumer party.[754] This expansive stance, which is symptomatic of the consumer protection prerogative, stands in contrast to the recent *Aquino* ruling where the "widest discretion" doctrine was truncated by the inadmissibility of claims before a highest instance of appeal.[755]

3.2.2.6 Protection of individuals against enforcement of EU law

We have thus far principally considered circumstances in which individuals benefit from the application of EU law in the context of litigation against other private or public parties. By contrast, in *reverse* vertical litigation, public authorities endeavor to enforce EU law *against* individuals. Such legal relationships have prompted a scholarly deliberation on effective and dissuasive sanctions, not in the perspective of granting individual protection of Union law rights, but of enforcing Union law against individuals in a proportionate manner (i.e. not *excessively* effective/dissuasive).[756]

The requirement of proportionality is essential in view of the conflict of interest between effective enforcement of EU law (public interest) and the protection of the individual against whom it is being enforced. Whether or not this is denoted proportionality, the latter may come in the form of procedural protection. The present section illustrates how the requirement of full effectiveness is balanced against procedural protection according to a reasoning analogous with the procedural rule-of-reason.[757]

---

754 CJEU judgment in *Banco Primus SA v. Jesús Gutiérrez García*, C-421/14, EU:C:2017:60, 50-52.

755 CJEU judgment in *Lucio Cesare Aquino v. Belgische Staat*, C-3/16, EU:C:2017:209, 41-45.

756 See e.g. S. Prechal (2017 a), 402; M. Dougan (2011 a), 426; M. Dougan (2012), 108, in reference to the line of case-law based on CJEU judgment in *Commission v. Greece (Greek Maize)*, 68/88, EU:C:1989:339.

757 CJEU judgment in *Commission v. Greece (Greek Maize)*, 68/88, EU:C:1989:339.

The issue of *ex officio* enforcement of EU law *against* individuals was first dealt with in the 2008 judgment in *Heemskerk and Schaap*.[758] Relevant Union law provisions would, if applied *ex officio*, ultimately have led to an outcome less favorable to the individual applicant in second instance than the appealed decision. The referring court's move to apply EU law *ex officio* was in breach of a general procedural tenet prohibiting *reformatio in pejus*, also contained in Dutch procedural law: "an individual bringing an action must not be placed in a less favorable position than if he had not brought that action".[759] The question put to the Court of Justice was accordingly whether the national court was nonetheless obliged to apply EU law of its own motion.

Advocate General Bot had proposed a different reference point than the principal case-law on *ex officio* review, since the pressing matter was not whether an individual had been granted the opportunity to raise a plea based on EU law, but whether he could avoid its application by declining to introduce EU law in his litigation.[760] The pertinent question, according to the Advocate General, was whether the public stakes would require Union law to be effectively enforced *(ex officio)* against the concerned individual. The Opinion proposed examining whether the prohibition against *reformatio in pejus* was liable to "undermine the application or the effectiveness of Union law".[761]

The chosen path – based on full effectiveness – required that enforcement be effective and non-discriminatory, subject to objective justifications.[762] This formula features prominently in a line of case-law concerning the recovery of unlawfully paid subsidies (in the typology of this work

758 CJEU judgment in *Heemskerk BV and Firma Schaap v. Productschap Vee en Vlees*, C-455/06, EU:C:2008:650; Y. Houyet (2010), 74-75; T. Corthaut (2012), 213-15; V. Couronne (2015), 407-8; H. Schebsta (2010), 874; S. Cazet, 'Le relevé d'office et la protection du justiciable', *Revue du droit de l'Union européenne* 3 (2017), 58ff.

759 CJEU judgment in *Heemskerk BV and Firma Schaap v. Productschap Vee en Vlees*, C-455/06, EU:C:2008:650, 44.

760 Opinion of Advocate General Bot in *Heemskerk BV and Firma Schaap v. Productschap Vee en Vlees*, C-455/06, EU:C:2008:258, 123-24.

761 Ibid., 130.

762 On the requirements of effectiveness and non-discrimination, see K. Lenaerts, I. Maselis, and K. Gutman (2014), 137; J. Jans, R. de Lange, S. Prechal, and R. Widdershoven (2007), 206-213.

belonging to the field of institutional autonomy).[763] EU law was there similarly enforced by public bodies against individuals, the endeavor of recovery representing a Union prerogative. The applicable tests of full effectiveness and non-discrimination were worded in similar language to the *Rewe* formula. The *Rewe* sibling is, however, a *faux ami*, as the legal relationship is inverted in the relevant tests (i.e. safeguarding the effectiveness of public bodies' measures against individual claimants, instead of, as in *Rewe*, protecting individual beneficiaries of EU law):[764]

> in the absence of provisions of Community law, disputes concerning the recovery of amounts wrongly paid under Community law must be decided by national courts in application of their own domestic law, subject to the limits imposed by Community law, on the basis that the rules and procedures laid down by domestic law must not have the effect of making it practically impossible or excessively difficult to recover the aid not due and that the national legislation must be applied in a manner which is not discriminatory as compared to procedures for deciding similar national disputes.

Full effectiveness (in this guise) allows at least a measure of flexibility through a reasoning akin to the procedural rule-of-reason: Legal certainty, legality, and legitimate expectations may be considered,[765] although they will only justify encroachments to the extent that "full account is taken of the interests of the Community."[766] In e.g. the strand of case-law leading up to *VNOSW*, the procedural rule-of-reason was not applied, although the context entailed balancing individuals' procedural protection against effective enforcement of Union law. The Court of Justice there laid down strict guidelines as to what was required in order for national authorities to disregard the obligation of recovery in order to safeguard individuals' legal certainty – amounting to a requirement that invoked derogations form part of Union law notions of legal protection and be treated in accordance

763 The case-law is treated as belonging to national institutional autonomy due to the overarching issue of organization and competences (of revocation) of public bodies, see J. M. Davidson (2008).

764 CJEU judgment in *Stichting ROM-projecten v. Staatssecretaris van Economische Zaken*, C-158/06, EU:C:2007:370, 23; see also CJEU judgment in *Steff-Houlberg Export and Others*, C-366/95, EU:C:1998:216, 15.

765 CJEU judgment in *Deutsche Milchkontor*, joined cases 205 to 215/82, EU:C:1983:233.

766 Opinion of Advocate General Bot in *Heemskerk BV and Firma Schaap v. Productschap Vee en Vlees*, C-455/06, EU:C:2008:258, 137; CJEU judgment in *Vereniging Nationaal Overlegorgaan Sociale Werkvoorziening and Others (VNOSW)*, joined cases C-383/06 to C-385/06, EU:C:2008:165, 52.

with rules of EU law.[767] In other words, not any derogations could be accepted; only justifications that formed part of recognized general principles of EU law.[768] Although the Court of Justice might defer to the national judge to make a final appraisal, the level of *de facto* discretion was strongly circumscribed by the strict interpretation of legitimate justifications, together with the obligation (irrespective of competences under national law) to grant Union law full effect.[769]

This is the legal background against which, in *Heemskerk and Schaap*, the Advocate General suggested that taking "full account" of the general interests vested in the correct application of EU law required that the national court review of its own motion the calculation method applied by the national authorities, even if this meant setting aside the prohibition against *reformatio in pejus*.[770] The relatively stricter justification test under the full effectiveness approach amounted to giving the enforcement of Union law priority over rules of procedure put in place to ensure legal certainty, which may otherwise have been treated as justified under the procedural rule-of-reason.

The Court of Justice, by contrast, endorsed the justification based on the national prohibition against *reformatio in pejus*, finding that Union law cannot oblige national courts to carry out *ex officio* review when so doing would be contrary to the rights of defense, legal certainty and the protection of legitimate expectations.[771] Weighing the effective application of Union law against these considerations, the Court of Justice did not clarify

767 CJEU judgment in *Vereniging Nationaal Overlegorgaan Sociale Werkvoorziening and Others (VNOSW)*, joined cases C-383/06 to C-385/06, EU:C:2008:165, 52-53; based on CJEU judgment in *Stichting ROM-projecten v. Staatssecretaris van Economische Zaken*, C-158/06, EU:C:2007:370, 24; see J. M. Davidson (2008), 119.

768 CJEU judgment in *Stichting ROM-projecten v. Staatssecretaris van Economische Zaken*, C-158/06, EU:C:2007:370, 24; see also CJEU judgment in *Deutsche Milchkontor*, joined cases 205 to 215/82, EU:C:1983:233; CJEU judgment in *Flemmer and Others*, joined cases C-80/99, C-81/99 and C-82/99, EU:C:2001:525, 60; CJEU judgment in *Republik Österreich v. Martin Huber*, C-336/00, EU:C:2002:509, 56.

769 CJEU judgment in *Vereniging Nationaal Overlegorgaan Sociale Werkvoorziening and Others (VNOSW)*, joined cases C-383/06 to C-385/06, EU:C:2008:165, 55-57.

770 Opinion of Advocate General Bot in *Heemskerk BV and Firma Schaap v. Productschap Vee en Vlees*, C-455/06, EU:C:2008:258, 140-46.

771 CJEU judgment in *Heemskerk BV and Firma Schaap v. Productschap Vee en Vlees*, C-455/06, EU:C:2008:650, 46-47.

its choice between the two justification formulas.[772] The issue of effective enforcement versus procedural protection was thus resolved by giving priority to the latter; yet the implications of this choice are unclear when we do not know which balancing test was applied.

Recognition of the fundamental status of the prohibition against *reformatio in pejus* may at the same time explain and distinguish *Heemskerk and Schaap* from a later ruling concerning *ex officio* review to the disadvantage of individuals. In *Online Games*, the outcome was different, whereas *reformatio in pejus* was not on the table.[773] The referring court wondered whether the principle of effective judicial protection was opposed to the use of *ex officio* review when considering derogations from fundamental freedoms under EU law. Despite the judgment's fundamental rights approach, the individual litigant was not helped by the balancing exercise between administrative courts' truth-seeking mission on the one side, and judicial impartiality under Art. 47 CFR on the other. With respect to the latter, the Court held that[774]

> there is no reason to consider that such a procedural system is such as to give rise to doubts as to the impartiality of the national court, in so far as that court is required to investigate the case before it, not in order to support the prosecution, but to establish the truth. Moreover, that system is based, in essence, on the idea that the court is not only the arbiter of a dispute between the parties but represents the general interest of society.

By the time this ruling was delivered in 2017, the fundamental rights approach for which the Court opted was mainstream, perhaps making the choice between full effectiveness and *Rewe*-effectiveness somewhat redundant. Despite endorsing *ex officio* review pursuant to a reasoning on principle, the ruling was concluded with a caveat about the limits of this review, which should be carried out "provided that such a system does not have the consequence that that court is required to substitute itself for the competent authorities of the Member State concerned".[775]

---

772 In fact, no case-law was evoked by the Court of Justice in this part of its reasoning; ibid., 44-48.

773 CJEU judgment in *Online Games Handels GmbH*, C-685/15, EU:C:2017:452.

774 Ibid., 64.

775 Ibid., 67. Such language is commonplace with respect to the EU judiciary's review of Commission decisions in competition proceedings (see e.g. P. van Cleynenbreugel (2015), 54) whereas, within the auspices of a preliminary ruling, the reservation appears a bit out of place as general commentary on the institutional distribution of responsibilities between national courts and authorities.

In sum, the matter of public authorities' competences activated a relatively strict test that *prima facie* discards some national justifications, leaving relatively little discretion for national courts in making the balancing exercise. This context of national institutional autonomy offered alternative solutions to the first research question,[776] allowing the Court of Justice to precede the national judge by ruling on whether national justifications are recognized in EU law and treated in accordance with equivalent Union notions, instead of deferring to the national judge to balance effective enforcement against procedural protection under national law. Still, the Court on occasion permitted essential procedural safeguards under national law to trump the interest of effective enforcement of Union law. This translated into striking a balance in favor of procedural protection on the basis of relevant justifications provided in national law, or at least deferring the matter of scrutiny to the national judge. Yet, it is not clear whether an initial choice between full effect, *Rewe*-effectiveness and the fundamental rights approach instructed such outcomes, or whether the variation is rather explained by an autonomous assessment as to the significance or status of the procedural safeguard.

3.2.3 *Ex officio* review to safeguard public policy

Public policy is a chameleon concept. It changes its colors depending on the circumstances it is relied upon[.][777]

Public policy considerations can be invoked in a variety of contexts, recurrently by Member States when attempting to justify deviation from EU internal market law.[778] Member States' possibilities to derogate from obligations under EU law are justified by the existence of public policy or public order considerations[779] – that is, rules and principles put in place "to protect the fundamental values of a legal and political order".[780]

---

776 *How is the balance struck between substantive and procedural protection in the Court of Justice's case-law on* ex officio *review?*

777 S. Prechal and N. Shelkoplyas (2004), 600.

778 See e.g. P. Craig and G. de Búrca (2011 a), 670-71; R. de Lange (2007), 9.

779 H. Lindahl, 'Discretion and Public Policy: Timing the Unity and Divergence of Legal Orders', in *The Coherence of EU law,* eds. Prechal, S. and B. van Roermund (New York: 2008), 291-313.

780 T. Corthaut (2012), 190.

In the context of Member State procedural law, however, the tables are turned. Since procedural law does not belong to the fields of EU competence, the central query is instead the conditions under which the notion of public policy can be used to derogate from *national* procedural rules posing obstacles to the effective enforcement of EU law. The present version of public policy exceptions can be functionalized to promote compliance with substantive EU law, by derogation from national procedural law. Consider the following examples:

- Arbitration proceedings make it possible for parties to decline entirely from subjecting their judicial interactions to the rule or applicability of EU law. But could it not be reasonable to require that an ordinary court in the context of annulment or enforcement of an arbitration award ensure that EU law be given adequate effect? This question is often, both internationally and in domestic legislation, resolved by recourse to the notion of public policy or public order.[781]
- As we have seen in the present chapter, courts may be barred from raising issues of EU law by the circumstance that the parties have not invoked the relevant provisions. Rules preventing judges from expanding the ambit of the proceedings by considering legal or factual claims *ex officio* may sometimes be foreseen with an exception based on the protected interests triggered by the barred claims – again, in the interest of providing a substantively correct judgment for litigants and third parties.[782]

781 S. Whittaker (2012), 46. An instance of this is Art. 34(2)(b) of the 1985 United Nations Commission on International Trade Law Model Law on International Commercial Arbitration (1985) (UNCITRAL), United Nations document A140117, annex I, as adopted by the United Nations Commission on International Trade Law on 21 June 1985, as amended in 2006. National variations will be discussed further below.

782 T. Corthaut (2012), 208ff. Another example (belonging to procedural public policy but falling outside the scope of this work) is that final decisions and judgments should be reviewed in special circumstances only, to protect legitimate expectations and foster viable legal precedents. Yet, faulty final judgments give rise to incorrect legal effects and precedents for future courts to rely on. The notion of public policy designates exceptional circumstances in which ensuring substantively correct legal precedents may trump the finality of judgments and decisions; ibid., 239-44.

These problems are resolved through legal derogations from the basic principles described above[783] – here referred to as procedural public policy rules. The topic of this section is how the connection between national and EU public policy has evolved in the Court of Justice's case-law on *ex officio* review. In the wake of the second line of case-law, a handful of judgments were delivered by the Court of Justice on the matter of public policy grounds for *ex officio* review. These cases focused on the issue of whether to allow more far-reaching review of Union law to protect national or Union public policy. The judgments belonging to this third line of case-law thus concern the extent to which the Court of Justice was ready to require national courts to introduce rules of EU law of their own motion, in order to safeguard a public interest vested in their enforcement.[784]

The present section first introduces relevant uses of public policy (for the purposes of this work), in which it affects the boundaries of Member State procedural autonomy.[785] First, internal procedural public policy will be examined in its function of allowing national judges to deviate from the principle of party disposition, so as to take into account public policy norms that have not been invoked by the parties. This hinges on the notion of public policy within the meaning of mandatory contract law (3.2.3.1). Second, the capacity of public policy norms to extend the powers of review granted ordinary courts when dealing with enforcement or annulment of arbitration awards will be described (3.2.3.2).[786] Finally, the case-law of the Court of Justice concerning *ex officio* review in general and administrative proceedings will be analyzed, particularly examining how the requirement of *Rewe*-equivalence may be applied to national public policy norms (3.2.3.3).

783 Regarding for example the English, German and French rules, see S. Whittaker (2012), 6-22.

784 J. Engström (2008), 79.

785 This work does not deal with three important uses of public policy in the international and EU law context, namely public policy as an exception to obligations to recognize foreign judgments, public policy as basis for derogating from fundamental rights and public policy as basis for deviating from the Treaty-based freedoms of movement within the EU. This delimitation is not intended to indicate their lesser importance, but follows from the scope of my study, whose focus on procedural autonomy necessitates a focalization on the interplay of public policy with rules of national procedural law.

786 This notion of public policy is not entirely internal, i.e. based on national law, due to the oftentimes international nature of arbitration litigation.

3.2.3.1 Identifying procedural public policy via mandatory contract law

There are various roles for public policy in Member States' domestic procedural settings. Insofar as there exist rules in national law that private parties are precluded from waiving by private contract, there are corresponding responsibilities for national courts to ensure that the same rules not be evaded via litigation tactics. This responsibility of control will in some instances require a national court to take a more active stance than would otherwise follow from domestic procedural law. The public policy notion is here used to instruct civil courts not to enforce agreements that have been entered in breach of mandatory contract law governing the litigation, not to accept arbitration awards that enforce such contracts, and not to recognize foreign judgments that disregard mandatory law.[787] The reason for this lies in the necessity to safeguard specific interests which parties should not be allowed to set aside contractually.[788]

A traditional typological divide concerning the function of procedural public policy derogations is found between common law and continental law.[789] In the common law, it is often assumed that courts will remain passive and that the principle of *jura novit curia*[790] does not apply. Yet, common law courts will also of their own motion take into account points of public policy,[791] even in the absence of an autonomous definition of public policy or public order for this purpose.[792] In e.g. the UK, the notion of public policy latches onto the requirements for nullity or illegality of a contract: If a contract is illegal, it will not be enforced irrespective of whether any ground of illegality was invoked – entailing that it is up to the seized court to apply the mandatory law despite its absence in the submissions of the parties.[793]

---

787 S. Prechal and N. Shelkoplyas (2004), 602.

788 Ibid., 600.

789 F. C. de la Torre (2005), 397-99. J. H. Jans, R. de Lange, S. Prechal, and R. J. G. M. Widdershoven (2007), 308-16, emphasize that this divide should not be exaggerated.

790 The presumption that the courts know and will apply applicable law in its entirety irrespective of the legal bases invoked by parties. J. Engström (2008), 67.

791 Opinion of Advocate General Jacobs in *van Schijndel v. Stichting Pensioenfonds voor Fysiotherapeuten*, joined cases C-430/93 and C-431/93, EU:C:1995:185, 35-36.

792 T. Corthaut (2012), 18, 20.

793 "[I]f, from the plaintiff's own stating or otherwise, the cause of action appears to arise ex turpi causa, or the transgression of a positive law of this country, there the Court says he has no right to be assisted." Lord Mansfield in Judgment of the Court of King's Bench (UK) in *Holman v. Johnson*, (1775) 1 Cowp 341, per

Continental courts subscribe to the principle of *jura novit curia*, and therefore apply any appropriate rule based on the facts presented by the parties, while there are limits to the possibility of introducing new grounds – increasingly so with later stages of the proceedings.[794] This rule is sometimes provided with an exemption for pleas or grounds based on rules of public policy.[795] Under the same conditions, to safeguard public policy, it is also possible for courts to take into consideration legal bases not activated by the factual claims within the ambit of the proceedings.[796] For example, in the Netherlands, administrative courts are only allowed to examine grounds that have not been raised by the parties in the light of rules of public policy.[797] By contrast, in Swedish administrative proceedings, far-reaching discretion is conferred on the judge to investigate or review matters of law or fact which have not been invoked.[798] Even civil proceedings may in some cases be denoted "non-dispositive", meaning that there are other considerations, beyond the interests of the parties, vested in their outcome. The interests of the public would in this case correspond to "public policy" within the relevant meaning.[799]

The extent to which the notion of public policy surfaces in the context of *ex officio* review is thus dependent on the legal system of the Member State in question. Public policy rules of this nature vary in both function

Lord Mansfield, 343, cited in S. Whittaker (2012), 11. *Ex turpi causa non oritur action* lays down that a cause of action cannot arise from a dishonorable act or measure, thus precluding plaintiffs from pursuing legal remedies on the basis of their own unlawful actions. See e.g. C. Barnard and O. Odudu, *The Outer Limits of European Law* (Oxford: Hart Publishing, 2009), 419.

794 Although also usually in continental law systems, the subject-matter of the case limits the legal bases that can be considered by the court; J. Engström (2008), 67. Therefore, the dispositions of the parties play an important role in continental law as well; J. H. Jans, R. de Lange, S. Prechal, and R. J. G. M. Widdershoven (2007), 308-9.

795 E.g. in the Netherlands before higher courts and in France and Belgium before the *Cour de Cassation*.

796 T. Corthaut (2012), 18; S. Prechal and N. Shelkoplyas (2004), 599.

797 Art. 8:69 of the General Administrative Law Act of the Netherlands [*Algemene Wet Bestuursrecht*], wet van 4 juni 1992, als gewijzigd, cited in J. H. Jans, R. de Lange, S. Prechal, and R. J. G. M. Widdershoven (2007), 313.

798 U. von Essen (2009), 107ff.

799 Meaning that not only the rights and obligations of the parties are at stake, which is why the court cannot take into account solely the arguments invoked by the parties to the dispute whilst disregarding the effects of the decision on a third party or the wider public; ibid.

and origin and may be filled with both substantive and procedural content.[800]

The line between substantive and procedural public policy rules is not always clear-cut. For instance, the Dutch *Hoge Raad* in several instances asked the Court of Justice whether the possibility of *ex officio* review of matters of public policy, as follows from Dutch procedural law,[801] should be interpreted as including Union public policy.[802] Dutch reform of administrative procedure in 1994 substantially limited the possibilities of *ex officio* review – which were further narrowed down through legal precedents allowing administrative courts to supplement the facts of their own initiative on grounds of public policy only. Dutch public policy refers to matters of court jurisdiction, admissibility of the action, and competence of the administrative body whose decision is contested – which would normally preclude substantive public policy grounds such as the contested decision being contrary to applicable law. However, the possibility of reviewing the "competence" of the body having taken the contested decision was, on occasion, interpreted widely by Dutch courts so as to include lack of competence to render a substantively unlawful decision. The rationale would then be that if an administrative body grants an application that runs contrary to relevant substantive law, the unlawfulness of the decision would be considered equivalent to lack of competence to render the con-

800 Protective prerogatives are capable of justifying far-reaching court intervention in Swedish administrative proceedings where the substantive interests protected by relevant legislation patently fill the concept of public policy with a *substantive* content; C. Diesen and A. Lagerqvist Veloz Roca, *Bevis 7: Bevisprövning i förvaltningsmål* (Stockholm: Norstedts juridik, 2003), 86. In Dutch administrative procedure, the concept of public policy is, by contrast, filled with a *procedural* content. See e.g. J. H. Jans, R. de Lange, S. Prechal, and R. J. G. M. Widdershoven (2007), 313.

801 Under Dutch procedural law, national courts are required to remain within the subject-matter of the dispute before it. Art. 48 of the Code of Civil Procedure (Arbitration Act of the Netherlands – Code of Civil Procedure [*Wetboek van Burgerlijke Rechtsvordering (Rv) – Boek IV. Arbitrage*] wet van 1 december 1986, herziening van 2011) allows national courts to raise points of law of their own motion, but the fundamental principle governing civil procedure is nonetheless the principle of judge passivity.

802 The bulk of references on *ex officio* review have been referred by Dutch courts; e.g. CJEU judgment in *van Schijndel v. Stichting Pensioenfonds voor Fysiotherapeuten*, joined cases C-430/93 and C-431/93, EU:C:1995:441; CJEU judgment in *Eco Swiss China Time Ltd v. Benetton International NV*, C-126/97, EU:C:1999:269 and CJEU judgment in *van der Weerd and Others v. Minister van Landbouw, Natuur en Voedselkwaliteit*, joined cases C-222/05 to C-225/05, EU:C:2007:318.

tested decision.[803] The example illustrates how national notions of public policy with a procedural content give rise to powers of substantive review by functionalizing the notion of public policy.

If, under national law, courts are normally precluded from *ex officio* review, but there exist provisions for exceptional circumstances in which *ex officio* review is required or allowed, the ensuing question is how this provision can be functionalized to ensure that Union law be applied *ex officio*.[804] Various answers may be found in the case-law on national procedural autonomy, where the Court has sometimes taken upon itself to determine whether a national procedural rule has to be set aside by a national judge in order to ensure substantive Union public policy. As already seen, rules of judge passivity have been scrutinized with recourse to the *Rewe* formula paired with the procedural rule-of-reason.[805] This determination has presumed (on the basis of the principle of equivalence) the pre-existence of a national procedural rule allowing or instructing a national court to take into account, of its own motion, national rules of public policy: If private contracts that encroach on national public policy or order cannot be relied on to derogate from what follows from the general law, then it must equally be expected that Member States do not allow national procedural law to oblige courts to enforce contracts configured in breach of Union public policy.[806]

803 J. H. Jans and A. T. Marseille 234 (2009), 854-56.

804 As is seen in Art. 48 of the Procedural Code of the Netherlands. Recent case-law of the Court of Justice of the EU (discussed below) limits the possibilities of such functionalization, particularly as a matter of equivalence; CJEU judgment in *Abdelhafid Bensada Benallal v. État belge*, C-161/15, EU:C:2016:175, 34-35.

805 CJEU judgment in *van Schijndel v. Stichting Pensioenfonds voor Fysiotherapeuten*, joined cases C-430/93 and C-431/93, EU:C:1995:441, 13-14; S. Prechal, (1998), 690-93.

806 Taking e.g. consumer protection, where Art. 6(1) of the Unfair Terms Directive (Council Directive 93/13/EEC of 5 April 1993 on unfair terms in consumer contracts, Official Journal L 095, 21/04/1993, 29) prescribes that contract clauses corresponding to the directive's definition of unfair consumer terms not be binding on the consumer. The effect of nullity based on Union legislation would (at least in this context) trigger an obligation for national courts to set aside otherwise applicable rules on time-limits and preclusion of pleas; CJEU judgment in *Cofidis SA v. Jean-Louis Fredout*, C-473/00, EU:C:2002:705, 35-38; CJEU judgment in *Elisa María Mostaza Claro v. Centro Móvil Milenium SL*, C-168/05, EU:C:2006:675, 35-39.

3.2.3.2 Public policy in ordinary courts' review of arbitration awards

The notion of public policy may also arise in the context of national courts' review of arbitration awards in proceedings for annulment or enforcement – first of all, concerning what aspects are reviewable by ordinary courts, and second of all, regarding what matters may be examined *ex officio*.

The two aspects are interlinked, but they will nonetheless be distinguished in the present section. The question of which aspects of arbitration awards are reviewable by ordinary courts hinges on the notion of mandatory contract law, as examined in the previous section. For instance, the nature of the Union's prohibition on anti-competitive agreements under Art. 101 TFEU has been attributed importance for determining the public policy character of the said provision – making an award susceptible to substantive review in annulment or enforcement proceedings.[807]

Having established that an arbitration award should be annulled or cannot be enforced due to being contrary to public policy, one must refer to the national procedural framework to determine the conditions for *ex officio* review. Annulment based on substantive review of arbitration awards is normally highly limited – a key exception being so as to examine whether the award complies with public policy.[808] Mirroring the US Supreme

807 When the Court of Justice, in CJEU judgment in *Eco Swiss China Time Ltd v. Benetton International NV*, C-126/97, EU:C:1999:269, 36, referred to "fundamental provision which is essential for the accomplishment of the tasks entrusted to the Community", it was denoting the fact that the Treaty's cartel prohibition could not be set aside by parties agreeing to engage in anti-competitive practices.

808 In Dutch legislation, at issue in ibid., an arbitration award may be set aside under the Arbitration Act of the Netherlands – Code of Civil Procedure [*Wetboek van Burgerlijke Rechtsvordering (Rv) – Boek IV. Arbitrage*] wet van 1 december 1986, herziening van 2011, in the event that the award violates public policy. Art. 1065 of the Netherlands Code of Civil Procedure establishes that: "1. Setting aside of the award can take place only on one or more of the following grounds: (a) absence of a valid arbitration agreement; (b) the arbitral tribunal was constituted in violation of the rules applicable thereto; (c) the arbitral tribunal has not complied with its mandate; (d) the award is not signed or does not contain reasons in accordance with the provisions of Art. 1057; (e) the award, or the manner in which it was made, violates public policy or good morals." Translated in Y. Brulard and Y. Quintin, 'European Community Law and Arbitration – National Versus Community Public Policy', *J. Int'l Arb.*, 18 (2001), fn. 2.

Court with respect to the Sherman Act,[809] the Court of Justice has required national courts to safeguard Union public policy by reviewing of their own motion whether the arbitration award complied with Union competition law, even though national procedural law required seized judges to abstain from reviewing arbitration awards in substance: national courts, in their role as guardians of Union law, must ensure that Union competition law not be circumvented by parties choosing arbitration over ordinary court litigation.[810]

An award delivered by an arbitral tribunal can also come before an ordinary court seized by an individual who seeks enforcement against his counter-party. Similarly to the context of international private law public policy, the underlying idea is to carry out limited review, in order to ensure some level of predictability for parties who have chosen to litigate via arbitration, by cutting short the cycle of appeals.[811] Also in national litigation, courts seized to enforce arbitration awards are sometimes required by national law to abstain from doing so if their enforcement would run contrary to public policy. As e.g. anti-competitive agreements are sanctioned by absolute nullity, it is up to regular courts to ensure that they are not enforced for the sole reason that the parties concede to the lawfulness or validity of the agreement.[812] This test corresponds to that carried out in the aforementioned context of annulment of arbitration awards.

3.2.3.3 Procedural public policy in the case-law of the Court of Justice

The national procedural rules described in the previous sections illustrate the problems arising in identifying on the one hand, what is the content or origin of public policy, and on the other hand, how to deal with it. These difficulties are exacerbated in their encounter with Union law prerogatives, as illustrated by numerous preliminary references asking whether certain matters of EU law carry such importance that they must be applied *ex officio*, even when the national court is precluded from considering them of its own motion. The present section examines the extent to which

809 US Supreme Court in *Mitsubishi Motors Corporation v. Soler Chrysler Plymouth*, Inc., 473 U.S. 614, 628 (1985).

810 CJEU judgment in *Eco Swiss China Time Ltd v. Benetton International NV*, C-126/97, EU:C:1999:269; see Y. Brulard and Y. Quintin (2001), 532-33.

811 T. Corthaut (2012), 25.

812 Y. Brulard and Y. Quintin (2001), 537-38.

the Court of Justice has been willing, in the context of considering claims based on EU law, to allow the national judge to fill the concept of public policy with a domestic content as foreseen by national law.

EU competition law had not been regarded in *van Schijndel* as belonging to public policy, and therefore not as capable of justifying deviation from the ambit of the proceedings, similarly to the way in which other public policy concepts would have been under Dutch procedural law.[813] In *Kraaijeveld*,[814] the Court of Justice subsequently opened a door to aligning Union environmental protection requirements with national "binding" rules, albeit under the condition that national law provide a procedural public policy exception for the purpose of *ex officio* review.[815] In the controversial case of *Eco Swiss*, a court of the Netherlands requested that the Court of Justice address the relationship between public policy under national procedural law applicable to ordinary courts' review of arbitration awards,[816] and Union public policy, particularly Union competition law.[817] The ruling in *Eco Swiss* aligned with *Kraaijeveld*, indicating that also with regard to *ex officio* review of arbitration awards, the dividing point is *whether* there exists a public policy exception under national law, apparent-

813 CJEU judgment in *van Schijndel v. Stichting Pensioenfonds voor Fysiotherapeuten*, joined cases C-430/93 and C-431/93, EU:C:1995:441; see comments in S. Prechal and N. Shelkoplyas (2004), 603. Whereas the question had also been posed in CJEU judgment in *Peterbroeck, Van Campenhout & Cie v. Belgian State*, C-312/93, EU:C:1995:437, 11, the Court of Justice there left it unanswered (22).

814 CJEU judgment in *Aannemersbedrijf P.K. Kraaijeveld BV e.a. v. Gedeputeerde Staten van Zuid-Holland*, C-72/95, EU:C:1996:404; see comments by M. Dougan (2004), 41-45; A. Beka (2018), 56; T. Tridimas and P. Nebbia, *European Union Law for the Twenty-First Century. Rethinking the New Legal Order* (Oregon: Hart Publishing, 2004), 226-32; P. Wennerås (2007), 123, 77; A. Rosas, E. Levits, and Y. Bot (2013), 71, 297; A. Wallerman (2016), 347ff.

815 CJEU judgment in *Aannemersbedrijf P.K. Kraaijeveld BV e.a. v. Gedeputeerde Staten van Zuid-Holland*, C-72/95, EU:C:1996:404, 57-62. This reasoning was recalled in e.g. the Opinion of Advocate General Mengozzi in *Abdelhafid Bensada Benallal v. État belge*, C-161/15, EU:C:2016:3, 52-53, in order to propose that Union public policy norms be "ranked" in reference to national categories of public policy, as part of the equivalence test.

816 Art. 1065 of the Netherlands Code of Civil Procedure.

817 The referring court had in this case taken the view that the public policy exception was applicable only to awards whose "terms or enforcement conflict with a mandatory rule so fundamental that no restrictions of procedural nature should prevent its application", this normally not meaning that anti-competitive agreements are contrary to Dutch public policy within the meaning of Art. 1065 of the Netherlands Code of Civil Procedure. CJEU judgment in *Eco Swiss China Time Ltd v. Benetton International NV*, C-126/97, EU:C:1999:269, 24.

ly attaching no importance to the national content with which this provision is filled.[818]

The possibility of substituting Union public policy for national procedural public policy would ultimately be resolved via the principle of equivalence – in other words, not boiling down to a balancing test between effectiveness and procedural protection, but to non-discrimination between claims based on national and Union law. A first indication of this came in *van der Weerd*,[819] where the Court clarified that *Eco Swiss* had hinged on the principle of equivalence – for which a conservative rule of application was prescribed (which is nonetheless difficult to reconcile with the path actually taken in *Eco Swiss*).[820] The turbulence that this divergent case-law gave rise to, settled through the ruling in *Benallal*,[821] in response to the question as to whether the right to be heard constitutes Union public policy for the purposes of a procedural public policy exception in Belgian law.

Interestingly, the Advocate General in *Benallal* had given a different interpretation of the ruling in *van der Weerd*, by extending equivalent treatment to rules of equivalent "ranking", rather than equivalent substance:

> Although domestic rules of procedure are more stringent and make the examination of a plea of a court's own motion conditional on the rule of domestic law which was infringed being classified as a public policy rule, a plea alleging infringement of EU law must also, if it is to be treated in an equivalent man-

818 Ibid., 36-37. The difference in approach *vis-à-vis van Schijndel* has also been understood to imply that standard court proceedings may be dealt with differently than arbitration awards; J. H. Jans, R. de Lange, S. Prechal, and R. J. G. M. Widdershoven (2007), 308-16.

819 CJEU judgment in *van der Weerd and Others v. Minister van Landbouw, Natuur en Voedselkwaliteit*, joined cases C-222/05 to C-225/05, EU:C:2007:318. See further X. Groussot (2008), 8ff.

820 The relevant public policy notion only pertained to matters of admissibility and powers of the courts and administrative bodies (i.e. fundamental procedural aspects), whereas the protective provisions contained in the Union secondary legislation were of substantive rather than procedural character. Therefore, the Court found that "[t]hose provisions cannot [...] be considered as being equivalent to the national rules of public policy referred to above." CJEU judgment in *van der Weerd and Others v. Minister van Landbouw, Natuur en Voedselkwaliteit*, joined cases C-222/05 to C-225/05, EU:C:2007:318, 31.

821 CJEU judgment in *Abdelhafid Bensada Benallal v. État belge*, C-161/15, EU:C:2016:175; cf. X. Groussot, G. T. Petursson, and J. Hettne, 'General Principles and the Many Faces of Coherence: Between Law and Ideology in the European Union', *Lund University Legal Research Paper Series*, (2016), 14.

ner by national courts, allege infringement of a rule which occupies a 'similar position' or is of the 'same ranking' under EU law.[822]

The question referred in *Benallal* had the potential of giving rise to notable tensions, had the Court of Justice endorsed this method of ranking rules of EU law by recourse to normative hierarchies in national law. Instead, the judgment in *Benallal* affirmed the narrow understanding of the equivalence test laid down in *van der Weerd*,[823] so as to require *ex officio* review *only* when, under similar circumstances, the same would have been required under national law, taking into account the *content* (rather than the ranking) of the domestic notion of public policy.[824]

In conclusion, the relevant test of equivalent treatment of national and Union public policy rules does not trigger the tensions foreseen in the first research question,[825] in view of the course that the case-law has taken. While earlier case-law had indicated that national public policy exceptions from *ex officio* review must be extended to a vast category of mandatory EU law,[826] later case-law would maintain a narrow and conservative approach to equivalence.[827] Although the designation of a particular rule as belonging to public policy embodies a key justification of exceptional *ex officio* review, that particular perspective does not arise when applying the equivalence test.

822 Opinion of Advocate General Mengozzi in *Abdelhafid Bensada Benallal v. État belge*, C-161/15, EU:C:2016:3, 54.

823 The Belgian definition of public policy for the purposes of allowing *ex officio* review is wider than the Dutch definition at issue in the *van der Weerd* case; the Belgian version including individual procedural protection contained in the rights of defense and other fundamental rights, whereas the Dutch rule allowing a court of appeal to more narrowly review matters of competence and jurisdiction.

824 I.e. equivalence in terms of similarity of purpose and cause of action, as laid down in CJEU judgment in *ET Agrokonsulting-04-Velko Stoyanov v. Izpalnitelen direktor na Darzhaven fond «Zemedelie» - Razplashtatelna agentsia*, C-93/12, EU:C:2013:432, 39. The method of comparison is systematically explained in Opinion of Advocate General Maduro in *van der Weerd and Others v. Minister van Landbouw, Natuur en Voedselkwaliteit*, joined cases C-222/05 to C-225/05, EU:C:2007:124, 33-41.

825 *How is the balance struck between substantive and procedural protection in the Court of Justice's case-law on* ex officio *review?*

826 CJEU judgment in *Eco Swiss China Time Ltd v. Benetton International NV*, C-126/97, EU:C:1999:269.

827 CJEU judgment in *Abdelhafid Bensada Benallal v. État belge*, C-161/15, EU:C:2016:175.

Based on the latter understanding, for the purposes of weighing effectiveness of Union law against effective judicial protection of litigants, the public policy status of the relevant rule can no longer be regarded as a key factor. This prediction is made with respect to the vast procedural context affected by the above-described case-law: administrative proceedings, civil litigation and ordinary courts' review of arbitration awards. By contrast, the same cannot be said of the field of EU consumer protection law – whether the litigation concerns summary proceedings, ordinary civil litigation or arbitration awards, efforts have been made to encourage *ex officio* review to the benefit of consumers. The protective prerogatives in consumer-to-business litigation (to be addressed in the forthcoming section) have crystallized as a potential form of EU public policy with capacity to impel *ex officio* review.[828]

3.2.4 Protection of the weaker party in consumer-to-business litigation

The ambitious endeavor of consumer protection under EU law is characterized by three specificities necessary to consider in their legislative context: harmonization at the EU level, resulting diminution of Member State competence, and an explicit protective prerogative governing both secondary law and the case-law of the Court of Justice:

1. The EU legislative field is exceptional in depth and reach, thus far achieved through wide-ranging harmonization. We have seen two types of harmonization with stark implications for consumer litigation within the Member States: increasing legislative activity within the field of judicial co-operation in civil matters, and important movements towards harmonization of procedure through sector-specific competence bases ("sectoral proceduralization"[829]). The main goals of EU consumer legislation were originally of substantive character, in the spirit of protection against e.g. unfair advertisement, distance contracts, unfair consumer clauses, unfair credit clauses etc. Although the protective prerogatives were embedded in favorable substantive treatment of consumers in legal relationships with business contract partners, the original idea

828 See e.g. CJEU judgment in *Pohotovosť s.r.o. v. Iveta Korčkovská (I)*, C-76/10, EU:C:2010:685, 49-51, CJEU judgment in *Gutiérrez Naranjo and Others*, joined cases C-154/15, C-307/15 and C-308/15, EU:C:2016:980, 53-55, CJEU judgment in *Banco Primus SA v. Jesús Gutiérrez García*, C-421/14, EU:C:2017:60, 40-43.

829 M. Tulibacka (2015).

was that legal redress on the basis of the secondary legislation – including court litigation – was to be governed by Member State procedural law as would normally follow from the principle of national procedural autonomy.[830] The reality of consumer litigation would however, with time, reveal that national procedural law could not be counted on to provide sufficient protection of consumers, let alone correct implementation of the applicable Union legislation.[831] As a result, consumer law is an area in which EU regulation has reached one of its most extensive levels of legal integration through substantive, sectoral measures, with a clear emphasis on ancillary procedural issues such as access to court.[832] Harmonization is not based on a unified legislative act, but rather dispersed through a variety of instruments addressing various contexts; still, there is a singular focus to match the enforcement of rights with the provision of remedies.[833]

2. The reach of this legislation has the effect of restricting the Member States' remaining discretion, i.e. procedural autonomy. Even though rules dealing with the modalities of consumer adjudication *prima facie* fall within the area of national procedural autonomy, this is one area in which it can less easily be argued that procedural autonomy is to be exercised "in the absence of Community rules on the subject".[834] The remaining competence of the Member States is thus more strongly circumscribed than in procedural law applicable to other types of litigation.[835]

3. Consumer adjudication is an instance of procedural "special treatment", both under the national law of many Member States and under

---

830 E. Storskrubb (2008), 28.

831 J. Lindholm, "DCFR, Please Meet National Procedure': Enforcing the Frame of Reference Using National Procedural Law', in *The Foundations of European Private Law*, eds. Brownsword, R., H.-W. Micklitz, L. Niglia, and S. Weatherill (Oxford: Hart, 2011); M. Loos, 'Individual Private Enforcement of Consumer Rights in Civil Courts in Europe', in ibid.

832 E. Storskrubb (2008), 27; S. Law, 'The Transformation of Consumer Law in Times of Crisis: The Ex Officio Control of Unfair Contract Terms', in *Transformation of Civil Justice*, eds. Uzelac A. and C. van Rhee (Chem: Springer, 2018), 284-87.

833 F. Wilman, (2015), 146.

834 CJEU judgment in *Rewe v. Landwirtschaftskammer für das Saarland*, 33/76, EU:C:1976:188, 5; CJEU judgment in *Comet BV v. Produktschap voor Siergewassen*, 45/76, EU:C:1976:191, 13.

835 S. Weatherill (2011).

EU law, comprising protective elements of both procedural and contractual/substantive character.[836] The reason for special treatment is straightforward: We are in an emblematic "poor client" dilemma, discussed conceptually in section 3.1.1 above – a matter of increased urgency in the wake of the 2008 financial crisis which hit consumers particularly hard.[837] This protective prerogative is enshrined throughout the legislative framework as well as throughout the case-law in which it is interpreted, giving rise to a special emphasis on legal remedies as common denominator and key objective.

The forthcoming sections consider the consumer protection prerogative in terms of its consequences for national judges' EU law mandate of *ex officio* review. Section 3.2.4.1 introduces the origins and legal basis of the *ex officio* mandate. The latter's reach would follow the substantive scope of EU consumer legislation (3.2.4.2) in which national courts' power to examine e.g. unfair consumer terms would successively be developed into an obligation (3.2.4.3). Although the protective prerogative is increasingly denoted as EU public policy, its effect at the decentralized level hinges on the existence of national public policy exceptions that permit *ex officio* review in the first place. Section 3.2.4.4 will describe how the national comparator for the equivalence principle was construed relatively extensively in the consumer case-law, as compared to the restrictive test developed in the general case-law. Section 3.2.4.5 will consider the avenues for justification of encroachments on the *ex officio* mandate, which have increasingly emphasized a fundamental rights perspective above and beyond the *Rewe* formula.

The choices made in the case-law examined below were founded on two perspectives on consumer litigation, which shape the ideology of EU policy within the area. The first view (a bottom-up perspective) emphasizes the role of individual consumers as guardians of the collective interest of upholding Union law, including Union consumer policy. By contrast, the top-down perspective designates the protection of vulnerable litigants as autonomous objective of the adjudication. The final section (3.2.4.6) considers these collective and individual rationales behind the consumer imperative.

---

836 E. Storskrubb (2008), 27; C. Warin (2019), 476.

837 S. Law (2018), 284.

3.2.4.1 Origins of the Union mandate of *ex officio* review in consumer litigation

The seminal case on *ex officio* review in consumer litigation was *Océano*,[838] where the seized court of first instance had referred the matter of its own jurisdiction by virtue of the Unfair Terms Directive[839] to the Court of Justice. Since summons had not been served on the defendant consumer before a preliminary reference was made, the national court's consideration of its own jurisdiction had to be carried out *ex officio*, an exercise tainted with ambiguity under Spanish jurisprudence.[840]

The Opinion had entertained a critical discussion on the proposition that a defendant, not having appeared before the national court, should forgo his right to invoke lack of jurisdiction.[841] In the view of the Advocate General, it would be consistent with the overall spirit of the directive "to preclude the attachment of decisive significance to the consumer's behavior in court proceedings",[842] e.g. the failure to invoke unfairness of a contract term. In the case of unfair jurisdictional clauses, assigning such responsibility to a consumer would give rise to a paradox; obliging the consumer to defend his case before a court far away from his place of domicile for the precise purpose of challenging the clause obliging him to do so.[843] This reasoning was the first intimation that the protective prerogative could entail an exception from the procedural dictum of *ius vigilantibus*

838 CJEU judgment in *Océano Grupo Editorial and Salvat Editores*, joined cases C-240/98 to C-244/98, EU:C:2000:346; see further M. Ebers, 'ECJ (First Chamber) 6 October 2009, Case C-40/08, Asturcom Telecomunicaciones SL v. Cristina Rodríguez Nogueira – From Océano to Asturcom: Mandatory Consumer Law, *Ex officio* Application of European Union Law and *Res judicata*', *Eur. Rev. Pr. L.*, (2010), 195; A. Beka (2018), 130-43; S. Weatherill 'Interpretation of the Directives: The Role of the Court', in *Towards a European Civil Code*, eds. Hartkamp, A. S., M. Hesselink, E. H. Hondius, C. Mak and E. du Perron (Alphen aan den Rijn: Kluwer, 2011); A. Wallerman (2019), Ch. 3.1.

839 Council Directive 93/13/EEC of 5 April 1993 on unfair terms in consumer contracts, Official Journal L 095, 21/04/1993, 29.

840 CJEU judgment in *Océano Grupo Editorial and Salvat Editores*, joined cases C-240/98 to C-244/98, EU:C:2000:346, 18.

841 Opinion of Advocate General Saggio in *Océano Grupo Editorial and Salvat Editores*, joined cases C-240/98 to C-244/98, EU:C:1999:620, 21.

842 Ibid., 23.

843 Ibid., 24.

scriptum est ("use it or lose it") which by default places the responsibility with the defendant to explicitly raise jurisdictional objections.[844]

The Court of Justice followed the overall lead of the Advocate General, responding that the jurisdiction clause constituted an unfair contract term within the meaning of the Directive, which precludes terms having as object or producing the effect of "excluding or hindering the consumer's right to take legal action or exercise any other legal remedy."[845] Although the directive did not include any particular provision explicitly requiring a national court to examine its jurisdiction *ex officio*,[846] the Court of Justice concurred that many consumers would not know to challenge the jurisdiction of the seized court.[847] To ensure that unfair jurisdictional clauses were not applied contrary to the Directive, the Court of Justice held that "effective protection of the consumer may be attained only if the national court acknowledges that it has power to evaluate terms of this kind of its own motion."[848]

The *Océano* judgment had not specified a legal basis separate from the Unfair Terms Directive for the mandate of *ex officio* review, referring mainly to the "system of protection" offered by the latter.[849] Although subse-

---

844 Cf. CJEU Judgment in *VB Pénzügyi Lízing Zrt. v. Ferenc Schneider*, C-137/08, EU:C:2010:659, 52-56.

845 Art. 1(q), Annex to Council Directive 93/13/EEC of 5 April 1993 on unfair terms in consumer contracts, Official Journal L 095, 21/04/1993, 29.

846 Unlike the Convention of 27 September 1968 on jurisdiction and the enforcement of judgments in civil and commercial matters (Brussels Convention), OJ L 299, 31/12/1972, see CJEU judgment in *Ferdinand M.J.J. Duijnstee v. Lodewijk Goderbauer*, 288/82, EU:C:1983:326.

847 By contrast, if the defendant *does* enter an appearance without contesting jurisdiction, the seized court is not obliged to ascertain of its own motion whether the defendant was aware of or intended to tacitly accept jurisdiction, provided that a basis for tacit prorogation rule is explicitly provided in applicable secondary law; CJEU judgment in *Česká podnikatelská pojišťovna as, Vienna Insurance Group v. Michal Bilas*, C-111/09, EU:C:2010:290.

848 CJEU judgment in *Océano Grupo Editorial and Salvat Editores,* joined cases C-240/98 to C-244/98, EU:C:2000:346, 27.

849 Although the duty of sincere co-operation was denoted in reference to the implementation period of the Directive (CJEU judgment in *Océano Grupo Editorial and Salvat Editores*, joined cases C-240/98 to C-244/98, EU:C:2000:346, 30-32), the Directive itself represented the legal basis for the duty of *ex officio* review (26-29).

quent case-law shows some variation in this respect,[850] the *Rewe* formula in its "excessively difficult" threshold would be adopted at an early stage, for a long time designating the duty of sincere co-operation as preferred legal basis.[851]

3.2.4.2 Substantive scope of the *ex officio* mandate

That the spirit of the Unfair Terms Directive requires national courts to review unfair consumer clauses of their own motion has since been upheld in reference to unfair jurisdictional clauses,[852] although jurisdictional rules unfavorable to consumers do not in all circumstances need to be set aside.[853]

The Court's interpretation of the Unfair Terms Directive would be transposed both to the enforcement of other unfair consumer terms than jurisdiction clauses,[854] and to other EU instruments whose underlying ob-

850 E.g. reverting to the principle of full effectiveness in CJEU judgment in *Rampion and Godard*, C-429/05, EU:C:2007:575, 61-65; CJEU judgment in *Pannon GSM Zrt. v. Erzsébet Sustikné Győrfi*, C-243/08, EU:C:2009:350, 32; CJEU judgment in *Banif Plus Bank Zrt v. Csaba Csipai*, C-472/11, EU:C:2013:88, 28 (the latter denoting *Rewe*-effectiveness, full effectiveness as well as effective judicial protection).

851 CJEU judgment in *Cofidis SA v. Jean-Louis Fredout*, C-473/00, EU:C:2002:705, 36-37; CJEU judgment in *Asturcom Telecomunicaciones SL v. Cristina Rodríguez Nogueira*, C-40/08, EU:C:2009:615, 39-48; CJEU judgment in *Asociación de Consumidores Independientes de Castilla y León*, C-413/12, EU:C:2010:739, 30, 53; CJEU judgment in *BBVA SA v. Pedro Peñalva López*, C-8/14, EU:C:2015:731, 40-41, CJEU judgment in *Jorge Sales Sinués v. Caixabank*, joined cases C-381/14 and 385/14, EU:C:2016:252, 34-41.

852 CJEU judgment in *Pannon GSM Zrt. v. Erzsébet Sustikné Győrfi*, C-243/08, EU:C:2009:350, 41-44; CJEU Judgment in *VB Pénzügyi Lízing Zrt. v. Ferenc Schneider*, C-137/08, EU:C:2010:659.

853 CJEU judgment in *Erika Jőrös v. Aegon Magyarország Hitel Zrt.*, C-397/11, EU:C:2013:340, 52-53; CJEU judgment in *Baczó and Vizsnyiczai*, C-567/13, EU:C:2015:88, 59.

854 CJEU judgment in *Cofidis SA v. Jean-Louis Fredout*, C-473/00, EU:C:2002:705, 32-36; CJEU judgment in *Dirk Frederik Asbeek Brusse*, C-488/11, EU:C:2013:341, 34 (consumer-to-business tenacy contracts); CJEU judgment in *Elisa María Mostaza Claro v. Centro Móvil Milenium SL*, C-168/05, EU:C:2006:675, 28-30 (arbitration clauses).

jectives correspond to those of the Directive.[855] Consequently, within the scope of application of Union legislation serving the consumer protective prerogative, be it consumer credit[856] distance sales[857] or consumer sales,[858] national courts must, in principle, be free to review the validity of unfair consumer clauses.

Amid recent controversy concerning the division of responsibility for *ex officio* review between court instances on the one hand and enforcement authorities and other administrative instances on the other, the Court has nevertheless revealed that the reach of *Océano* is not without limit. This case-law essentially indicates that the *ex officio* mandate must be carried out at some stage of the proceedings, while consumers do not have an unfettered right to have a contract's compliance checked against the unfair terms directive at the stage of their choice, or for that matter, at all stages.[859] While the protective prerogative requires that courts, if necessary of their own motion, supplement the review carried out by other organs,[860] registrars etc. belonging to the latter category have ultimately not been required to autonomously carry out *ex officio* review.[861]

855 CJEU judgment in *Rampion and Godard,* C-429/05, EU:C:2007:575, 62-63: the reason for prescribing *ex officio* review of unfair consumer terms, is the element of risk that the consumer is "unaware of his rights or may encounter difficulties in exercising them" which could also be said of the protection provided by the Consumer Credit Directive; cf Opinion of Advocate General *Mengozzi* in *Rampion and Godard,* C-429/05, EU:C:2007:199, 102ff.

856 CJEU judgment in *Rampion and Godard,* C-429/05, EU:C:2007:575, 62-63.

857 CJEU judgment in *Eva Martín Martín v. EDP Editores SL,* C-227/08, EU:C:2009:792.

858 CJEU judgment in *Froukje Faber,* C-497/13, EU:C:2015:357, 42-48; CJEU judgment in *Soledad Duarte Heuros*, C-32/12, EU:C:2013:637, 40-43.

859 CJEU judgment in *Finanmadrid EFC SA v. Jesús Vicente Albán Zambrano and Others*, C-49/14, EU:C:2016:98, 45; CJEU judgment in *EOS KSI Slovensko*, C-448/17, EU:C:2018:745, 49.

860 CJEU judgment in *Finanmadrid EFC SA v. Jesús Vicente Albán Zambrano and Others*, C-49/14, EU:C:2016:98; CJEU judgment in *ERSTE Bank Hungary Zrt. v. Attila Sugár,* C-32/14, EU:C:2015:637; CJEU judgment in *EOS KSI Slovensko*, C-448/17, EU:C:2018:745.

861 CJEU judgment in *ERSTE Bank Hungary Zrt. v. Attila Sugár,* C-32/14, EU:C:2015:637; CJEU judgment in *Ramón Margarit Panicello*, C-503/15, EU:C:2017:126, 42.

3.2.4.3 *Ex officio* review as mandatory Union mandate

Having addressed the scope of the *Océano* doctrine, we return to the issue of power versus obligation of *ex officio* review which, for consumer protection purposes, was first entertained in *Rampion*. A French tribunal had consulted the Court of Justice on the objective and aim of the Consumer Credit Directive, acknowledging that it was allowed to apply the relevant provisions of its own motion, as soon as a Union objective in the category of *règles d'ordre public de direction* could be established.[862] Case-law of the French *Cour de cassation* draws a distinction between two types of public policy rules: *règles d'ordre public de protection* and *règles d'ordre public de direction*. The first category applies to rules protecting specific groups; litigants belonging to the designated category of protection may raise arguments relating to such rules of protection. The second set of rules is adopted to observe a general interest and may therefore be raised by a court of its own motion.[863] Since consumer credit law belongs within the first category according to the French typology, courts would be precluded from raising it *ex officio*.

The Court of Justice, having additionally assigned consumer protection to the second category (*ordre public de direction*), responded that the Directive "must be interpreted as *allowing* national courts to apply of their own motion the provisions transposing Art. 11(2) of Directive 87/102".[864] Considering that the French legislation only precluded *ex officio* review for the purposes of *règles d'ordre public de protection*, the use of the term "allowing" was appropriate yet abstruse; a response as to whether national designations which in circumstances such as those at hand precluded *ex officio* review could be *tolerated* might have been more to the point. Similar facultative language has also been employed in cases where the referring court essentially asked whether EU law *permitted* it to take protective measures to benefit consumer litigants.[865]

In the ruling in *Pannon*, it would in any event be spelled out with regards to measures necessary to reach the consumer legislation's minimum

862 CJEU judgment in *Rampion and Godard*, C-429/05, EU:C:2007:575, 16.

863 Ibid., 58.

864 Ibid., 69 (here emphasized).

865 CJEU judgment in *Eva Martín Martín v. EDP Editores SL*, C-227/08, EU:C:2009:792, 34-36; CJEU judgment in *Jana Pereničová and Vladislav Perenič*, C-453/10, EU:C:2012:144, 34-35.

requirements that Member State courts' *ex officio* mandate is in fact an obligation:[866]

> The role thus attributed to the national court by Community law in this area is not limited to a mere power to rule on the possible unfairness of a contractual term, but also consists of the obligation to examine that issue of its own motion [...]

Considering that *ex officio* review of jurisdiction was time-barred and would have necessitated national procedural law to be set aside in the circumstances at issue,[867] the above formula reached beyond the limited use of conform interpretation of national law. The Court of Justice has since favored a language of obligation – both in cases where seized national courts were required to act outside their powers under national law, and in situations where national courts' *power or discretion* under national law was functionalized into a Union law *obligation* of *ex officio* review.[868] For instance, in *Banco Español* a national court's lack of power under national legislation did not stop the Court of Justice from requiring review of its own motion.[869] The solution is more far-reaching than the general case-law on the relationship between discretion under national law and obligation under Union law,[870] especially in instances where *ex officio* review has been formulated as an obligation even without considering avenues for justification foreseen by the procedural rule-of-reason.[871]

By contrast, in case-law concerning review of arbitration awards (considered in the forthcoming section), the principle of equivalence was understood as requiring a national court to review the unfairness of an arbitration clause *only to the extent* that the court has the power to carry out an

866 CJEU judgment in *Pannon GSM Zrt. v. Erzsébet Sustikné Győrfi*, C-243/08, EU:C:2009:350, 32.

867 Ibid., 18-19, 27.

868 CJEU judgment in *Asturcom Telecomunicaciones SL v. Cristina Rodríguez Nogueira*, C-40/08, EU:C:2009:615, 53, 59; CJEU judgment in *Pohotovosť s.r.o. v. Iveta Korčkovská (I)*, C-76/10, EU:C:2010:685, 51-53. See also S. Law (2018), 305.

869 CJEU judgment in *Banco Español de Crédito SA v. Joaquín Calderón Camino*, C-618/10, EU:C:2012:349, 43, 57; see also CJEU judgment in *Banif Plus Bank Zrt v. Csaba Csipai*, C-472/11, EU:C:2013:88, 23.

870 Cf. CJEU judgment in *van Schijndel v. Stichting Pensioenfonds voor Fysiotherapeuten*, joined cases C-430/93 and C-431/93, EU:C:1995:441 and CJEU judgment in *Kühne & Heitz NV v. Produktschap voor Pluimvee en Eieren*, C-453/00, EU:C:2004:17, discussed earlier in this chapter.

871 CJEU judgment in *Pannon GSM Zrt. v. Erzsébet Sustikné Győrfi*, C-243/08, EU:C:2009:350, 32-35; CJEU judgment in *EOS KSI Slovensko*, C-448/17, EU:C:2018:745.

equivalent review in similar actions of domestic nature under national rules of procedure.[872] This solution prescribes an obligation of *ex officio* review in cases "where the domestic legal system grants a national court a discretion to consider of its own motion whether such a clause is in conflict with national public policy rules"[873] and has, as is familiar, been confirmed as the appropriate equivalence test for claims based on Union public policy outside the field of consumer law.[874]

In conclusion, the examined case-law did not modify the second tier of the *van Schijndel* formula (*may* = *must*), indicating that any level of discretion remaining in the hands of the national judges must be functionalized to safeguard the consumer protective prerogative. On the other hand, the relevant case-law has made it more difficult for Member State legislatures to circumvent the requirements following from EU consumer law by choosing mandatory (instead of facultative) legislative formulas.[875] By precluding national obstacles to *ex officio* review without considering possible justifications, the third tier of the *van Schijndel* formula (*may not* = *must not*) has been modified for the present purposes, inhibiting the autonomy otherwise retained by the domestic legislature. In most cases, obstacles to *ex officio* review have nonetheless been disallowed only after applying the procedural rule-of-reason, i.e. remaining within the *van Schijndel* framework.[876]

872 CJEU judgment in *Asturcom Telecomunicaciones SL v. Cristina Rodríguez Nogueira*, C-40/08, EU:C:2009:615, 52, 57-59.

873 M. Ebers (2010), 835. See also H. L. MacQueen, 'Illegality and Immorality in Contracts: Towards European Principles', in *Towards a European Civil Code*, ed. Hartkamp, A. S., M. Hesselink, E. H. Hondius, C. Mak, and E. du Perron (Alphen aan den Rijn: Kluwer, 2011) on mandatory rules for illegality of contracts as basis for Union public policy.

874 CJEU judgment in *Abdelhafid Bensada Benallal v. État belge*, C-161/15, EU:C:2016:175.

875 Cf. Wallerman (2016).

876 CJEU judgment in *Sanchez Morcillo and Abril García (I)*, C-169/14, EU:C:2014:2099, 34; CJEU judgment in *Pohotovosť s. r. o. v. Miroslav Vašuta (II)*, C-470/12, EU:C:2014:101, 51; CJEU judgment in *Baczó and Vizsnyiczai*, C-567/13, EU:C:2015:88, 49; CJEU judgment in *Finanmadrid EFC SA v. Jesús Vicente Albán Zambrano and Others*, C-49/14, EU:C:2016:98, 43-46.

3.2.4.4 Consumer protection as Union public policy

Already in the *Océano* Opinion, a classification of "mandatory rules of economic public policy" had been derived from the requirement of ensuring that unfair consumer clauses be treated as non-binding.[877] While the initial case-law following *Océano* had been preoccupied with the scope of protection of consumers enshrined in secondary EU law, legal typologies in national frameworks successively triggered the question whether the *ex officio* mandate in fact hinged on a common notion of consumer protection as public policy.[878]

In the above-discussed *Rampion* case, the referring court had asked whether the objective of the Consumer Credit Directive "extends beyond consumer protection alone to the organization of the market".[879] The Court and the Advocate General concurred that the Consumer Credit Directive was adopted for dual purposes; the creation of a common consumer credit market (corresponding to *ordre public de direction*) as well as "the protection of consumers who avail themselves of such credit" (corresponding to *ordre public de protection*).[880] This response would, as is familiar, have allowed the French tribunal to consider the relevant rules of its own motion, as rules of *ordre public de direction* may be raised *ex officio* according to the French case-law. However, the *ex officio* mandate in *Rampion* hinged on procedural labels occurring in the French legal tradition, whereas the understanding of consumer protection as common public policy would have implications for any legal tradition allowing *ex officio* review in order to safeguard public policy rules.

The consequences of public policy designations are most palpable in arbitration proceedings, where substantive review is in most jurisdictions limited to instances of public policy violations. In *Mostaza*, delivered a year earlier, the Court of Justice had recalled that *if* domestic rules prescribe deviation from normal review standards for purposes of upholding rules of national public policy, then the *Eco Swiss* dictum required that such ex-

877 Opinion of Advocate General Saggio in *Océano Grupo Editorial and Salvat Editores*, joined cases C-240/98 to C-244/98, EU:C:1999:620, 25-26.

878 CJEU judgment in *Elisa María Mostaza Claro v. Centro Móvil Milenium SL*, C-168/05, EU:C:2006:675, 34-38; CJEU judgment in *Asturcom Telecomunicaciones SL v. Cristina Rodríguez Nogueira*, C-40/08, EU:C:2009:615, 52-55; CJEU judgment in *Pohotovosť s.r.o. v. Iveta Korčkovská (I)*, C-76/10, EU:C:2010:685, 50-51.

879 CJEU judgment in *Rampion and Godard*, C-429/05, EU:C:2007:575, 16.

880 Ibid., 59; see also Opinion of Advocate General *Mengozzi* in *Rampion and Godard*, C-429/05, EU:C:2007:199, 88.

emptions be applied also for the purpose of safeguarding Union public policy.[881] In *Eco Swiss*, the ensuing nullity/voidness of anti-competitive market arrangements had served as an indicator of the public policy status of Art. 101 TFEU.[882] The mandatory character of the consumer protection prerogative was, in turn, indicated by the fact that unfair consumer clauses shall not be binding on the consumer according to the wording of the Unfair Terms Directive, whose protection was deemed "essential to the accomplishment of the tasks entrusted to the community and, in particular, to raising the standard of living and the quality of life in its territory". [883]

The task of ensuring that consumers not be bound by unfair contract terms required that a national court not be precluded from re-examining arbitration awards upholding or applying such unfair clauses, even in instances when the consumer had forfeited the opportunity to object to litigation before an arbitral tribunal.[884] Yet, when asked whether a national court in exceptional cases could be required to review arbitration awards even once they had become final (in order to desist enforcement), the pain limit of the consumer protective prerogative appeared to have been reached. The Court of Justice attributed key importance to the principle of *res judicata* as justification for the opposite outcome:[885]

> the need to comply with the principle of effectiveness cannot be stretched so far as to mean that [...] a national court is required not only to compensate for a procedural omission on the part of a consumer who is unaware of his rights [...] but also to make up fully for the total inertia on the part of the consumer concerned who, like the defendant in the main proceedings, neither participated in the arbitration proceedings nor brought an action for annulment of the arbitration award, which therefore has become final.

In 2009, this formulation constituted a rare instance of enforcing the principle of *ius vigilantibus scriptum est* against consumers, where lenience was otherwise called for due to the embedded procedural inequalities in con-

---

881 CJEU judgment in *Elisa María Mostaza Claro v. Centro Móvil Milenium SL*, C-168/05, EU:C:2006:675, 35; CJEU judgment in *Eco Swiss China Time Ltd v. Benetton International NV*, C-126/97, EU:C:1999:269, 37.

882 CJEU judgment in *Eco Swiss China Time Ltd v. Benetton International NV*, C-126/97, EU:C:1999:269, 36-37.

883 CJEU judgment in *Elisa María Mostaza Claro v. Centro Móvil Milenium SL*, C-168/05, EU:C:2006:675, 37-38.

884 Ibid., 30.

885 CJEU judgment in *Asturcom Telecomunicaciones SL v. Cristina Rodríguez Nogueira*, C-40/08, EU:C:2009:615, 47.

sumer-to-business litigation.[886] The weight attributed to the finality of arbitration awards in *Asturcom* would resonate in subsequent case-law concerning the finality of judgments and decisions more widely:[887]

> consumer protection is not absolute [...] EU law does not require a national court to disapply domestic rules of procedure conferring finality on a decision, even if to do so would make it possible to remedy an infringement of a provision, regardless of its nature, contained in Directive 93/13[.]

This token of deference was in *Asturcom* and *Pohotovosť I* accompanied by the caveat that national procedural rules on *res judicata* are subject to the requirements of effectiveness and equivalence. National procedural law already having prescribed a possibility of public policy review of arbitration awards in the circumstances of those cases, the Court of Justice indicated that Union consumer protection legislation holds a similar rank to national public policy, and must (as a matter of equivalence) be reviewed *ex officio*.[888] The rulings in *Asbeek Brusse* and *Faber* confirmed the national comparator thus proposed:[889]

> in view of the nature and importance of the public interest underlying the protection which the directive confers on consumers, Article 6 thereof must be regarded as a provision of equal standing to national rules which rank, within the domestic legal system, as rules of public policy[...] It must be held that that classification extends to all the provisions of the directive which are essential for the purpose of attaining the objective pursued [...][890]

---

886 See e.g. Opinion of Advocate General Szpunar in *Finanmadrid EFC SA v. Jesús Vicente Albán Zambrano and Others*, C-49/14, EU:C:2015:746, 43.

887 CJEU judgment in *Banco Primus SA v. Jesús Gutiérrez García*, C-421/14, EU:C:2017:60, 47-49; see also CJEU judgment in *Gutiérrez Naranjo and Others*, joined cases C-154/15, C-307/15 and C-308/15, EU:C:2016:980 (67-68), whose outcome is explained not by the litigants' passivity, but a restrictive temporal limitation for restitution claims which the CJEU deemed contrary to the Unfair Terms Directive (70-74).

888 CJEU judgment in *Asturcom Telecomunicaciones SL v. Cristina Rodríguez Nogueira*, C-40/08, EU:C:2009:615, 49-52; CJEU judgment in *Pohotovosť s.r.o. v. Iveta Korčkovská (I)*, C-76/10, EU:C:2010:685, 48-54.

889 CJEU judgment in *Dirk Frederik Asbeek Brusse*, C-488/11, EU:C:2013:341, 44; CJEU judgment in *Froukje Faber*, C-497/13, EU:C:2015:357, 56-57; see also CJEU judgment in *Banco Primus SA v. Jesús Gutiérrez García*, C-421/14, EU:C:2017:60, 42, which retained this formulation on rank while examining the principle of effective judicial protection.

890 CJEU judgment in *Dirk Frederik Asbeek Brusse*, C-488/11, EU:C:2013:341, 44.

That the consumer protection prerogative constituted autonomous Union public policy was hence accepted, on occasion even without resort to any comparator in terms of rank or substance.[891] This stance deviates from the ruling in *Benallal*, which had in fact mitigated the effects of *Eco Swiss*;[892] *ex officio* review had there been required only insofar as national public policy provisions were similar in *substance*, not *rank*, to rules of EU public policy.[893] The public policy designation is therefore of greater practical import under the consumer protective prerogative than in the general procedural case-law, where the *ex officio* mandate hinges on a substantively similar national comparator.

3.2.4.5 A fundamental rights approach to justifications

In most of the cases thus far discussed, the Court of Justice's preferred tool for assessing procedural obstacles to *ex officio* review was the *Rewe* criteria of effectiveness and equivalence.[894] As is familiar, also procedural rules contrary to the *Rewe* criteria can be justified by their role, progress and features in the national legal system. In the rulings based on the *Rewe* formula, the balance was often ultimately tilted by the procedural rule-of-reason.[895]

891 CJEU judgment in *Erika Jőrös v. Aegon Magyarország Hitel Zrt.*, C-397/11, EU:C:2013:340, 30; CJEU judgment in *Gutiérrez Naranjo and Others*, joined cases C-154/15, C-307/15 and C-308/15, EU:C:2016:980, 54.

892 CJEU judgment in *Eco Swiss China Time Ltd v. Benetton International NV*, C-126/97, EU:C:1999:269.

893 CJEU judgment in *Abdelhafid Bensada Benallal v. État belge*, C-161/15, EU:C:2016:175, 31-35.

894 See e.g. CJEU judgment in *Asturcom Telecomunicaciones SL v. Cristina Rodríguez Nogueira*, C-40/08, EU:C:2009:615, 39-48; CJEU judgment in *Asociación de Consumidores Independientes de Castilla y León*, C-413/12, EU:C:2010:739, 30, 53; CJEU judgment in *BBVA SA v. Pedro Peñalva López*, C-8/14, EU:C:2015:731, 40-41, CJEU judgment in *Jorge Sales Sinués v. Caixabank*, joined cases C-381/14 and 385/14, EU:C:2016:252, 34-41.

895 CJEU judgment in *Banco Español de Crédito SA v. Joaquín Calderón Camino*, C-618/10, EU:C:2012:349, 49; commented by A. Beka, 'Commentary Note on Case C-618/10 Banco Español de Crédito SA v. Joaquín Calderón Camino, Judgment of 14 June 2012', *Zeitschrift für Gemeinschaftsprivatrecht*, 9 (2012). See also CJEU judgment in *Mohamed Aziz v. Caixa d'Estalvis de Catalunya*, C-415/11, EU:C:2013:164, 53-55; CJEU judgment in *Sanchez Morcillo and Abril García (I)*, C-169/14, EU:C:2014:2099, 34; CJEU judgment in *ERSTE Bank Hungary Zrt. v. Attila Sugár*, C-32/14, EU:C:2015:637, 51-63.

Also the consumer case-law was nevertheless influenced by a general trend towards increased use of fundamental rights. While Art. 47 CFR grants a right to effective judicial protection, Art. 38 CFR prescribes a high level of consumer protection in Union policies – both mandatory requirements applicable in Member States implementation of the EU consumer legislation.[896] The case of *Finanmadrid*[897] sheds light on how consumers' fundamental right to defense may be accounted for either under the procedural rule-of-reason, or through a fundamental rights approach. This was the first in a series of rulings in which the scope of review at the enforcement stages has been treated as supplementary to the review carried out by earlier judicial or administrative instances.[898]

The case before the referring court concerned the execution of a payment order, in which substantive review of the terms of the underlying consumer contract was barred. Advocate General Szpunar had been hesitant to expand the scope of review – first of all because in the context of enforcement proceedings the seized court rarely has the necessary factual elements before it; and secondly, because re-visiting the contract terms would be contrary to the principle of *res judicata*.[899] The Opinion nonetheless identified a vital gap in the scope of review carried out at the first stage (by the registrar) leading to "the total absence of a review of unfair terms by a court acting of its own motion at all stages of the procedure leading to

896 CJEU judgment in *Monika Kušionová v. SMART Capital a.s.*, C-34/13, EU:C:2014:2189, 47.

897 CJEU judgment in *Finanmadrid EFC SA v. Jesús Vicente Albán Zambrano and Others*, C-49/14, EU:C:2016:98, commented in P. Hacker and M. F. Starke, 'European Union Litigation', *European Review of Contract Law*, 12 (2016), 149.

898 CJEU judgment in *Jana Pereničová and Vladislav Perenič*, C-453/10, EU:C:2012:144; CJEU judgment in *Dirk Frederik Asbeek Brusse*, C-488/11, EU:C:2013:341; CJEU judgment in *Árpád Kásler v. OTP*, C-26/13, EU:C:2014:282; CJEU judgment in *Unicaja Banco and Caixabank*, C-482/13, EU:C:2015:21; CJEU judgment in *Banco Primus SA v. Jesús Gutiérrez García*, C-421/14, EU:C:2017:60.

899 European standards for intra-state enforcement orders embody the same mechanisms, including the limits of review applied at the enforcement stage of the proceedings, making these standards difficult to consolidate with expanding the powers of a seized court for the purpose of national enforcement proceedings; Regulation (EC) 805/2004 of the European Parliament and of the Council of 21 April 2004 creating a European Enforcement Order for uncontested claims, OJ L 143, 30/4/2004, 15; Regulation (EC) 1896/2006 of the European Parliament and of the Council of 12 December 2006 creating a European order for payment procedure, OJ L 399, 30/12/2006, 1.

an adoption of an order for payment".[900] For this reason, national courts should after all be entrusted to compensate for the lack of effective judicial protection at that initial stage by reviewing the terms of the contract at the execution stage.

The fact that the consumer could have objected to the payment order before it gained finality and formed the basis for an execution order, did not stop the Court of Justice from ruling that the Spanish prohibition against *ex officio* review at the execution stage was precluded. In particular, the time-limit for lodging an objection was exceptionally short, the costs of litigation high, and the possibility of consumers being unaware of their rights under Union legislation was altogether capable of deterring consumers from litigating.[901]

The above reasoning was both in the ruling and in the Opinion carried out under the procedural rule-of-reason.[902] Advocate General Szpunar additionally addressed the question of overlap between Art. 47 CFR and the *Rewe* principles, noting that the principle of effectiveness also "embodies" the principle of effective judicial protection.[903] A subsidiary reasoning offers insight on how the same problem could have been solved under Art. 47 CFR. The Advocate General underlined that review of the compatibility of the national procedural rules with the Charter would not allow the same conclusion as would the principle of effectiveness with regard to the provisions of the Unfair Terms Directive (combined with the procedural rule-of-reason), since the Directive grants a higher level of protection than does Art. 47 CFR.[904] In particular, the Directive itself contains specific

900 Opinion of Advocate General Szpunar in *Finanmadrid EFC SA v. Jesús Vicente Albán Zambrano and Others*, C-49/14, EU:C:2015:746, 66.

901 CJEU judgment in *Finanmadrid EFC SA v. Jesús Vicente Albán Zambrano and Others*, C-49/14, EU:C:2016:98, 5.

902 Ibid., 44 (referring to case-law which can be back-tracked to CJEU judgment in *Peterbroeck, Van Campenhout & Cie v. Belgian State*, C-312/93, EU:C:1995:437). By contrast, in CJEU judgment in *EOS KSI Slovensko*, C-448/17, EU:C:2018:745, the Court came to this conclusion without recourse to the rule-of-reason.

903 Opinion of Advocate General Szpunar in *Finanmadrid EFC SA v. Jesús Vicente Albán Zambrano and Others*, C-49/14, EU:C:2015:746, 85, also emphasizing that the requirement of effective judicial protection remains applicable to "all legal actions seeking to safeguard the rights conferred on individuals under EU law", in response to the observation that the field of national procedural autonomy falls outside the scope of application of the Charter (83). See comments by J. Krommendijk (2016), 1411.

904 Opinion of Advocate General Szpunar in *Finanmadrid EFC SA v. Jesús Vicente Albán Zambrano and Others*, C-49/14, EU:C:2015:746, 89.

provisions implicitly obliging national courts to carry out *ex officio* review in order to extend procedural support to the weaker consumer party.[905] Modalities and exigencies of the Directive aside, the Opinion underlined what would be the outcome of a balancing between the rights of defense in the hypothetical Art. 47 CFR test, stressing that "observance of the rights of the defense is not absolute and may be subject to restrictions", the latter under certain circumstances including the possibility of holding proceedings in the absence of the defendant.[906]

The hypothetical reasoning of the Advocate General indicated that the principle of effectiveness may benefit a litigant relying on favorable procedural rights codified in EU secondary law.[907] By contrast, the weighing of interests under Art. 47 CFR may (hypothetically) be less generous than the procedural rule-of-reason. Although these hypotheses would be validated in case-law from other substantive fields of law,[908] the consumer case-law is ambivalent. In e.g. *Banif Plus*, the right to effective judicial protection had previously required that any considerations made by national courts of their own motion be subject to scrutiny and possible objections by litigants on both sides (*audi alteram partem*). In other words, introducing Charter rights did not exclusively protect the consumer litigant.[909] Although the case mentioned the *Rewe* criteria, it shifted into a reasoning about both full effectiveness of the Directive and effective judicial protection under the Charter, which explains why the procedural rule-of-reason did not figure in this balancing exercise.

By contrast, in *Sanchez Morcillo I and II*, the right to defense figured in explicit reference to the procedural rule-of-reason.[910] Yet, in *Sanchez Morcil-*

905 Ibid., 93.

906 Namely, that reasonable attempts had been made to summon the defendant and that the decision delivered *in absentia* be susceptible to review (ibid., 94-95), i.e. the same requirements as in CJEU judgment in *Hypoteční banka a.s. v. Udo Mike Lindner*, C-327/10, EU:C:2011:745.

907 As was the case in e.g. CJEU judgment in *Asturcom Telecomunicaciones SL v. Cristina Rodríguez Nogueira*, C-40/08, EU:C:2009:615; CJEU judgment in *Banco Español de Crédito SA v. Joaquín Calderón Camino*, C-618/10, EU:C:2012:349 and CJEU judgment in *Finanmadrid EFC SA v. Jesús Vicente Albán Zambrano and Others*, C-49/14, EU:C:2016:98.

908 To be developed in Chapter 5 of the present work.

909 CJEU judgment in *Banif Plus Bank Zrt v. Csaba Csipai* C-472/11, EU:C:2013:88, 29, 36.

910 CJEU judgment in *Sanchez Morcillo and Abril García (I)*, C-169/14, EU:C:2014:2099, 34; CJEU judgment in *Sanchez Morcillo and Abril García (II)*, C-539/14, EU:C:2015:508, 35.

lo I, the ensuing reasoning again shifted into a discussion of whether the cornerstones of the right to effective judicial protection required that procedural rules be set aside to benefit the consumer litigant (and not whether they were justified):[911]

> the principle of equality of arms, together with, among others, the principle *audi alteram partem*, is no more than a corollary of the very concept of a fair hearing that implies an obligation to offer each party a reasonable opportunity of presenting its case in conditions that do not place it in a clearly less advantageous position compared with its opponent[.]

By contrast, in *Sanchez Morcillo II*, the protection of fundamental rights remained in the foreground of the Court of Justice's application of the procedural rule-of-reason, which ultimately justified the national legislation under scrutiny.[912]

In conclusion, introducing fundamental rights into the equation cuts both ways. On the one hand, the procedural rule-of-reason can be dispensed with – yet must not necessarily be – making it more difficult to justify encroachments on the protection offered by EU consumer legislation. On the other hand, once fundamental rights are in the game, both consumers and commercial litigants can use them[913] – this is at the very core of the principle of equality of arms. The wider consequences of the choice between *Rewe*-effectiveness and effective judicial protection under the Charter will be explored in Chapter 5.

3.2.4.6 Rationale and reach of the consumer protection prerogative

The backdrop of the examined case-law is far-reaching harmonization and the protective prerogatives enshrined in the EU legislative context, both of which are here revisited on a concluding note.

The harmonization of consumer protection law has several consequences. Art. 6 of the Unfair Terms Directive, and similar provisions in other consumer regulations, indirectly govern the issue of *ex officio* application of EU secondary legislation to the benefit of the consumer party in

911 CJEU judgment in *Sanchez Morcillo and Abril García (I)*, C-169/14, EU:C:2014:2099, 49.

912 CJEU judgment in *Sanchez Morcillo and Abril García (II)*, C-539/14, EU:C:2015:508, 35-36, 50.

913 CJEU judgment in *Banif Plus Bank Zrt v. Csaba Csipai* C-472/11, EU:C:2013:88, 34-36.

consumer-to-business contracts. Because of the binding force of the applicable rules of secondary EU law, the Court of Justice has adopted a firm language in the form of an overall *obligation* to apply EU law, rather than a *power* to do so.[914]

Although the *Rewe* formula has been predominant, the Court of Justice has, in its resolution of procedural and remedial matters, sometimes opted for the "full effect" approach.[915] This has shifted emphasis away from national procedural autonomy (which hardly exists any more within the area) towards ensuring the enforcement of secondary legislation within a domain that is broadly harmonized. In other instances, a fundamental rights approach has permeated either the *Rewe* test, the full effect requirement, or both.[916]

When examining the present litigation type, it is not clear that far-reaching analogies can be made outside the field of consumer-to-business litigation. On the one hand, the case-law deals with secondary legislation whose implementation is compulsory for the Member States and regulated in some detail. Progressive as this line of case-law may be, its implications are limited *not* to instances of weaker litigants needing procedural protection, but to the substantive context of consumer adjudication.[917] In other words, transposition to other areas of law appears to be beyond reach – at least in the absence of harmonization with similar protective prerogatives.[918]

On the other hand, provisions requiring that legal remedies be made available may be specified in general terms in the EU legislative acts, while not governing their modalities: "the powers of these organizations, their

---

914 K. Lenaerts, I. Maselis, and K. Gutman (2014), 134-36.

915 Ibid., see e.g. CJEU judgment in *Océano Grupo Editorial and Salvat Editores*, joined cases C-240/98 to C-244/98, EU:C:2000:346, 27; CJEU judgment in *Rampion and Godard*, C-429/05, EU:C:2007:575, 65; CJEU judgment in *Banif Plus Bank Zrt v. Csaba Csipai* C-472/11, EU:C:2013:88, 27-28.

916 CJEU judgment in *Banif Plus Bank Zrt v. Csaba Csipai* C-472/11, EU:C:2013:88; CJEU judgment in *Sanchez Morcillo and Abril García (I)*, C-169/14, EU:C:2014:2099, 34; CJEU judgment in *Sanchez Morcillo and Abril García (II)*, C-539/14, EU:C:2015:508.

917 The scope of the *ex officio* mandate has limits even within the context of consumer litigation, where exercise of the judicial function serves as dividing line; CJEU judgment in *ERSTE Bank Hungary Zrt. v. Attila Sugár*, C-32/14, EU:C:2015:637, 47.

918 Cf. A. Beka (2018), 347-52, arguing that an extrapolation is possible for the protection of weak litigants insofar as a criterion of general interest and an element of protection is articulated by the EU legislator, e.g. in EU employment law and other legislation with a view to combat discrimination and structural imbalances.

operation and financing, as well as those of administrative authorities remains subject to national discretion."[919] Under the Unfair Terms Directive, provisions on access to court, and on adequate and effective powers of courts and authorities for preventing abuse, lay down minimum standards based on existing case-law, whereas the means to achieve these goals are up to the Member States.[920] It is from this perspective that analogies in the opposite direction are viable, i.e. *from* the general case-law on national procedural autonomy, which guides not only national procedural law at large, but also procedural rules applicable to litigation under the consumer directives. Consumer case-law may accordingly draw on the general case-law as soon as procedural rules are at stake, whereas the general case-law cannot as easily draw on the consumer case-law.

By contrast, analogies are possible in neither direction when determining the national comparator for the equivalence test, where the general case-law has opted for similar content/substance as benchmark,[921] whereas the consumer case-law has opted for rules of similar rank.[922] The proposition of consumer protection belonging to common Union "public policy" analogously to Union competition law anticipated the same treatment as anti-competitive agreements: nullity or voidness (to be examined *ex officio*).[923] The public policy label was rationalized by the protective imperative of EU consumer law, justifying from a procedural equity perspective the importance and consequences that the designation brings with it for the seized judge. The consumer case-law has lent support to "ranking" protective consumer legislation as Union public policy, even beyond the re-

919 M. Tulibacka (2015), 62, referring to Art. 7 of the Unfair Terms Directive (Council Directive 93/13/EEC of 5 April 1993 on unfair terms in consumer contracts, Official Journal L 095, 21/04/1993, 29); see, by analogy CJEU judgment in *Joan Cuadrench Moré v. Koninklijke Luchtvaart Maatschappij NV*, C-139/11, EU:C:2012:741, where substantive rights were regulated in secondary law while the procedural modalities were left unregulated, leaving room for national procedural rules to reign.

920 Arts. 6 and 7 Council Directive 93/13/EEC of 5 April 1993 on unfair terms in consumer contracts, Official Journal L 095, 21/04/1993, 29.

921 CJEU judgment in *Abdelhafid Bensada Benallal v. État belge*, C-161/15, EU:C:2016:175.

922 CJEU judgment in *Froukje Faber*, C-497/13, EU:C:2015:357, 57; cf. S. Law (2018), 297, reaching the opposite conclusion.

923 E.g. CJEU judgment in *Elisa María Mostaza Claro v. Centro Móvil Milenium SL*, C-168/05, EU:C:2006:675, 35; CJEU judgment in *Eco Swiss China Time Ltd v. Benetton International NV*, C-126/97, EU:C:1999:269, 36.

view of arbitration awards.[924] Still, it does not follow that the categorization of consumer protection as Union public policy autonomously triggers an obligation of *ex officio* review as general Union law prerogative, this obligation embedded already in applicable EU secondary legislation.[925]

By helping consumers gain access to national courts, the seized judge can step into his role as Union judge in order to give effect to rules of Union public policy – attributing the consumer a central function in triggering the enforcement of Union law. This idea is encapsulated in the view of individual litigants as private policemen,[926] instrumental in the decentralized enforcement of Union law by bringing the consumer directives to the litigation forum.[927] Viewed from this perspective, the consumer imperative instrumentalizes the consumer so as to bring consumer protection directives before the national judge.

This "bottom-up" approach encourages individual consumers as well as consumer associations to act as private enforcers of Union law.[928] From this vantage point, access to courts is not only an individual right, but also a path via the courts to which a wider category of litigants have been granted access, with the potential to promote Union law to the benefit of the

924 CJEU judgment in *Pohotovosť s.r.o. v. Iveta Korčkovská (I)*, C-76/10, EU:C:2010:685, 48-51; CJEU judgment in *Banco Primus SA v. Jesús Gutiérrez García*, C-421/14, EU:C:2017:60, 42.

925 This issue is developed in B. U. Graf and A. E. Appleton, 'Elisa Marioa Mostaza Claro v. Centro Móvil Milenium: EU Consumer Law as a Defence against Arbitral Awards, ECJ Case C-168/05', *ASA Bulletin*, 25 (2007). See also CJEU judgment in *Rampion and Godard*, C-429/05, EU:C:2007:575, 58; CJEU judgment in *Pohotovosť s.r.o. v. Iveta Korčkovská (I)*, C-76/10, EU:C:2010:685, 49-51.

926 See M. Burley and W. Mattli (1993), 60 f.; M. Dougan (2012); F. Wilman, 'The Vigilance of Individuals: How, When and Why the EU Legislates to Facilitate the Private Enforcement of EU Law before National Courts' (Leiden University, 2014), 4; C. Warin (2019), 464-65.

927 On private enforcement through consumer litigation, see F. Wilman (2014), 146-92; A. P. Komninos (2002) and N. Reich, 'Legal protection of individual and collective consumer interests', in *European Consumer Law*, eds. Reich, N., H. Micklitz, P. Rott, and K. Tonner (Intersentia, 2014); F. Cafaggi, 'Towards Collaborative Governance of European Remedial and Procedural law', *Theoretical Inquiries in Law*, 19 (2018).

928 On the complementarity between individual and collective redress in consumer litigation, see further F. Cafaggi (2018), 235-60.

wider collective of consumers.[929] The present perspective encapsulates the idea described in section 3.1.2, namely that mandatory rules should not be circumvented through litigating strategies of "savvy lawyers" who wish to see Union law left unapplied, at least as concerns their clients' legal affairs. It should nevertheless be noted that the Court of Justice has been decreasingly inclined to grant consumer associations standing etc. in the same way as it had individual consumers, since the former are not considered to have deficits in knowledge and resources and are therefore not covered by the protective prerogative (even though their cause is).[930]

The mandate of *ex officio* review also triggers a "top-down" perspective, in which the consumer protection imperative directly serves the individual litigant. As recalled by the Court on numerous occasions, consumers are not necessarily well-informed of their rights or capable of navigating the national and international framework of consumer law. They rarely have the resources to seek legal representation by a lawyer – contrary to commercial actors who often have internal or external lawyers at their regular disposal. In order to compensate for these and other disadvantages, it is the responsibility of national courts to consider of their own motion certain relevant and (for the consumer) advantageous legal grounds, insofar as the consumer or his lawyer has not managed to invoke them. The Court's emphasis on significant imbalances between litigants in consumer-to-business contractual relationships expresses the initially described theoretical construction of the "poor client".[931] National judges have an important function in ensuring that consumers' rights are given effective protection, even when the consumer is not himself aware of these rights.

The present perspective emphasizes the interest of protecting vulnerable litigants, which ultimately gives rise to an adjudication objective of delivering substantively correct judgments in compliance with applicable Union

929 CJEU judgment in *Commission v. Italian Republic*, C-372/99, EU:C:2002:42, 14; CJEU judgment in *Nemzeti Fogyasztóvédelmi Hatóság v. Invitel Távközlési Zrt*, C-472/10, EU:C:2012:242, 36-37. The case-law has also juxtaposed the interests of individual consumers and consumer protection associations; CJEU judgment in *Jorge Sales Sinués v. Caixabank*, joined cases C-381/14 and 385/14, EU:C:2016:252 (individual standing *vis-à-vis litis pendens* of proceedings brought by consumer association).

930 CJEU judgment in *Asociación de Consumidores Independientes de Castilla y León*, C-413/12, EU:C:2010:739, 50-53; see also CJEU judgment in *Pohotovosť s. r. o. v. Miroslav Vašuta (II)*, C-470/12, EU:C:2014:101 and CJEU judgment in *EOS KSI Slovensko*, C-448/17, EU:C:2018:745.

931 J. Engström (2008), 81. See also CJEU judgment in *Cofidis SA v. Jean-Louis Fredout*, C-473/00, EU:C:2002:705, 33.

consumer legislation. Although *procedural* protection is instrumental towards reaching this result, the Court of Justice's frequent emphasis on ensuring that the beneficiary is granted procedural protection hinges on the identification of the consumer as beneficiary of *substantive* Union law. Against this background, it is not surprising that the priority of safeguarding the beneficiary of substantive EU legislation has visibly transpired throughout the case-law on *ex officio* review. The present chapter has demonstrated that the Court of Justice's balancing of interests, when developing the *ex officio* mandate, has overall prioritized the substantive interests of consumers (especially when litigating on their own).

This rule is not without exception in the wider case-law on EU consumer litigation.[932] For instance, in *Lindner*, the Court of Justice weighed the procedural rights of the defendant against those of the commercial applicant party, finding that the rights of defense (to be present at the hearing) did not trump the right of the applicant to bring proceedings *in absentia*.[933] Also in case-law on *ex officio* review, other considerations including the procedural protection of the opposing commercial party have been permitted to hold back the consumer cause.[934] Whether under the procedural rule-of-reason[935] or under the fundamental rights approach,[936] limitations to consumer protection are on the rise as the Court of Justice increasingly appears to draw a line instead of further pushing the boundaries of the consumer imperative.

3.3 Interim conclusions

The mandate of *ex officio* review was examined in the perspective of the ideological stakes in a court's choice to consider rules of law or matters of fact not invoked by the parties. When *ex officio* review is carried out to protect a vulnerable litigant, it is done in the collective interest of enforcing

932 CJEU judgment in *Hypoteční banka a.s. v. Udo Mike Lindner*, C-327/10, EU:C:2011:745, 53-54; CJEU judgment in *Biuro podróży 'Partner'*, C-119/15, EU:C:2016:987, 27.

933 CJEU judgment in *Hypoteční banka a.s. v. Udo Mike Lindner*, C-327/10, EU:C:2011:745, 54, discussed by L. M. Ravo (2012), 120-22.

934 CJEU judgment in *Banif Plus Bank Zrt v. Csaba Csipai*, C-472/11, EU:C:2013:88.

935 CJEU judgment in *Baczó and Vizsnyiczai*, C-567/13, EU:C:2015:88; CJEU judgment in *Finanmadrid EFC SA v. Jesús Vicente Albán Zambrano and Others*, C-49/14, EU:C:2016:98, 52.

936 CJEU judgment in *Banif Plus Bank Zrt v. Csaba Csipai*, C-472/11, EU:C:2013:88.

substantive rules and rights, in the court's role of guarantor of the "truth" and for the purpose of establishing precedents that comply with substantive law and respect individual rights, irrespective of the beneficiary's capacity to vindicate them. It is done in the private interest of ensuring not only procedural equality (playing according to the rules) but also procedural equity (compensating for pre-existing procedural inequalities) *in casu*. By contrast, when *ex officio* review is carried out against the wishes of "savvy lawyers" on one or both sides, this is done in the collective interest of safeguarding rules of public policy, where those interests are unrepresented in the ongoing litigation.

The appropriateness of *ex officio* review depends on the seized court's role in truth-seeking or dispute resolution. Whether emphasis should be on the former or the latter depends on the legal tradition governing the litigation; still, truth-seeking has been recognized as increasingly important in the rise of "public law litigation".[937]

With regard to the type of litigation as indicator of the judge's appropriate level of interventionism, a dividing line is drawn in the scholarship between horizontal and vertical litigation. In horizontal litigation, the task of dispute resolution is emphasized in the spirit of party disposition. In vertical litigation, any individual litigant embodies the theoretical construction of a "poor client", facing a resourceful public authority. In the latter context, *ex officio* review is more widely accepted, assuming that it is carried out to the benefit of the private party, and not the public party to the proceedings.

Whether or not this can be done also depends on the ambit of the proceedings. Although courts are assumed to know the law, it is principally and practically problematic for them to investigate of their own motion facts that have not been put forward by the parties. In many cases where a national court poses the question whether an element of law can be considered *ex officio*, the actual obstacle lies in the circumstance that the court cannot take into account facts necessary to substantiate the sought application of the law. Insofar as the ambit of the proceeding is delimited by legal claims, similar problems arise if a narrow claim precludes the investigation into alternative legal bases.

While the language of adversarialism, placed under the umbrella of the right to a fair trial by the ECtHR, would appear to give food to an argument that *ex officio* review should be practiced with caution, it has been

---

937 A. Chayes (1976), 1281; see recently CJEU judgment in *Online Games Handels GmbH*, C-685/15, EU:C:2017:452, 64.

demonstrated that the ECtHR has in fact embraced the practice. The standard of judge impartiality by no means precludes *ex officio* review as long as the requirement of due notice is satisfied. As a result, the case-law of the ECtHR cannot in its own right be used to argue that *ex officio* review is contrary to the right to a fair trial nor, by extension, the EU law general principle of effective judicial protection.[938]

The present chapter also examined the EU mandate of *ex officio* review in view of the balance to be struck between effectiveness of EU law and procedural protection. As initially clarified, the findings of the Court are nuanced and the final choice is often left to the national judge. The case-law highlighted conditions and factors of particular significance towards making a prioritization between the goals at issue, an exercise which is at most capable of answering the question as to *how* the balance is struck, but not *where*.

In the first line of case-law, ambiguities between various versions and legal bases of the principle of effectiveness were discussed in light of the Court of Justice's initial statements on *ex officio* review. The constitutional mandate required that all national courts act as constitutional courts with the power to review the compatibility of national law with the Treaties. As part of constitutional review, compatibility of national law with EU law should also be carried out *ex officio*. National courts should moreover disregard obstacles to making a preliminary reference under the *Rheinmühlen* mandate, and preliminary references need not be triggered by a party's demand for a reference to be made – although parties' omission to invoke EU law is capable of placing the latter outside the ambit of the proceedings.[939]

The first line of case-law also indicated that neither the *Rheinmühlen* mandate nor the constitutional mandate was sufficient to give rise to an *obligation* of *ex officio* review – but rather a *power*.[940] The issue of power versus obligation would nevertheless be reconsidered under the duty of sin-

938 CJEU judgment in *Online Games Handels GmbH*, C-685/15, EU:C:2017:452, 66-67 recently supported the stance that *ex officio* review is not in itself contrary to adversarialism, albeit emphasizing the substitution of grounds as pain limit as opposed to due notice as precondition.

939 That is, if the plea was inadmissible in the national proceedings, as at least implied in CJEU judgment in *Lucio Cesare Aquino v. Belgische Staat*, C-3/16, EU:C:2017:209, 44-46.

940 CJEU judgment in *Verholen and Others v. Sociale Verzekeringsbank Amsterdam*, joined cases C-87/90, C-88/90 and C-89/90, EU:C:1991:314; CJEU judgment in *Ferdinand M.J.J. Duijnstee v. Lodewijk Goderbauer*, 288/82, EU:C:1983:326, 54.

cere co-operation, moving away from the doctrine of full effect in favor of the *Rewe* formula.[941] The constitutional mandate brought about a negative obligation by constraining the legislator, while empowering the national judge.[942]

The second line of case-law allowed the Court of Justice to guide national judges through policy choices between active adjudication to promote effectiveness and judge passivity/party autonomy.[943] Several principles crystallized as key factors towards deciding whether *ex officio* review is a power or obligation under the remedial mandate. These factors indicated how the balance was struck between effectiveness and procedural protection in the present context, thus addressing the first research question.[944] A first such key factor was the interest of *ensuring access to court*, discussed above.

Secondly, the presence of *procedural omissions* proved capable of tilting the balance towards procedural protection, at the expense of Union law effectiveness. However, litigants' inertia did not lead to a full forfeiture of the substantive protection provided through *ex officio* review.[945] For the purposes of the *Rheinmühlen* mandate, a national court's responsibility is not – in principle – reduced by omissions by the beneficiary. The effectiveness of the Art. 267-procedure requires national judges to have an uninhibited right following the Treaties to consult the Court of Justice on matters of interpretation and validity of EU law, which is essential in order to ensure that the objective of uniform application of EU law is reached in collaboration between the national judge and the Court of Justice.[946] In practice, however, forfeiture placing claims based on EU law outside the ambit of the national proceedings may render a preliminary reference hypothetical and thus inadmissible before the Court of Justice.[947]

---

941 CJEU judgment in *Peterbroeck, Van Campenhout & Cie v. Belgian State*, C-312/93, EU:C:1995:437; CJEU judgment in *van Schijndel v. Stichting Pensioenfonds voor Fysiotherapeuten*, joined cases C-430/93 and C-431/93, EU:C:1995:441.

942 CJEU judgment in *Silvia Georgiana Câmpean*, C-200/14, EU:C:2016:494.

943 J. Engström (2008), 72.

944 *How is the balance struck between substantive and procedural protection in the Court of Justice's case-law on* ex officio *review?*

945 CJEU judgment in *Willy Kempter KG v. Hauptzollamt Hamburg-Jonas*, C-2/06, EU:C:2008:78.

946 CJEU judgment in *Pasquale Foglia v. Mariella Novello*, 244/80, EU:C:1981:302, 16; CJEU judgment in *Associação Sindical dos Juízes Portugueses v. Tribunal de Contas*, C-64/16, EU:C:2018:117, 33.

947 CJEU judgment in *Lucio Cesare Aquino v. Belgische Staat*, C-3/16, EU:C:2017:209, 44-46.

A third factor of significance was the presence of national rules containing procedural safeguards precluding *ex officio* review, to be taken into account in a weighing exercise by the national judge. The procedural rule-of-reason does not disclose *where* the balance should be struck between effectiveness and procedural protection, but defers to the national judge. It has nevertheless been argued retrospectively that the rule-of-reason was used as a "tool to enhance [the] effectiveness" of EU law, inviting national courts to take on the role of guardians of policy objectives rather than of procedural rights.[948] Returning to the terminology defined in the initial part of this chapter, this may also trigger a choice between *recours objectif* and *recours subjectif*,[949] prompting the Court of Justice to venture into core procedural ideologies in Member State traditions, including defining the fundamental role of courts.[950] Although *van Schijndel* – usually considered the founding judgment for the Union mandate of *ex officio* review – did demonstrate deference to national procedural principles, the rule-of-reason test would subsequently be used to justify both interventionism and deference.

In the third line of case-law, the Court of Justice made an initial move to elevate parts of EU law to public policy status, in order to further strengthen the *ex officio* mandate. Ultimately, though, this expansive stance was maintained only in the area of consumer protection, whereas the designation of public policy rules was otherwise allocated to the national legislator. Hence, a rule's public policy status did not prove to be a key parameter for balancing effectiveness against procedural protection.[951] A narrow interpretation of the principle of equivalence was prescribed for public policy rules, based on their content/substance under national law.[952] We may expect that the *ex officio* application of public policy rules may continue to be foreseen with a narrow interpretation of the national comparator, at least outside the auspices of EU consumer law. Therefore, in its contemporary construction, the equivalence test does not necessarily trigger tensions

---

948 S. Prechal (1998), 706; J. Engström (2008), 74-75.

949 J. Engström (2008), 76.

950 Ibid., 72.

951 Aside from the interpretation following from CJEU judgment in *Eco Swiss China Time Ltd v. Benetton International NV*, C-126/97, EU:C:1999:269, which was not sustained in terms of transplanting public policy; see CJEU judgment in *Abdelhafid Bensada Benallal v. État belge*, C-161/15, EU:C:2016:175, 31-35.

952 CJEU judgment in *Abdelhafid Bensada Benallal v. État belge*, C-161/15, EU:C:2016:175.

between Union law effectiveness and procedural protection when based on national public policy substance, rather than rank.

By contrast, in the fourth line, the designation of the consumer imperative as public policy was pivotal – even though the case-law also hinged on the presence of public policy exceptions in national procedural law. Another factor that has been stressed in the scholarship was the prevalence of litigation omissions at the source of procedural preclusion.[953] In the consumer case-law, litigants' procedural omissions in effect crystallized as a significant dividing line, although the strong imperative to protect weak litigating parties was taken into consideration before sanctioning inertia.[954] Finally, the most crucial aspect was the fact that secondary legislation indirectly regulated the matter of *ex officio* review. This was justified by the overarching imperative of protecting the weak consumer, in combination with the codification of the right to effective remedies and access to court, leaving a lesser degree of discretion for national courts to carry out the balancing exercise. This initially tilted the balance in favor of substantive effectiveness over procedural protection of the commercial litigant, whereas the case-law has been increasingly responsive to fundamental rights considerations that protect procedural interests on both sides of the litigation.[955]

953 K. Lenaerts, I. Maselis, and K. Gutman (2014), 135.

954 Compare e.g. CJEU judgment in *Finanmadrid EFC SA v. Jesús Vicente Albán Zambrano and Others*, C-49/14, EU:C:2016:98, 52 with CJEU judgment in *ERSTE Bank Hungary Zrt. V. Attila Sugár*, C-32/14, EU:C:2015:637, 62.

955 CJEU judgment in *Banif Plus Bank Zrt v. Csaba Csipai*, C-472/11, EU:C:2013:88; CJEU judgment in *Biuro podróży 'Partner'*, C-119/15, EU:C:2016:987, 27.

4 Personal scope of effectiveness and effective judicial protection

The present chapter disentangles the beneficiaries of effectiveness, effective judicial protection, and procedural safeguards under national law and the ECHR. This approach is based on a methodology described in section 4.1 below; namely to trace the protective and personal scope of Union rights via their beneficiaries.[956] Section 4.2 approaches the EU *ex officio* mandate from the vantage point of beneficiaries of the principle of *effectiveness*. Section 4.3 transposes this reasoning to the personal scope of *effective judicial protection*, emphasizing differences and potential conflicts between beneficiaries of effectiveness and procedural protection. The previous chapter introduced a variety of factors intervening in the Court of Justice's respective emphasis on substantive or procedural protection. The most important of these factors are next elaborated, in particular view of the protective or personal scope of relevant legal sources, which had additional implications for beneficiaries of national courts' *ex officio* mandate. Parameters governing these prioritizations are distilled in light of the evolution of the principle of effective judicial protection: the procedural equity perspective[957] (4.3.1), the designation of vulnerable litigants as EU law beneficiaries (4.3.2) and responsibilities for flagrant litigation lapses (4.3.3).

4.1 Tracing beneficiaries through the protective scope of substantive rights

When the principle of effective judicial protection is understood as protecting solely or primarily the beneficiary of Union law, the interest of effectiveness is given greater due than procedural principles sorting under the umbrella of judicial protection. The priority of the effectiveness element is the enforcement of substantive Union law; intended, in other words, to protect those individuals who enjoy substantive rights under Union law. Even if procedural protection is held in mind when asking

956 M. Dougan (2012), 73.
957 N. H. Andrews (2003), 128ff.

whether national rules of *procedure* have the consequence of rendering enjoyment of rights "virtually impossible or excessively difficult", that assessment limits itself to regarding the consequences of national rules of procedure for the opportunity to enjoy *substantive* rights derived from Union law:[958]

> the concept of effectiveness refers primarily to the enforcement of Union rights *per se*, protecting the individual's rights (if at all) only instrumentally or incidentally.

By contrast, if effective judicial protection is to be emphasized in its character of fundamental right,[959] its protective scope reaches a wider category of beneficiaries, and its rationale shifts from ensuring effectiveness of Union law to ensuring the integrity and legal certainty of judicial proceedings.

Consider the examples of injunctions against rival companies breaching Union law and liability arising from anti-competitive agreements.[960] This context of litigation between private parties gives rise to the same tension as do horizontal direct effects:[961] namely that a litigant typically seeks to benefit from Union law-derived rights at the expense of another individual litigant, whose legal interests are equally in the hands of the national court. Such situations raise complex questions about whether the enforcement of Union law through setting aside national procedural rules may actually come at the expense of equality of arms between parties.[962]

A related difficulty arises in inverse vertical relationships between litigants, i.e. in which an individual is litigating against a public body seeking to enforce Union law. The seized court is here entrusted to protect both the parties' procedural rights (under national law) and their substantive

---

958 M. Dougan (2011 a), 425; see also P. Nebbia, 'The Double Life of Effectiveness', *Cambridge Yearbook of European Legal Studies*, 10 (2008); C. Warin, 'Individual rights under Union law. A study on the relation between rights, obligations and interests in the case law of the Court of Justice' (University of Luxembourg, 2017), 57ff.; cf. J-U. Franck (2017), 1876-77.

959 See L. M. Ravo (2012), 101.

960 CJEU judgment in *Muñoz and Superior Fruiticola*, C-253/00, EU:C:2002:497; CJEU judgment in *Courage Ltd v. Bernard and Crehan*, C-453/99, EU:C:2001:465. See also C.A. Jones, 'Into the Parallel Universe: Procedural Fairness in Private Litigation after the Damages Directive' in *Procedural Fairness in Competition Proceedings*, eds. Nihoul, P. and T. Skozcy (Cheltenham: Elgar, 2015), 209ff.

961 As was the situation in CJEU judgment in *CIA Security International SA v. Signalson SA and Securitel SPRL*, C-194/94, EU:C:1996:172.

962 M. Dougan (2011 a), 425.

rights and obligations (including under Union law). As in horizontal litigation, the enforcement of substantive Union law may here come at the expense of the procedural rights of an individual litigant.[963] As is familiar, the Court of Justice has compelled Member States to provide "effective, proportionate and dissuasive" sanctions against breaches of Union law (also by individuals).[964] This requirement sought to ensure that procedural rules be sanctioned sufficiently severely through appropriate penalties or other measures against legal or physical persons who violated them. However, the proportionality limb of the test prevented undermining the legal standing of individuals through *excessive* sanctions. In such case, safeguarding Union law effectiveness would come at too high an expense for an individual litigating party (through advantaging the opposing public party). The principle of effectiveness, protecting the public interest, was instead counteracted by the principle of proportionality, which stepped in to protect individual interests.[965]

Dougan has dealt widely with decentralized enforcement by attempting to systematize the protective scope of Treaty provisions as applied by national judges.[966] He proposes a methodology for answering questions concerning access to Member State courts for Union law-based claims: Which category of persons are entitled to seek enforcement of substantive Treaty provisions before national courts, i.e. who are the intended beneficiaries of Union law rights? The answer to this question is found in the object of the Treaty provision in question: Does it seek to protect individual or collective interests? The latter case opens for a second category of beneficiaries entitled to bring proceedings – on the state side, public authorities etc., and on the private side, protective private bodies acting (as third parties) on account of other individuals, or acting in their sphere of interest.[967]

Dougan's next step is to examine what role private and public actors play in enforcing the interests at stake. Looking first at the appropriate role

---

963 As was in the case in e.g. CJEU judgment in *Commission v. Greece (Greek Maize)*, 68/88, EU:C:1989:339 and, in the context of *ex officio* review, CJEU judgment in *Heemskerk BV and Firma Schaap v. Productschap Vee en Vlees*, C-455/06, EU:C:2008:650; CJEU judgment in *Online Games Handels GmbH*, C-685/15, EU:C:2017:452.

964 CJEU judgment in *Commission v. Greece (Greek Maize)*, 68/88, EU:C:1989:339, 24; CJEU judgment in *Ivo Taricco and Others*, C-105/14, EU:C:2015:555, 39-43.

965 M. Dougan (2011 a), 426; M. Dougan (2012), 108; CJEU judgment in *M.A.S.*, C-42/17, EU:C:2017:936, 51-59.

966 M. Dougan (2012), 108.

967 Ibid., 82-86.

for private actors, it is common that Union law itself designates a circle of relevant beneficiaries, either in secondary law or through case-law.[968] In other instances, the Court of Justice defers to national courts, also on matters concerning access to justice. Whether the intended beneficiaries are pre-defined in applicable secondary law or specified by the Court, the matter of standing before national courts is normally left for the national jurisdiction to determine,[969] including the criteria of legal interest decisive for rules on standing.[970]

With regard to the requirement of effective judicial protection, an important differentiation is made between the matter of effective access to courts and the more general effectiveness of Union law. On the one hand, some national procedural rules may have (negative) consequences for the effectiveness of Union law, but oftentimes such rules must be tolerated insofar as they form part of the rules applying to national proceedings. Therefore, as concerns e.g. time-limits for bringing appeals, we can largely live with their inherent limitations on the enforcement of Union law, which would justify a higher level of deference to national law.[971] On the other hand, as concerns fundamental access to justice, the Court has purportedly been less likely to show deference, since access is in itself a prerequisite for intended beneficiaries of Union law to be able to avail themselves of their rights.[972] Jolowicz has (in other contexts) suggested that the right of standing is the most basic of procedural rights, since denial of standing has the capacity to cut short access to a substantive right even before the claimant has had a chance to make any material arguments.[973]

Whereas the above reasoning distinguishes between more versus less disruptive rules, we may also ask which type of (substantive) Union rule or right is activated in a given litigation context. When the enforcement of economic norms is at stake, it has been argued that the Court of Justice will be less likely to leave a wide discretion to the national court, because of a supposed bias towards eliminating distortions of the common market.

968 This is normally the case for substantive provisions having direct effect; ibid., 82ff.

969 To be differentiated from the situation in which also the matter of access to justice is explicitly governed in secondary law measures, or when the central substantive rule or right is in itself the objective of access to justice.

970 On legal interest and standing under EU law, see C. Warin (2019), 463.

971 See e.g. CJEU judgment in *Joan Cuadrench Moré v. Koninklijke Luchtvaart Maatschappij NV*, C-139/11, EU:C:2012:741, 24-26.

972 M. Dougan (2012), 76.

973 J. A. Jolowicz (2005), 552.

As for other "socially oriented" Union interests, the Court of Justice has (ostensibly) been less inclined to instate autonomous standing rights, instead relying more heavily on the procedural prerogatives of the Member States.[974]

Two factors have thus been discerned which may affect the Court of Justice's willingness to intervene in Member State procedural autonomy: the consequences of the procedural rule limiting access to courts and the substance/nature of the Union rule at stake. A third parameter can be added that hinges on the nature of the Union rule: whether it endeavors to protect individual or collective interests. While rules protecting private interests normally grant standing for individual beneficiaries, rules put in place to protect public interests imply standing rights for collective bodies seeking enforcement on behalf of the public.[975] Yet, third parties such as NGO's may be able to invoke not only public, but also private interests on behalf of a community of victims, indicating that private interests can be transformed into collective interests of the wider population of private beneficiaries.[976]

In distinct fields of EU law such as environmental law, whose general logic is protective of common welfare, collective standing has already materialized – even where national rules prescribe individual standing.[977]

---

974 M. Dougan (2012), 94.

975 CJEU judgment in *Bund für Umwelt und Naturschutz Deutschland, Landesverband Nordrhein-Westfalen (Trianel)*, C-115/09, EU:C:2011:289, 45-59; see commentary by C. Warin (2019), 466ff.

976 CJEU judgment in *Bund für Umwelt und Naturschutz Deutschland, Landesverband Nordrhein-Westfalen (Trianel)*, C-115/09, EU:C:2011:289, 46: "[i]f, as is clear from that provision, those organisations must be able to rely on the same rights as individuals, it would be contrary to the objective of giving the public concerned wide access to justice and at odds with the principle of effectiveness if such organisations were not also allowed to rely on the impairment of rules of EU environment law solely on the ground that those rules protect the public interest."

977 In CJEU judgment in *Bund für Umwelt und Naturschutz Deutschland, Landesverband Nordrhein-Westfalen (Trianel)*, C-115/09, EU:C:2011:289, the Court held that even though domestic legislation can limit standing only to individuals, the objective of environmental protection foreseen in EU secondary law required that NGOs not be excluded from standing – procedural autonomy was in this regard 'limited' (45-46, 50). EU environmental law thus conferred rights not only on individuals, but as is acceptable under the logic of environmental law, also on the wider public represented by an NGO, to whom domestic legislation must not deny standing (48, 56-57, 59). See also less apodictically, yet steering in this direction, CJEU judgment in *Djurgården-Lilla Värtans Miljöskyddsförening v. Stockholms kommun genom dess marknämnd*, C-263/08, EU:C:2009:631.

This may be explained by reference either to the type of right protected (public goods) or to the judicial protection of the beneficiary.[978] The context of collective standing has prompted a distinction between minor procedural constraints that we have to "live with" versus more fundamental rules of access to courts with the capacity of excluding categories of beneficiaries from the protective scope of Union rights.[979] This would provide a rationale for extending access to courts; namely to expand the range of individuals capable of seizing national courts for the particular purpose of vindicating rights (on their own behalf or on others') in order to bring claims into the judicial sphere. If the requirement of effective judicial protection is accordingly regarded as a method for instrumentalizing claims made by individuals or third-party associations as "private policemen"[980] for the enforcement of Union law, the ensuing question will be what uses such litigants are instrumentalized for.[981]

The perspective of private versus collective interests is muddled by the wider public's vested interest in the outcome of private litigation – a point which is true for the enforcement of national law and Union law equally. Collective interests or rights suggest a wider personal scope in the form of a right to standing; yet, the moment the protection of individual rights derived from EU law is designated a collective interest by default, this risks putting in place an *actio popularis* applicable to essentially all rules of Union law.[982] Although the typology of a litigation form as "non-disposi-

---

978 CJEU judgment in *ClientEarth*, C-404/13, EU:C:2014:2382; CJEU judgment in *Lesoochranárske zoskupenie VLK (II)*, C-243/15, EU:C:2016:838.

979 M. Dougan (2012), 76.

980 "[T]he notion that legal actions brought by private parties can be instrumental in strengthening compliance with EU law is as old as the very foundations of that law. This implies that private parties can be recruited as the EU's 'private attorneys general' or 'private policemen'. That means in turn that "*the vast potential resources of the general European population [are] enlisted to supplement the Commission in its efforts to secure the uniform and effective application of [EU] law*". Implicit in this private enforcement model is that these proceedings are to be brought before the competent courts of the Member States." F. Wilman (2014), 4, citing M. Dougan (2004), 76; see also M. Burley and W. Mattli (1993), 60 f.

981 M. Dougan (2012), 92-93.

982 See P. Wenneräs (2007), 108-10; C. Warin (2019), 471-74.

tive"[983] or "mandatory"[984] – i.e. as entailing public law effects[985] – may have consequences for the barring of claims (as was seen in Chapter 3), the case-law does not indicate that e.g. consumer associations can derive a right to intervene already from individual interests protected by EU secondary litigation.[986]

4.2 Beneficiaries of effectiveness under the *ex officio* mandate

Let us then consider, for the purposes of *ex officio* review, the implications of Dougan's suggested path via the beneficiaries. As described above, this path covers the personal scope of EU legislation, its substantive scope, the interests protected by the contested rule, and the character of the legal relationship at stake.[987]

Starting with horizontal relationships, the Court of Justice has been sensitive to national rules fostering judge passivity in civil litigation, prompting it to introduce the procedural rule-of-reason instead of invariably or automatically impelling *ex officio* review.[988] The *van Schijndel* ruling – for a while – remained the main dictum on *ex officio* review, signaling that effec-

983 On mandatory or binding civil law rules in Swedish procedural law, see e.g. P. O. Ekelöf and H. Edelstam (2002), 54; U. von Essen (2009), 107ff.; A. Wallerman (2019), Ch. 2.

984 H. L. MacQueen (2011). Under Art. 6 of the Napoleonic Code, French Civil Code [Code Napoléon, Code civil de Français] ordonné le 21 mars 1804 (used in Belgium, Luxembourg and France), "*on ne peut pas déroger, par des conventions particulières, aux lois qui intéressent l'ordre public et les bonnes moeurs*"/EN: "one cannot derogate by private agreement from the laws of public order and morality." Such an agreement would, to that extent, be considered null and void (in the Napoleonic orders) due to serving the cause of contravening either "the political and moral order, i.e., the organization of the State, the family and public morality" or "the economic and social order, which mainly focuses on the correct functioning of the markets." See T. Corthaut (2012), 17. The Italian system gives a similar definition in Art. 1343 of its Civil Code [*Codice Civile*] Regio Decreto 16 marzo 1942, n. 262, aggiornato il 21 aprile 2015, defining illicit contracts as such clauses that are contrary to public policy, public morality or imperative laws: "*La causa è illecita quando è contraria a norme imperative, all'ordine pubblico o al buon costume.*"

985 See A. Chayes (1976), 1281.

986 CJEU judgment in *EOS KSI Slovensko*, C-448/17, EU:C:2018:745, 41 f.

987 M. Dougan (2011 a), 425.

988 CJEU judgment in *Van Schijndel v. Stichting Pensioenfonds voor Fysiotherapeuten*, joined cases C-430/93 and C-431/93, EU:C:1995:441, 19-22.

tiveness may in some situations give way to procedural protection. Even when solely applying the *Rewe* formula, safeguards constituting basic tenets for the procedural side of effective judicial protection intervened in the effectiveness test. In horizontal litigation, additional interests than those of the litigants could be identified – such as mandatory competition rules under Union law. In *Eco Swiss*,[989] declaring the contentious contract void would promote effectiveness, but also reinforce the legal position of one party at the expense of another. The central element, with the potential of thwarting the balance between the parties, is the intervention of a common Union interest capable of justifying "appreciable enhancement of one party's legal position to the detriment of another."[990] The interests protected by the contested rule (incidentally, one litigant's interests), were in any event capable of taking the form of a collective and, where relevant, third-party interest.[991] Advocate General Saggio took into account both of these factors in his Opinion, addressing (in reference to *Rewe*) the role of the judge when intervening in relationships between private parties:[992]

> These requirements are bound up with the passive role assigned to the courts, the rules governing the relationship between the pleas of the parties and the decision handed down, and the need to safeguard the rights of the defence and ensure the proper conduct of proceedings. Moreover, arbitrators, being appointed by the parties to an agreement to settle a dispute, are under an even greater obligation to comply with the parties' wishes than a court would be, so it does not seem reasonable to require them as a matter of course to consider issues that are outside the ambit of the dispute as defined by the parties.

As in *van Schijndel*,[993] the issue at stake was not only which of the parties could potentially benefit from the decentralized enforcement of EU law, but also whether other procedural considerations, all inherent in the principle of effective judicial protection, could justify encroaching upon Union

989 CJEU judgment in *Eco Swiss China Time Ltd v. Benetton International NV*, C-126/97, EU:C:1999:269.

990 M. Dougan (2011 a), 425, referring to the issue of litigation on anti-competitive agreements in the context of CJEU judgment in *Courage Ltd v. Bernard and Crehan*, C-453/99, EU:C:2001:465.

991 M. Dougan (2012), 81.

992 The Opinion of Advocate General Saggio in *Eco Swiss China Time Ltd v. Benetton International NV*, C-126/97, EU:C:1999:97, 22, took note that "in arbitration proceedings too, these rules […] ensure proper conduct of proceedings by, in particular, protecting them from the delays inherent in examination of new pleas" – a procedural consideration benefitting the counter-party wishing to avoid *ex officio* review.

993 On which the Opinion relied.

law effectiveness. If so, this would be in the interest of the procedural rights of the parties, but to the collective detriment of beneficiaries of the Union law provisions at stake:[994]

> This appears to be even less justified in the case of competition rules, when one considers the interest of ensuring strict application of the provisions contained in Article 85 et seq. of the Treaty, an interest that clearly extends beyond the interests of private parties to those of other undertakings, potential competitors and consumers. [T]he need to supervise arbitration awards to ensure that they are compatible with Community law is particularly great in an area, such as competition, where there is a general interest in observance of the rules to ensure the smooth functioning of the common market.

The present reasoning illustrates how the protective scope of the contested rule (protection of the internal market and of victims of anti-competitive behavior) led to the prioritization of the effective enforcement of substantive EU law over the proper or efficient conduct of arbitration proceedings. The beneficiary of effectiveness was the public, whereas the designation of individuals as beneficiaries was incidental, or even instrumental (private litigation triggering public enforcement).[995] Examples from the consumer case-law also lend support to Dougan's emphasis on the substantive scope of the rule at stake, applying itself with particularly strong force when its protective scope is of collective character.[996] The beneficiary of the principle of effectiveness is thus to be sought with reference to the protective scope of applicable substantive Union law.

The ruling in *Peterbroeck* initially reinforced the picture painted above, insofar that the invoked EU rule was granted effectiveness through requiring that procedural obstacles be set aside to the advantage of the private beneficiary.[997] The beneficiary of the substantive right coincided with the beneficiary of the principle of effectiveness (which in that case had no im-

---

994 Opinion of Advocate General Saggio in *Eco Swiss China Time Ltd v. Benetton International NV*, C-126/97, EU:C:1999:97, 35; see also CJEU judgment in *Eco Swiss China Time Ltd v. Benetton International NV*, C-126/97, EU:C:1999:269, 41 (note, however, that the Court did accept the justification of *res judicata*, with regards to the final interim award, 43-47).

995 M. Dougan (2011 a), 425 (in reference to other cases); C. Warin (2017), 53-57.

996 As discussed in Chapters 3-4 above, EU consumer legislation has as clear prerogative to protect consumers against abuse by commercial contractual parties. Procedural safeguards were in that case-law explicitly linked to strengthening the beneficiary falling within the protective scope of the substantive rights. See e.g. C. Warin (2019), 475 f. on collective standing in EU consumer litigation.

997 CJEU judgment in *Peterbroeck, Van Campenhout & Cie v. Belgian State*, C-312/93, EU:C:1995:437, 21.

mediately implicated other beneficiaries even though the freedom of establishment might be deemed a collective interest). However, in other instances of administrative proceedings, the public interest vested in the outcome of the case did not prompt the Court of Justice to deviate from the *van Schijndel* dictum.[998] Collective interests hence do not always tilt the balance towards Union law effectiveness over due conduct of procedure; nor does the vertical nature of the litigation automatically grant investigative powers to administrative courts.

4.3 Beneficiaries of effective judicial protection under the *ex officio* mandate

The right or capacity to seek enforcement of EU law – which is commonly discussed in terms of direct effect – was in Dougan's typology instead linked to the matter of standing. This procedural context allows the reasoning to be extrapolated to the notions of effectiveness and effective judicial protection. The beneficiaries of *effectiveness* were, in the examined case-law, individual litigants – although sometimes substantive rules at the origin of the litigation were intended to protect a wider public of beneficiaries, including collectives of litigants. If the substantive rules at stake are given variable importance based on whether they constitute purely individual or also collective interests, this will trigger an estimation of how far-reaching sacrifices may be made to legitimately protect them without protracting from other litigants' rights of procedural and substantive nature.

In the interest of systematic clarity, this issue must be kept apart from the legal relationship between litigants – to be approached from the perspective of *effective judicial protection*. The horizontal versus vertical relationship between litigants does not change the beneficiary of the substantive right(s), nor does it – as above argued – necessarily change the priorities in applying the principle of *effectiveness*. However, the legal relationship between the parties may affect the possibilities of preserving the substantive interests of the identified beneficiary of Union rights. *Horizontal* relationships can make it necessary to accept encroachments on substantive rules of Union law in the interest of protecting the legal certainty of the opposing party. These considerations would become more explicit un-

998 CJEU judgment in *Aannemersbedrijf P.K. Kraaijeveld BV e.a. v. Gedeputeerde Staten van Zuid-Holland*, C-72/95, EU:C:1996:404, 57-60.

der the fundamental rights approach – even in horizontal litigation.[999] The latter case-law widened the view on beneficiaries of the procedural side of effective judicial protection above and beyond the reach of designated beneficiaries of substantive EU law.[1000]

Vertical litigation raises similar concerns for procedural protection of individual litigants as do horizontal relationships, whereas procedural protection of public bodies carries less weight as against individuals' substantive protection.[1001] In inverse vertical litigation, the need for proportionate and dissuasive measures against violations of EU law is opposed to the protection of individual parties against public authorities' encroachments on their rights.[1002] Where relevant EU legislation creates individual *obligations* – rather than *rights* – the beneficiary of the principle of effectiveness, following the reasoning proposed above, is the public. The Court of Justice has nonetheless been sensitive to the preservation of procedural rights of applicants that form part of the very essence of the principle of effective judicial protection.[1003] Still, this does not mean that *ex officio* review can be dispensed with as soon as it would have negative consequences for any litigant.[1004] Both the foundational case-law and more recent rulings demonstrate an ambivalence between effectiveness of EU law and due process, pinpointing an incompatibility between the beneficiaries of the substantive and procedural side of effective judicial protection.[1005]

---

999 CJEU judgment in *Sanchez Morcillo and Abril García (I)*, C-169/14, EU:C:2014:2099, 49.

1000 CJEU judgment in *Banif Plus Bank Zrt v. Csaba Csipai*, C-472/11, EU:C:2013:88, 34-36.

1001 Yet, this does not automatically lead to investigative *obligations* as compared to use of existing *powers*, as follows from a comparison between CJEU judgment in *Aannemersbedrijf P.K. Kraaijeveld BV e.a. v. Gedeputeerde Staten van Zuid-Holland*, C-72/95, EU:C:1996:404, 57-60 and CJEU judgment in *Peterbroeck, Van Campenhout & Cie v. Belgian State*, C-312/93, EU:C:1995:437, 21.

1002 M. Dougan (2012), 104-7, discussing the line of case-law starting with CJEU judgment in *Commission v. Greece (Greek Maize)*, 68/88, EU:C:1989:339.

1003 CJEU judgment in *Heemskerk BV and Firma Schaap v. Productschap Vee en Vlees*, C-455/06, EU:C:2008:650, 47.

1004 CJEU judgment in *Online Games Handels GmbH*, C-685/15, EU:C:2017:452.

1005 The Opinion of Advocate General Bot in *Heemskerk BV and Firma Schaap v. Productschap Vee en Vlees*, C-455/06, EU:C:2008:258, 119-20, took into account the substantive interests justifying obligations under EU law whereas the Court of Justice focalized on justifications for the procedural prohibition against *reformatio in pejus*; CJEU judgment in *Heemskerk BV and Firma Schaap v. Productschap Vee en Vlees*, C-455/06, EU:C:2008:650, 47. Cf. CJEU judgment in *Online Games Handels GmbH*, C-685/15, EU:C:2017:452.

The above representation of divergent beneficiaries suggests that insofar as the substantive side of the principle of effective judicial protection is given priority over its procedural side, this might have the effect of limiting the principle's protective scope to the beneficiaries of EU substantive law. Prioritizing the procedural side of the principle of effective judicial protection, by contrast, may extend its protective scope to any litigant hoping for a proper conduct of proceedings. The forthcoming section will show how a balance was struck between procedural equality and procedural equity through both concrete and abstract assessments of exclusionary litigation costs.

4.3.1 Financially weak beneficiaries of EU law

The issue of costs for litigation is on the borderline between procedural obstacles and encroachments on Art. 47 CFR, seeing as prohibitive expenses are capable of negating access to court.[1006] The case of *DEB*[1007] – which founded the fundamental rights approach – concerned national legislation that only allowed legal aid insofar as lack of representation would run counter to public interests. This limitation, in conjunction with court fees, made the cause of action for State liability unavailable to a litigant with limited financial resources, purportedly amounting to a denial of justice.

The ruling shifted the emphasis from effective implementation of EU law to access to venues of litigation. Instead of treating the national legislation as a "traditional" obstacle to the effectiveness of EU law, the Court of Justice required that the arsenal of legal matter giving substance to the principle of effective judicial protection be utilized; its foundation in the constitutional traditions of the Member States and in Art. 6 ECHR, as well as its reinforced legal status following its codification in EU primary

1006 J. Krommendijk (2016), 1413 f. uses the differentiation between soft and hard exclusionary rules to explain the differences of outcome in e.g. CJEU judgment in *Liivimaa Lihaveis MTÜ v. Eesti-Läti programmi 2007-2013 Seirekomitee*, C-562/12, EU:C:2014:2229 (prohibitive ban) versus CJEU judgment in *ET Agrokonsulting-04-Velko Stoyanov v. Izpalnitelen direktor na Darzhaven fond «Zemedelie» - Razplashtatelna agentsia*, C-93/12, EU:C:2013:432 (access to single court with exclusive jurisdiction).

1007 CJEU judgment in *Deutsche Energiehandels- und Beratungsgesellschaft mbH v. Bundesrepublik Deutschland (DEB)*, C-279/09, EU:C:2010:811; commented by H. C.H. Hofmann (2014 a) and J. Engström (2011), 53.

law.[1008] The ruling instructed the national court to balance the right to effective judicial protection against the legitimacy and proportionality of the national rule limiting access to legal aid.[1009]

A strong link was thus identified between the cost and realization of litigation. Yet how poor must a litigant be and how debilitating are the litigation costs for access to court? The Court has elsewhere addressed both the general effects of the litigation costs and the financial situation of a given litigant. Although effective remedies must not be "prohibitively expensive",[1010] the financial situation of a claimant is not the sole factor for assessing whether judicial protection has been granted:[1011]

> the national court [...] may also take into account the situation of the parties concerned, whether the claimant has a reasonable prospect of success, the importance of what is at stake for the claimant and for the protection of the environment, the complexity of the relevant law and procedure, the potentially frivolous nature of the claim at its various stages, and the existence of a national legal aid scheme or a costs protection regime.

Combatting "frivolous" claims is thus a valid reason for restricting access to court, in the interest of the efficient conduct of proceedings. However, prohibitive effects are to be assessed on principle, and not *in casu:* "the fact that a claimant has not been deterred, in practice, from asserting his claim is not of itself sufficient to establish that the proceedings are not prohibitively expensive for him."[1012]

That burdensome litigation costs are to be assessed in the abstract was confirmed with respect to court fees in public procurement, where the financial capacity of tenderers was also evoked. The resulting balancing exercise took moderate account of litigants' financial situation. On the one hand, the Court was satisfied that the proportionality between the imposed charges and the tendered contract meant that the costs would be "modest" for smaller contracts, which (it can be induced) would attract

---

1008 CJEU judgment in *Deutsche Energiehandels- und Beratungsgesellschaft mbH v. Bundesrepublik Deutschland (DEB)*, C-279/09, EU:C:2010:811, 29-31. See also CJEU judgment in *Vladimir Peftiev*, C-314/13, EU:C:2014:1645, 25-29 (limiting the discretion of national authorities when applying secondary EU legislation in a manner contrary to Art. 47 CFR).

1009 Ibid., 60-62. This concern also transpired throughout the case-law on consumer protection starting with CJEU judgment in *Océano Grupo Editorial and Salvat Editores*, joined cases C-240/98 to C-244/98, EU:C:2000:346, 26-28.

1010 CJEU judgment in *Edwards and Pallikaropoulos*, C-260/11, EU:C:2013:221, 33.

1011 Ibid., 46.

1012 Ibid., 47.

smaller tenderers. Any inhibitive effect of such fees were, under this rationale, easier to accept, in view of their objective of dissuading what was in *Edwards* designated "frivolous" claims.[1013] On the other hand, in the interest of predictability and non-discrimination (foundational tenets of EU public procurement), the Court rejected arguments for further shielding litigants with *de facto* "weak financial capacity"[1014], supporting the view already taken in this work that protective prerogatives in secondary law do not by default extend to all financially weak EU law litigants.

4.3.2 Legal bases for protecting procedurally vulnerable beneficiaries

Besides keen concern for the deterrent cost of litigation, the area of consumer law has in common with the above-discussed public procurement cases a pragmatic use of legal sources for customized levels of protection.[1015] The seminal ruling in *Océano* had relied directly on the protective prerogative foreseen in the Unfair Terms Directive, requiring the national judge to ensure this objective through its interpretation of national procedural law.[1016] This reasoning was recalled throughout the consumer protection case-law, referring interchangeably to specific provisions of consumer protection directives, their functioning in the national procedural framework, and the directives' overall objective of granting procedural protection of consumers.[1017] Effective consumer protection and legal protection of consumers in these rulings translated *inter alia* into a requirement of full effectiveness of Union objectives.[1018]

1013 CJEU judgment in *SC Star Storage SA and Others*, joined cases C-439/14 and C-488/14, EU:C:2016:688, 58-61; CJEU judgment in *Orizzonte Salute*, C-61/14, EU:C:2015:655, 56.

1014 CJEU judgment in *Orizzonte Salute*, C-61/14, EU:C:2015:655, 62-64.

1015 Ibid.; CJEU judgment in *SC Star Storage SA and Others*, joined cases C-439/14 and C-488/14, EU:C:2016:688, 61.

1016 CJEU judgment in *Océano Grupo Editorial and Salvat Editores*, joined cases C-240/98 to C-244/98, EU:C:2000:346, 28.

1017 See e.g. CJEU judgment in *Elisa María Mostaza Claro v. Centro Móvil Milenium SL*, C-168/05, EU:C:2006:675, 28; CJEU judgment in *Rampion and Godard*, C-429/05, EU:C:2007:575, 61-65.

1018 CJEU judgment in *Rampion and Godard*, C-429/05, EU:C:2007:575, 61-65; CJEU judgment in *Banif Plus Bank Zrt v. Csaba Csipai*, C-472/11, EU:C:2013:88, 28; CJEU judgment in *Ernst Georg Radlinger v. Finway a.s.*, C-377/14, EU:C:2016:283, 79.

Other consumer case-law exclusively or additionally examined whether national rules made it virtually impossible or excessively difficult to enjoy the legal protection foreseen in the directives, i.e. the *Rewe* formula.[1019] In rulings prescribing the *van Schijndel* test for weighing the protective imperative against the role and purposes of national rules of procedure, the effectiveness of relevant directives was repeatedly granted priority over national procedural law.[1020]

Although their legal bases differ, both full effectiveness and *Rewe*-effectiveness were in these strands of case-law preoccupied with the vulnerable litigating position of consumers whose protection was the overarching objective of EU secondary law.[1021] Since the vulnerable litigant and the beneficiary of substantive law coincided, the Court's rationalizations merged the protective prerogative with an instrumental language of deterrence:[1022]

> in a system [...] intended to put a stop to unfair terms detrimental to consumers' interests, the court's power to determine of its own motion whether a term is unfair must be regarded as constituting a proper means both of achieving the result sought by Article 6 of the Directive, namely, preventing an individual consumer from being bound by an unfair term, and of contributing to achieving the aim of Article 7, since if the court undertakes such an examination, that may act as a deterrent and contribute to preventing unfair terms[.]

The principle of effective judicial protection – including the right to an effective remedy as laid down in EU secondary law – has increasingly afforded an additional basis for formulating protective imperatives governing na-

1019 See e.g. CJEU judgment in *Cofidis SA v. Jean-Louis Fredout*, C-473/00, EU:C:2002:705, 33; CJEU judgment in *Banco Español de Crédito SA v. Joaquín Calderón Camino*, C-618/10, EU:C:2012:349, 49, 53; CJEU judgment in *Mohamed Aziz v. Caixa d'Estalvis de Catalunya*, C-415/11, EU:C:2013:164, 52-63; CJEU judgment in *Erika Jőrös v. Aegon Magyarország Hitel Zrt.*, C-397/11, EU:C:2013:340, 32.

1020 CJEU judgment in *Banco Español de Crédito SA v. Joaquín Calderón Camino*, C-618/10, EU:C:2012:349, 54; see also CJEU judgment in *Cofidis SA v. Jean-Louis Fredout*, C-473/00, EU:C:2002:705, 35-37 and CJEU judgment in *Mohamed Aziz v. Caixa d'Estalvis de Catalunya*, C-415/11, EU:C:2013:164, 58, 63 (with regard only to the first question posed by the national court).

1021 CJEU judgment in *Océano Grupo Editorial and Salvat Editores*, joined cases C-240/98 to C-244/98, EU:C:2000:346, 28 (full effectiveness); CJEU judgment in *Banco Español de Crédito SA v. Joaquín Calderón Camino*, C-618/10, EU:C:2012:349, 54 (*Rewe*-effectiveness).

1022 CJEU judgment in *Océano Grupo Editorial and Salvat Editores*, joined cases C-240/98 to C-244/98, EU:C:2000:346, 28.

tional judges' EU mandate of *ex officio* review.[1023] In many instances, the choice of legal source from which to derive an obligation of judicial protection appeared to be of limited importance for the final priority of protecting consumers, through ensuring the correct application of the relevant directives. The resilient protective agenda of the consumer case-law explains why national courts seized in consumer-to-business litigation have, by comparison, more often been asked to set aside procedural obstacles, than in the general case-law on *ex officio* review. The beneficiaries of *Rewe*-effectiveness, *Simmenthal*-effectiveness and effective judicial protection here routinely coincide – judicial protection is in and of itself furthered by ensuring the effective implementation and enforcement of EU secondary law. This observation aligns with the approach of tracing the beneficiaries of effectiveness back to the source of the substantive right at stake; hence focusing on judicial protection or provision of legal remedies as quasi-substantive right.[1024]

That is not to say that effectiveness and effective judicial protection must *always* coincide when secondary Union law unequivocally identifies its beneficiaries. As already discussed in Chapter 3, the interests of a vulnerable litigant have sometimes clashed with the judicial protection of the seller or creditor against whom he is litigating. The case-law has increasingly emphasized the need to take the interests of opposing parties, who may be

1023 Effective judicial protection was evoked in connection with *Rewe*-effectiveness in CJEU judgment in *ERSTE Bank Hungary Zrt. v. Attila Sugár*, C-32/14, EU:C:2015:637 and CJEU judgment in *Ernst Georg Radlinger v. Finway a.s.*, C-377/14, EU:C:2016:283, whereas it was raised distinctly from full effectiveness in CJEU judgment in *Banif Plus Bank Zrt v. Csaba Csipai*, C-472/11, EU:C:2013:88, 29-34 (referring to CJEU judgment in *Commission v. Ireland*, C-89/08 P, EU:C:2009:742, 50, 54 concerning *ex officio* review by the General Court).

1024 These requirements are quasi-substantive in their legal-technical construction – constituting a key objective in Council Directive 93/13/EEC of 5 April 1993 on unfair terms in consumer contracts, OJ L 095, 21/04/1993, 29 (Preamble and Art. 7), and an autonomous objective in Directive 2009/22/EC of the European Parliament and of the Council of 23 April 2009 on injunctions for the protection of consumers' interests, OJ L 110, 01/05/2009, 30. The merging of substantive goals and procedural means is not exclusive to consumer protection law; with more patent examples in e.g. Council Directive 97/80/EC of 15 December 1997 on the burden of proof in cases of discrimination based on sex, OJ L 14, 20/1/1998, 6; Council Directive 89/665/EEC of 21 December 1989 on the coordination of the laws, regulations and administrative provisions relating to the application of review procedures to the award of public supply and public works contracts, OJ L 395, 30/12/1989.

disadvantaged by the exercise of *ex officio* review, into account.[1025] The objective of deterring "frivolous" claims can potentially also protect public and private defendants.[1026]

Moreover, in the presence of secondary law with the capacity to protect the creditor, the procedural interests of the consumer may be slighted.[1027] This constellation displays a competition for effective judicial protection between consumers' right to defense and creditors' access to court; also the latter in capacity of beneficiaries of the effectiveness of secondary Union law.[1028]

The principle of effective judicial protection, as legal basis, increasingly emphasizes individual procedural protection in the abstract when, as in the example above, there are beneficiaries of EU substantive law on both sides of the litigation. Under an individual fundamental rights approach (i.e. which does not distinguish between beneficiaries and non-beneficiaries of EU law) there is greater room to take other procedural factors into account that may disadvantage an EU law beneficiary. One such key consideration is procedural equity grounds for sanctioning litigants' inertia. We have seen in Chapter 3 how consumer protection required national courts to compensate for consumers' knowledge deficits.[1029] But where do we draw the line towards the type of inertia that would justify deviation from the forgiving standard sustained in the consumer case-law? This question is considered in the forthcoming section.

1025 CJEU judgment in *Banif Plus Bank Zrt v. Csaba Csipai*, C-472/11, EU:C:2013:88, 34-36; Opinion of Advocate General Szpunar in *Finanmadrid EFC SA v. Jesús Vicente Albán Zambrano and Others*, C-49/14, EU:C:2015:746, 94.

1026 CJEU judgment in *Edwards and Pallikaropoulos*, C-260/11, EU:C:2013:221, 42.

1027 CJEU judgment in *Hypoteční banka a.s. v. Udo Mike Lindner*, C-327/10, EU:C:2011:745, 53-54; in reference to Council Regulation (EC) No 44/2001 of 22 December 2000 on jurisdiction and the recognition and enforcement of judgments in civil and commercial matters (Brussels I Regulation), OJ L 012, 16/01/2001, 1.

1028 E.g. under Council Regulation (EC) No 44/2001 of 22 December 2000 on jurisdiction and the recognition and enforcement of judgments in civil and commercial matters (Brussels I Regulation), OJ L 012, 16/01/2001, 1.

1029 E.g. CJEU judgment in *Océano Grupo Editorial and Salvat Editores*, joined cases C-240/98 to C-244/98, EU:C:2000:346, 26.

4.3.3 Responsibility for litigation lapses by the EU law beneficiary

Although the Court's reasoning in e.g. *Peterbroeck* was limited to compliance with the *Rewe* principles, effective judicial protection as today understood was in fact the central issue.[1030] As previously argued in this work, the pertinent connection to effective judicial protection was whether "genuine opportunity to raise a plea based on Community law" had been given[1031] – if not, then access to a court or tribunal had not been granted for the purpose of having the EU law-based plea tried.

Auxiliary to the obligation to provide genuine opportunity, is what the result will be if this opportunity is not relied upon by its beneficiary: Do procedural omissions tilt the balance in favor of procedural formalism[1032] over the overlooked aspect of Union law effectiveness? In the case of consumers, the Court's initial answer was no:[1033]

> While it is the case that, in a number of Member States, procedural rules enable individuals to defend themselves in such proceedings, there is a real risk that the consumer, particularly because of ignorance of the law, will not challenge the term pleaded against him on the grounds that it is unfair.

Linking onto this, does a "weak" litigant who is also EU law beneficiary forfeit his right to effective judicial protection when he is *flagrantly* lethar-

---

1030 See also CJEU judgment in *van der Weerd and Others v. Minister van Landbouw, Natuur en Voedselkwaliteit*, joined cases C-222/05 to C-225/05, EU:C:2007:318, 41.

1031 Opinion of Advocate General Bot in *Heemskerk BV and Firma Schaap v. Productschap Vee en Vlees*, C-455/06, EU:C:2008:258, 126; see also CJEU judgment in *van der Weerd and Others v. Minister van Landbouw, Natuur en Voedselkwaliteit*, joined cases C-222/05 to C-225/05, EU:C:2007:318, 41; Opinion of Advocate General Mengozzi in *Abdelhafid Bensada Benallal v. État belge*, C-161/15, EU:C:2016:3, 42.

1032 The notion of procedural formalism is here used synonymously with procedural idiosyncrasy, drawing on the definition of legal formalism put forwards by C. J. Peters (2015), 24: "the idea that judges and other decisionmakers should decide particular cases, to the extent possible, by the mechanical application of existing legal rules. Those existing rules might come from constitutional provisions, from statutes, from treaties, from administrative regulations, or from the decisions of prior courts [...] There is, then, a quite literal relationship of semantic or logical entailment between pure legal formalism and judicial constraint."

1033 See e.g. CJEU judgment in *Océano Grupo Editorial and Salvat Editores*, joined cases C-240/98 to C-244/98, EU:C:2000:346, 26.

gic? As has been reaffirmed in multiple rulings and Opinions,[1034] "the need to comply with the principle of effectiveness cannot be stretched so far as to mean that [...] a national court is required [...] to make up fully for the total inertia on the part of the consumer".[1035] Even though this case-law was already covered in Chapter 3 above, a few reflections are in place relating to the nature of national courts' responsibilities. When a substantive EU law beneficiary could be identified, the latter's procedural status (in the consumer law, emblematic financial vulnerability), sharpened the court's responsibility for *ex officio* review – yet did not automatically require the principle of *res judicata* to be transgressed, i.e. for a closed case to be re-opened.[1036] The possibility to re-open the proceedings as well as the ambit of the proceedings under national law guided what remedies were available to consumers.

With respect to access to the preliminary reference mechanism, the Court initially maintained that this remains the responsibility of the national court only – sanctions against beneficiaries in response to procedural omissions do not go so far as to preclude the seized judge from making a preliminary reference.[1037] An inadvertent beneficiary of Union law could thus expect a preliminary reference to be made – irrespective of national rules limiting the ambit of the proceedings – since the appraisal of need for guidance from the Court of Justice is to be "completely independent of any initiative by the parties",[1038] under the conditions laid down in

1034 E.g. in CJEU judgment in *Finanmadrid EFC SA v. Jesús Vicente Albán Zambrano and Others*, C-49/14, EU:C:2016:98, 51-52; CJEU judgment in *Monika Kušionová v. SMART Capital a.s.*, C-34/13, EU:C:2014:2189, 56; CJEU judgment in *ERSTE Bank Hungary Zrt. v. Attila Sugár*, C-32/14, EU:C:2015:637, 62; Opinion of Advocate General Szpunar in *Finanmadrid EFC SA v. Jesús Vicente Albán Zambrano and Others*, C-49/14, EU:C:2015:746, 43; Opinion of Advocate General Mengozzi in *Abdelhafid Bensada Benallal v. État belge*, C-161/15, EU:C:2016:3, 42.

1035 CJEU judgment in *Asturcom Telecomunicaciones SL v. Cristina Rodríguez Nogueira*, C-40/08, EU:C:2009:615, 47.

1036 CJEU judgment in *Banco Primus SA v. Jesús Gutiérrez García*, C-421/14, EU:C:2017:60, 49.

1037 CJEU judgment in *Willy Kempter KG v. Hauptzollamt Hamburg-Jonas*, C-2/06, EU:C:2008:78, 41.

1038 CJEU judgment in *Cartesio Oktató és Szolgáltató bt*, C-210/06, EU:C:2008:723, 90; see also CJEU judgment in *Patrick Kelly v. National University of Ireland*, C-104/10, EU:C:2011:506, 62; CJEU judgment in *Consiglio nazionale dei geologi and Autorità garante della concorrenza e del mercato*, C-136/12, EU:C:2013:489, 28.

Art. 267 TFEU.[1039] In practice, however, if a national court considers a claim to be time-barred or outside the ambit of the proceedings, the Court of Justice will deem the matter hypothetical, and therefore that aspect of a preliminary reference inadmissible.[1040] In this respect, even if national courts maintain the widest possible discretion – independent of party initiative – to pose a question to the Court of Justice, the beneficiary of EU law will have no guarantee that the referring court's question will be answered.

4.4 Interim conclusions

The present chapter has contemplated the personal scope of protection of Union-origin rules and rights, commenting on the scholarly contention that the respective principles of effectiveness and effective judicial protection differ in subjective scope.[1041] Against this backdrop, the beneficiaries of effectiveness and effective judicial protection have as far as possible been distinguished. The method of tracking beneficiaries of those principles and norms proved useful in order to understand their content and reach.

Examining the principle of *effectiveness* from the viewpoint of its beneficiaries required taking a path via the substantive rule at stake; particularly its protective scope.[1042] In the case-law on *ex officio* review, the priority of substantive protection through Union law effectiveness singled out the litigant benefitting from EU law as beneficiary of the principle of effectiveness.

The priority of procedural protection had a wider range of beneficiaries, both due to the broad construction of the principle of effective judicial protection under EU law, and due to the latter's variety of origins in EU, international and national law. Codification efforts directed the analysis towards secondary legislation laying down substantive and quasi-substantive rules and rights. The principle of effective judicial protection demon-

1039 CJEU judgment in *Puligienica Facility Esco SpA (PFE) v. Airgest SpA*, C-689/13, EU:C:2016:199, 34; see also CJEU judgment in *Aziz Melki and Sélim Abdeli*, joined cases C-188/10 and C-189/10, EU:C:2010:363, 42, and CJEU judgment in *Georgi Ivanov Elchinov v. Natsionalna zdravnoosiguritelna kasa*, C-173/09, EU:C:2010:581, 27.

1040 CJEU judgment in *Lucio Cesare Aquino v. Belgische Staat*, C-3/16, EU:C:2017:209, 44-46.

1041 M. Dougan (2011 a), 424-25, 431.

1042 M. Dougan (2012), 87-94.

strated capacity to protect both procedural and substantive interests of litigants, whereas quandaries arose when effectiveness benefitted one party at the same time as procedural protection benefitted another.

Three factors were examined that hinged on the personal scope of substantive or quasi-substantive rights: the normative prerogative to protect unresourceful litigants, the need to compensate for procedural inequality,[1043] and the responsibility for litigation lapses and/or inertia. The concern for procedural protection transpired throughout the case-law on consumer protection, and also resonated in assessments as to whether prohibitive costs for legal representation and litigation amounted to *de facto* exclusion from access to court.[1044]

Yet, these concerns may strike in both directions, tilting the scale towards effectiveness in order to require *ex officio* review in the face of "significant" imbalances,[1045] or towards procedural protection interpreted as access to justice.[1046] Whereas in the consumer case-law, useful effect/full effect, *Rewe*-effectiveness and effective judicial protection frequently converged towards protecting the (coinciding) beneficiary of substantive and procedural rights, the present chapter has also identified instances of ambivalence as a result of opposing prerogatives and beneficiaries. The final aspect of procedural omissions raised an important matter of principle – the unfairness against the other litigating party entailed by the court compensating for litigation errors. Although the principle of effective judicial protection on occasion required a national court to apply Union law of its own motion, this did not mean compensating for complete inertia on the side of the beneficiary party.[1047] Protecting a party who had a chance, but

---

1043 CJEU judgment in *Mohamed Aziz v. Caixa d'Estalvis de Catalunya*, C-415/11, EU:C:2013:164, 76.

1044 CJEU judgment in *Edwards and Pallikaropoulos*, C-260/11, EU:C:2013:221; CJEU judgment in *Deutsche Energiehandels- und Beratungsgesellschaft mbH v. Bundesrepublik Deutschland (DEB)*, C-279/09, EU:C:2010:811; CJEU judgment in *Vladimir Peftiev*, C-314/13, EU:C:2014:1645, 29. CJEU judgment in *Orizzonte Salute*, C-61/14, EU:C:2015:655.

1045 E.g. CJEU judgment in *Elisa María Mostaza Claro v. Centro Móvil Milenium SL*, C-168/05, EU:C:2006:675, 36-38.

1046 Opinion of Advocate General Szpunar in *Finanmadrid EFC SA v. Jesús Vicente Albán Zambrano and Others*, C-49/14, EU:C:2015:746, 43 (effectiveness), 94; cf. CJEU judgment in *Hypoteční banka a.s. v. Udo Mike Lindner*, C-327/10, EU:C:2011:745.

1047 CJEU judgment in *Asturcom Telecomunicaciones SL v. Cristina Rodríguez Nogueira*, C-40/08, EU:C:2009:615, 47; CJEU judgment in *Monika Kušionová v. SMART Capital a.s.*, C-34/13, EU:C:2014:2189, 56.

did not use it, would tilt the balance from appropriate use of investigative powers to potential excess, by implication thwarting the procedural rights of the opposing party.[1048]

1048 *Hypoteční banka a.s. v. Udo Mike Lindner*, C-327/10, EU:C:2011:745, 53-54.

5 Effective judicial protection in the service of effectiveness or procedural protection?

There is a dual role for effective judicial protection: on the one hand, protection of the beneficiary of EU law (general principle) and on the other, protection of the integrity of the proceedings (fundamental right). The present chapter explores various forms in which the principle of effective judicial protection has surfaced, fitting the above considered case-law on *ex officio* review into the context of wider legal developments. While the effectiveness of substantive EU law and the requirements of effective judicial protection are not systematically opposed,[1049] this chapter focuses on situations where they do conflict or where there is at least a tension between their respective beneficiaries.

In section 5.1, terminological distinctions are made between effectiveness and effective judicial protection, including their mechanisms of complementarity. An alternative view on effective judicial protection as independent from substantive rights of EU law emphasizes its procedural justice aspect, which may or may not coincide with protecting the Union law beneficiary.[1050] The section also links various components of effective judicial protection to its present legal bases.

Section 5.2 illustrates additional tensions that arise when effective judicial protection is understood in its contemporary character of fundamental right. Three types of conflict are considered that are symptomatic to the fundamental rights approach: tensions between various guises of procedural protection; tensions between procedural protection and effectiveness of substantive EU law, and tensions between individual procedural protection and the effectiveness of EU procedural frameworks.

While the status of the right to judicial protection has ostensibly been reinforced, its codification in the Charter may in fact have activated a de-

1049 Tensions are similarly traced by S. Prechal (2016), while H. C.H. Hofmann (2014 a), 1222, emphasizes convergence in their common endeavor to "avoid situations of denial of justice in cases of rights under EU law"; see also Opinion of Advocate General Wahl in *Sanchez Morcillo and Abril García (I)*, C-169/14, EU:C:2014:2110, 77-78.

1050 See L. M. Ravo (2012), 101.

cline in *de facto* individual procedural protection.[1051] Section 5.3 explains this contradiction by recourse to available avenues for justification of encroachments on effectiveness, effective judicial protection, and full effect.

A few conceptual clarifications are in place, before embarking on this jurisprudence.

5.1 Origins of the principle of effective judicial protection

While *Rewe*-effectiveness is based on the long-since codified duty of sincere co-operation, the principle of effective judicial protection was first codified in the Charter in 2000 and granted Treaty status through the Lisbon Treaties in 2009. The right to effective judicial protection has since been derived directly from Art. 47 CFR, whereas Art. 19(1) is increasingly evoked either together with Art. 47 CFR or autonomously.[1052]

Art. 19(1) TEU prescribes a distinct obligation (national judges included) to provide legal protection in the fields covered by EU law. The provision describes the mandate of national courts, rather than defining the notion of judicial protection itself. Essentially it links judicial protection to substantive Union prerogatives[1053] (as does Art. 51(1) CFR in reference to the implementation of EU law).[1054] At the same time, both Art. 51(1) CFR and Art. 19(1) TEU remind that the fields covered by EU law are granted effectiveness through the provision of a remedy, so that judicial protection

1051 On the development of effective judicial protection from general principle to codified and self-standing fundamental right, see section 2.3 of the present work.

1052 See e.g. CJEU judgment in *Associação Sindical dos Juízes Portugueses*, C-64/16, EU:C:2018:117 (Art. 19 paired with Art. 47); CJEU judgment in *Slowakische Republik v. Achmea BV*, C-284/16, EU:C:2018:158 and CJEU judgment in *Carlos Escribano Vindel v. Ministerio de Justicia*, C-49/18, EU:C:2019:106 (Art. 19 used autonomously).

1053 Art. 19(1) TEU: "Member States shall provide remedies sufficient to ensure effective legal protection in the fields covered by Union law."

1054 Art. 51(1) CFR: "The provisions of this Charter are addressed to the institutions and bodies of the Union with due regard for the principle of subsidiarity and to the Member States *only when they are implementing* Union law. They shall therefore respect the rights, observe the principles and promote the application thereof in accordance with their respective powers" (here emphasized).

and effectiveness of rules and rights under EU law converge in the mandate of the national judge.[1055]

While Art. 19(1) TEU has been on the rise as legal basis, ancillary justifications for compliance with it have in instances been sought elsewhere. A new perspective transpires in the recent emphasis on mutual trust in shared common values (particularly, the rule of law), placing minimum standards on the national judiciaries.[1056]

5.1.1 Complementarity between *Rewe*-effectiveness and effective judicial protection

It is sometimes asserted that the principles of effectiveness and effective judicial protection *enshrine*, *embody* or *mutually reinforce* each other.[1057] In the case-law and scholarship, it is possible to delineate (more or less) distinctive takes on their interrelationship.

There is, first of all, the understanding that the principle of effective judicial protection represents an umbrella requirement including – but not limited to – the *Rewe* criteria of equivalence and effectiveness. Effectiveness should consequently fall under the principle of effective judicial protection – an "aspect or sub-principle" of the latter.[1058] This would mean that failure to comply with either of the *Rewe* criteria represents an encroachment on effective judicial protection; a view that appears to be on the decline in the case-law of the Court of Justice, although it prevails in some Opinions.[1059]

1055 CJEU judgment in *Carlos Escribano Vindel v. Ministerio de Justicia*, C-49/18, EU:C:2019:106, 62.

1056 CJEU judgment in *Associação Sindical dos Juízes Portugueses,* C-64/16, EU:C:2018:117, 30-32; see also CJEU judgment in *Slowakische Republik v. Achmea BV*, C-284/16, EU:C:2018:158, 34; CJEU judgment in *LM (Judicial independence in Poland),* C-216/18 PPU, EU:C:2018:586 (both pairing Art. 2 with Art. 19(1) TEU).

1057 See e.g. Opinion of Advocate General Cruz Villalón in *Coty Germany GmbH*, C-580/13, EU:C:2015:243, fn. 16; CJEU judgment in *Alassini and Others*, C-317/08, EU:C:2010:146, 46.

1058 J. Krommendijk (2016), 1409.

1059 CJEU judgment in *i-21 Germany*, joined cases C-392/04 and C-422/04, EU:C:2006:586, 170; CJEU judgment in *Unibet*, C-432/05, EU:C:2007:163, 37-44; CJEU judgment in *Impact v. Minister for Agriculture and Food and Others*, C-268/06, EU:C:2008:223, 48; CJEU judgment in *Deutsche Energiehandels- und Beratungsgesellschaft mbH v. Bundesrepublik Deutschland (DEB)*, C-279/09,

A second interpretation is that the principle of effective judicial protection is a sub-category of the principle of effectiveness – the former representing an extension of the *Rewe* criteria.[1060] This perspective regards the *Rewe*-requirements as *umbrella*, meaning that effective judicial protection must be safeguarded in order to conclude that the effectiveness leg of the *Rewe* test has been complied with.[1061] The reasoning is more intuitive than it may appear at first glance; one way of ensuring that rights derived from Union law can be effectively relied upon is to require that effective access to court be granted, which is but one of several paths for vindicating rights. The legal bases of the respective principles have been reconciled in the following way: While Art. 19(1) TEU requires Member States to provide a system of judicial/legal remedies that sufficiently ensures substantive Union rights, this obligation is ancillary to the responsibility of Member States to construct their more detailed rules of procedure in a manner that at the same time complies with the *Rewe* principles.[1062]

A third view is that the three principles are cumulative and must all be met – an understanding founded on case-law in which the Court of Justice tests the three principles autonomously, while requiring compliance on all counts.[1063] National procedural rules complying with the *Rewe* test, "even

EU:C:2010:811, 29, 33, 58-59; Opinion of Advocate General Jääskinen in *Liivimaa Lihaveis*, C-562/12, EU:C:2014:155, 47, 57; Opinion of Advocate General Bot in *ET-Agrokonsulting-04*, C-93/12, EU:C:2013:172, 30; Opinion of Advocate General Jääskinen in *Orizzonte Salute*, C-61/14, EU:C:2015:307, 24.

1060 J. H. Jans, R. de Lange, S. Prechal, and R. J. G. M. Widdershoven (2007), 51; S. Prechal and N. Shelkoplyas (2004), 591; see e.g. CJEU judgment in *Unibet (London) Ltd and Unibet (International) Ltd v. Justitiekanslern*, C-432/05, EU:C:2007:163, 37-38 and CJEU judgment in *Silvia Georgiana Câmpean*, C-200/14, EU:C:2016:494, 70, in which separate legal bases for *inter alia* the principle of effective judicial protection were considered, whereas the Court of Justice took its conclusive point of departure in the duty of sincere co-operation.

1061 CJEU judgment in *Orizzonte Salute*, C-61/14, EU:C:2015:655, 48.

1062 S. Prechal and R. Widdershoven (2011 a), 293; in this vein, see CJEU judgment in *ET Agrokonsulting-04-Velko Stoyanov v. Izpalnitelen direktor na Darzhaven fond «Zemedelie» - Razplashtatelna agentsia*, C-93/12, EU:C:2013:432 and CJEU judgment in *Orizzonte Salute*, C-61/14, EU:C:2015:655.

1063 E.g. CJEU judgment in *Alassini and Others*, C-317/08, EU:C:2010:146, 50-66 (see discussion by S. Prechal and R. Widdershoven (2011 a), 293); CJEU judgment in *Banif Plus Bank Zrt v. Csaba Csipai*, C-472/11, EU:C:2013:88, 26-29; CJEU judgment in *Direcţia Generală Regională a Finanţelor Publice Braşov v. Vasile Toma*, C-205/15, EU:C:2016:49, 54-59 (ambiguous on the relationship between *Rewe*-equivalence and Arts. 20 and 21 CFR, 35-38).

without representing an obstacle to the enforcement of EU law before national courts, may still be regarded as a substantive infringement of the principle of judicial protection, when their application determines a restriction to one of the rights enshrined in the principle."[1064] This third interpretation recognizes effective judicial protection as a self-standing rule with various legal bases, aside from the duty of sincere co-operation.[1065]

The *Rewe* principles and the principle of effective judicial protection have, fourthly, been understood as *separate or subsidiary sets of requirements*, to be tested independently or alternatively.[1066] Separation between the two tests may in practice lead to different outcomes due to their varying levels of protection.[1067] In this vein, compliance with the *Rewe* criteria has sometimes been assessed without bringing effective judicial protection into the picture.[1068] In other instances – and this appears to be the contemporary trend – requirements on the judiciary have been exclusively handled as a matter of judicial protection (paired with Art. 19(1) TEU).[1069] The reason for separating effective judicial protection from *Rewe*-effectiveness is that the respective principles pursue different objectives. The principle of effectiveness seeks to promote substantive Union law in the context of decentralized enforcement. Effective judicial protection, on the other hand, seeks to safeguard the judicial status of litigants either as individual funda-

1064 L. M. Ravo (2012), 111.

1065 S. Prechal and R. Widdershoven (2011 b), 37.

1066 CJEU judgment in *Mono Car Styling SA, in liquidation v. Dervis Odemis and Others*, C-12/08, EU:C:2009:466, 49; CJEU judgment in *Alassini and Others*, C-317/08, EU:C:2010:146, 47-60, 61-66; cf. CJEU judgment in *Silvia Georgiana Câmpean*, C-200/14, EU:C:2016:494, 56, 69-70, where encroachment on the *Rewe* principles obviated the need to examine compliance with the Charter, notwithstanding the latter's potential applicability.

1067 Opinion of Advocate General Szpunar in *Finanmadrid EFC SA v. Jesús Vicente Albán Zambrano and Others*, C-49/14, EU:C:2015:746, 89-95; cf. Opinion of Advocate General Wahl in *Sanchez Morcillo*, C-169/1, EU:C:2014:2110, 77-78, where the two tests were separated, albeit not leading to opposing outcomes.

1068 CJEU judgment in *Evelyn Danqua v. Minister for Justice and Equality*, C-429/15, EU:C:2016:789; CJEU judgment in *EOS KSI Slovensko*, C-448/17, EU:C:2018:745; CJEU judgment in *Nikolay Kantarev v. Balgarska Narodna Banka*, C-571/16, EU:C:2018:807, 118ff.

1069 CJEU judgment in *Associação Sindical dos Juízes Portugueses*, C-64/16, EU:C:2018:117, 35-36; CJEU judgment in *LM (Judicial independence in Poland)*, C-216/18 PPU, EU:C:2018:586, both commented by V. Roeben (2019), 10-11.

mental right,[1070] or to preserve the rule of law at a common Union standard.[1071]

5.1.2 Components of effective judicial protection

Leaving aside for the moment the *sources* of effective judicial protection, we will now attend to its *components* originating in Union law as source. The principle of effective judicial protection encompasses elements that are both connected to the possibility of effectively vindicating substantive rights (primarily, access to a court to hear claims based on such rights) and to what was in Chapter 2 referred to as elements of *quality* of the court proceedings, including due process and judicial independence.[1072] The principle has thus been broken down into two elements, the first pertaining to the principle of effectiveness with the objective of avoiding obstacles to reliance on rights derived from EU law, whereas the second one intended to more generally guarantee respect for the rule of law through the proper conduct of proceedings.[1073] It has for this reason been suggested that the two elements of the principle also differ in scope of applicability: the requirement of effectiveness applies only within the area of *implementation or enforcement* of rights under EU law, whereas procedural protection ostensibly remains applicable "irrespective of its effects on EU law."[1074]

A potential tension between the elements pertaining to enforcement by courts of substantive rights and those put in place to ensure procedural justice and judicial integrity is contained already in the three legs of Art. 47 CFR, which protects:

1070 See e.g. L. M. Ravo (2012), 109-10.

1071 V. Roeben (2019), 5, 11-12.

1072 J. Krommendijk (2016), 1406; L. M. Ravo (2012), 102; see most recently CJEU judgment in *Carlos Escribano Vindel v. Ministerio de Justicia*, C-49/18, EU:C:2019:106.

1073 L. M. Ravo (2012), 111; see more recently CJEU judgment in *Associação Sindical dos Juízes Portugueses*, C-64/16, EU:C:2018:117.

1074 L. M. Ravo (2012), 112. This interpretation does not follow strictly from the Charter, which remains applicable within the scope of substantive EU law, albeit in a wider sense than only its "implementation"; see Art. 51(1) CFR, construed widely in *Åklagaren v. Hans Åkerberg Fransson*, C-617/10, EU:C:2013:105, CJEU judgment in *Eugenia Florescu v. Casa Judeţeană de Pensii Sibiu*, C-258/14, EU:C:2017:448, 48 and CJEU judgment in *Associação Sindical dos Juízes Portugueses*, C-64/16, EU:C:2018:117, 29-34.

1. the "right to an effective remedy" (hinging on the procedural protection of substantive rights granted under Union law);
2. the right to a "fair and public hearing [...] by an independent and impartial tribunal" (linking to the characteristics and quality of the said protection);
3. the right to legal representation, so as to ensure effective access to justice.[1075]

The Charter's provisions regarding equality before the law and non-discrimination[1076] have supplemented the principle of effective judicial protection,[1077] in addition to which codification of the principle in EU secondary law has contributed to both articulating its components and restricting its reach.[1078]

The discussed components of effective judicial protection correspond to standards and concepts of national and international law, capable of intervening both as competing layers of rights and as interpretative substance for the Union-origin right. As laid down in Art. 6(3) TEU, the rights of the Charter endorse constitutional traditions of the Member States as well as the meaning prescribed by the ECHR:[1079]

> Fundamental rights, as guaranteed by the European Convention for the Protection of Human Rights and Fundamental Freedoms and as they result from the constitutional traditions common to the Member States, shall constitute general principles of the Union's law.

1075 Art. 47 CFR. On the second and third legs of effective judicial protection under Union law, see e.g. F. Wilman (2015), 41ff.

1076 Arts. 20 and 21 CFR.

1077 CJEU judgment in *Direcţia Generală Regională a Finanţelor Publice Braşov v. Vasile Toma*, C-205/15, EU:C:2016:499.

1078 E.g. Opinion of Advocate General Szpunar in *Finanmadrid EFC SA v. Jesús Vicente Albán Zambrano and Others*, C-49/14, EU:C:2015:746, 94; CJEU judgment in *E.G. v. Republika Slovenija*, C-662/17, EU:C:2018:847, 43-46.

1079 See also Preamble, CFR: "This Charter reaffirms, with due regard for the powers and tasks of the Community and the Union and the principle of subsidiarity, the rights as they result, in particular, from the constitutional traditions and international obligations common to the Member States, the Treaty on European Union, the Community Treaties, the European Convention for the Protection of Human Rights and Fundamental Freedoms, the Social Charters adopted by the Community and by the Council of Europe and the case-law of the Court of Justice of the European Communities and of the European Court of Human Rights."

Art. 6(3) TEU also bridges standards of judicial protection originating in national law, incorporating domestic conceptions of its substance and hence increasing the level of complexity.[1080] For the purposes of this chapter, effective judicial protection based on conceptions stemming from national law will as far as possible be distinguished from its Union law origins. It might have been more appropriate to choose a different term to describe norms of judicial protection originating in national law. This would alas have detracted from their additional authority foreseen by Art. 6(3) TEU, resulting from national convergence with the Union notion. This is illustrated by the threshold rule of Art. 53 CFR:

> Nothing in this Charter shall be interpreted as restricting or adversely affecting human rights and fundamental freedoms as recognised, in their respective fields of application, by Union law and international law and by international agreements to which the Union, the Community or all the Member States are party, including the European Convention for the Protection of Human Rights and Fundamental Freedoms, and by the Member States' constitutions.

Insofar as fundamental rights contained in the Charter are duplicated in national law or in the ECHR, the double layering should – in theory[1081] – promote a higher level of individual protection. E.g. legal certainty and the equality of arms (both recognized as forming part of judicial protection under national law), should in principle activate Art. 53 CFR – making it relevant to keep, rather than reject, effective judicial protection as an umbrella term. Such notions originate both in national concepts thereof, and in the right to a fair and public hearing by an independent and impartial tribunal under Art. 47 CFR, representing its Union law origin.[1082]

5.2 A fundamental rights approach to effective judicial protection

It was in Chapter 4 above suggested that the beneficiaries of various substantive instruments subject to *effectiveness* do not necessarily coincide,

1080 As in CJEU judgment in *Stefano Melloni v. Ministerio Fiscal*, C-399/11, EU:C:2013:107; CJEU judgment in *Atanas Ognyanov (I)*, C-614/14, EU:C:2016:514; CJEU judgment in *ML/Generalstaatsanwaltschaft*, C-220/18 PPU, EU:C:2018:589.

1081 Albeit subject to a restrictive interpretation in CJEU judgment in *Stefano Melloni v. Ministerio Fiscal*, C-399/11, EU:C:2013:107.

1082 F. Wilman, (2015), 43ff; CJEU judgment in *Carlos Escribano Vindel v. Ministerio de Justicia*, C-49/18, EU:C:2019:106.

sometimes triggering a balancing test between their respective interests. The same has been observed regarding *effective judicial protection*, whose divergence of sources makes the identification of its beneficiaries more difficult than under the effectiveness approach. Effective judicial protection is abstruse not only in relationship to the principle of effectiveness, but also contains ambiguities in and of itself – the most prominent one surfacing in its element of general rule of EU law versus fundamental right. While Dougan has noted that the principle of effectiveness primarily serves Union law beneficiaries,[1083] a transversal purview for the principle of effective judicial protection has been suggested by other scholars.[1084]

> The Court appeared to be more committed to grant effectiveness of the right of the individual to judicial protection as such, rather than linking its reasoning to the effectiveness of EU law. In such cases, the application of the principle was linked to a fundamental right and implied a balance between competing interests.[1085]

The possibility of tensions between competing claims to effective judicial protection on both sides of the litigation will be discussed in the forthcoming sections. Section 5.2.1 discusses instances of tension between procedural protection derived from legal sources at different levels. Section 5.2.2 compares this type of clash with instances where the effectiveness of EU substantive law was given priority over expressions of procedural protection granted under Member State law. Section 5.2.3 considers tensions between individual procedural protection on the one hand, and the effectiveness of EU procedural mechanisms on the other. Reviewing the case-law in these perspectives reveals legitimate prerogatives above and beyond the procedural protection of beneficiaries of EU substantive law.

5.2.1 Procedural protection vs. (other) procedural protection

A line of case-law relating to the Brussels Convention and Brussels I Regulation illustrates tensions between the rights of defense and the right to bring proceedings on the basis of Art. 47 CFR as codified in EU secondary

1083 M. Dougan (2011 a), 425 and (2012), 116.

1084 V. Roeben (2019), 1; L. M. Ravo (2012), 118. By contrast, J-U. Franck (2017), 1876-77, suggests that effective judicial protection cannot protect public interests in enforcement against individual litigants, whereas the principle of effectiveness is capable of protecting interests on both sides.

1085 L. M. Ravo (2012), 118.

instruments.[1086] While the fundamental rights approach – which permeated this case-law – has perhaps promoted procedural protection for a wider circle of beneficiaries, we may be surprised by who benefits from it *in casu*.

Lindner and *A v. B* concerned the procedural protection of defendants *in absentia*, whose right to be heard etc. was addressed by the designation of guardians *ad litem*, yet not necessarily fully safeguarded. On the other side were the interests of the claimants who would not be able to bring claims unless the national court asserted jurisdiction. While this was a situation to which *substantive* EU law was essentially neutral,[1087] the applicants in both cases had attempted to rely on the Brussels I Regulation in pursuit of the defendants. The interest in access to a court seizing jurisdiction was consequently on the side of the applicants, whereas the procedural interests of the defendants were jeopardized through adjudication in their absence – both procedural components of effective judicial protection finding themselves on a colliding path.

The Court of Justice's fundamental rights approach "with the view to ensuring a fair balance between the rights of the applicant and those of the defendant"[1088] was in the present cases consequential:[1089]

> the requirement that the rights of the defence be observed, as laid down also in Article 47 of the Charter of Fundamental Rights of the European Union, must be implemented in conjunction with respect for the right of the applicant to bring proceedings before a court in order to determine the merits of its claim.

Procedural rights of applicants were weighed against those of defendants, not under the rule-of-reason, but instead as a matter of effective judicial

1086 CJEU judgment in *Marco Gambazzi v. DaimlerChrysler Canada Inc. and CIBC Mellon Trust Company*, C-394/07, EU:C:2009:219 (on the Convention of 27 September 1968 on jurisdiction and the enforcement of judgments in civil and commercial matters (Brussels Convention), OJ L 299, 31/12/1972, 32); CJEU judgment in *Hypoteční banka a.s. v. Udo Mike Lindner*, C-327/10, EU:C:2011:745 and CJEU judgment in *A v. B and Others*, C-112/13, EU:C:2014:2195 (both concerning Council Regulation (EC) No 44/2001 of 22 December 2000 on jurisdiction and the recognition and enforcement of judgments in civil and commercial matters (Brussels I Regulation), OJ L 012, 16/01/2001, 1).

1087 See L. M. Ravo (2012), 120.

1088 Ibid., 121, in reference to CJEU judgment in *Hypoteční banka a.s. v. Udo Mike Lindner*, C-327/10, EU:C:2011:745.

1089 CJEU judgment in *Hypoteční banka a.s. v. Udo Mike Lindner*, C-327/10, EU:C:2011:745, 49.

protection.[1090] On both sides of the scale were considerations tightly linked to ensuring access to court – on the defendants' side, the right to be heard, and on the applicants', the right to bring proceedings before a competent court. If the balance would have been struck in favor of absolute protection of the absent defendant, this would not give due consideration to the protection of the applicant, who "runs the risk of being deprived of all possibility of recourse", in contrast to the defendant who remained free to oppose the judgment, should he later choose to make an appearance.[1091] The Court of Justice, in *Lindner* designating the interests of creditors to initiate proceedings as an "objective of public interest," found that disproportionate favoritism of the consumer would amount to a denial of justice.[1092] A precedent was thus set for balancing the judicial protection of litigants on both sides.[1093]

Case-law on *ex officio* review followed a similar track. As already seen in Chapter 3, the Union mandate of *ex officio* review was, to a large extent, founded on the principles of *Rewe*-effectiveness and/or full effectiveness. Yet, *ex officio* review has not only triggered tensions between substantive effectiveness and procedural principles under national law; procedural safeguards also occasionally found themselves on the colliding course against each other. The right to be heard is illustrative also in this context by forming, on the one hand, an integral component of the right to defense whereas it must, on the other hand, be weighed against procedural rules relating to the ambit of the proceedings – the latter ensuring procedural stability with regards to the object of the litigation.

Has then the fundamental rights approach strengthened the EU law *ex officio* mandate? Starting in 2013 with the *Banif Plus* ruling, the *Rewe* principles in conjunction with the requirement of full effect founded an obligation of *ex officio* review to the benefit of the consumer.[1094] Yet, the principle of effective judicial protection activated the right to be heard as pro-

---

1090 Ibid.; CJEU judgment in *A v. B and Others*, C-112/13, EU:C:2014:2195, 61.

1091 CJEU judgment in *Hypoteční banka a.s. v. Udo Mike Lindner*, C-327/10, EU:C:2011:745, 54.

1092 Ibid., 51 and 55; see similar reasoning in CJEU judgment in *A v. B and Others*, C-112/13, EU:C:2014:2195, 60.

1093 The claimants' right to bring proceedings was somewhat less pronounced in CJEU judgment in *Marco Gambazzi v. DaimlerChrysler Canada Inc. and CIBC Mellon Trust Company*, C-394/07, EU:C:2009:219, which nevertheless emphasized that the right to be heard is not absolute (29).

1094 CJEU judgment in *Banif Plus Bank Zrt v. Csaba Csipai*, C-472/11, EU:C:2013:88, 26-28.

cedural safeguard, to be enjoyed also by the opposing party. The ruling thus isolated elements dealt with under the fundamental rights approach, in which equation substantive prerogatives of Union law (viz. consumer protection) did not figure.[1095]

In *Benallal*, two procedural requirements were likewise balanced against each other, this time entirely without recourse to the effectiveness of underlying substantive rights: the right to be heard versus rules limiting access to higher courts.[1096] Whilst the principle of effective judicial protection was not mentioned, a fundamental rights approach can be traced in the language of the ruling:[1097]

> respect for the rights of the defence is, in all proceedings initiated against a person which are liable to culminate in a measure adversely affecting that person, a fundamental principle of EU law which must be guaranteed even in the absence of any rules governing the proceedings in question. That principle requires that the addressees of decisions which significantly affect their interests should be placed in a position in which they may effectively make known their views.

Despite this firm language, the *Benallal* judgment ultimately deferred to national procedural law, leaving to the national court to ascertain whether the principle of equivalence requires *ex officio* consideration of the right to be heard.[1098] Although that particular case hinged on the rather technical matter of how to apply the equivalence principle to national rules of public policy, the choice of deference was consistent with a stance that would be reinforced in subsequent case-law – namely, that the right to defense does not entail an absolute right to be heard.[1099]

In *Online Games*,[1100] procedural protection in one guise was also weighed against another in the context of administrative proceedings against an individual. Although the case was *not* neutral to substantive ef-

1095 Ibid., 29-36.

1096 CJEU judgment in *Abdelhafid Bensada Benallal v. État belge*, C-161/15, EU:C:2016:175.

1097 Ibid., 33. This reference to adversarial procedure has its foundation in Art. 6 ECHR, following the case-law of the ECtHR; however, neither the ECHR nor Art. 47 CFR were named in the present judgment.

1098 Ibid., 34-35; see also CJEU judgment in *Deutsche Energiehandels- und Beratungsgesellschaft mbH v. Bundesrepublik Deutschland (DEB)*, C-279/09, EU:C:2010:811, 60-62 and *Orizzonte Salute*, C-61/14, EU:C:2015:655, 77, deferring to the national court.

1099 E.g. CJEU judgment in *Moussa Sacko*, C-348/15, EU:C:2017:591, 38-40.

1100 CJEU judgment in *Online Games Handels GmbH*, C-685/15, EU:C:2017:452.

fectiveness of EU law (*ex officio* review favoring the enforcement of EU law), the circumstances of the case more explicitly than before juxtaposed one type of procedural prerogative (truth-seeking) with another (objectivity).[1101] The Court of Justice held that the "internal" aspect of judicial independence

> is linked to 'impartiality' and seeks to ensure a level playing field for the parties to the proceedings and their respective interests with regard to the subject matter of those proceedings. That aspect [...] requires objectivity and the absence of any interest in the outcome of the proceedings apart from the strict application of the rule of law.[1102]

The Court of Justice accordingly considered whether the national court could carry out *ex officio* review without repudiating its impartiality. Although there were limits to administrative courts' truth-seeking mission; within these limits, arguments relating to judicial impartiality could not shield individual litigants from *ex officio* review in their disadvantage.[1103]

5.2.2 Procedural protection vs. effectiveness of EU substantive law

The *Taricco* line of case-law, concerning penalties for tax fraud, activated tensions between fundamental rights under the Charter and effectiveness of Union substantive law.[1104] In *Taricco*, short statutory limitations had allowed the defendants in the main proceedings to avoid prosecution, why the referring court sought to have ascertained whether such impunity in effect constituted a VAT exemption in violation of EU law. Observations had been submitted based on Art. 49 CFR, affirming the principle of non-retroactive penalties in criminal law and requiring criminal sanctions to be lawful and proportionate. Referring to case-law of the ECtHR, the Court of Justice rejected the precept that statutory limitations cannot be retroactively modified or overridden:[1105]

1101 Cf. CJEU judgment in *Heemskerk BV and Firma Schaap v. Productschap Vee en Vlees*, C-455/06, EU:C:2008:650.

1102 CJEU judgment in *Online Games Handels GmbH*, C-685/15, EU:C:2017:452, 61.

1103 Ibid., 64-67.

1104 CJEU judgment in *Åklagaren v. Hans Åkerberg Fransson*, C-617/10, EU:C:2013:105; CJEU judgment in *Ivo Taricco and Others*, C-105/14, EU:C:2015:555; CJEU judgment in *Luca Menci*, C-524/15, EU:C:2018:197; CJEU judgment in *M.A.S.*, C-42/17, EU:C:2017:936.

1105 CJEU judgment in *Ivo Taricco and Others*, C-105/14, EU:C:2015:555, 55.

> the sole effect of the disapplication of the national provisions at issue would be to not shorten the general limitation period in the context of pending criminal proceedings, to allow the effective prosecution of the alleged crimes, and to ensure, if necessary, that penalties intended to protect the financial interests of the European Union and those intended to protect the financial interests of the Italian Republic are treated in the same way. Such a disapplication of national law would not infringe the rights of the accused, as guaranteed by Article 49 CFR.

The Court deemed the relevant limitation periods for VAT fraud offences "liable to have an adverse effect on the fulfillment of the Member States' obligations under Article 325(1) and (2) TFEU if that national rule prevents the imposition of effective and dissuasive penalties in a significant number of cases of serious fraud affecting the financial interests of the EU". In view of these Union stakes, the Court demanded that the national court give full effect to the relevant Treaty provisions, if need be by disapplying national legislation.[1106]

The argument based on Art. 49 CFR was in *Taricco* dealt with, not by balancing it against the effectiveness of Union law or by considering available objective limitations, but instead by stating *tout court* that Union law must be granted full effect[1107] – whereas in its sequel, *M.A.S.*, an avenue for justification was developed.[1108] This response was in line with the prior ruling in *Belvedere*,[1109] balancing the effectiveness of penalties for VAT fraud against the principle of legality in criminal proceedings. The latter were time-barred after having been pending for more than 10 years, a rule put in place to ensure the judicial protection of defendants, in their right to due process within reasonable time under the ECHR. As in the *Taricco* line, the statutory limitation benefitted the defendants who would be able to walk away from the demands of the tax authorities, whereas the effective application of Union provisions would suffer setbacks because VAT could consequently not be collected. The *Belvedere* ruling weighed the effectiveness of Union fiscal legislation against the interests of individual

1106 Ibid., 58; see also CJEU judgment in *M.A.S.*, C-42/17, EU:C:2017:936, 36-38.

1107 CJEU judgment in *Ivo Taricco and Others*, C-105/14, EU:C:2015:555, 57. The argument made by the Court on the absence of violation of the ECHR is not convincing, as the ECtHR case-law to which the Court of Justice referred, concerned the *extension* of statutory limitations under the prohibition against retroactive criminal sanctions, whereas what the Court of Justice in effect was proposing was the *disapplication* of such limitations.

1108 CJEU judgment in *M.A.S.*, C-42/17, EU:C:2017:936, 48ff.

1109 CJEU judgment in *Ufficio IVA di Piacenza v. Belvedere Costruzioni Srl*, C-500/10, EU:C:2012:186; see further L. M. Ravo (2012), 120.

parties in having proceedings brought against them within reasonable time, relying specifically on Art. 47 CFR in reference to procedural requirements derived from the ECHR. The Court concluded that Member States are bound to comply with the Charter when implementing EU law,[1110] entailing an additional obligation also to comply with Art. 6 ECHR.[1111] Although the codified avenues for limiting Charter rights were not evoked, the Court's *de facto* consideration of stakes and rights of the defendants permitted a finding that the statutory limitations were justified. In conclusion, whether implicit (as in *Belvedere*) or explicit (as in *M.A.S.*), a fundamental rights approach towards justifying encroachments on EU substantive law is crystallizing in parallel with the fundamental rights approach to judicial protection (see, further, section 5.3).[1112]

5.2.3 Individual procedural protection vs. effectiveness of EU procedural mechanisms

A distinct line of case-law on the European arrest warrant additionally reinforces the impression that the fundamental rights approach will not necessarily increase individual procedural protection. The effectiveness of EU law also features in these rulings, albeit in a different guise than the effectiveness of *substantive* EU law examined in the previous section. This line of case-law relates rather to what we may call effectiveness of EU procedural mechanisms or frameworks, in which effective judicial protection figures as a quasi-substantive right, according to the terminology used in previous chapters. The point of interest is hence the balancing exercise between, on the one hand, individual procedural protection and, on the other hand, effective judicial protection as quasi-substantive right or standard.

The seminal ruling in *Melloni* concerned a defendant's surrender between authorities of two Member States.[1113] Pursuant to the Framework

1110 See, however, CJEU judgment in *Associação Sindical dos Juízes Portugueses*, C-64/16, EU:C:2018:117, which founded rights under Art. 47 CFR directly on Art. 19(1) TEU, obviating the need differentiate between "implementation" and "in the fields covered by Union law".

1111 CJEU judgment in *Ufficio IVA di Piacenza v. Belvedere Costruzioni Srl*, C-500/10, EU:C:2012:186, 23-24.

1112 CJEU judgment in *M.A.S.*, C-42/17, EU:C:2017:936, 47-51.

1113 CJEU judgment in *Stefano Melloni v. Ministerio Fiscal*, C-399/11, EU:C:2013:107; see further E. Spaventa, 'The interpretation of Article 51 of the EU Charter of Fundamental Rights: the dilemma of stricter or broader applica-

decision,[1114] Member States are precluded from refusing surrender, save under specific circumstances.[1115] While surrender would have allowed the arrest warrant to function effectively, the rights of defense (as perceived by the referring court) were ostensibly jeopardized by the level of judicial protection prescribed in the issuing state. In the spirit of judicial co-operation, which demands mutual trust between Member States for the system to be efficient, the Court of Justice opted for the requirement of *Simmenthal*-effectiveness.[1116]

Although the ruling was controversial at the time of its delivery, a series of judgments weighing fundamental rights against the functioning of the arrest warrant has since confirmed it.[1117] The Court of Justice was recently asked, in *TC*, whether release from custody was possible after 90 days without breaching the arrest warrant *and* whether it was possible to hold a detainee beyond that period without violating the Charter, i.e. pinpointing a clash between the arrest warrant and Charter rights. The Court responded that while an *automatic* release after this time-period would be incompatible with the European arrest warrant, postponing release for an unforesee-

---

tion of the Charter to national measures', A Study for the European Parliament's PETI Committee (15/02/2016); E. Dubout, 'Le niveau de protection des droits fondamentaux dans l'Union européenne: unitarisme constitutif versus pluralisme constitutionnel – Réflexions autour de l'arrêt Melloni', *Cah. dr. eur.*, 49 (2013), 293-317; D. Ritleng, 'De l'articulation des systèmes de protection des droits fondamentaux dans l'Union. Les enseignements des arrêts Akerberg Fransson et Melloni', *Revue trimestrielle de droit européen*, 49 (2013), 267.

1114 Council Framework Decision 2002/584/JHA of 13 June 2002 on the European arrest warrant and the surrender procedures between Member States, OJ L 190, 28/07/2002, 20.

1115 As in CJEU judgment in *LM (Judicial independence in Poland)*, C-216/18 PPU, EU:C:2018:586, 73-79 and CJEU judgment in *Pal Aranyosi*, joined cases C-404/15 and C-659/15 PPU, EU:C:2016:198, 82; see comments by S. Prechal, 'Mutual Trust Before the Court of Justice of the European Union', *Mutual Recognition and Mutual Trust: Reinforcing EU Integration? (Second Part) European Papers* 2 (2017 b), 87 f.

1116 CJEU judgment in *Stefano Melloni v. Ministerio Fiscal*, C-399/11, EU:C:2013:107, 59: "by virtue of the principle of primacy of EU law, which is an essential feature of the EU legal order […] rules of national law, even of a constitutional order, cannot be allowed to undermine the effectiveness of EU law on the territory of that State."

1117 E.g. CJEU judgment in *Minister for Justice and Equality v. Francis Lanigan*, C-237/15 PPU, EU:C:2015:474; CJEU judgment in *Pal Aranyosi*, joined cases C-404/15 and C-659/15 PPU, EU:C:2016:198; CJEU judgment in *IK*, C-551/18 PPU, EU:C:2018:991, 67-70.

able time would only be contrary to the Charter in the face of inhuman or degrading detention conditions.[1118]

Below this pain threshold (and other grounds for mandatory and optional non-execution)[1119] disparate standards of judicial protection between Member States is something that we must perhaps live with. It is consequently not up to each Member State to weigh the arrest warrant's effectiveness against the interest in safeguarding procedural protection at each executing State's standard. When asked specifically, in *Ognyanov II*, whether Member States cooperating in the Framework decision on enforcement of criminal sentences[1120] could offer more lenient sentencing than foreseen by EU law,[1121] the Court of Justice underscored that the system of mutual trust would be undermined by any executing state granting sentence reductions not prescribed by the issuing state.[1122]

These difficulties are perhaps symptomatic to the European arrest warrant and similar mechanisms, whose reliance on a system of mutual trust and recognition has evolved into a presumption of compliance with a defined standard of judicial protection[1123] from which collaborating Member States can deviate only exceptionally.[1124] Yet, mutual trust is not reserved

1118 CJEU judgment in *TC*, C-492/18 PPU, EU:C:2019:108, 77; see also CJEU judgment in *ML/Generalstaatsanwaltschaft*, C-220/18 PPU, EU:C:2018:589; CJEU judgment in *RO (Brexit/European arrest warrant)*, C-327/18 PPU, EU:C:2018:733.

1119 Recital 13 Preamble and Arts. 3-4 of Council Framework Decision 2002/584/JHA of 13 June 2002 on the European arrest warrant and the surrender procedures between Member States, OJ L 190, 28/07/2002, 20.

1120 Council Framework Decision 2008/909/JHA of 27 November 2008 on the application of the principle of mutual recognition to judgments in criminal matters imposing custodial sentences or measures involving deprivation of liberty for the purpose of their enforcement in the European Union, OJ L 327, 5/12/2008, 27.

1121 CJEU judgment in *Atanas Ognyanov (II)*, C-554/14, EU:C:2016:835, 54.

1122 Ibid., 51.

1123 See e.g. A. Efrat, 'Assessing Mutual Trust among EU Members: Evidence from the European Arrest Warrant', *JEPP* (2018), https://doi.org/10.1080/13501763.2018.1478877, 1.

1124 As in CJEU judgment in *LM (Judicial independence in Poland)*, C-216/18 PPU, EU:C:2018:586, 73-79; cf. CJEU judgment in *Pal Aranyosi*, joined cases C-404/15 and C-659/15 PPU, EU:C:2016:198, 82.

for the area of EU criminal law.[1125] In Opinion 2/13, the Court customized the *Melloni* take on Art. 53 CFR for wider interpretational purposes:[1126]

> In so far as Article 53 of the ECHR[1127] essentially reserves the power of the Contracting Parties to lay down higher standards of protection of fundamental rights than those guaranteed by the ECHR, that provision should be coordinated with Article 53 of the Charter, as interpreted by the Court of Justice, so that the power granted to Member States by Article 53 of the ECHR is limited — with respect to the rights recognised by the Charter that correspond to those guaranteed by the ECHR — to that which is necessary to ensure that the level of protection provided for by the Charter and the primacy, unity and effectiveness of EU law are not compromised.

Also in *Achmea,* the Court resorted to the notion of mutual trust in common values to require that Member States refrain from outsourcing the resolution of EU litigation to other international bodies, conceptually preserving judicial protection and autonomy through the proper functioning of the preliminary reference mechanism itself.[1128] The ruling in *Ognyanov I* stressed that disparate standards of procedural protection cannot be permitted to overturn the effectiveness of the preliminary reference procedure. The referring court had worried that its preliminary reference necessitated it to voice premature opinions on factual and legislative elements prior to its sentence, giving rise to doubts about its impartiality.[1129] Without exactly juxtaposing national procedural protection and EU law effec-

---

1125 On mutual trust within the European Asylum system, see e.g. CJEU judgment in *Bashar Ibrahim,* joined cases C-297/17, C-318/17, C-319/17 and C-438/17, EU:C:2019:219 and S. Prechal (2017 b), 77 f. With respect to the failed agreement on EU accession to ECHR, see ibid., 91 f.

1126 CJEU Opinion *delivered pursuant to Article 218(11) TFEU,* 2/13, EU:C:2014:2454, 189.

1127 Art. 53 ECHR: "Nothing in this Convention shall be construed as limiting or derogating from any of the human rights and fundamental freedoms which may be ensured under the laws of any High Contracting Party or under any other agreement to which it is a party."

1128 CJEU judgment in *Slowakische Republik v. Achmea BV,* C-284/16, EU:C:2018:158, 34-37, 58; cf. CJEU Opinion *delivered pursuant to Article 218(11) TFEU,* 2/13, EU:C:2014:2454, 192-199; see e.g. E. Neframi and M. Gatti, 'Autonomy and EU Competences in the Context of Free Trade Investment Agreements', in *Negotiation and Conclusion of the New Generation Trade Agreements,* eds. Bosse Platière, I. and C. Rapoport (Edward Elgar, forthcoming 2019).

1129 CJEU judgment in *Atanas Ognyanov (I),* C-614/14, EU:C:2016:514, 13. See also CJEU judgment in *Emil Milev,* C-310/18 P, EU:C:2018:732, where pre-trial assessments as to "reasonable grounds" were not considered contrary to the pre-

tiveness, the Court of Justice dismissed the notion of protection evoked by the national court as safeguard for effective judicial protection because it was contrary to the co-operation required by the national court in formulating its preliminary reference.[1130]

In conclusion, the interest in effectiveness of Union law was given priority over procedural protection provided under national law, insofar as this should come at the expense of effective collaboration in Union law frameworks. The present section has explained this phenomenon by reference to the proper functioning and efficacy of procedural mechanisms founded on a presumption of mutual trust. Still, mutual trust was only part of the equation whereas the Court of Justice additionally relied on various legal bases in the Charter as well as in secondary EU law to justify encroachments on procedural protection. In the forthcoming analysis, available justifications for obstacles to *Rewe*-effectiveness will be compared with the fundamental rights approach to limitations, based directly on the Charter or on provisions of secondary law supplementing Charter rights.

5.3 Balancing effectiveness against procedural protection via objective justifications

The procedural rule-of-reason, described in Chapters 2 and 3, for a long time remained commonplace for weighing a substantive EU right against the *raisons d'être* behind a national procedural obstacle. The forthcoming section 5.3.1 traces the Court's prioritizations between effectiveness and procedural protection in case-law applying the rule-of-reason, conceived to introduce a component of proportionality in the *Rewe* formula.[1131]

Even in this case-law, the underlying rationale was sometimes *de facto* effective judicial protection.[1132] Yet, the *van Schijndel* formula does not lend itself to justification for encroachments on the principle of effective

---

sumption of innocence enshrined in *inter alia* Art. 47 CFR, as long as no provisional statement on the defendant's guilt was made.

1130 CJEU judgment in *Atanas Ognyanov (I)*, C-614/14, EU:C:2016:514, 23-25.

1131 CJEU judgment in *Levez v. Jennings Ltd*, C-326/96, EU:C:1998:577, 44 (equivalence); CJEU judgment in *Van Schijndel v. Stichting Pensioenfonds voor Fysiotherapeuten*, joined cases C-430/93 and C-431/93, EU:C:1995:441, 19 (effectiveness).

1132 See e.g. Opinion of Advocate General Jacobs in *Peterbroeck, Van Campenhout & Cie v. Belgian State*, C-312/93, EU:C:1995:437, 43.

judicial protection, despite common denominators.[1133] This is the topic of sections 5.3.2-3, which examine case-law in which fundamental rights were limited on the basis of interpretations of the Charter's horizontal provisions. Most of these rulings also hinged on provisions of EU secondary law, where the "substantive" rule or right in itself included the objective of access to court (i.e. a quasi-substantive right, subject to codified modalities, also considered in section 5.3.3).

Examples of related balancing tests have been applied in the context of institutional autonomy – neither relying on the rule-of-reason, nor explicitly taking recourse to lawful and proportionate limitations of Charter rights. Section 5.3.4 considers this full effect-strand of case-law in which effectiveness was balanced against legal certainty.

5.3.1 Justifications for procedural obstacles based on the rule-of-reason

In its seminal ruling in *van Schijndel*, the Court of Justice found that national courts, when considering whether the setting aside of a national procedural rule would be necessary to ensure the correct application of EU law, must balance the triggered Union right against the interest of procedural protection, insofar as it is embedded in or justifies the existence of the contested national procedural rule.[1134]

Throughout the case-law on *ex officio* review, the Court of Justice helped national courts identify relevant factors and considerations towards deciding how to deal with procedural obstacles. Although the Court sometimes required the national judge to prioritize the effective application of EU law by setting aside national rules precluding *ex officio* review,[1135] the rule-of-reason was frequently left to the national judge to apply, without clear instruction as to where to strike the balance – yet with the implicit go-ahead to prioritize procedural rules of national law when justified and proportionate.[1136] The Court of Justice thus accepted that procedural protection may sometimes prevail over Union law effectiveness, as long as this was

---

1133 CJEU judgment in *Alassini and Others*, C-317/08, EU:C:2010:146, 63, with case-law there cited.

1134 CJEU judgment in *Van Schijndel v. Stichting Pensioenfonds voor Fysiotherapeuten*, joined cases C-430/93 and C-431/93, EU:C:1995:441, 19.

1135 CJEU judgment in *Peterbroeck, Van Campenhout & Cie v. Belgian State*, C-312/93, EU:C:1995:437.

1136 E.g. CJEU judgment in *Van Schijndel v. Stichting Pensioenfonds voor Fysiotherapeuten*, joined cases C-430/93 and C-431/93, EU:C:1995:441, 22; CJEU judg-

not done automatically, but only after careful consideration of the competing interests at stake.

In the consumer case-law, the Court was, at least initially, hesitant to allow national procedural principles to trump Union law effectiveness (thereby also trumping the legal interests of procedurally vulnerable litigants).[1137] Yet, under the procedural rule-of-reason, the consumer case-law dealt not only with the issue of Union law effectiveness versus procedural protection of individuals, but also with the effective protection of consumers versus the procedural protection of creditors.[1138] In other instances, the rule-of-reason triggered forfeiture of the consumer protection foreseen in Union secondary legislation, taking into account inertia on the side of the consumer party.[1139] Following this divergence, Advocate General Szpunar proposed that the rule-of-reason be applied, to the effect of "strik[ing] a balance between the notion that a court should compensate for a procedural omission on the part of a consumer who is unaware of his rights and the notion that it should make up fully for the consumer's total inertia."[1140]

On balance, the consumer case-law has tended to prioritize the coinciding procedural *and* substantive protection of the consumer (based on the protective prerogative in the Union consumer legislation), whereas it will exceptionally allow the procedural protection of an opposing commercial party to prevail in the face of reasonable justifications – however, the *van*

---

ment in *van der Weerd and Others v. Minister van Landbouw, Natuur en Voedselkwaliteit*, joined cases C-222/05 to C-225/05, EU:C:2007:318, 33.

1137 As noted by S. Weatherill, (2011), section IV), "the introduction of the *consumer* into the fact pattern typically diminishes the Court's willingness to respect national procedural autonomy and its concern for legal certainty."

1138 CJEU judgment in *Banco Español de Crédito SA v. Joaquín Calderón Camino*, C-618/10, EU:C:2012:349, 51.

1139 CJEU judgment in *Asturcom Telecomunicaciones SL v. Cristina Rodríguez Nogueira*, C-40/08, EU:C:2009:615, 39, 48; CJEU judgment in *Monika Kušionová v. SMART Capital a.s.*, C-34/13, EU:C:2014:2189, 56; CJEU judgment in *ERSTE Bank Hungary Zrt. v. Attila Sugár*, C-32/14, EU:C:2015:637, 62-63.

1140 Opinion of Advocate General Szpunar in *Finanmadrid EFC SA v. Jesús Vicente Albán Zambrano and Others*, C-49/14, EU:C:2015:746, 43. In the end, though, the Advocate General prioritized the effectiveness of Union law through the protection of the consumer, over the interests of legal certainty enshrined in the principle of *res judicata* underlying the contested national procedural rule (77) – a solution also ultimately favored by the Court albeit without reference to the rule-of-reason (CJEU judgment in *Finanmadrid EFC SA v. Jesús Vicente Albán Zambrano and Others*, C-49/14, EU:C:2016:98, 55).

Schijndel formula was not utilized in rulings where such was the outcome.[1141] The main tenet in the *general* (non-consumer) case-law on *ex officio* review, by contrast, in principle allows procedural protection to trump Union law effectiveness as long as the national court, pursuant to the rule-of-reason, gives due weight to priorities on both sides.

The above observations are valid with respect to the balancing test between substantive and procedural protection under the rule-of-reason, whereas the considered case-law additionally activates the effective judicial protection of litigants, including consumers, under Art. 47 CFR. The forthcoming sections will examine the implications of a related balancing exercise carried out *outside* the auspices of the *Rewe* test, starting with the Court's interpretation of the level of protection required under Art. 53 CFR.

5.3.2 Art. 53 CFR and the level of effective judicial protection

In the earlier discussed *Melloni* ruling,[1142] the Court of Justice considered the relationship between Arts. 47 and 53 CFR, the latter laying down a threshold rule according to which the Charter shall not be interpreted as encroaching on human rights and fundamental freedoms as follow from e.g. the standards of Member State constitutions. As is familiar, the Court of Justice did not recognize the need for a higher level of judicial protection according to the executing State's view of the ECHR's requirements:[1143]

> allowing a Member State to avail itself of Article 53 of the Charter to make the surrender of a person convicted *in absentia* conditional upon the conviction being open to review in the issuing Member State, a possibility not provided for under [the arrest warrant], in order to avoid an adverse effect on the right to a fair trial and the rights of the defence guaranteed by the constitution of the executing Member State, by casting doubt on the uniformity of the standard of protection of fundamental rights as defined in that framework decision, would undermine the principles of mutual trust and recognition which

1141 CJEU judgment in *Hypoteční banka a.s. v. Udo Mike Lindner*, C-327/10, EU:C:2011:745; CJEU judgment in *Banif Plus Bank Zrt v. Csaba Csipai*, C-472/11, EU:C:2013:88; CJEU judgment in *Biuro podróży 'Partner'*, C-119/15, EU:C:2016:987, 27.

1142 CJEU judgment in *Stefano Melloni v. Ministerio Fiscal*, C-399/11, EU:C:2013:107.

1143 Ibid., 63-64.

> that decision purports to uphold and would, therefore, compromise the efficacy of that framework decision.

Art. 53 CFR was thus construed in a manner that abridged procedural protection within the meaning foreseen in Art. 6 ECHR – at least as interpreted by the referring court. The judgment has been criticized for turning what was supposed to be a minimum threshold in the Charter's horizontal provisions into an absolute standard, according to which neither more nor less protection may be granted at the cost of effectiveness of the arrest warrant.[1144]

Although this outcome can be explained by recourse both to the Framework decision's modalities and to the system of mutual trust, it has already been suggested in this work that the *Melloni* take on Art. 53 CFR is not limited to its legislative context.[1145] Recall *Ognyanov I*, where the referring court had been inclined to disqualify itself from ruling in criminal proceedings, in the interest of ensuring the defendant's right to a fair trial – i.e. his procedural protection. In fact, the referring court had provocatively asked the Court of Justice whether the relevant procedural safeguard was precluded "on the ground that that rule ensures a higher degree of protection of the parties' fundamental rights."[1146] While rejecting the presumptions underlying this question, the Court of Justice's reasoning did not forecast any retreat from the threshold rule established in *Melloni*.[1147] The Court of Justice avoided confrontation between levels of protection by *prima facie* rejecting the procedural safeguard provided by national law, reinforcing the impression that Member States ultimately cannot exceed the minimum threshold foreseen in Art. 47 CFR in order to provide a higher level of protection (again, insofar as this would come at the expense of the effectiveness of EU law).

In conclusion, Art. 53 CFR is not necessarily capable of granting the most generous level of protection available to individual litigants when weighed against the underlying interest of ensuring the effective application of EU law – contrary to a literal construction of it, Art 53(1) CFR may lead to the de-prioritization of Charter rights. The same may be said of recent case-law in which Art. 52(3) CFR has been referred to as benchmark

1144 E. Dubout (2013), 308. Although the constitutional imperative of respecting the Union legislator is highly relevant, exploration of this potential motive for the judgment falls outside the scope of the present work.

1145 CJEU judgment in *Atanas Ognyanov (I)*, C-614/14, EU:C:2016:514, 25.

1146 Ibid., 31.

1147 Ibid., 31-32.

for other EU secondary legislation.[1148] According to its heading ("Scope of guaranteed rights"), Art. 52 designates scope rather than level of protection under the Charter; yet its third paragraph is worded similarly to Art. 53(1) CFR:

> In so far as this Charter contains rights which correspond to rights guaranteed by the Convention for the Protection of Human Rights and Fundamental Freedoms, the meaning and scope of those rights shall be the same as those laid down by the said Convention. This provision shall not prevent Union law providing more extensive protection.

A decline in individual procedural protection has been observed with respect to yet another horizontal Charter provision: Art. 52(1) CFR. It remains to be seen whether the balance could (re-)shift, although dynamic interpretations of Art. 19(1) TEU, as discussed in Chapter 2, cannot be expected to dislocate remedies from Union rights, if put to the test.[1149] The consequences of supplementary norms in secondary Union legislation for fundamental rights protection has been further developed in case-law in which limitations to Art. 47 CFR were contained in the applicable secondary legislation itself.

5.3.3 Art. 52(1) CFR and modulation of judicial protection in EU secondary law

In the case-law examined in the present section, the effectiveness of EU secondary law was again put to the test through claims based on the Charter, including its Art. 47. Secondary law provisions either codifying the right to effective judicial protection, or containing context-specific limitations to it, were considered against Art. 52(1) CFR:

> Any limitation on the exercise of the rights and freedoms recognised by this Charter must be provided for by law and respect the essence of those rights and freedoms. Subject to the principle of proportionality, limitations may be made only if they are necessary and genuinely meet objectives of general inter-

---

1148 I.e. in support of a presumption of compliance with a Union-common standard of fundamental rights protection; see CJEU judgment in *M.A. v. International Protection Appeals Tribunal*, C-661/17, EU:C:2019:53, 83-86.

1149 As the remedial mandate is functionalized to promote substantive Union law, it is better equipped to serve beneficiaries of the principle of effectiveness, see Art. 19(1) TEU: "Member States shall provide remedies sufficient to ensure effective legal protection in the fields covered by Union law."

> est recognised by the Union or the need to protect the rights and freedoms of others.

The principle of proportionality is hence one of several requirements on limitations to Charter rights. Despite common denominators with the rule-of-reason, differences in both rationale and protective capacity are revealed already by the provision's reference to recognition of objectives by the Union and the protection of "others".

Particularly case-law concerning legal protection of tenderers in public procurements contributed to defining the Charter's protective scope, by clarifying the requirements on any restrictions on fundamental rights. In *Orizzonte* and *Star Storage*, the matter of compliance with the Charter was activated by applicable secondary legislation in which effective judicial protection represented a key objective.[1150] National regulations were in *Orizzonte* considered against the *Rewe*-requirements of effectiveness and equivalence; however, the justification exercise was not based on the *van Schijndel* rule-of-reason, instead considering Art. 47 CFR in light of mechanisms and safeguards contained in secondary law. The relevant test was, as per Advocate General Jääskinen, whether national rules posing obstacles to access to court under Art. 52(1) CFR satisfy "the principle of proportionality, namely pursuit of a legitimate purpose, necessity, aptness for purpose, and confinement to what is required to secure the legitimate purpose."[1151] This assessment was made with respect to the directive's objectives.[1152]

The Court of Justice found that although the Directive must be interpreted in light of the Charter, the answer as to whether effective judicial protection had been safeguarded coincided with the examination of the

---

1150 CJEU judgment in *Orizzonte Salute*, C-61/14, EU:C:2015:655; CJEU judgment in *SC Star Storage SA and Others*, joined cases C-439/14 and C-488/14, EU:C:2016:688, both concerning Directive 2007/66/EC of the European Parliament and of the Council of 11 December 2007 amending Council Directives 89/665/EEC and 92/13/EEC with regard to improving the effectiveness of review procedures concerning the award of public contracts, OJ L 335, 20/12/2007, 31; see Recital 36: "This Directive respects the fundamental rights and observes the principles recognised by the [Charter]. In particular, this Directive seeks to ensure full respect for the right to an effective remedy and to a fair hearing, in accordance with the first and second subparagraphs of Article 47 of the [Charter]."

1151 Opinion of Advocate General Jääskinen in *Orizzonte Salute*, C-61/14, EU:C:2015:307, 36.

1152 Ibid., 54.

Rewe principles. The Court considered the rationale of the court fees, taking into account the Directive's purposes and objectives:[1153]

> Such levying contributes to the proper functioning of the judicial system, since it amounts to a source of financing for the judicial activity of the Member States and discourages the submission of claims which are manifestly unfounded or which seek only to delay the proceedings.

Without express mention of proportionality in its examination of the amounts and cumulation of court fees, the Court found the latter justified only when linked clearly to additional costs for the seized court, due to the enlargement of the ambit of the proceedings.[1154] The Court of Justice in fact appeared to be following the solution proposed by the Advocate General; namely, whether the levying of court fees could be justified and was proportionate (albeit implying, through the context of the relevant reasoning, that it formed part of the *Rewe*-effectiveness test rather than a test of justified limitations of Charter rights). Whereas the Advocate General had envisaged that compliance with Art. 47 CFR be appraised by recourse to Art. 52(1) CFR, it is not clear whether the Court of Justice's insistence on the *Rewe* principles was to be interpreted as also activating its ancillary procedural rule-of-reason.[1155]

Similarly to Advocate General Jääskinen in *Orizzonte*, Advocate General Sharpston subsequently observed in *Star Storage* that the applicable litigation fees constituted a limitation to the right to an effective remedy under Art. 47 CFR. Therefore, it was necessary to examine whether such limitations were provided by law, respected the essence of the right, were proportionate and necessary and met objectives of general interest, i.e. opting for a fundamental rights approach to limitations under Art. 52 CFR.[1156] The Court of Justice followed this methodology, examining particularly the prevalence of objective interests and the measure of proportionality.

1153 CJEU judgment in *Orizzonte Salute*, C-61/14, EU:C:2015:655, 73.

1154 Ibid., 74-74: "Those objectives justify the multiple application of court fees such as those at issue in the main proceedings only where the subject-matter of the actions or supplementary pleas are in fact separate and amount to a significant enlargement of the subject-matter of the dispute that is already pending. By contrast, if that is not the case, an obligation of additional payment of such court fees because of the submission of such actions or pleas is contrary to the availability of legal remedies ensured by Directive 89/665 and to the principle of effectiveness."

1155 As noted by J. Krommendijk (2016), 1407.

1156 Opinion of Advocate General Sharpston in *SC Star Storage SA and Others*, joined cases C-439/14 and C-488/14, EU:C:2016:307, 37-38.

The former prompted the Court of Justice to recognize the combating of abuse of remedies as an objective interest contributing to the proper administration of justice.[1157] The latter proportionality test hinged on whether the amounts imposed could reasonably be borne by the applicant or were prohibitively dissuasive, i.e. making litigation excessively costly (an inquiry which we can recognize from *Orizzonte*).[1158]

Recent developments have given two indications about legitimate justifications for encroachments on the right to effective judicial protection.

Firstly, when deriving effective judicial protection directly from secondary Union legislation with the explicit objective of safeguarding Art. 47 CFR (i.e. as a quasi-substantive right), the justification exercise is to be carried out not pursuant to *van Schijndel*, but under Art. 52(1) CFR, or at least in the spirit of the latter.[1159] Although recourse to the *Rewe* test may still be relevant in the future, justifications under the fundamental rights approach have been on the rise in the decade following *Varec* and *Alassini*,[1160] and continue to be in subsequent case-law concerning modulations of effective judicial protection in EU secondary law.[1161]

Secondly, it is not evident that justification under the Charter will, in practice, bolster the procedural protection of individuals. Recall the two alternative scenarios drawn up by Advocate General Szpunar in *Finanmadrid*, pinpointing the differences between the rule-of-reason and justification under the fundamental rights approach.[1162] Relying on effective judicial protection pursuant to the Charter impacted the rights of defense in the Opinion's hypothetical Art. 47 test – the latter including, under certain circumstances, the possibility of holding proceedings in the absence of the defendant.[1163] This comparison indicated that the principle of effectiveness

1157 CJEU judgment in *SC Star Storage SA and Others,* joined cases C-439/14 and C-488/14, EU:C:2016:688, 53.

1158 Ibid., 55-63.

1159 Ibid.; CJEU judgment in *Orizzonte Salute,* C-61/14, EU:C:2015:655.

1160 CJEU judgment in *Alassini and Others*, C-317/08, EU:C:2010:146, 62ff.; CJEU judgment in *Varec SA v. Belgian State*, C-450/06, EU:C:2008:91.

1161 CJEU judgment in *TC*, C-492/18 PPU, EU:C:2019:108, 77.

1162 Opinion of Advocate General Szpuar in *Finanmadrid EFC SA v. Jesús Vicente Albán Zambrano and Others,* C-49/14, EU:C:2015:746, 94-95.

1163 This was subject to the *proviso* that reasonable attempts had been made to summon the defendant and that the decision delivered *in absentia* be susceptible to review (Opinion of Advocate General Szpuar in *Finanmadrid EFC SA v. Jesús Vicente Albán Zambrano and Others,* C-49/14, EU:C:2015:746, 94-95), i.e. the same requirements as in CJEU judgment in *Hypoteční banka a.s. v. Udo Mike Lindner*, C-327/10, EU:C:2011:745.

may benefit a litigant relying on favorable procedural rights granted in EU secondary law,[1164] whereas the fundamental right laid down in the Charter potentially offers a lower level of protection.[1165]

The risk of reduced individual protection appears particularly tangible when applicable secondary legislation contains provisions upon which such limitations can be construed and justified. Returning to *Melloni*, its restrictive outcome in fact hinged not primarily on Art. 53 CFR, but on rules contained in the European arrest warrant itself, whose compliance with the Charter was analyzed in detail:[1166]

> [T]he solution which the EU legislature found, consisting in providing an exhaustive list of the circumstances in which the execution of a European arrest warrant issued in order to enforce a decision rendered *in absentia* must be regarded as not infringing the rights of the defence, is incompatible with any retention of the possibility for the executing judicial authority to make that execution conditional on the conviction in question being open to review in order to guarantee the rights of defence of the person concerned.

The Framework decision, in other words, granted effective judicial protection as a quasi-substantive right, albeit equipped with limitations in the exhaustive list to which the Court referred in the above quotation. Recent case-law similarly shows how modalities in the level of judicial protection can be derived from the conditions under which surrender may be refused in order to safeguard defendants' rights.[1167] Rulings relating to asylum procedures also align with *Melloni et seq.* by relying on limitations to the right to be heard contained in secondary Union law (even without considering compliance with the Charter requirements contained in Art. 52(1) CFR).[1168]

1164 As was the case in e.g. CJEU judgment in *Asturcom Telecomunicaciones SL v. Cristina Rodríguez Nogueira*, C-40/08, EU:C:2009:615; CJEU judgment in *Banco Español de Crédito SA v. Joaquín Calderón Camino*, C-618/10, EU:C:2012:349 and CJEU judgment in *Finanmadrid EFC SA v. Jesús Vicente Albán Zambrano and Others*, C-49/14, EU:C:2016:98.

1165 Subsequently confirmed in e.g. CJEU judgment in *Moussa Sacko*, C-348/15, EU:C:2017:591, 38-49.

1166 CJEU judgment in *Stefano Melloni v. Ministerio Fiscal*, C-399/11, EU:C:2013:107, 58.

1167 CJEU judgment in *LM (Judicial independence in Poland)*, C-216/18 PPU, EU:C:2018:586; CJEU judgment in *Zlawomir Andrzej Zdziaszek*, C-271/17 PPU, EU:C:2017:629.

1168 CJEU judgment in *M. v. Minister for Justice and Equality*, C-560/14, EU:C:2017:101; CJEU judgment in *Moussa Sacko*, C-348/15, EU:C:2017:591, 44-45.

5.3.4 Balancing effectiveness against legal certainty under the full effect approach

A final aspect related to justifications of procedural obstacles is the method applied within a line of case-law relying on full effect. Even though it is most commonly used in substantive EU law contexts,[1169] the principle has had a renaissance in the presence of procedural and institutional obstacles.[1170] For the latter purposes, the principle of full effect has been described in the scholarship as wider than that of *Rewe*-effectiveness,[1171] whereas the present work has portrayed it rather as a sharper tool allowing greater encroachments on procedural autonomy.

Section 3.2.2.6 described a distinct rationale for justifying obstacles to the enforcement of EU law *against* individuals that was developed in a line of case-law pertaining to the recovery of unlawfully paid subsidies. It resembled the procedural rule-of-reason insofar that it envisaged a balancing test between EU law effectiveness and national expressions of procedural protection. This line of case-law took into account national law to fill out the notions of legal certainty and legitimate expectations:[1172]

> it is clear from a study of the national laws of the Member States [...] that the concern to strike a balance, albeit in different ways, between the principle of legality on the one hand and the principles of legal certainty and the protection of legitimate expectation on the other is common the laws of the Member States.

This approach promised broad possibilities and lent interpretative substance to justifying "institutional" obstacles to Union law effectiveness.[1173] The Court of Justice, however, took as starting point a common status and recognition of the principle of legal certainty,[1174] and would later clarify

1169 E.g. CJEU judgment in *Dansk industri*, C-441/14, EU:C:2016:278.

1170 Institutional autonomy: e.g. CJEU judgment in *Ministero dell'Industria, del Commercio e dell'Artigianato v. Lucchini SpA*, C-119/05, EU:C:2007:434. Procedural autonomy: e.g CJEU judgment in *Banif Plus Bank Zrt v. Csaba Csipai*, C-472/11, EU:C:2013:88, 28; CJEU judgment in *Ernst Georg Radlinger v. Finway a.s.*, C-377/14, EU:C:2016:283, 79.

1171 J. Krommendijk (2016), 1404.

1172 CJEU judgment in *Deutsche Milchkontor*, joined cases 205 to 215/82, EU:C:1983:233, 30.

1173 J. M. Davidson (2008), 119.

1174 CJEU judgment in *Deutsche Milchkontor*, joined cases 205 to 215/82, EU:C:1983:233, 31: "The first point to be made in this regard is that the principles of the protection of legitimate expectation and assurance of legal certainty

that this balancing test hinged on interpretations and understandings of it derived from Union law and jurisprudence,[1175] whereas the procedural rule-of-reason test deferred to national law to fill the notions thereunder protected with content.[1176] The result of this was that "[o]nly aspects of national procedural law that coincide with the general principles of Community law are protected under the principle of procedural autonomy and may therefore limit the full effect of Community law."[1177] The principles of legality, legitimate expectations and legal certainty were, in principle, permitted to encroach on the full effect of Union law "*since* those principles form part of the legal order of the Community."[1178]

The full effect requirement has also proven potent in cases dealing not with *institutional* autonomy within the meaning of this work, but rather *procedural* autonomy. The rulings in *Taricco* and *A v. B* required national courts to disapply procedural provisions, even without mentioning avenues for justification.[1179] In yet other case-law applying the full effect approach, the Court separated the *Rewe* principles, the full effect requirement and the Charter right of effective judicial protection, whereas it proceeded to a single balancing test between the consumer imperative and the right to be heard, apparently opting for the fundamental rights justification test while dispensing with the others.[1180] Also in *M.A.S.*, the full effect approach was used whereas the ruling's discussion about justifications incorporated a fundamental rights language. When considering fundamental

---

are part of the legal order of the Community. The fact that national legislation provides for the same principles to be observed in a matter such as the recovery of unduly-paid Community aids cannot, therefore, be considered contrary to that same legal order".

1175 See e.g. CJEU judgment in *Stichting ROM-projecten v. Staatssecretaris van Economische Zaken*, C-158/06, EU:C:2007:370, 24-26.

1176 E.g. CJEU judgment in *Shirley Preston v. Wolverhampton Healthcare NHS Trust*, C-78/98, EU:C:2000:247, 62-63.

1177 J. M. Davidson (2008), 119, refers to procedural autonomy also in reference to case-law that, in this work, sorts under institutional autonomy: e.g. CJEU judgment in *Stichting ROM-projecten v. Staatssecretaris van Economische Zaken*, C-158/06, EU:C:2007:370.

1178 CJEU judgment in *Stichting ROM-projecten v. Staatssecretaris van Economische Zaken*, C-158/06, EU:C:2007:370, 24 (here emphasized). See commentary by E. Paunio, *Legal Certainty in Multilingual EU Law: Language, Discourse and Reasoning at the European Court of Justice* (New York: Routledge, 2016), 67.

1179 CJEU judgment in *Ivo Taricco and Others*, C-105/14, EU:C:2015:555, 58; CJEU judgment in *A v. B and Others*, C-112/13, EU:C:2014:2195, 36-46.

1180 CJEU judgment in *Banif Plus Bank Zrt v. Csaba Csipai*, C-472/11, EU:C:2013:88, 27-30.

rights protection, the Court emphasized its dual basis under national and Union law.[1181] The fundamental rights approach and the full effect approach to justifications in this respect converge.[1182]

This outcome can be compared to the ruling in *Heemskerk and Schaap* (also concerning enforcement of EU law against individuals). As is familiar, the Court did not disclose whether it envisaged the rule-of-reason or the full effect approach when contemplating whether the national provision was justified. If *Heemskerk and Schaap* is understood as a procedural law case, then national procedural autonomy and the role of the *reformatio in pejus* prohibition in the *national* legal system may be understood to have tilted the balance. If it is instead viewed as a case of institutional autonomy, the convergence of Union and national standards of procedural protection may instead have been determinative.[1183]

Although the balancing exercise between effectiveness and legal certainty are similar under the application of the respective *Simmenthal* and *Rewe* requirements, the *van Schijndel* rule-of-reason is, in conclusion, more generous towards the interests of procedural protection, both due to its deference to the national judge, and, inter-relatedly, to national notions filling the concept of procedural protection with a content whose modification is reserved for the national legislator.[1184] Therefore, the need is lesser than under the full effect approach to examine whether the protected national notion is normatively endorsed by the Treaties or the Union legislator. By contrast, justification under the fundamental rights approach to limitations may be said to implicitly *presume* dual recognition or legal basis (at Union and Member State level), while justification under the full effect approach explicitly *requires* it.

1181 CJEU judgment in *M.A.S.*, C-42/17, EU:C:2017:936, 47-52.

1182 This is not surprising in view of the requirement in Art. 52(1) CFR that limitations to fundamental rights "meet objectives of general interest recognized by the Union".

1183 CJEU judgment in *Heemskerk BV and Firma Schaap v. Productschap Vee en Vlees*, C-455/06, EU:C:2008:650.

1184 This difference is perhaps not surprising since areas characterized by a greater degree of Member State autonomy, as has been institutional autonomy compared to procedural autonomy (C. Kakouris (1997), 1411), will also, where necessary, have to be grappled with sharper tools.

5.4 Interim conclusions

The answer as to how the balance was struck between substantive and procedural protection depended on a variety of factors, whereas no overall choice or priority was made between the substantive and procedural sides of effective judicial protection. The examination of the case-law identified three central factors:

1. Whether the principle was seen as a general principle or a fundamental right;
2. Its origin and legislative context;
3. Available rules allowing limitations and justifications.

On the first issue (*general principle or fundamental right*), the Court of Justice balanced the interest of judicial protection against other procedural tenets serving as justification for limitations under the fundamental rights approach. The Court referred to various sources of effective judicial protection: its reinforced legal status as EU primary law, constitutional traditions of the Member States, Art. 6 ECHR,[1185] and increasingly, the remedial mandate[1186], equality before the law[1187] (Art. 20 CFR) and respect for the rule of law[1188] (Art. 2 TEU). Yet, this perspective did not always lead to stronger individual protection.[1189]

This finding hinges on the second factor identified in the *origin and context* of the applied notion of procedural or judicial protection. Particularly case-law on the European arrest warrant presented a three-way clash between the effectiveness of Union secondary law, judicial protection under Art. 47 CFR (which was presumed to be safeguarded by participating Member States and the Union legislator), and judicial protection through the right to a fair trial pursuant to national constitutional law. The system

1185 E.g. CJEU judgment in *Deutsche Energiehandels- und Beratungsgesellschaft mbH v. Bundesrepublik Deutschland (DEB)*, C-279/09, EU:C:2010:811, 29-31.

1186 Art. 19(1) TEU: CJEU judgment in *Associação Sindical dos Juízes Portugueses*, C-64/16, EU:C:2018:117; CJEU judgment in *Carlos Escribano Vindel v. Ministerio de Justicia*, C-49/18, EU:C:2019:106.

1187 Art. 20 CFR: CJEU judgment in *Direcția Generală Regională a Finanțelor Publice Brașov v. Vasile Toma*, C-205/15, EU:C:2016:499, 36.

1188 Art. 2 TEU: CJEU judgment in *Associação Sindical dos Juízes Portugueses*, C-64/16, EU:C:2018:117, 32-36.

1189 CJEU judgment in *Brahim Samba Diouf v. Ministre du Travail, de l'Emploi et de l'Immigration*, C-69/10, EU:C:2011:524, 65; CJEU judgment in *Orizzonte Salute*, C-61/14, EU:C:2015:655.

of mutual trust singularly tilted the balance in favor of effectiveness of EU law over procedural safeguards pursuant to Member State law – both with respect to the arrest warrant and to other EU procedural frameworks.[1190]

The level of protection depended on the third factor listed above – namely the premises of *rules allowing limitations* to the effectiveness of EU law, its full effect, and the right to effective judicial protection.

The procedural rule-of-reason proved capable of tilting the balance towards procedural protection over effectiveness of EU law. Still, the *van Schijndel* formula – despite common denominators – no longer lends itself to justification for encroachments on the *right* to (as opposed to *principle* of) effective judicial protection.[1191] Along with a fundamental rights approach to procedural obstacles has accordingly followed a fundamental rights approach to justifications, under which Charter provisions frequently figured as a benchmark for encroachments founded on EU secondary law. On occasion, however, the requirements of the Charter were weighed against Union secondary law even without referring to possible justifications for limitations based on the Charter's own provisions.[1192]

In response to preliminary references implicitly or explicitly evoking the threshold rule contained in Art. 53 CFR, the Court of Justice in several instances allowed the effectiveness of EU law to trump national procedural safeguards. In *Melloni*, the effectiveness and correct application of the European arrest warrant was prioritized over individual procedural protection to avoid "undermin[ing] the principle of the primacy of EU law inasmuch as it would allow a Member State to disapply EU legal rules which are fully in compliance with the Charter where they infringe the fundamental rights guaranteed by that State's constitution."[1193] In *Ognyanov I and II*, the Court again dismissed the referring court's measures to provide a higher level of judicial protection than that prescribed by EU law, insisting that national courts abide by EU procedural frameworks.[1194]

1190 CJEU judgment in *Atanas Ognyanov (II)*, C-554/14, EU:C:2016:835; CJEU judgment in *Associação Sindical dos Juízes Portugueses*, C-64/16, EU:C:2018:117, 30.

1191 CJEU judgment in *Alassini and Others*, C-317/08, EU:C:2010:146, 63, with case-law there cited.

1192 CJEU judgment in *A v. B and Others*, C-112/13, EU:C:2014:2195, questions 2 and 3 (47-61).

1193 CJEU judgment in *Stefano Melloni v. Ministerio Fiscal*, C-399/11, EU:C:2013:107, 58.

1194 CJEU judgment in *Atanas Ognyanov (I)*, C-614/14, EU:C:2016:514, 25; CJEU judgment in *Atanas Ognyanov (II)*, C-554/14, EU:C:2016:835.

Another overall observation was that the Charter's horizontal provisions paired with secondary EU law appear to have provided a lower level of individual procedural protection as compared to competing notions in national law. In the previous Chapter 4, this was explained *inter alia* by recourse to competition between different beneficiaries of EU substantive law. The present chapter has additionally examined competition between beneficiaries of effectiveness on the one hand and effective judicial protection on the other, arguing that they do not always coincide even when secondary Union law identifies its beneficiaries. The fundamental rights approach to effective judicial protection did not always *de facto* strengthen the latter when secondary law designates not only beneficiaries, but also modalities capable of limiting individual judicial protection, which may tilt the balance towards ensuring the public interest in the efficient conduct of proceedings.[1195]

Justifications in the context of institutional autonomy and/or under the full effect approach were also less generous (than the rule-of-reason) towards national procedural safeguards, such as legal certainty and the protection of legitimate expectations. Convergence between national law and Union law was traditionally required for justifications to be accepted.[1196] In later case-law applying the full effect approach, the Court's guidelines for the balancing exercise integrated a fundamental rights language.[1197] On a comparative note, the full effect formula in principle *required* duplication or overlap between national and EU law, whereas the fundamental rights approach *presumed* such a dual basis.

1195 CJEU judgment in *Orizzonte Salute*, C-61/14, EU:C:2015:655, 73; CJEU judgment in *SC Star Storage SA and Others*, joined cases C-439/14 and C-488/14, EU:C:2016:688; CJEU judgment in *Moussa Sacko*, C-348/15, EU:C:2017:591, 44-45.

1196 See e.g. CJEU judgment in *Stichting ROM-projecten v. Staatssecretaris van Economische Zaken*, C-158/06, EU:C:2007:370, 24.

1197 CJEU judgment in *Banif Plus Bank Zrt v. Csaba Csipai,* C-472/11, EU:C:2013:88; CJEU judgment in *M.A.S.*, C-42/17, EU:C:2017:936, 48ff.

6 Conclusion

In a liberal democratic society, regulatory goals may be promoted by public powers on condition that the constitutional values are also respected. Adherence to these values to the requisite degree ensures that the pursuit of the regulatory goals by society is legitimate.[1198]

The present work has examined the encounter between the effectiveness of EU law and procedural protection, as dealt with by the Court of Justice within the judicial dialogue of the preliminary reference procedure. National courts' mandate of decentralized enforcement contributes to overall regulatory goals, whereas choices made by national courts must also take into account constitutional values, including due process and the proper conduct of proceedings.[1199] Striking an appropriate balance is necessary to ensure the legitimacy of the judiciary[1200] – all of whose functions hinge on the willingness of the public to turn to the court system in the first place.

Within the sphere of institutional and procedural autonomy, a language of deference has been employed by the Court of Justice so as to leave room for judicial discretion, as well as autonomy for the national legislator. Nevertheless, the Court of Justice has not left national judges adrift – instead, a number of tools evolved throughout the case-law, intended to help the seized courts navigate the choices left within their discretion. The principles that were examined in Chapter 2 provide useful tools for national courts, to be used when balancing the effectiveness of EU law against the protective prerogatives behind procedural "obstacles". The general case-law in the procedural domain therefore already prompts reflection about the priorities implied in the choice of tools offered. With respect to each of these tools, the question may be posed whether they primarily serve the interests of substantive protection of Union rights, or procedural protection

1198 S. Drake (2016), 20, here referring to constitutional values by way of including judicial protection and procedural safeguards.

1199 Ibid., 18.

1200 A nuanced discussion about the capacity of legal formalism versus procedural safeguards for bolstering the legitimacy of the judiciary may be found in C. J. Peters (2015), 23-44; see also S. Drake, 17-20 (2016).

in its various guises; and the resolution may instruct the seized national judge in his adjudication.

Returning therefore briefly to the key principles examined in Chapter 2, most belong to a category of tools giving priority to effective enforcement of Union law; particularly, the requirement of full/useful effect and the duty of sincere co-operation, functionalized for granting equal procedural treatment to claims based on EU law,[1201] for not making rights under Union law virtually impossible or excessively difficult to vindicate,[1202] and for providing effective, dissuasive and proportionate sanctions against breaches of EU law.[1203] Such tools represent an obligation of result in which the priority of effectiveness is inherent.[1204]

Yet other formulas were specifically devised to allow the national judge to carry out a balancing exercise between effectiveness and procedural protection through e.g. legal certainty. Examples of this are the procedural rule-of-reason[1205] and the balancing exercise prescribed for the requirement of full effect.[1206] Both of these justification tests can be understood as deferential in the margin granted national judges to take into account national procedural safeguards. Yet, they can also be interpreted as encouraging national judges to take a critical stance on national procedural law, by heightening the standard of scrutiny.[1207] Viewed from this perspective, they may represent a greater degree of interventionism in pursuit of effectiveness rather than, as is sometimes purported, increased deference.[1208]

Finally, Art. 19(1) TEU, requiring effective remedies to be provided in the fields covered by EU law, and the fundamental right to effective judicial protection, endorse both the priorities of procedural protection and ef-

1201 CJEU judgment in *Evelyn Danqua v. Minister for Justice and Equality*, C-429/15, EU:C:2016:789, 30; CJEU judgment in *EOS KSI Slovensko*, C-448/17, EU:C:2018:745, 36-40.

1202 CJEU judgment in *BBVA SA v. Pedro Peñalva López*, C-8/14, EU:C:2015:731, 26, 40-42.

1203 CJEU judgment in *Commission v. Greece (Greek Maize)*, 68/88, EU:C:1989:339, 23-25.

1204 See e.g. CJEU judgment in *M.A.S.*, C-42/17, EU:C:2017:936, 29-38.

1205 CJEU judgment in *Van Schijndel v. Stichting Pensioenfonds voor Fysiotherapeuten*, joined cases C-430/93 and C-431/93, EU:C:1995:441; CJEU judgment in *Peterbroeck, Van Campenhout & Cie v. Belgian State*, C-312/93, EU:C:1995:437.

1206 CJEU judgment in *Deutsche Milchkontor*, joined cases 205 to 215/82, EU:C:1983:233; CJEU judgment in *M.A.S.*, C-42/17, EU:C:2017:936, 48-53.

1207 M. Dougan (2004), 31-32.

1208 Ibid.; see also P. Wennerås (2007), 88-90.

fectiveness.[1209] Whereas limitations are also foreseen in the Charter, the Court's interpretations have been non-deferential towards national law, justifying the examination of ways in which the balance was concretely struck.

6.1 *Ex officio* review: Striking a balance between substantive and procedural protection

It is clear that allowing or requiring a national court to examine applicable Union law is the solution that best promotes its effective implementation, and, by consequence, substantive protection. Yet it is a sensitive obligation to lay down, because it may also require national judges to set aside applicable national principles of judge passivity and party disposition. National rules of procedure concerning *ex officio* review express a policy choice between full-fledged adversarialism and quasi-adversarial hybrids.[1210] Requiring national judges to override party disposition in the spirit of effective enforcement of Union law may come at the expense of procedural equal treatment, potentially pushing Member States a step closer to inquisitorialism.[1211] Still, the latter model is not (despite its reputation) all bad:[1212]

> both the adversarial and the inquisitorial systems may, if care is not taken, give rise to difficulties as regards compliance with Article 6 of the ECHR and Article 47 of the Charter. [...] But, if managed properly, each is a system for ascertaining the truth; they simply do so in different ways.

The first research question[1213] did not easily lend itself to operationalization, due to the deferential stance of the Court of Justice (in the absence of clear instructions, no balance has in effect been struck). When singling out key factors in the balancing exercise, the casuistic character of the relevant case-law (produced by e.g. the equivalence test and the rule-of-reason) must be kept in mind. Chapter 3 nevertheless revealed some factors to be

1209 CJEU judgment in *Slowakische Republik v. Achmea BV*, C-284/16, EU:C:2018:158, 36; CJEU judgment in *Associação Sindical dos Juízes Portugueses*, C-64/16, EU:C:2018:117, 29-34.

1210 Opinion of Advocate General Sharpston in *Online Games Handels GmbH*, C-685/15, EU:C:2017:201, 40.

1211 Ibid., 38-39.

1212 Ibid., 45 (remarked with respect to administrative sanctions classified as "criminal" in nature within the meaning of the ECHR).

1213 *How is the balance struck between substantive and procedural protection in the Court of Justice's case-law on* ex officio *review?*

more significant than others. For instance, notwithstanding its theoretical import, the distinction between civil and administrative proceedings did not appear to have been decisive to the EU law mandate of *ex officio* review; nor did the hierarchy of judicial levels of appeal.[1214]

The focal factor was the role and status of national rules containing procedural safeguards promoting the proper conduct of proceedings, legal certainty or due process. The procedural rule-of-reason[1215] and the balancing exercise prescribed for the requirement of full effect[1216] did not disclose where the balance should be struck between effectiveness and procedural protection. In practice, the rule-of-reason, as applied in the case-law on *ex officio* review, is nevertheless more generous towards national procedural safeguards, while the alternative test requires them to coincide with principles of Union law.[1217]

A second vital factor was access to a court or a tribunal within the meaning of Art. 267 TFEU, in Chapter 3 interpreted as both a matter of effective judicial protection, and effectiveness of the preliminary reference mechanism, in terms of its availability to the seized court. Both interpretations promote Union law effectiveness for the beneficiary,[1218] whereas constraints on *ex officio* review serve the procedural protection of the opposing party.[1219]

A third factor was the circumstance of procedural omissions by the litigant benefitting from EU law. The general case-law on *ex officio* review had indicated that national courts need not necessarily compensate for proce-

---

1214 See e.g. Opinion of Advocate General Maduro in *van der Weerd and Others v. Minister van Landbouw, Natuur en Voedselkwaliteit*, joined cases C-222/05 to C-225/05, EU:C:2007:124. By contrast, criminal proceedings have their own set of procedural requirements that, alas, mostly fall outside the scope of this thesis.

1215 CJEU judgment in *Van Schijndel v. Stichting Pensioenfonds voor Fysiotherapeuten*, joined cases C-430/93 and C-431/93, EU:C:1995:441; CJEU judgment in *Peterbroeck, Van Campenhout & Cie v. Belgian State*, C-312/93, EU:C:1995:437.

1216 CJEU judgment in *Deutsche Milchkontor*, joined cases 205 to 215/82, EU:C:1983:233; CJEU judgment in *M.A.S.*, C-42/17, EU:C:2017:936.

1217 Following from CJEU judgment in *Stichting ROM-projecten v. Staatssecretaris van Economische Zaken*, C-158/06, EU:C:2007:370, 24.

1218 CJEU judgment in *Peterbroeck, Van Campenhout & Cie v. Belgian State*, C-312/93, EU:C:1995:437, aligning with the *Rheinmühlen* mandate.

1219 Opinion of Advocate General Szpunar in *Finanmadrid EFC SA v. Jesús Vicente Albán Zambrano and Others*, C-49/14, EU:C:2015:746, 43, 94; CJEU judgment in *Banif Plus Bank Zrt v. Csaba Csipai* C-472/11, EU:C:2013:88.

dural omissions.[1220] This represented an insistence on procedural formalism,[1221] tacitly tilting the balance towards procedural protection of the opposing party in the spirit of due process. Although litigants' inertia was not consistently decisive, it bears potential implications for national courts' duty to make a preliminary reference, as well as the prospect of enjoying a response in substance from the Court of Justice.[1222]

As a matter of effectiveness, the public policy status of the relevant rule did not crystallize as key factor in the general case-law, although it clearly did in the test of equivalence.[1223] Whilst the designation of a particular rule as belonging to national public policy or Union public policy embodies a key justification of exceptional *ex officio* review, that particular perspective did not arise when applying the equivalence test. For the moment, therefore, the use of the equivalence test for public policy rules has limited significance in the context of balancing Union law *effectiveness* against procedural protection. This stance, in the general case-law, does not exclude for the future that the balancing exercise between effectiveness and procedural protection could potentially take into account the importance of the public policy rules at stake when applying the rule-of-reason, or a similar test. In this circumstance, collective interests vested in compliance with public policy rules (including under Union law) could be weighed against procedural safeguards precluding their examination *ex officio*.

Similar parameters surfaced in the context of consumer protection, where the Court of Justice fine-tuned and moderated their application, as compared to the general case-law on *ex officio* review. The designation of public policy status by "rank" rather than substance/content under national law strengthened the *ex officio* mandate in the consumer case-law even

1220 CJEU judgment in *van der Weerd and Others v. Minister van Landbouw, Natuur en Voedselkwaliteit*, joined cases C-222/05 to C-225/05, EU:C:2007:318, 41. See also Opinion of Advocate General Maduro in *van der Weerd and Others v. Minister van Landbouw, Natuur en Voedselkwaliteit*, joined cases C-222/05 to C-225/05, EU:C:2007:124, 29-30, construing the neglected "genuine opportunity" as dividing line between CJEU judgment in *van Schijndel v. Stichting Pensioenfonds voor Fysiotherapeuten*, joined cases C-430/93 and C-431/93, EU:C:1995:441 and CJEU judgment in *Peterbroeck, Van Campenhout & Cie v. Belgian State*, C-312/93, EU:C:1995:437.

1221 Within the meaning foreseen by C. J. Peters (2015), 24ff.

1222 CJEU judgment in *Lucio Cesare Aquino v. Belgische Staat*, C-3/16, EU:C:2017:209, 54-56.

1223 CJEU judgment in *Abdelhafid Bensada Benallal v. État belge*, C-161/15, EU:C:2016:175.

within the premises of the equivalence test.[1224] The rationale of *ius vigilantibus scriptum est* was also employed in the consumer protection case-law. Here, lower requirements of vigilance were levied on the beneficiary – drawing the line at "total inertia" and consequently oftentimes giving priority to the effectiveness of EU law at the potential expense of the procedural protection of the opposing party.[1225]

Although consumer protection was not an unfettered prerogative, legislative efforts and judges' compensation for procedural imbalances bolstered both the procedural and substantive protection of the consumer.[1226] This is explained by the convergence of beneficiaries of sources of procedural and substantive protection through the codification of quasi-substantive rights – it is judicial protection itself that is furthered by ensuring the enforcement of EU secondary law.[1227]

6.2 Beneficiaries of *ex officio* review and effective judicial protection

The present work approached both research questions from the perspective of beneficiaries of various overlapping norms of substantive and proce-

1224 CJEU judgment in *Asturcom Telecomunicaciones SL v. Cristina Rodríguez Nogueira*, C-40/08, EU:C:2009:615, 49-52; CJEU judgment in *Pohotovosť s.r.o. v. Iveta Korčkovská (I)*, C-76/10, EU:C:2010:685, 48-54; CJEU judgment in *Dirk Frederik Asbeek Brusse,* C-488/11, EU:C:2013:341, 44; CJEU judgment in *Froukje Faber,* C-497/13, EU:C:2015:357, 56-57; CJEU judgment in *Banco Primus SA v. Jesús Gutiérrez García*, C-421/14, EU:C:2017:60, 42 (the latter applying the same reasoning to the principle of effective judicial protection).

1225 See e.g. CJEU judgment in *Asturcom Telecomunicaciones SL v. Cristina Rodríguez Nogueira*, C-40/08, EU:C:2009:615, 47; CJEU judgment in *Monika Kušionová v. SMART Capital a.s.*, C-34/13, EU:C:2014:2189, 56; CJEU judgment in *Finanmadrid EFC SA v. Jesús Vicente Albán Zambrano and Others*, C-49/14, EU:C:2016:98, 52.

1226 CJEU judgment in *Elisa María Mostaza Claro v. Centro Móvil Milenium SL*, C-168/05, EU:C:2006:675, 36-38; cf., CJEU judgment in *Mohamed Aziz v. Caixa d'Estalvis de Catalunya*, C-415/11, EU:C:2013:164, 76 (on significant imbalance); CJEU judgment in *Hypoteční banka a.s. v. Udo Mike Lindner*, C-327/10, EU:C:2011:745, 53-54 and CJEU judgment in *Biuro podróży 'Partner'*, C-119/15, EU:C:2016:987, 27 (on access to justice/judicial protection for the commercial counterparty).

1227 E.g. in Directive 2009/22/EC of the European Parliament and of the Council of 23 April 2009 on injunctions for the protection of consumers' interests, OJ L 110, 01/05/2009, 30 and Council Directive 93/13/EEC of 5 April 1993 on unfair terms in consumer contracts, OJ L 095, 21/04/1993, 29 (Preamble and Art. 7).

dural protection. The analysis distilled, and where relevant distinguished between, the personal and protective scope of the principles of effectiveness and effective judicial protection under EU law (the latter subscribing to national and ECHR standards of procedural protection). This allowed the research problems to be resolved as a choice between ensuring procedural protection for all litigants and ensuring substantive protection of the Union law beneficiary. The former corresponds to the legal-technical notion of procedural *equality* whereas the latter – at least with respect to vulnerable litigants – encapsulates the theoretical notion of procedural *equity*.[1228]

The EU law mandate of *ex officio* review was permeated by the notion of procedural equity, which was in turn rationalized by reference to the protective scope of Union rules and rights.[1229] The identification of beneficiaries of *effectiveness* took a path via substantive legislation, whose personal scope depends on the construction and interpretation of the underlying substantive provision.[1230] When Union legislation envisaged the creation of rights, as seen in the consumer protection legislation, it identified its own personal *and* protective scope, at the origin of the Court of Justice's interpretative guidelines. The need to ensure that the effectiveness of the substantive goals was not undermined by a prohibitive procedural framework required the co-operation of national judges in compensating for procedural imbalances.

The conceptual approach via the identification of beneficiaries of effective judicial protection was also fruitful towards resolving the central research problem of striking a balance between procedural and substantive protection. The priority of *substantive* protection through Union law effectiveness singled out the litigant gaining from EU law as beneficiary of effective judicial protection. The priority of *procedural* protection envisaged a wider scope of potential beneficiaries. Particularly the advent of the fundamental rights approach proved capable of protecting litigants on both sides:[1231]

- Litigants' effective judicial protection was strongly linked to their capacity to litigate. This procedural equity aspect resonated throughout both the Court of Justice's case-law on *ex officio* review and the broader

1228 N. H. Andrews (2003), 128ff.

1229 I.e. lending support to the method proposed by M. Dougan (2012), 87ff., 113.

1230 Ibid., 87-94.

1231 *Hypoteční banka a.s. v. Udo Mike Lindner*, C-327/10, EU:C:2011:745, 53-54; CJEU judgment in *Biuro podróży 'Partner'*, C-119/15, EU:C:2016:987, 27ff.

case-law on effective judicial protection.[1232] Prohibitive litigation costs, viewed *inter alia* in terms of litigants' capacity to meet them, were considered an obstacle towards access to justice and therefore a key factor. Although this reasoning may tilt the balance towards procedural protection, competing considerations may tilt it towards substantive protection.

- A decisive factor was whether or not the beneficiaries of substantive and procedural protection coincided, as seen in secondary consumer legislation where judicial protection and effective remedies themselves represent the targets of the requirement of full/useful effect.[1233] The notion of legal remedies as quasi-substantive rights was based on a convergence of the legal instruments' personal scope.
- The consumer protection imperative also rationalized the need to compensate for procedural imbalances, pivotal in the Court of Justice's reactions to procedural omissions. Although litigation errors were evaluated on a case-by-case basis, the circumstance of belonging to the personal scope of protective legislation allowed margin for special treatment.

These prioritizations denote a distinction between beneficiaries of substantive rights under Union law (be they litigants or third parties) versus a wider population of litigants with claims to procedural protection, irrespective of whether they are addressees of Union law rights. Such differentiation is, in conclusion, the result of an interaction between various levels of protection pursuant to EU primary law, secondary law and Member State constitutional standards.

6.3 Effective judicial protection: Striking a balance between substantive and procedural protection

The second research question does not lend itself to establishing an unambiguous priority, which was also the reason behind the methodological

1232 CJEU judgment in *Deutsche Energiehandels- und Beratungsgesellschaft mbH v. Bundesrepublik Deutschland (DEB)*, C-279/09, EU:C:2010:811; CJEU judgment in *Orizzonte Salute*, C-61/14, EU:C:2015:655.

1233 E.g. in Directive 2009/22/EC of the European Parliament and of the Council of 23 April 2009 on injunctions for the protection of consumers' interests, OJ L 110, 01/05/2009, 30 and Council Directive 93/13/EEC of 5 April 1993 on unfair terms in consumer contracts, OJ L 095, 21/04/1993, 29 (Preamble and Art. 7).

choice to ask *how* – rather than *where* – *the balance is struck between substantive and procedural protection in the Court of Justice's case-law on effective judicial protection*. In Chapter 5, the answer to this question would also depend on a variety of factors. The following typology was distilled from the examination of relevant parameters: 1) the construction of the principle of effective judicial protection as a general principle or fundamental right; 2) the origin/legal source of the principle (EU primary law, EU secondary law, the ECHR and national law); and 3) available limitations and objective justifications for encroachments.

On the first issue *(general principle or fundamental right)*, it was observed that the fundamental rights perspective has gained ground. Its status of fundamental right did not in itself change the constituent elements of effective judicial protection. However, the latter's advent has to a certain point been accompanied by the decline of the principle of effectiveness. I use the word decline because effective judicial protection has not entirely replaced the principle of effectiveness, whereas the parameters for and legal consequences of choosing between them has become increasingly opaque.[1234]

In practice, the fundamental rights perspective did not necessarily bring about a stronger level of individual procedural protection, the latter primarily hinging on the origin of effective judicial protection as applicable in a given case. The examination of the second issue *(source and legislative context)* demonstrated the function and *de facto* vigor of the horizontal limitations and threshold rules contained in the Charter.

On the third issue *(justifications and limitations)* it was observed that the procedural rule-of-reason gave rise to far-reaching possibilities to justify encroachments on substantive protection. Whereas the principle of effectiveness (at least once equipped with its rule-of-reason) displayed a sensitive and nuanced approach towards national procedural safeguards, the fundamental rights approach – in addition to proportionality – required recognition and legitimacy as Union law prerogatives. This finding supports the proposition that the *Rewe* formula had greater potential for safeguarding procedural protection under national law than does the Charter.[1235]

It was moreover observed that encroachments on procedural protection following the fundamental rights approach were often founded on hori-

---

1234 S. Prechal (2017 a), 396; see e.g. CJEU judgment in *Banif Plus Bank Zrt v. Csaba Csipai* C-472/11, EU:C:2013:88; CJEU judgment in *Orizzonte Salute,* C-61/14, EU:C:2015:655.

1235 See e.g. J. Krommendijk (2012), 1395.

zontal provisions of the Charter allowing limitations to its Art. 47. Although limitations to fundamental rights are to be interpreted restrictively, both Art. 52 and 53 CFR were interpreted in a way that limited individuals' procedural protection. A similar observation was made when EU secondary law granted effective judicial protection, based on the Charter but adding modalities:[1236] the latter facilitated far-reaching limitations to the procedural protection of individuals.

Finally, comparison between the respective prospects for justification under the rule-of-reason, and the balancing test for the requirement of full effect, indicated that the former is more generous than the latter. This observation is in line with the level of deference shown by the Court of Justice throughout the case-law on *ex officio* review, illustrating the consequences of resolving a matter as pertaining to procedural autonomy. The comparison prompted the conclusion that while the full effect doctrine tilted the balance in favor of substantive protection by rejecting or downplaying national notions of procedural protection,[1237] the *Rewe* test was more inclined to allow national judges to grant priority to procedural protection under national law.[1238] There are, however, indications that also the full effect requirement is in the process of being usurped by the fundamental rights approach, at least with respect to avenues for justification.[1239]

6.4 Procedural harmonization of the principle of party disposition?

A contemplation of the benefits and perils of approximation of national laws on judge passivity vs. interventionism is merited in view of their pursuit of procedural versus substantive justice. The present work juxtaposed the said adjudication objectives, employing the related terms of substantive and procedural protection. Choices made by the Court of Justice in-

---

1236 CJEU judgment in *Orizzonte Salute*, C-61/14, EU:C:2015:655; CJEU judgment in *Stefano Melloni v. Ministerio Fiscal*, C-399/11, EU:C:2013:107.

1237 CJEU judgment in *Stichting ROM-projecten v. Staatssecretaris van Economische Zaken*, C-158/06, EU:C:2007:370, 24; CJEU judgment in *Ivo Taricco and Others*, C-105/14, EU:C:2015:555, 54-58.

1238 E.g. CJEU judgment in *Shirley Preston v. Wolverhampton Healthcare NHS Trust*, C-78/98, EU:C:2000:247, 62-63; S. Prechal (2017 a), 395 (in reference to the *Rewe* test).

1239 CJEU judgment in *Banif Plus Bank Zrt v. Csaba Csipai*, C-472/11, EU:C:2013:88; CJEU judgment in *M.A.S.*, C-42/17, EU:C:2017:936, 48ff.

cluded prioritizations between overall objectives and functions of the judiciary; between its role as adjudicator and truth-seeker.[1240] Therefore, the conditioned obligation of *ex officio* review that evolved throughout the case-law examined in this work has the capacity of prescribing a role for the national judge with which he is not familiar. The search for the "truth" as the judge's mission is highly contested, and may in the most extreme instances be called an externality to adjudication,[1241] whereas the obligation of *ex officio* review, integrated in EU law as an obligation of result, internalizes the task.

Therefore, the directions given in the case-law on *ex officio* review may, when implemented by the national judge, have different implications according to the procedural tradition in which he carries out his function.[1242] Without the legislator validating the said instructions, a court's deviation from national procedural law may have consequences for the domestic legitimacy of the court system,[1243] the individual and public perception of judge passivity and independence,[1244] and national concepts of procedural protection.[1245]

As described by Thibaut, the role of the judiciary varies between different litigation forms and types of conflict – so, depending on the tradition in which a judge serves, the balancing exercise foreseen in the jurisprudence may or may not fit the type of litigation for which he is seized.[1246] The avenues for justification explored in this work allow such aspects to be evaluated by national judges, even at the cost of Union law effectiveness. Taking these ideological implications into account, it is appropriate to allow national courts to continue to adjudicate "according to the rule-

1240 J. Thibaut and L. Walker (1978); A. Jolowicz (2005); see CJEU judgment in *Online Games Handels GmbH*, C-685/15, EU:C:2017:452.

1241 See Jolowicz (2005), 564, summarizing both ends of this spectrum within the scholarly debate.

1242 As warned in Opinion of Advocate General Jacobs in *van Schijndel v. Stichting Pensioenfonds voor Fysiotherapeuten*, joined cases C-430/93 and C-431/93, EU:C:1995:185, 37-38.

1243 A. Arnull (2013), 211-32; see also S. Drake (2016), 17-20.

1244 N. H. Andrews (1988), 125-40; S. Buhai, (2008).

1245 J. Engström, (2008), 73.

1246 J. Thibaut and L. Walker (1978)

book".[1247] The Court's choice to sort the present issue under the *Rewe* formula or under the Charter is of increasing importance.[1248]

When contemplating whether substantive rights must give way to procedural protection, the present study has demonstrated the importance of weighing the interests *on each side* of the scale: the individual or collective import of the substantive rights at jeopardy, and the weight of the procedural rule standing in the way of its realization. Tempting as it may be to regulate procedural law in order for that balance to be carried out in a uniform manner, consistency is likely to come at the expense of legal certainty. This prompted Wallerman to observe that procedural law "is not, and should not be reduced to being, only a servant of substantive law."[1249] Although no transversal rule can be envisaged with sufficient nuance for any probable or possible scenario, a rule of deference leaving the decentralized judge a measure of discretion is the closest we can expect to come. The second closest is deferring to the national legislator to choose between compulsory and facultative formulas.[1250]

The complexity of these parameters together with the ideological stakes triggered by *ex officio* review have led e.g. Storskrubb to contend that technical rules of procedure should not be harmonized.[1251] The findings of the present work lend support to this view. Procedural formalism or idiosyncrasy *should* be nurtured – not for its own sake[1252] but in order to respect the constitutional values and traditions of the Member States,[1253] and allow the legitimacy of the national court systems, as perceived within the Member States, to be safeguarded.

1247 On the stakes and the need for procedural safeguards inducing judicial restraint: E. Storskrubb, (2008), 21; C. J. Peters (2015), 23.

1248 Opinion of Advocate General Szpunar in *Finanmadrid EFC SA v. Jesús Vicente Albán Zambrano and Others*, C-49/14, EU:C:2015:746; CJEU judgment in *Orizzonte Salute*, C-61/14, EU:C:2015:655.

1249 A. Wallerman (2016), 359.

1250 CJEU judgment in *van Schijndel v. Stichting Pensioenfonds voor Fysiotherapeuten*, joined cases C-430/93 and C-431/93, EU:C:1995:441, 20-22 (*may not* = *must not*).

1251 E. Storskrubb (2008), 21.

1252 Cf. Judgment of the Court of Appeal (UK) in *Dresser UK Ltd v. Falcongate Ltd* (1992) QB 502 522 H, CA, per Bingham L.J.

1253 Art. 4(2) TEU requires loyalty on the Union side towards the Member States' constitutional identity: "the Union shall respect the equality of Member States before the Treaties as well as their national identities, inherent in their fundamental structures, political and constitutional, inclusive of regional and local self-government."

6.5 Looking ahead

How can effectiveness be promoted without making too big an ask of national judges? The present work has accused the fundamental rights approach of promising *inter alia* improved procedural protection while delivering (as usual) Union law effectiveness. Still, with the increased emphasis on due process,[1254] equality of arms,[1255] equality before the law,[1256] judicial independence,[1257] the rule of law,[1258] with perhaps more to come, it cannot be credibly vied that the Court of Justice does not take individual procedural protection seriously.

> the view that procedural and remedial law always serves the substantive effectiveness of EU law has by now been refined. While, for instance, effective judicial protection may look like a vehicle for the effectiveness of EU [law], in reality, this principle has a self-standing meaning and may equally protect against EU law and limit its effectiveness.[1259]

van Cleynenbreugel has made a compelling case that due process is increasingly built into the institutional design of enforcing EU law, where procedural fairness is regarded as a policy goal instead of an imposed threshold.[1260] The case-law considered in the present work has shown some horizontal provisions available under the fundamental rights approach to be untenable as thresholds in their conventional sense,[1261] whereas the underlying framework (i.e. the Charter rights) to which these threshold rules apply, places due process in the foreground.

1254 P. van Cleynenbreugel (2015), 45.

1255 CJEU judgment in *Banif Plus Bank Zrt v. Csaba Csipai* C-472/11, EU:C:2013:88, 29-36, CJEU judgment in *Sanchez Morcillo and Abril García (I)*, C-169/14, EU:C:2014:2099, 48-50.

1256 CJEU judgment in *Direcţia Generală Regională a Finanţelor Publice Braşov v. Vasile Toma*, C-205/15, EU:C:2016:499, 35ff.; CJEU judgment in *Bashar Ibrahim*, joined cases C-297/17, C-318/17, C-319/17 and C-438/17, EU:C:2019:219, 66.

1257 CJEU judgment in *Associação Sindical dos Juízes Portugueses*, C-64/16, EU:C:2018:117, 45-52; CJEU judgment in *Carlos Escribano Vindel v. Ministerio de Justicia*, C-49/18, EU:C:2019:106, 61ff.

1258 V. Roeben (2019), 32; CJEU judgment in *Associação Sindical dos Juízes Portugueses*, C-64/16, EU:C:2018:117; 30-36.

1259 S. Prechal (2017 a), 403.

1260 At least in EU competition law; P. van Cleynenbreugel (2015), 44, 68-72.

1261 Particularly Art. 53 CFR pursuant to CJEU judgment in *Stefano Melloni v. Ministerio Fiscal*, C-399/11, EU:C:2013:107 *et seq.*, but, as argued in Chapter 5, also Art. 52(1) and perhaps Art. 52(3) CFR.

van Cleynenbreugel's proposal is that if we cherish procedural fairness, we might get effectiveness on the house.[1262]

> As complementary standards, justice requirements guarantee a *procedurally sound* framework through which a perception of *fairness* is attached to efficient outcomes. Fairness necessarily complements without completely replacing effectiveness considerations.

It could, in this vein, be expected that a perception of legitimacy of the EU fundamental rights framework may render national judges more willing to participate in the preliminary reference procedure, i.e. making EU law more enforceable by bringing more cases under the Court of Justice's purview. The reasoning is reminiscent of Burley and Mattli's classic sketch of national judges' endorsement of direct effect and primacy: If national judges see an opportunity to promote individual or fundamental rights, cooperation in the enforcement of EU law will empower them as "public policemen" – i.e. a rationalist means to achieve enforcement.[1263] Insofar as the EU legal framework is perceived by national courts as legitimate in its priorities and construction, a similar argument can be advanced with respect to participation in the preliminary reference system. Both mechanisms of "reciprocal empowerment"[1264] between the Court of Justice and the national judiciary have the same endgame: increased effectiveness of EU law.

How can then my earlier argument in favor of deference (with respect to *ex officio* review) be reconciled with van Cleynenbreugel's case for institutionally consolidating and strengthening procedural rights? It is increasingly observed that institutionalization of the norm of effective judicial protection has brought about a federalization of the Union judicature:[1265]

> Judicial protection welds the organizationally separate EU and Member States['] judicatures into one coherent judicial function, on which the rule of law in the EU comes to rest.

1262 P. van Cleynenbreugel (2015), 71, refers to such measures of increased objective legitimacy as a "sweetener".

1263 M. Burley and W. Mattli (1993), 63-64, depict a purposive appeal from the Court of Justice to national courts to protect the "little guy" or the underdog against the state.

1264 Ibid., 64-65.

1265 V. Roeben (2019), 32.

A corollary image is the Court of Justice as constitutional court, scrutinizing Member States' as well as the EU legislature's compliance with fundamental rights protection (including procedural rights).

Yet, the Court's recent dealings with common constitutional values of the EU – including references to mutual trust[1266] – is capable of cutting both ways. In case-law relating to the European arrest warrant, presumptions of compliance with fundamental rights in fact led to reduced scrutiny.[1267] On the other hand, rather functionalist justifications previously accepted[1268] have been superseded by case-law in which fundamental rights encroachments were concretely – and sometimes strictly – reviewed.[1269]

The recent surge in references to presumptions of compliance with the foundational values enumerated in Art. 2 TEU – both within and outside the context of the European arrest warrant – have arguably placed the Court's standards of review in the spotlight. It is an urgent undertaking for future research to tackle the flipside of presumptions of compliance with procedural standards; i.e., where applicable, to systematize the avenues for rebutting them.[1270] Propositions that limitations to Art. 47 CFR should be reviewed particularly intensely,[1271] that serious interferences prompt stricter review,[1272] and that its intensity should take account of the benefi-

1266 Viz. Art. 2 TEU, see CJEU judgment in *Slowakische Republik v. Achmea BV*, C-284/16, EU:C:2018:158, 34; CJEU judgment in *Bashar Ibrahim*, joined cases C-297/17, C-318/17, C-319/17 and C-438/17, EU:C:2019:219, 83ff.; CJEU judgment in *Associação Sindical dos Juízes Portugueses*, C-64/16, EU:C:2018:117, 30-32.

1267 CJEU judgment in *Minister for Justice and Equality v. Francis Lanigan*, C-237/15 PPU, EU:C:2015:474, 36-42.

1268 CJEU judgment in *Brahim Samba Diouf v. Ministre du Travail, de l'Emploi et de l'Immigration*, C-69/10, EU:C:2011:524, 65.

1269 CJEU judgment in *Liivimaa Lihaveis MTÜ v. Eesti-Läti programmi 2007-2013 Seirekomitee*, C-562/12, EU:C:2014:2229, 72-76; CJEU judgment in *Vladimir Peftiev*, C-314/13, EU:C:2014:1645, 25-29; CJEU judgment in *E.G. v. Republika Slovenija*, C-662/17, EU:C:2018:847, 50; CJEU judgment in *Bashar Ibrahim*, joined cases C-297/17, C-318/17, C-319/17 and C-438/17, EU:C:2019:219, 88-89. See also, within the European arrest warrant framework, CJEU judgment in *LM (Judicial independence in Poland)*, C-216/18 PPU, EU:C:2018:586, 44-47, prescribing exceptional derogation from the presumption of compliance with Art. 47 CFR, subject to review by the national court.

1270 S. Prechal (2017 b), 85-90; see also A. Efrat (2019) 16 f., presenting empirical evidence against the mutual trust presumption in Member State practices.

1271 J-U. Franck (2017), 1877.

1272 CJEU judgment in *Bashar Ibrahim*, joined cases C-297/17, C-318/17, C-319/17 and C-438/17, EU:C:2019:219, 88-90.

ciary of the fundamental right *vis-à-vis* the interests shielded by the limitation[1273] draw attention to the layers involved in the Court of Justice's judicial scrutiny. As observed by Prechal: "Finding a fair balance between two (fundamental) rights is arguably a different issue than balancing the protection of a right and an objective of general interest."[1274]

With respect to the intensity of review, restrictions on e.g. judicial protection (be they prescribed by the EU or the national legislator within the scope of application of EU law[1275]), must be distinguished from unilateral attempts to derogate from fundamental rights limitations laid down in EU secondary law. The latter attempts, in effect, do not at all represent a restriction, but rather a (professed) domestic advancement of individual rights.[1276] Such "derogations" do not conceptually fall under the fundamental rights approach to justifications, but should rather enjoy moderate scrutiny within the context of implementation of EU law, or – outside the realm of EU competence – deference.

1273 S. Prechal (2016), 153.

1274 Ibid.

1275 CJEU judgment in *Hampshire County Council v. C.E. and N.E.*, joined cases C-325/18 PPU and C-375/18 PPU, EU:C:2018:739, 63-75.

1276 As were relevant in CJEU judgment in *Stefano Melloni v. Ministerio Fiscal*, C-399/11, EU:C:2013:107; CJEU judgment in *Atanas Ognyanov (I)*, C-614/14, EU:C:2016:514; CJEU judgment in *Atanas Ognyanov (II)*, C-554/14, EU:C:2016:835; CJEU judgment in *Bashar Ibrahim*, joined cases C-297/17, C-318/17, C-319/17 and C-438/17, EU:C:2019:219.

Bibliography

Monographs

Andrews, Neil H., *English Civil Procedure: Fundamentals of the New Civil Justice System* (Oxford: Oxford University Press, 2003).

Beka, Anthi, *The Active Role of Courts in Consumer Litigation. Applying EU Law of the National Courts' Own Motion* (Cambridge: Intersentia, 2018).

Bernitz, Ulf, and Anders Kjellgren, *Europarättens grunder* (Vällingby: Norstedts juridik AB, 2007).

Bertrand, Brunesse, *Le juge de l'Union européenne, juge administratif* (Brussels: Bruylant, 2012).

Cadiet, Loïc, Jacques Normand, Soraya Amrani-Mekki, and Jacques Normand, *Théorie générale du procès* (Paris: Presses Universitaires de France, 2013).

Claes, Monica, *The National Courts' Mandate in the European Constitution* (Oregon: Hart Publishing, 2006).

Corrias, Luigi, *The Passivity of Law. Competence and Constitution in the Court of Justice* (Amsterdam: Springer, 2011).

Corthaut, Tim, *EU Ordre Public* (Croydon: Kluwer Law International, 2012).

Craig, Paul, and Gráinne de Búrca, *EU Law: Text, Cases, and Materials*. 5 edn. (New York: Oxford University Press, 2011 a).

Craig, Paul, *EU Administrative Law*. Vol. 2 (New York: Oxford University Press, 2012).

Diesen, Christian, and Annika Lagerqvist Veloz Roca, *Bevis 7: Bevisprövning i förvaltningsmål* (Stockholm: Norstedts juridik, 2003).

Dougan, Michael, *National Remedies before the Court of Justice: Issues of Harmonisation and Differentiation*, *Modern studies in European law* (Oxford: Hart, 2004).

Douglas-Scott, Sionaidh, *Constitutional Law of the European Union* (Harlow: Longman, 2002).

Ekelöf, Per Olof, and Henrik Edelstam, *Rättegång: Första häftet* (Stockholm: Norstedts Juridik, 2002).

Ergec, Rusen, and Jacques Velu, *Convention européenne des droits de l'homme* (Brussels: Bruylant, 2014).

Esaiasson, Peter, Mikael Gilljam, Henrik Oscarsson, and Lena Wängnerud, *Metodpraktikan. Konsten att studera samhälle individ och marknad.* 2 edn. (Stockholm: Nordstedts Juridik, 2004).

von Essen, Ulrik, *Processramen i förvaltningsmål: ändring av talan och anslutande frågor* (Stockholm: Norstedts juridik, 2009).

Galetta, Diana-Urania, *Procedural Autonomy of EU Member States: Paradise Lost? A Study on the "Functionalized Procedural Competence" of EU Member States* (Heidelberg: Springer, 2010).

Gilliaux, Pascal, *Droit(s) européen(s) à un procès équitable* (Brussels: Bruylant, 2012).

Gray, John Chipman, *The Nature and Sources of the Law*. Vol. 2 (New York: Macmillan, 1921).

Harris, David, Michael O'Boyle, Edward Bates, and Carla Buckley, *Harris, O'Boyle & Warbrick: Law of the European Convention on Human Rights* (Oxford: Oxford University Press, 2009).

Hay, Colin, *Political Analysis. A Critical Introduction* (Hampshire: Palgrave, 2002).

Hofmann, Herwig C.H., Gerard C. Rowe, and Alexander Türk, *Administrative Law and Policy of the European Union* (Oxford: Oxford University Press, 2011).

Jans, Jan H., Roel de Lange, Sacha Prechal, and Robert J. G. M. Widdershoven, *Europeanisation of Public Law* (Groningen: Europa Law Publishing, 2007).

Kaczorowska-Ireland, Alina, *European Union Law* (Routledge, 2012).

Klamert, Marcus, *The Principle of Loyalty in EU Law* (New York: Oxford University Press, 2014).

Lenaerts, Koen, Ignace Maselis, and Kathleen Gutman, *EU Procedural Law* (New York: Oxford University Press, 2014).

Lind, Allan, and Tom Tyler, *The Social Psychology of Procedural Justice* (New York: Plenum Press, 1988).

Motulsky, Henri, Gérard Cornu, Jean Foyer, Berthold Goldman, and Philippe Fouchard, *Ecrits* (Paris: Dalloz, 1973).

Paunio, Elina, *Legal Certainty in Multilingual EU Law: Language, Discourse and Reasoning at the European Court of Justice* (New York: Routledge, 2016).

Prechal, Sacha, *Directives in EC Law. 2 edn* (New York: Oxford University Press, 2005).

Robberstad, Anne, *Mellom tvekamp og inkvisisjon: straffeprosessens grunnstruktur belyst ved fornærmedes stilling* (Oslo: Universitetsforlaget, 1998).

Schermers, Henry G., and Denis Waelbroeck, *Judicial Protection in the European Union*. 6 edn. (The Hague: Kluwer Law International, 2001).

Schütze, Robert, *European Constitutional Law* (Cambridge: Cambridge University Press, 2012).

Schütze, Robert, *European Union Law* (Cambridge: Cambridge University Press, 2015).

Storskrubb, Eva, *Civil Procedure and EU Law: A Policy Area Uncovered* (New York: Oxford University Press, 2008).

Tridimas, Takis, and Paolisa Nebbia, *European Union Law for the Twenty-First Century. Rethinking the New Legal Order*. Vol. 1. Constitutional and Public Law External Relations (Oregon: Hart Publishing, 2004).

Tridimas, Takis, *The General Principles of EU Law* (New York: Oxford University Press, 2006).

Wallerman, Anna, *Om fakultativa regler. En studie av svensk och unionsrättslig reglering av skönsmässigt beslutsfattande i processrättsliga frågor* (Uppsala: Iustus förlag, 2015).

Ward, Angela, *Judicial Review and the Rights of Private Parties in EC Law* (New York: Oxford University Press, 2000).

Wejedal, Sebastian, and Allison Östlund, *Advokatens roll. Om ändamålsenlig rollfördelning i mål om tvångsvård av barn* (Stockholm: Santérus, 2016).

Wennerås, Pål, *The Enforcement of EC Environmental Law* (New York: Oxford University Press, 2007).

Werlauff, Erik, *Common European Procedural law. European Law requirements imposed on national administration of Justice* (Gylling: DJOF Publishing Copenhagen 1999).

Westberg, Peter, *Civilrättskipning* (Stockholm: Norstedts juridik, 2013).

White, Robin C. A., and Claire Ovey, *Jacobs, White & Ovey: The European Convention on Human Rights*. 5 edn. (Oxford: Oxford University Press, 2010).

Wilman, Folkert, *Private Enforcement of EU Law before National Courts: The EU Legislative Framework* (Northampton: Elgar European Law and Practice, 2015).

Edited books and book chapters

Andrews, Neil H., 'Nurturing Civil Justice', in *Festschrift für Rolf Sturner zum 70. Geburtstag. 2. Teilband*, eds. Bruns, A., C. Kern, J. Münch, A. Piekenbrock, A. Stadler and D. Tsikrikas (Tübingen: Mohr Siebeck, 2013), 1393.

Arabadjiev, Alexander, Marko Pavliha, Marko Ilešič, Ada Polajnar-Pavčnik, and Boštjan Koritnik, eds., *Challenges of Law in Life Reality, Liber Amicorum Marko Ilešič* (Ljublana: Pravna faculteta Univerze v Ljubljani, 2017).

Arnull, Anthony, 'Judicial Activism and the European Court of Justice: How Should Academics Respond?', in *Judicial Activism at the European Court of Justice*, eds. de Witte, B., E. Muir and M. Dawson (Cheltenham: Edward Elgar Publishing, 2013).

Arnull, Anthony, Catherine Barnard, Michael Dougan, and Eleanor Spaventa, eds., *A Constitutional Order of States? Essays in EU Law in Honour of Alan Dashwood* (Cornwall: Hart Publishing, 2011).

Avbelj, Matej, and Jan Komárek, eds., *Constitutional Pluralism in the European Union and Beyond* (Portland: Hart Publishing, 2012).

Barnard, Catherine and Okeoghene Odudu, eds., *The Outer Limits of European Law* (Oxford: Hart Publishing, 2009).

Barnard, Catherine, ed., *The Fundamentals of EU Law Revisited: Assessing the Impact of the Constitutional Debate* (New York: Oxford University Press, 2007).

Bobek, Michal, 'Why There is no Principle of 'Procedural Autonomy' of the Member States', in *The European Court of Justice and the Autonomy of the Member States*, eds. de Witte, B. and H. Micklitz (Antwerp: Intersentia, 2012).

Brenninkmeijer, Alex Franciscus Maria, 'The Influence of Court of Justice Case Law on the Procedural Law of the Member States', in *Administrative Law Application and Enforcement of Community Law in the Netherlands*, eds. Vervaele, J. A. E. and K.-A. Andrean-Gellert (Deventer-Boston: Kluwer Law and Taxation Publ., 1994).

Brownsword, Roger, Hans-W Micklitz, Leone Niglia, and Stephen Weatherill, eds., *The Foundations of European Private Law* (Oxford: Hart, 2011).

Bruns, Alexander, Christoph Kern, Joachim Münch, Astrid Stadler, Andreas Piekenbrock, and Dimitrios Tsikrikas, eds., *Festschrift für Rolf Stürner zum 70. Geburtstag* (Tübingen: Mohr Siebeck, 2013).

de Búrca, Grainne, 'National Procedural Rules and Remedies: The Changing Approach of the Court of Justice', in *Remedies for Breach of EC Law*, eds. Lonbay, J. and A. Biondi (Michigan: John Wiley & Sons, 1997).

Caoimh, Aindrias Ó, 'Issues of EU Law Raised by National Courts of their Own Motion', in *Constitutionalising the EU Judicial System: Essays in Honour of Pernilla Lindh*, eds. Cardonnel, P., A. Rosas and N. Wahl (Oxford: Hart Publishing, 2012).

van Cleynenbreugel, Pieter, 'Effectiveness through fairness? 'Due process' as an institutional precondition for effective decentralized EU competition law enforcement', in *Procedural Fairness in Competition Proceedings*, eds. Nihoul, P. and T. Skoczny (Northhampton: Elward Elgar, 2015).

Craig, Paul, and Gráinne de Búrca, eds., *The Evolution of EU Law*, Vol. 2 (Oxford: Oxford University Press, 2011 b).

Cremona, Marise, ed., *Compliance and the Enforcement of EU Law* (Oxford: Oxford University Press, 2012).

da Cruz Vilaça, José Luís, 'Le principe de l'effet utile du droit de l'Union dans la jurisprudence de la Cour', in *The Court of Justice and the Construction of Europe: Analyses and Perspectives on Sixty Years of Case-Law* (The Hague: Asser press, 2013).

Dougan, Michael, 'In Defence of Mangold?', in *A Constitutional Order of States?*, eds. Arnull, A., C. Barnard, M. Dougan and E. Spaventa (Cornwall: Hart Publishing, 2011 b).

Dougan, Michael, 'The Vicissitudes of Life at the Coalface: Remedies and Procedures for Enforcing Union Law before the National Courts', in *The Evolution of EU Law*, eds. Craig, P. and G. de Búrca (New York: Oxford University Press, 2011 a).

Drake, Sara, 'More Effective Private Enforcement of EU Law Post-Lisbon: Aligning Regulatory Goals and Constitutional Values', in *New Directions in the Effective Enforcement of EU Law and Policy*, eds. Drake, S. and M. Smith (Northampton: Edward Elgar Publishing, 2016).

Dubos, Olivier, 'Que reste-t-il de l'autonomie procédurale du juge national ? Histoire de l'attribution d'une compétence au nom de l'effectivité et de l'efficacité du droit de l'Union', in *Renvoi préjudiciel et marge d'appréciation du juge national*, ed. Neframi, E. (Brussels: Larcier, 2015 a).

Hartkamp, Arthur S., Martijn Hesselink, Ewoud H Hondius, Chantal Mak, and Edgar du Perron, eds., *Towards a European Civil Code.* Vol. 4 (Alphen aan den Rijn: Kluwer Law International, 2011).

Hofmann, Herwig C.H., 'Effective Judicial Remedies Before the National Courts' in *The EU Charter of Fundamental Rights*, eds. A. Ward, S. Peers, T. Harvey and J. Kenner, (Oxford: Hart Publishing, 2014 a).

Hofmann, Herwig C.H., 'The International Market in a Context of Deepening Integration – Long on Content and Short on Modes of Delivery?', in *Of Courts and Constitutions: Liber Amicorum in Honour Of Nial Fennelly*, eds. Bradley, K., N. Travers, A. Whelan and N. Fennelly (Oxford: Hart Publishing, 2014 b).

Jolowicz, John A., 'Da mihi factum dabo tibi jus: A Problem of Demarcation in English and French Law', in *On Civil Procedure*, ed. Jolowicz, J. A. (Cambridge: Cambridge University Press, 2000).

Jolowicz, John A., 'Substantive and Procedural Justice in Civil Litigation: A Measure of the Role of Civil Litigation', in *De tous horizons. Mélanges Xavier Blanc-Jouvan*, ed. Fauvarque-Cosson, B. (Paris: Société de législation comparée, 2005).

Jones, Clifford A., 'Into the Parallel Universe: Procedural Fairness in Private Litigation after the Damages Directive' in *Procedural Fairness in Competition Proceedings*, eds. Nihoul, P. and T. Skozcy (Cheltenham: Elgar, 2015).

Law, Stephanie, 'The Transformation of Consumer Law in Times of Crisis: The Ex Officio Control of Unfair Contract Terms', in *Transformation of Civil Justice*, eds. Uzelac A. and C. van Rhee (Chem: Springer, 2018).

Leczykiewicz, Dorota, 'Effectiveness of EU Law before National Courts: Direct Effect, Effective Judicial Protection, and Member State Liability', in *Oxford Handbook of European Union Law*, eds. Arnull, A. and D. Chalmers (Oxford: Oxford University Press, 2015).

Lindahl, Hans, 'Discretion and Public Policy: Timing the Unity and Divergence of Legal Orders', in *The Coherence of EU law*, eds. Prechal, S. and B. van Roermund (New York: 2008).

Lindholm, Johan, ''DCFR, Please Meet National Procedure': Enforcing the Frame of Reference Using National Procedural Law', in *The Foundations of European Private Law*, eds. Brownsword, R., H.-W. Micklitz, L. Niglia and S. Weatherill (Oxford: Hart, 2011).

Loos, Marco, 'Individual Private Enforcement of Consumer Rights in Civil Courts in Europe', in *The Foundations of European Private Law*, eds. Brownsword, R., H.-W. Micklitz, L. Niglia and S. Weatherill (Oxford: Hart, 2011).

MacQueen, Hector L., 'Illegality and Immorality in Contracts: Towards European Principles', in *Towards a European Civil Code*, eds. Hartkamp, A. S., M. Hesselink, E. H. Hondius, C. Mak and E. du Perron (Alphen aan den Rijn: Kluwer, 2011).

Meij, Arjen, 'The Rules of the Game. Party Autonomy in the EU Courts', in *De Regels en het Spel, Opstellen over Recht, Filosofie, Literatuur en Geschiedenis aangeboden aan Tom Eijsbouts*, eds. J-H. Reestman, A. Schrauwen, M. van Montfrans and J.H. Jans (The Hague: Asser, 2011).

Micklitz, Hans-Wolfgang, and Bruno de Witte, eds., *The European Court of Justice and the Autonomy of the Member States* (Cambridge: Intersentia, 2012).

Neframi, Eleftheria, 'Exigence de cohérence et action extérieure de l'Union européenne', in *Le Droit, les Institutions et les politiques de l'Union européenne face à l'impératif de coherence*, ed. V. Michel (Strasbourg: Presses Universitaires de Strasbourg, 2009).

Neframi, Eleftheria, 'La force intégrative du statut de l'Etat membre sur la fonction juridictionnelle', in *Le statut d'Etat membre de l'Union européenne*, ed. Potvin-Solis, L. (Brussels: Bruylant, 2018).

Neframi, Eleftheria, 'La rôle du juge national dans le cadre du renvoi préjudiciel : une marge d'appréciation?', in *Renvoi préjudiciel et marge d'appréciation du juge national*, ed. Neframi, E. (Brussels: Larcier, 2015).

Neframi, Eleftheria, 'Quelques réflexions sur l'article 19, paragraphe 1, alinéa 2, TUE et l'obligation de l'État membre d'assurer la protection juridictionnelle effective', in *La Constitution, l'Europe et le droit, Mélanges en l'honneur de Jean-Claude Masclet*, ed. Boutayeb, C. (Paris: Publications de la Sorbonne, 2013).

Neframi, Eleftheria, ed., *Renvoi préjudiciel et marge d'appréciation du juge national* (Brussels: Larcier, 2015).

Neframi, Eleftheria, and Mauro Gatti, 'Autonomy and EU Competences in the Context of Free Trade Investment Agreements', in *Negotiation and Conclusion of the New Generation Trade Agreements*, eds. I. Bosse Platière and C. Rapoport (Edward Elgar, forthcoming 2019).

Nihoul, Paul, and Tadeusz Skozcy, eds., *Procedural Fairness in Competition Proceedings* (Cheltenham: Elgar, 2015).

Peters, Christopher J, 'Legal Formalism, Procedural Principles, and Judicial Constraint in American Adjudication', in *General Principles of Law – The Role of the Judiciary*, ed. Pineschi, L. (Switzerland: Springer, 2015).

Pineschi, Laura, ed., *General Principles of Law – The Role of the Judiciary* (Switzerland: Springer, 2015).

Piquani, Darinka, 'The Role of National Courts in Issues of Compliance', in *Compliance and the Enforcement of EU Law*, ed. Cremona, M. (Oxford: Oxford University Press, 2012).

Plender, Richard, 'The Role of National Judges in Implementing Uniform Rules of Jurisdiction and Choice of Law in the European Union', in *A Constitutional Order of States? Essays in EU Law in Honour of Alan Dashwood*, eds. Arnull, A., C. Barnard, M. Dougan and E. Spaventa (Cornwall: Hart Publishing, 2011).

Potvin-Solis, Laurence, ed., *Le statut d'Etat membre de l'Union européenne* (Brussels: Bruylant, 2018).

Prechal, Sacha, 'Between Effectiveness, Procedural Autonomy and Judicial Protection', in *Challenges of Law in Life Reality, Liber Amicorum Marko Ilešič*, eds. Alexander Arabadjiev, A., M. Pavliha, M. Ilešič; A. Polajnar-Pavčnik and B. Koritnik (Ljublana: Pravna faculteta Univerze v Ljubljani, 2017 a).

Prechal, Sacha, 'Direct effect, indirect effect, supremacy and the evolving constitution of the European Union', in *The Fundamentals of EU Law Revisited: Assessing the Impact of the Constitutional Debate*, ed. Barnard, C. (New York: Oxford University Press, 2007).

Prechal, Sacha, 'The Court of Justice and Effective Judicial Protection: What Has the Charter Changed?', in *Fundamental Rights in International and European Law*, eds. Paulussen, C., T. Takácz, V. Lazić and B. van Rompuy (The Hague: Springer, 2016).

Prechal, Sacha, and Rob Widdershoven, 'Effectiveness or Effective Judicial Protection: A Poorly Articulated Relationship', in *Today's Multi-layered Legal Order: Current Issues and Perspectives*, ed. Baumé, T. (Paris: Zutphen, 2011 a).

Ravo, Linda Maria, 'The Role of the Principle of Effective Judicial Protection in the EU and its Impact on National Jurisdictions', in *Sources of Law and Legal Protection* (Trieste: Edizioni Università di Trieste, 2012).

Reestman, Jan-Herman, Annette Schrauwen, Manet van Montfrans, and Jan H. Jans, eds., *De Regels en het Spel, Opstellen over Recht, Filosofie, Literatuur en Geschiedenis aangeboden aan Tom Eijsbouts* (The Hague: Asser Press, 2011).

Reich, Norbert, 'Legal protection of individual and collective consumer interests', in *European Consumer Law*, eds. Reich, N., H. Micklitz, P. Rott and K. Tonner (Cambridge: Intersentia, 2014).

Reich, Norbert, Hans-Wolfgang Micklitz, Peter Rott, and Klaus Tonner, eds., *European Consumer Law* (Cambridge: Intersentia, 2014).

Rosas, Allan, 'The National Judge as EU Judge: Opinion 1/09', in *Constitutionalising the EU Judicial System. Essays in Honour of Pernilla Lindh*, eds. Cardonnel, P., A. Rosas and N. Wahl (Oxford: Hart Publishing, 2012).

Rosas, Allan, Egils Levits, and Yves Bot, eds., *La Cour de Justice et la Construction de l'Europe : Analyses et Perspectives de Soixante Ans de Jurisprudence* (The Hague: Asser Press, 2013).

Schütze, Robert, 'Federalism as Constitutional Pluralism: 'Letter from America'', in *Constitutional Pluralism in the European Union and Beyond*, eds. Avbelj M. and J. Komárek, (Portland: Hart Publishing, 2012).

Skouris, Vassilios, 'The Principle of Procedural Autonomy and the Duty of Loyal Cooperation of National Judges under Article 10 EC', in *Tom Bingham and the Transformation of the Law: A Liber Amicorum*, eds. Andenæs, M. T., D. Fairgrieve, B. Markesinis, E. McKendrick and S. B. A. Rix (Oxford: Oxford University Press, 2009).

St Clair Bradley, Kieran, 'Powers and Procedures in the EU Constitution: Legal Bases and the Court', in *The Evolution of EU Law*, eds. Craig, P. and G. de Búrca (Oxford: Oxford University Press, 2011).

Vahlne Westerhäll, Lotta, ed., *Tvångsvård och psykisk ohälsa* (Gothenburg: School of Business, Economics and Law, Legal Publications series 012, 2012).

Vesterdorf, Bo, 'Le relevé d'office par le juge communautaire' in *Une Communauté de Droit. Festschrift für Gil Carlos Rodríquez Iglesias,* eds. Colneric, N., D. Edward, J.-P. Puissochet and D. Ruiz-Jarabo Colomer (Berlin: Berliner Wissenschafts-Verlag, 2003).

Wallerman, Anna, 'Manoeuvering Procedural Autonomy in Sweden: Is *Materielle Prozessleitung* the Answer?', in *Procedural autonomy: Room for Manoeuvre,* eds. Nylund, A. and B. Krans (Intersentia, forthcoming 2019).

Weatherill, Stephen, 'Interpretation of the Directives: The Role of the Court', in *Towards a European Civil Code*, eds. Hartkamp, A. S., M. Hesselink, E. H. Hondius, C. Mak and E. du Perron (Alphen aan den Rijn: Kluwer, 2011).

de Witte, Bruno, 'Treaty Revision Procedures after Lisbon', in *EU Law after Lisbon*, eds. Biondi, A., P. Eeckhout and S. Ripley (Oxford: Oxford University Press, 2012).

Zetterquist, Ola, 'Out with the New, in with the Old – Neo-Roman Constitutional Thought and the Enigma of Constitutional Pluralism in the EU', in *Constitutional pluralism in the European Union and beyond*, eds. Avbelj, M. and Komárek, J. (Portland: Hart Publishing, 2012).

Ziller, Jacques, 'Les concepts d'administration directe, d'administration indirecte et de co-administration et les fondements du droit administratif européen', in *Traité de droit administratif européen*, eds. Auby, J.-B. and J. Dutheil de la Rochère (Brussels: Bruylant, 2007).

Journal articles and papers

Accetto, Matej, and Stefan Zleptnig, 'The Principle of Effectiveness: Rethinking Its Role in Community Law', *European Public Law*, 11 (2005), 375.

Andrews, Neil H., 'The Passive Court and Legal Argument', *C.J.Q.*, 7 (1988), 125.

Arnull, Anthony, 'The Beat Goes On', *E.L. Rev.*, 12 (1987), 56.

Arnull, Anthony, 'The Principle of Effective Judicial Protection in EU law: An Unruly Horse?', *E.L. Rev.*, 36 (2011), 51.

Barents, René, 'EU Procedural Law and Effective Legal Protection', *CMLR*, 51 (2014), 1462.

Beka, Anthi, 'Commentary Note on Case C-618/10 Banco Español de Crédito SA v. Joaquín Calderón Camino, Judgment of 14 June 2012', *Zeitschrift für Gemeinschaftsprivatrecht*, 9 (2012), 326.

Beyer-Katzenberger, Malte, 'Judicial Activism and Judicial Restraint at the Bundesverfassungs-gericht: Was the *Mangold* Judgment of the European Court of Justice an *Ultra Vires* Act?', *ERA Forum*, 11 (2011), 517.

Biondi, Andrea, 'Effectiveness Versus Efficiency: Recent Developments on Judicial Protection in EC Law', *European Public Law*, 6 (2000), 311.

Bobek, Michal, 'Cartesio – Appeals Against an Order to Refer under Article 234 (2) EC Treaty Revisited', *C.J.Q.*, 29 (2010), 307.

Boccaccini, Marcus, Jennifer Boothby, and Stanley Brodsky, 'Development and Effects of Client Trust in Criminal Defense Attorneys: Preliminary Examination of the Congruence Model of Trust Development', *Behav. Sci. Law*, 22 (2004), 197.

van den Bossche, Anne-Marie, 'Private Enforcement, Procedural Autonomy and Article 19(1) TEU: Two's Company, Three's a Crowd', *YEL*, 33 (2014), 41.

Bossuyt, Marc, and Willem Verrijdt, 'The Full Effect of EU Law and of Constitutional Review in Belgium and France after the Melki Judgment', *ECL*, 7 (2011), 355.

Broberg, Morten, 'National Courts of Last Instance Failing to Make a Preliminary Reference: The (Possible) Consequences Flowing Therefrom', *European Public Law*, 22 (2016), 243.

Brulard, Yves, and Yves Quintin, 'European Community Law and Arbitration – National Versus Community Public Policy', *J. Int'l Arb.*, 18 (2001), 533.

Buhai, Sande, 'Access to Justice for Unrepresented Litigants: A Comparative Perspective', *Loy. L.A. L. Rev.*, 42 (2008), 979.

de Búrca, Gráinne, 'The Legal Effects of Directives: Policy, Rules and Exceptions', *ELR*, 34 (2009), 349.

Burley, Anne-Marie, and Walter Mattli, 'Europe before the Court: A Political Theory of Legal Integration', *International Organization*, 47 (1993), 41-76.

Cafaggi, Fabrizio, 'Towards Collaborative Governance of European Remedial and Procedural law', *Theoretical Inquiries in Law*, 19 (2018), 235.

Cazet, Safia, 'Le relevé d'office et la protection du justiciable', *Revue du droit de l'Union européenne*, 3 (2017), 53.

Chayes, Abram, 'The Role of the Judge in Public Law Litigation', *Harv. L. Rev.*, 89 (1976), 1281.

Claes, Monica, 'Constitutionalizing Europe at its Source: The 'European Clauses' in the National Constitutions: Evolution and Typology', *YEL*, 24 (2005), 81.

van Cleynenbreugel, Pieter, '"Meroni" Circumvented? Article 114 TFEU and EU Regulatory Agencies', *MJECL*, 21 (2014), 64.

van Cleynenbreugel, Pieter, 'Judge-Made Standards of National Procedure in the Post-Lisbon Constitutional Framework', *E.L. Rev.*, 12 (2012 a), 90.

van Cleynenbreugel, Pieter, 'The Confusing Constitutional Status of Positive Procedural Obligations in EU Law', *REALaw*, 5 (2012 b), 81.

Couronne, Vincent, 'L'autonomie procédurale des États membres de l'Union européenne à l'épreuve du temps', *Cah. dr. eur.*, 46 (2010), 273.

Coutron, Laurent, 'Cour de Justice, 13 janvier 2004, Kühne & Heitz NV/Productschap voor Pluimvee en Eieren', *Rev. Aff. Eur.*, 13 (2003-2004), 417.

Craig, Paul, 'The ECJ and *Ultra Vires* Action: A Conceptual Analysis', *CMLR*, 48 (2011), 395.

Davidson, Jenny M., 'The Full Effect of Community Law – An Increasing Encroachment upon National Law and Principles', *REALaw*, 1 (2008), 113.

Dederke, Julian, and Daniel Naurin, 'Friends of the Court? Why EU governments file observations before the Court of Justice', *EJPR* (2017), 1.

Díez-Picazo, L.M., 'Towards a Unified Judicial Protection in Europe (?)', *ERPL*, 9 (1997), 975.

Dougan, Michael, 'Who Exactly Benefits from the Treaties? The Murky Interaction Between Union and National Competence over the Capacity to Enforce EU Law', *Cambridge Yearbook of European Legal Studies*, 12 (2012), 73.

Dubey, Bernard, 'Administration indirecte et fédéralisme d'exécution en Europe', *Cah. dr. eur.*, 39 (2003), 87.

Dubos, Olivier, 'The Origins of the Proceduralisation of EU Law: A Grey Area of European Federalism', *REALaw*, 8 (2015 b), 7.

Dubout, Edouard, 'Le niveau de protection des droits fondamentaux dans l'Union européenne : unitarisme constitutif versus pluralisme constitutionnel – Réflexions autour de l'arrêt Melloni', *Cah. dr. eur.*, 49 (2013), 293.

Düsterhaus, Dominik, 'Procedural Primacy and Effective Judicial Protection – A Trilogue. Case C-112/13 A v. B and Others, EU:C:2014:2195', *MJECL*, 23 (2016), 317.

Ebers, Martin, 'ECJ (First Chamber) 6 October 2009, Case C-40/08, Asturcom Telecomunicaciones SL v. Cristina Rodríguez Nogueira – From Océano to Asturcom: Mandatory Consumer Law, Ex Officio Application of European Union Law and Res Judicata', *Eur. Rev. Pr. L.* (2010), 823.

Efrat, Asif, 'Assessing Mutual Trust among EU Members: Evidence from the European Arrest Warrant', *JEPP* (2018), https://doi.org/10.1080/13501763.2018.1478877, 1.

Eliantonio, Mariolina, 'Case C-240/09, Lesoochranárske zoskupenie VLK v. Ministerstvo životného prostredia Slovenskej republiky, Judgment of the Court of Justice (Grand Chamber) of 8 March 2011', *CMLR*, 49 (2012), 767.

Eliantonio, Marioloina, 'The Application of EC Law *Ex Officio* – Some News from the Italian Administrative Courts', *REALaw*, 1 (2008), 101.

Eliantonio, Mariolina, 'The Future of National Procedural Law in Europe: Harmonisation vs. Judge-Made Standards in the Field of Administrative Justice', *EJCL* (2009), 1.

Engström, Johanna, 'Effektivt rättsskydd i förvirring - Nationell process- och sanktionsrätt i ljuset av C-253/00 Muñoz', *ERT*, 1 (2003), 167.

Engström, Johanna, 'National Courts' Obligation to Apply Community Law Ex Officio – The Court Showing New Respect for Party Autonomy and National Procedural Autonomy?', *REALaw*, 1 (2008), 67.

Engström, Johanna, 'The Principle of Effective Judicial Protection after the Lisbon Treaty. Reflection in the Light of Case C-279/09 DEB Deutsche Energiehandels- und Beratungsgesellschaft mbH', *REALaw*, 4 (2011), 53.

Ereciński, Tadeusz, 'When Must National Judges Raise European Law Issues on Their Own Motion?', *ERA Forum*, 11 (2011), 525.

Franck, Jens-Uwe, 'Rights, remedies and effective enforcement in air transportation: *Ruijsenaars*. Joined Cases C-145/15 and C-146/15, *K. Ruijssenaars and Others v. Staatssecretaris van Infrastructuur en Milieu*, Judgment of the Court (Eighth Chamber) of 17 March 2016, EU:C:2016:187', *CMLR*, 54 (2017), 1867.

Fuller, Lon L., 'The Forms and Limits of Adjudication', *Harv. L. Rev.*, 92 (1978), 353.

Galetta, Diana-Urania, 'The Jurisprudence of the European Court of Justice on the Procedural Autonomy of EU Member States', *Ius Publicum Network Review* (2011), 1.

Gattinara, Giacomo, and Fabrice Picod, 'L'autorité de la chose jugée après l'arrêt Pizzarotti', *Rev. Aff. Eur.*, 3 (2014), 623.

Gerbrandy, Anna, 'The Dual Identity of National Judges in the EU and the Implausibility of Uniform and Effective Application of European Law throughout the European Union', *REALaw*, 7 (2014), 33.

van Gerven, Walter, 'Of Rights, Remedies and Procedures', *CMLR*, 37 (2000), 501.

Graf, Bernd U., and Arthur E. Appleton, 'Elisa Marioa Mostaza Claro v. Centro Móvil Milenium: EU Consumer Law as a Defence against Arbitral Awards, ECJ Case C-168/05', *ASA Bulletin*, 25 (2007), 48.

Groussot, Xavier, and Timo Minssen, 'Res Judicata in the Court of Justice Case-Law: Balancing Legal Certainty with Legality', *ECL*, 3 (2007), 385.

Groussot, Xavier, 'Spirit, Are You There? Reinforced Judicial Dialogue and the Preliminary Ruling Procedure', *The Eric Stein Working Papers* (2008), 1.

Groussot, Xavier, Gunnar Thor Petursson, and Jörgen Hettne, 'General Principles and the Many Faces of Coherence: Between Law and Ideology in the European Union', *Lund University Legal Research Paper Series* (2016), 1.

Hacker, Philipp, and Max Fabian Starke, 'European Union Litigation', *European Review of Contract Law*, 12 (2016), 141.

Hallberg, Jonas, and Östlund, Allison, 'Början på slutet för skiljeförfaranden i internationella investeringsskyddsavtal? EU-domstolens avgörande i *Achmea*', *JT*, 4 (2017/2018), 841.

Hancox, Emily, 'Meaning of Implementing EU Law under Article 51 (1) of the Charter: Åkerberg Fransson', *CMLR*, 50 (2013), 1411.

van Harten, Herman, 'National Judicial Autonomy: The Example of National European Law Precedents in the Dutch Case-Law on the Free Movement of Services and the Freedom of Establishment', *REALaw*, 2 (2009), 135.

Heukels, Ton, 'Joined Cases C-430/93 and C-431/93, van Schijndel and van Veen v. Stichting Pensioenfonds voor Fysiotherapeuten; and Case C-312/93, Peterbroeck, van Campenhout & Cie SCS v. Belgian State, Both Judgments of the Court of 14 December 1995 (Full Court)', *CMLR*, 33 (1996), 337.

Hinton, Eric F, 'Strengthening the Effectiveness of Community Law: Direct Effect, Article 5 EC, and the European Court of Justice', *JILP*, 31 (1998), 307.

Hofmann, Herwig C.H., 'Legislation, Delegation and Implementation under The Treaty of Lisbon: Typology Meets Reality', *European Law Journal*, 15 (2009), 482.

Hoskins, Mark, 'Tilting the Balance, Supremacy and National Procedural Rules', *E.L. Rev.*, 21 (1996), 365.

Houyet, Yves, 'L'application d'office du droit de l'Union européenne par les juges nationaux', *J.D.E.*, 3 (2010), 69.

Jans, Jan H., and Albert. T. Marseille, 'Joined Cases C-222-225/05, Van der Weerd and others v. Minister van Landbouw, Natuur en Voedselkwaliteit, Judgment of the Court (Fourth Chamber) of 7 June 2007, [2007] ECR I-14233', *CMLR*, 234 (2009), 853.

Kakouris, Constantinos, 'Do the Member States Possess Judicial Procedural "Autonomy"?', *CMLR*, 34 (1997), 1389.

Kitsos, John, 'Public Procurement – Meaning of 'Public Works Contract' – Scope of the Principle of '*Res Judicata*'', *Eur. Procurement & Pub. Private Partnership L. Rev.*, 10 (2015), 207.

Kleist, David, and Sebastian Wejedal, 'Tala är silver, tiga är guld. Om muntlig förhandling i förvaltningsmål, särskilt i skattemål', *FT*, 4 (2013), 345.

Kmiec, Keenan D, 'The Origin and Current Meanings of "Judicial Activism"', *CLR*, 92 (2004), 1441.

Komninos, Assimakis P., 'New Prospects for Private Enforcement of EC Competition Law: Courage v. Crehan and the Community Right to Damages', *CMLR*, 39 (2002), 447.

Krommendijk, Jasper, 'Is There Light on the Horizon? The Distinction Between "Rewe Effectiveness" and the Principle of Effective Judicial Protection in Article 47 of the Charter after Orizzonte', *CMLR*, 53 (2016), 1395.

Lang, John Temple, 'The Duties of National Authorities under Community Constitutional Law', *E.L. Rev.*, 23 (1998), 109.

de Lange, Roel, 'The European Public Order, Constitutional Principles and Fundamental Rights', *Erasmus Law Review*, 1 (2007), 4.

Lauwaars, Richard, 'The Application of Community Law by National Courts Ex Officio', *Fordham International Law Journal*, 31 (2007), 1161.

Mahlmann, Matthias, 'The Politics of Constitutional Identity and its Legal Frame – the Ultra Vires Decision of the Federal Constitutional Court', *German Law Journal*, 11 (2010), 1407.

Mann, Frederick A., 'Fusion of the Legal Professions?', *Law Quarterly Review*, 93 (1977), 367.

Martin, Raymond M., 'La crise du contradictoire entre juge et avocat', *La Gazette du Palais*, 1 (1978), 419.

le Masson, Jean-Marc, 'La recherche de la vérité dans le procès civil', *Droit et société*, 38 (1998), 21.

Mohr, Pamela, 'Report of the Working Group on the Allocation of Decision Making', *Fordham Law Review*, 64 (1996), 1325.

Mounts, Suzanne E, 'Public Defender Programs, Professional Responsibility, and Competent Representation', *Wisconsin Law Review* (1982), 473.

Nebbia, Paolisa, 'The Double Life of Effectiveness', *Cambridge Yearbook of European Legal Studies*, 10 (2008), 287.

Neframi, Eleftheria, 'L'État membre au service de l'Union', *Annuaire de droit européen 2004* (2006), 51.

Neframi, Eleftheria, 'Principe de coopération loyale et principe d'attribution dans le cadre de la mise en œuvre du droit de l'Union', *Cah. dr. eur.*, 1 (2016), 221.

Nový, Zdeněk, 'Arbitration Clause as Unfair Contract Term: Some Observations on the ECJ's Claro case', *Cofola*, 1 (2008), 76.

Ortlep, Rolf, and Maartje Verhoeven, 'The Principle of Primacy Versus the Principle of National Procedural Autonomy', *Netherlands Administrative Law Library*, April-June (2012).

Prechal, Sacha, 'Community Law in National Courts: The Lessons from van Schijndel', *CMLR*, 35 (1998), 681.

Prechal, Sacha, 'Does Direct Effect Still Matter?', *CMLR*, 37 (2000), 1047.

Prechal, Sacha, 'Mutual Trust Before the Court of Justice of the European Union', *Mutual Recognition and Mutual Trust: Reinforcing EU Integration? (Second Part) European Papers*, 2 (2017 b), 75.

Prechal, Sacha, and Kees Cath, 'The European Acquis of Civil Procedure: Constitutional Aspects', *Uniform Law Review – Revue de droit uniforme*, 19 (2014), 179.

Prechal, Sacha, and Natalya Shelkoplyas, 'National Procedures, Public Policy and EC Law. From Van Schijndel to Eco Swiss and Beyond', *Eur. Rev. Pr. L.*, 5 (2004), 589.

Prechal, Sacha, and Widdershoven, Rob, 'Redefining the Relationship between "Rewe-effectiveness" and Effective Judicial Protection', *REALaw*, 4 (2011 b), 31.

Ritleng, Dominique, 'De l'articulation des systèmes de protection des droits fondamentaux dans l'Union. Les enseignements des arrêts Akerberg Fransson et Melloni', *Revue trimestrielle de droit européen*, 49 (2013), 267.

Roeben, Volker, 'Judicial Protection as the Meta-Norm in the EU Judicial Architecture', *Hague J Rule Law* (2019), https://doi.org/10.1007/s40803-019-00085-3, 1.

Šadl, Urška, 'The Role of Effet Utile in Preserving the Continuity and Authority of European Union Law: Evidence from the Citation Web of the Pre-Accession Case Law of the Court of Justice of the EU', *European Journal of Legal Studies*, 8 (2015), 18.

Šadl, Urška, and Sabine Mair, 'Mutual Disempowerment: Case C-441/14 Dansk Industri, acting on behalf of Ajos A/S v Estate of Karsten Eigil Rasmussen and Case no. 15/2014 Dansk Industri (DI) acting for Ajos A/S v The estate left by A', *ECL*, 13 (2017), 347.

Safjan, Marek, and Dominik Düsterhaus, 'A Union of Effective Judicial Protection: Addressing a Multi-level Challenge through the Lens of Article 47 CFREU', *YEL* (2014), 1.

Sandefur, Rebecca, 'Effects of Representation on Trial and Hearing Outcomes in Two Common Law Countries', *International Sociological Association*, (2005), 1.

Sandefur, Rebecca, 'The Impact of Counsel: An Analysis of Empirical Evidence', *Seattle Journal for Social Justice*, 9 (2010), 51.

Sandin, Erik, 'Åberopsbörda i mål om offentlig upphandling? Två steg framåt, ett steg bakåt', *JT*, 10 (2009), 917.

Schebsta, Hanna, 'Does the National Court Know European Law? A Note on *Ex Officio* Application after *Asturcom*', *Eur. Rev. Pr. L.*, 4 (2010), 847.

Shin, Hyan S., 'Adversarial and Inquisitorial Procedures in Arbitration', *The RAND Journal of Economics*, 29 (1998), 378.

Simon, Denys, 'Autorité de chose jugée des décisions juridictionnelles nationales', *Europe*, 10 (2016).

Simon, Denys, 'Les fondements de l'autonomie du droit communautaire', *Droit international et droit communautaire. Perspectives actuelles* (2000), 228.

Smith, Susie, 'Impresa Pizzarotti v. Comune di Bari (Case C-213/13): Is a Contract for the Leasing of a Building which has not yet been Built a Works Contract, and must a National Court Revisit a Ruling which has led to a Situation which is Incompatible with EU Procurement Legislation?', *Public Procurement Law Review* (2014), 171.

Snyder, Francis, 'The Effectiveness of European Community Law: Institutions, Processes, Tools and Techniques', *The Modern Law Review*, 56 (1993), 19.

Spigelman, James, 'Judicial Accountability and Performance Indicators', *C.J.Q.*, 21 (2002), 18.

Thibaut, John, and Laurens Walker, 'A Theory of Procedure', *CLR*, 66 (1978).

Timmerman, Mikhel, 'Balancing Effective Criminal Sanctions with Effective Fundamental Rights Protection in Cases of VAT Fraud: Taricco', *CMLR*, 53 (2016), 779.

de la Torre, Fernando Castillo, 'Le relevé d'office par la juridiction communautaire', *Cah. dr. eur.*, 41 (2005), 395.

Tridimas, Takis, 'Constitutional Review of Member State Action: The Virtues and Vices of an Incomplete Jurisdiction', *I•CON*, 9 (2012), 737.

Tulibacka, Magdalena, 'Proceduralisation of EU Consumer Law and its Impact on European Consumers', *REALaw*, 8 (2015), 51.

Wallerman, Anna, 'Överklagande av beslut att begära förhandsavgörande: Några reflektioner med anledning av EFTA-domstolens avgörande i Irish Bank', *ERT*, 2 (2013), 308.

Wallerman, Anna, 'Towards an EU Law Doctrine on the Exercise of Discretion in National Courts? The Member States' Self-Imposed Limits on National Procedural Autonomy', *CMLR*, 53 (2016), 339.

Ward, Angela, 'Effective Sanctions in EC Law: A Moving Boundary in the Division of Competence', *ELJ*, 1 (1995), 205.

Warin, Catherine, 'Individual Rights and Collective Interests in EU Law: Three Approaches to a Still Volatile Relationship', *CMLR*, 56 (2019), 463.

Wattel, Peter J., 'National Procedural Autonomy and Effectiveness of EC Law: Challenge the Charge, File for Restitution, Sue for Damages?', *LIEI*, 35 (2008), 109.

Whittaker, Simon, 'Who Determines What Civil Courts Decide? Private Rights, Public policy and EU Law', *Oxford Legal Research Paper Series*, 46 (2012).

de Wilmars, J. Mertens, 'L'efficacité des différentes techniques nationales de protection juridique contre les violations du droit communautaire par les autorités nationales et les particuliers', *Cah. dr. eur.* (1981), 379.

Östlund, Allison, and Jonas Hallberg, 'Kan nya EU-domar läggas till grund för förnyad prövning av slutgiltiga internationella skiljedomar?', *JT*, 3 (2018/19), 675.

Theses

Clausen, Freja, 'Les moyens d'ordre public dans le contentieux relevant de la Cour de justice de l'Union européene' (Université Paris 2, 2017).

Couronne, Vincent, 'La compétence procédurale des Etats-membres de l'Union européenne' (Université Paris 1 Panthéon Sorbonne, 2015).

Lacchi, Clelia, 'Preliminary References to the Court of Justice of the EU and Effective Judicial Protection: Towards a More Protection-Oriented Approach of Article 267 TFEU' (University of Luxembourg, 2017).

Warin, Catherine, 'Individual rights under Union law. A study on the relation between rights, obligations and interests in the case law of the Court of Justice' (University of Luxembourg, 2017).

Wejedal, Sebastian, 'Rätten till biträde – Om biträdeskostnaders hantering vid svenska domstolar' (University of Gothenburg, 2017).

Wilman, Folkert Geert, 'The Vigilance of Individuals: How, When and Why the EU Legislates to Facilitate the Private Enforcement of EU Law before National Courts' (Leiden University, 2014).

Reports and official publications

Cazet, Safia, 'Relevé d'office', *Europe 2016*, Mai Comm. nº 5 (2016), 13.

European Parliament, 'The Principle of Subsidiarity', Fact Sheets on the European Union – 2017 (10/2016).

European Parliament Resolution of 9 July 2008 on the role of the national judge in the European judicial system (2007/2027(INI), OJ C 294 E, 3/12/2009, 27.

Final report of Working Group VII on External Action, 16 December 2002, Convention on the Future of Europe - Conv 459/02 – WGII 17, Bruxelles, 16/10/02.

Intersights, 'Right to a fair trial under the European Convention on Human Rights (Article 6)', in *Intersights Manual for Lawyers* (London: 2009).

Pescatore, Pierre, 'Court of Justice of the European Communities. References for preliminary rulings under Article 177 of the EEC Treaty and cooperation between the Court and national courts' (Luxembourg: Office for Official Publications of the European Communities, 1986).

Spaventa, Eleanor, 'The interpretation of Article 51 of the EU Charter of Fundamental Rights: the dilemma of stricter or broader application of the Charter to national measures', A Study for the European Parliament's PETI Committee (15/02/2016).

Records

Holy Bible, Deuteronomy 1:17, New International Version, Biblica (2011 version).

Holy Bible, Exodus 23: Laws of Justice and Mercy, New International Version, Biblica (2011 version).

EU primary law

Charter of Fundamental Rights of the European Union (Consolidated version), OJ C 202, 7/6/2016, 389.

Protocol (No 2) of the Treaty on the Functioning of the European Union (Consolidated version), on application of the principles of subsidiarity and proportionality, OJ C 115, 9/5/2008, 206.

Protocol (No 25) of the Treaty on the Functioning of the European Union (Consolidated version), on the exercise of shared competence, OJ C 115, 9/5/2008, 307.

Rules of Procedure of the Court of Justice of 25 September 2012, OJ L 265, 29/9/2012, as amended on 18 June 2013, OJ L 173, 26/6/2013, 65.

Treaty on European Union (Consolidated version), OJ C 202, 7/6/2016, 13.

Treaty on the Functioning of the European Union (Consolidated version), OJ C 202, 7/6/2016, 47.

EU secondary law

Council Directive 76/207/EEC of 9 February 1976 on the implementation of the principle of equal treatment for men and women as regards access to employment, vocational training and promotion, and working conditions, OJ L 39, 14/2/1976, 40.

Council Directive 85/337/EEC of 27 June 1985 on the assessment of the effects of certain public and private projects on the environment, OJ L 175, 5/7/1985, 40.

Council Directive 85/511/EEC of 18 November 1985 introducing Community measures for the control of foot-and-mouth disease, OJ L 315, 26/11/1985, 11.

Council Directive 85/577/EEC of 20 December 1985 to protect the consumer in respect of contracts negotiated away from business premises, OJ L 372, 31/12/1985, 31.

Council Directive 86/378/EEC of 24 July 1986 on the implementation of the principle of equal treatment for men and women in occupational social security schemes, OJ L 225, 12/08/1986, 40.

Council Directive 87/102/EEC of 22 December 1986 for the approximation of the laws, regulations and administrative provisions of the Member States concerning consumer credit, 'Official Journal L 042, 12/02/1987, 48.

Council Directive 89/665/EEC of 21 December 1989 on the coordination of the laws, regulations and administrative provisions relating to the application of review procedures to the award of public supply and public works contracts, OJ L 395, 30/12/1989, 33.

Council Directive 91/628/EEC of 19 November 1991 on the protection of animals during transport and amending Directives 90/425/EEC and 91/496/EEC, OJ L 340, 11/12/1991, 17.

Council Directive 92/13/EEC of 25 February 1992 coordinating the laws, regulations and administrative provisions relating to the application of Community rules on the procurement procedures of entities operating in the water, energy, transport and telecommunications sectors, OJ L 76, 23/3/1992, 14.

Council Directive 93/13/EEC of 5 April 1993 on unfair terms in consumer contracts, OJ L 095, 21/04/1993, 29.

Council Directive 97/80/EC of 15 December 1997 on the burden of proof in cases of discrimination based on sex, OJ L 14, 20/1/1998, 6.

Council Regulation (EC) 44/2001 of 22 December 2000 on jurisdiction and the recognition and enforcement of judgments in civil and commercial matters (Brussels I Regulation), OJ L 012, 16/01/2001, 1.

Council Regulation 2154/2002 of 28 November 2002 amending Regulation (EEC) No 4045/89 on scrutiny by Member States of transactions forming part of the system of financing by the Guarantee Section of the European Agricultural Guidance and Guarantee Fund, OJ L 328, 5/12/2002, 4.

Directive 2002/21/EC of the European Parliament and of the Council of 7 March 2002 on a common regulatory framework for electronic communications networks and services, OJ L 108, 24/4/2002, 33.

Council Framework Decision 2002/584/JHA of 13 June 2002 on the European arrest warrant and the surrender procedures between Member States, OJ L 190, 28/07/2002, 20.

Directive 2004/38/EC of the European Parliament and of the Council of 29 April 2004 on the right of citizens of the Union and their family members to move and reside freely within the territory of the Member States amending Regulation (EEC) No 1612/68 and repealing Directives 64/221/EEC, 68/360/EEC, 72/194/EEC, 73/148/EEC, 75/34/EEC, 75/35/EEC, 90/364/EEC, 90/365/EEC and 93/96/EEC, OJ L 229, 29/6/2004, 35.

Regulation (EC) 805/2004 of the European Parliament and of the Council of 21 April 2004 creating a European Enforcement Order for uncontested claims, OJ L 143, 30/4/2004, 15.

Council Directive 2005/85/EC of 1 December 2005 on minimum standards on procedures in Member States for granting and withdrawing refugee status, OJ L 326, 13/12/2005, 13.

Council Directive 2006/112/EC of 28 November 2006 on the common system of value added tax, OJ L 347, 11/12/2006, 1.

Regulation (EC) 1896/2006 of the European Parliament and of the Council of 12 December 2006 creating a European order for payment procedure, OJ L 399, 30/12/2006, 1.

Directive 2007/66/EC of the European Parliament and of the Council of 11 December 2007 amending Council Directives 89/665/EEC and 92/13/EEC with regard to improving the effectiveness of review procedures concerning the award of public contracts, OJ L 335, 20/12/2007, 31.

Council Framework Decision 2008/909/JHA of 27 November 2008 on the application of the principle of mutual recognition to judgments in criminal matters imposing custodial sentences or measures involving deprivation of liberty for the purpose of their enforcement in the European Union, OJ L 327, 5/12/2008, 27.

Directive 2009/22/EC of the European Parliament and of the Council of 23 April 2009 on injunctions for the protection of consumers' interests, OJ L 110, 01/05/2009, 30.

Case-law of the CJEU

CJEU judgment in *A v. B and Others*, C-112/13, EU:C:2014:2195.

CJEU judgment in *Aannemersbedrijf P.K. Kraaijeveld BV e.a. v. Gedeputeerde Staten van Zuid-Holland*, C-72/95, EU:C:1996:404.

CJEU judgment in *Abdelhafid Bensada Benallal v. État belge*, C-161/15, EU:C:2016:175.

CJEU judgment in *Adidas AG*, C-223/98, EU:C:1999:500.

CJEU judgment in *Åklagaren v. Hans Åkerberg Fransson*, C-617/10, EU:C:2013:105.

CJEU judgment in *Alassini and Others*, C-317/08, EU:C:2010:146.

CJEU judgment in *Amministrazione dell'Economia e delle Finanze and Agenzia delle entrate v. Fallimento Olimpiclub Srl*, C-2/08, EU:C:2009:506.

CJEU judgment in *Amministrazione delle finanze dello Stato v. Simmenthal*, 106/77, EU:C:1978:49.

CJEU judgment in *Árpád Kásler v. OTP*, C-26/13, EU:C:2014:282.

CJEU judgment in *Asociación de Consumidores Independientes de Castilla y León*, C-413/12, EU:C:2013:800.

CJEU judgment in *Associação Sindical dos Juízes Portugueses v. Tribunal de Contas*, C-64/16, EU:C:2018:117.

CJEU judgment in *Association de médiation sociale v. Union locale des syndicats CGT and Others (AMS)*, C-176/12, EU:C:2014:2.

CJEU judgment in *Asturcom Telecomunicaciones SL v. Cristina Rodríguez Nogueira*, C-40/08, EU:C:2009:615.

CJEU judgment in *Atanas Ognyanov (I)*, C-614/14, EU:C:2016:514.

CJEU judgment in *Atanas Ognyanov (II)*, C-554/14, EU:C:2016:835.

CJEU judgment in *Aziz Melki and Sélim Abdeli*, joined cases C-188/10 and C-189/10, EU:C:2010:363.

CJEU judgment in *Baczó and Vizsnyiczai*, C-567/13, EU:C:2015:88.

CJEU judgment in *Banco Español de Crédito SA v. Joaquín Calderón Camino*, C-618/10, EU:C:2012:349.

CJEU judgment in *Banco Primus SA v. Jesús Gutiérrez García*, C-421/14, EU:C:2017:60.

CJEU judgment in *Banif Plus Bank Zrt v. Csaba Csipai*, C-472/11, EU:C:2013:88.

CJEU judgment in *Bashar Ibrahim*, joined cases C-297/17, C-318/17, C-319/17 and C-438/17, EU:C:2019:219.

CJEU judgment in *BBVA SA v. Pedro Peñalva López*, C-8/14, EU:C:2015:731.

CJEU judgment in *Berlioz Investment Fund SA*, C-682/15, EU:C:2017:373.

CJEU judgment in *Biuro podróży 'Partner'*, C-119/15, EU:C:2016:987.

CJEU judgment in *Borrell*, C-104/91, EU:C:1992:202.

CJEU judgment in *Boxus and Others*, joined cases C-128/09 to C-131/09, C-134/09 and C-135/09, EU:C:2011:667.

CJEU judgment in *Brahim Samba Diouf v. Ministre du Travail, de l'Emploi et de l'Immigration*, C-69/10, EU:C:2011:524.

CJEU judgment in *Brasserie du Pêcheur v. Bundesrepublik Deutschland and The Queen / Secretary of State for Transport, ex parte Factortame and Others*, joined cases C-46/93 and C-48/93, EU:C:1996:79.

CJEU judgment in *Bund für Umwelt und Naturschutz Deutschland, Landesverband Nordrhein-Westfalen (Trianel)*, C-115/09, EU:C:2011:289.

CJEU judgment in *Bundeswettbewerbsbehörde v. Donau Chemie AG and Others*, C-536/11, EU:C:2013:366

CJEU judgment in *Byankov*, C-249/11, EU:C:2012:608.

CJEU judgment in *Carlos Escribano Vindel v. Ministerio de Justicia*, C-49/18, EU:C:2019:106.

CJEU judgment in *Cartesio Oktató és Szolgáltató bt*, C-210/06, EU:C:2008:723.

CJEU judgment in *Centrosteel Srl v. Adipol GmbH*, EU:C:2000:402.

CJEU judgment in *Česká podnikatelská pojišťovna as, Vienna Insurance Group v. Michal Bilas*, C-111/09, EU:C:2010:290.

CJEU judgment in *Chalkor v. Commission*, C-386/10 P, EU:C:2011:815.

CJEU judgment in *Chavez-Vilchez and Others*, C-133/15, EU:C:2017:354.

CJEU judgment in *CIA Security International SA v. Signalson SA and Securitel SPRL*, C-194/94, EU:C:1996:172.

CJEU judgment in *CILFIT v. Ministero della Sanità*, 283/81, EU:C:1982:335.

CJEU judgment in *Ciola*, C-224/97, EU:C:1999:212.

CJEU judgment in *Claude Chartry v. État belge*, C- 457/09, EU:C:2011:101.

CJEU judgment in *ClientEarth v. The Secretary of State for the Environment, Food and Rural Affairs*, C-404/13, EU:C:2014:2382.

CJEU judgment in *Cofidis SA v. Jean-Louis Fredout*, C-473/00, EU:C:2002:705.

CJEU judgment in *Comet BV v. Produktschap voor Siergewassen*, 45/76, EU:C:1976:191.

CJEU judgment in *Commission of the European Communities v. Anton Pieter Roodhuijzen*, T-58/80 P, EU:T:2009:385.

CJEU judgment in *Commission of the European Communities v. Council of the European Communities (ERTA)*, 22/70, EU:C:1971:32.

CJEU judgment in *Commission v. Greece (Greek Maize)*, 68/88, EU:C:1989:339.

CJEU judgment in *Commission v. Ireland*, C-89/08 P, EU:C:2009:742.

CJEU judgment in *Commission v. Italian Republic*, C-372/99, EU:C:2002:42.

CJEU judgment in *Consiglio nazionale dei geologi and Autorità garante della concorrenza e del mercato*, C-136/12, EU:C:2013:489.

CJEU judgment in *Costa v. E.N.E.L.*, 6/64, EU:C:1964:66.

CJEU judgment in *Courage Ltd v. Bernard and Crehan*, C-453/99, EU:C:2001:465.

CJEU judgment in *Criminal proceedings against Johannes Martinus Lemmens*, C-226/97, EU:C:1998:296.

CJEU judgment in *Criminal proceedings against Maria Pupino*, C-105/03, EU:C:2005:386.

CJEU judgment in *Cullet v. Leclerc*, C-231/83, EU:C:1985:29.

CJEU judgment in *Da Costa en Schaake NV, Jacob Meijer NV, Hoechst-Holland NV v. Netherlands Inland Revenue Administration*, joined cases 28/62 to 39/62 EU:C:1963:6.

CJEU judgment in *Dansk industri*, C-441/14, EU:C:2016:278.

CJEU judgment in *Deutsche Energiehandels- und Beratungsgesellschaft mbH v. Bundesrepublik Deutschland (DEB)*, C-279/09, EU:C:2010:811.

CJEU judgment in *Deutsche Milchkontor*, joined cases 205/82 to 215/82, EU:C:1983:233.

CJEU judgment in *Diageo Brands BV v. Simiramida-04 EOOD*, C-681/13, EU:C:2015:471.

CJEU judgment in *Digital Rights Ireland Ltd*, C-293/12.

CJEU judgment in *Direcţia Generală Regională a Finanţelor Publice Braşov v. Vasile Toma*, C-205/15, EU:C:2016:499.

CJEU judgment in *Dirk Frederik Asbeek Brusse*, C-488/11, EU:C:2013:341.

CJEU judgment in *Djurgården-Lilla Värtans Miljöskyddsförening v. Stockholms kommun genom dess marknämnd*, C-263/08, EU:C:2009:631.

CJEU judgment in *Dokter and Others v. Minister van Landbouw, Natuur en Voedselkwaliteit*, C-28/05, EU:C:2006:408.

CJEU judgment in *Dragoş Constantin Târşia v. Statul român and Serviciul Public Comunitar Regim Permise de Conducere si Inmatriculare a Autovehiculelor*, C-69/14, EU:C:2015:662.

CJEU judgment in *E.G. v. Republika Slovenija*, C-662/17, EU:C:2018:847.

CJEU judgment in *Eco Swiss China Time Ltd v. Benetton International NV*, C-126/97, EU:C:1999:269.

CJEU judgment in *Edwards and Pallikaropoulos*, C-260/11, EU:C:2013:221.

CJEU judgment in *Elisa María Mostaza Claro v. Centro Móvil Milenium SL*, C-168/05, EU:C:2006:675.

CJEU judgment in *Emil Milev*, C-310/18 P, EU:C:2018:732.

CJEU judgment in *Enderby v. Frenchay Health Authority and Secretary of State for Health*, C-127/92, EU:C:1993:859.

CJEU judgment in *EOS KSI Slovensko*, C-448/17, EU:C:2018:745.

CJEU judgment in *Erika Jőrös v. Aegon Magyarország Hitel Zrt.*, C-397/11, EU:C:2013:340.

CJEU judgment in *Ernst Georg Radlinger v. Finway a.s.*, C-377/14, EU:C:2016:283.

CJEU judgment in *ERSTE Bank Hungary Zrt. v. Attila Sugár*, C-32/14, EU:C:2015:637.

CJEU judgment in *ET Agrokonsulting-04-Velko Stoyanov v. Izpalnitelen direktor na Darzhaven fond «Zemedelie» - Razplashtatelna agentsia*, C-93/12, EU:C:2013:432.

CJEU judgment in *Eugenia Florescu v. Casa Judeţeană de Pensii Sibiu*, C-258/14, EU:C:2017:448.

CJEU judgment in *Europese Gemeenschap v. Otis NV and Others*, C-199/11, EU:C:2012:684.

CJEU judgment in *Eva Martín Martín v. EDP Editores SL*, C-227/08, EU:C:2009:792.

CJEU judgment in *Evelyn Danqua v. Minister for Justice and Equality*, C-429/15, EU:C:2016:789.

CJEU judgment in *Faccini Dori v. Recreb*, C-91/92, EU:C:1994:292.

CJEU judgment in *Fantask and Others v. Industriministeriet*, C-188/95, EU:C:1997:580.

CJEU judgment in *Fazenda Pública and Câmara Municipal do Porto*, C-446/98, EU:C:2000:691.

CJEU judgment in *Ferdinand M.J.J. Duijnstee v. Lodewijk Goderbauer*, 288/82, EU:C:1983:326.

CJEU judgment in *Finanmadrid EFC SA v. Jesús Vicente Albán Zambrano and Others*, C-49/14, EU:C:2016:98.

CJEU judgment in *Firma Gebrüder Lück v. Hauptzollamt Köln-Rheinau*, 34/67, EU:C:1968:24.

CJEU judgment in *Flemmer and Others*, joined cases C-80/99, C-81/99 and C-82/99, EU:C:2001:525.

CJEU judgment in *François De Coster v. Collège des bourgmestre et échevins de Watermael-Boitsfort*, C-17/00, EU:C:2001:651.

CJEU judgment in *Francovich and Bonifaci v. Italy*, joined cases C-6/90 and C-9/90, EU:C:1991:428.

CJEU judgment in *Fratelli Costanzo v. Comune di Milano*, 103/88, EU:C:1989:256.

CJEU judgment in *Froukje Faber*, C-497/13, EU:C:2015:357.

CJEU judgment in *Gabriel Alonso-Pérez v. Bundesanstalt für Arbeit*, C-394/93, EU:C:1995:400.

CJEU judgment in *Georgi Ivanov Elchinov v. Natsionalna zdravnoosiguritelna kasa*, C-173/09, EU:C:2010:581.

CJEU judgment in *Gerhard Köbler v. Republik Österreich*, C-224/01, EU:C:2003:513.

CJEU judgment in *Germany v. Parliament and Council (Tobacco advertising case)*, C-376/98, EU:C:2000:544.

CJEU judgment in *Gervais Larsy v. Institut national d'assurances sociales pour travailleurs indépendants*, C-118/00, EU:C:2001:368.

CJEU judgment in *Gesellschaft für Abfallentsorgungs-Technik GmbH (GAT) v. Österreichische Autobahnen und Schnellstraßen AG*, C-315/01, EU:C:2003:360.

CJEU judgment in *Gesellschaft für Antriebstechnik mbH & Co. KG*, C-4/03, EU:C:2006:457.

CJEU judgment in *Global Starnet Ltd v. Ministero dell'Economia e delle Finanze*, C-322/16, EU:C:2017:985.

CJEU judgment in *Graham J. Wilson v. Ordre des avocats du barreau de Luxembourg*, C-506/04, EU:C:2006:587.

CJEU judgment in *Gutiérrez Naranjo and Others*, joined cases C-154/15, C-307/15 and C-308/15, EU:C:2016:980.

CJEU judgment in *Hampshire County Council v. C.E. and N.E.*, joined cases C-325/18 PPU and C-375/18 PPU, EU:C:2018:739.

CJEU judgment in *Hans Just I/S v. Danish Ministry for Fiscal Affairs*, 68/79, EU:C:1980:57.

CJEU judgment in *Hansruedi Raimund v. Michaela Aigner*, C-425/16, EU:C:2017:776.

CJEU judgment in *Heemskerk BV and Firma Schaap v. Productschap Vee en Vlees*, C-455/06, EU:C:2008:650.

CJEU judgment in *Heylens*, 222/86, EU:C:1987:442.

CJEU judgment in *Hypoteční banka a.s. v. Udo Mike Lindner*, C-327/10, EU:C:2011:745.

CJEU judgment in *i-21 Germany GmbH and Arcor AG & Co. KG v. Bundesrepublik Deutschland*, joined cases C-392/04 and C-422/04, EU:C:2006:586.

CJEU judgment in *IK*, C-551/18 PPU, EU:C:2018:991.

CJEU judgment in *Impact v. Minister for Agriculture and Food and Others*, C-268/06, EU:C:2008:223.

CJEU judgment in *Impresa Pizzarotti & C. Spa v. Comune di Bari and Others*, C-213/13, EU:C:2014:2067.

CJEU judgment in *International Fruit Company*, joined cases 51/71 to 54/71, EU:C:1971:128.

CJEU judgment in *Inuit Tapiriit Kanatami*, C-283/11 P, EU:C:2013:625.

CJEU judgment in *Ivo Taricco and Others*, C-105/14, EU:C:2015:555.

CJEU judgment in *Jana Pereničová and Vladislav Perenič*, C-453/10, EU:C:2012:144.

CJEU judgment in *Jean-E. Humblet v. Belgian State*, 6/60, EU:C:1960:48.

CJEU judgment in *Joan Cuadrench Moré v. Koninklijke Luchtvaart Maatschappij NV*, C-139/11, EU:C:2012:741.

CJEU judgment in *Johnston*, 222/84, EU:C:1986:206.

CJEU judgment in *Jorge Sales Sinués v. Caixabank SA*, joined cases C-381/14 and 385/14, EU:C:2016:252.

CJEU judgment in *K. Ruijsenaars*, joined cases C-145/15 and 146/15, EU:C:2016:187.

CJEU judgment in *Karl Schwarz*, C-321/07, EU:C:2009:104.

CJEU judgment in *KME Germany and Others v. Commission*, C-272/09 P, EU:C:2011:810.

CJEU judgment in *Kraus*, C-19/92, EU:C:1993:125.

CJEU judgment in *Kühne & Heitz NV v. Produktschap voor Pluimvee en Eieren*, C-453/00, EU:C:2004:17.

CJEU judgment in *Leon Emile Gaston Carlos Debaecker and Berthe Plouvier v. Cornelis Gerrit Bouwman*, 49/84, EU:C:1985:252.

CJEU judgment in *Lesoochranárske zoskupenie VLK (Brown Bear)*, C-240/09, EU:C:2011:125.

CJEU judgment in *Lesoochranárske zoskupenie VLK (II)*, C-243/15, EU:C:2016:838.

CJEU judgment in *Levez v. Jennings Ltd*, C-326/96, EU:C:1998:577.

CJEU judgment in *Liivimaa Lihaveis MTÜ v. Eesti-Läti programmi 2007-2013 Seirekomitee*, C-562/12, EU:C:2014:2229.

CJEU judgment in *Littlewoods Retail Ltd and Others v. Her Majesty's Commissioners of Revenue and Customs*, C-591/10, EU:C:2012:478.

CJEU judgment in *LM (Judicial independence in Poland)*, C-216/18 PPU, EU:C:2018:586.

CJEU judgment in *LTU Lufttransportunternehmen GmbH & Co. KG v. Eurocontrol*, 29/76, EU:C:1976:137.

CJEU judgment in *Lucio Cesare Aquino v. Belgische Staat*, C-3/16, EU:C:2017:209.

CJEU judgment in *M. v. Minister for Justice and Equality*, C-560/14, EU:C:2017:101.

CJEU judgment in *M.A. v. International Protection Appeals Tribunal*, C-661/17, EU:C:2019:53.

CJEU judgment in *Marco Gambazzi v. DaimlerChrysler Canada Inc. and CIBC Mellon Trust Company*, C-394/07, EU:C:2009:219.

CJEU judgment in *Maribel Dominguez v. Centre informatique du Centre Ouest Atlantique and Préfet de la région Centre*, C-282/10, EU:C:2012:33.

CJEU judgment in *Marleasing v. Comercial Internacional de Alimentación*, C-106/89, EU:C:1990:395.

CJEU judgment in *Marshall v. Southampton and South-West Hampshire Area Health Authority (Marshall I)*, 152/84, EU:C:1986:84.

CJEU judgment in *Marshall v. Southampton and South-West Hampshire Area Health Authority (Marshall II)*, C-271/91, EU:C:1993:335.

CJEU judgment in *Massimo Orsi*, C-217/15, EU:C:2017:264.

CJEU judgment in *Mecanarte-Metalurgica da Lagoa v. Alfandega do Porto*, C-348/89, EU:C:1991:278.

CJEU judgment in *Mellor*, C-75/08, EU:C:2009:279.

CJEU judgment in *Ministero dell'Industria, del Commercio e dell'Artigianato v. Lucchini SpA*, C-119/05, EU:C:2007:434.

CJEU judgment in *Minister for Justice and Equality v. Francis Lanigan*, C-237/15 PPU, EU:C:2015:474.

CJEU judgment in *ML/Generalstaatsanwaltschaft*, C-220/18 PPU, EU:C:2018:589.

CJEU judgment in *Mohamed Aziz v. Caixa d'Estalvis de Catalunya*, C-415/11, EU:C:2013:164.

CJEU judgment in *Monika Kušionová v. SMART Capital a.s.*, C-34/13, EU:C:2014:2189.

CJEU judgment in *Mono Car Styling SA, in liquidation v. Dervis Odemis and Others*, C-12/08, EU:C:2009:466.

CJEU judgment in *Moussa Sacko*, C-348/15, EU:C:2017:591.

CJEU judgment in *MRAX*, C-459/99, EU:C:2002:461.

CJEU judgment in *Muñoz and Superior Fruiticola*, C-253/00, EU:C:2002:497.

CJEU judgment in *Nemzeti Fogyasztóvédelmi Hatóság v. Invitel Távközlési Zrt*, C-472/10, EU:C:2012:242.

CJEU judgment in *Nikolay Kantarev v. Balgarska Narodna Banka*, C-571/16, EU:C:2018:807.

CJEU judgment in *Nordsee v. Reederei Mond*, 102/81, EU:C:1982:107.

CJEU judgment in *ÖBB Personenverkehr*, C-417/13, EU:C:2015:38.

CJEU judgment in *Océano Grupo Editorial and Salvat Editores*, joined cases C-240/98 to C-244/98, EU:C:2000:346.

CJEU judgment in *Online Games Handels GmbH*, C-685/15, EU:C:2017:452.

CJEU judgment in *Orizzonte Salute – Studio Infermieristico Associato v. Azienda Pubblica di Servizi alla persona San Valentino – Città di Levico Terme and Others*, C-61/14, EU:C:2015:655.

CJEU judgment in *Pal Aranyosi*, joined cases C-404/15 and C-659/15 PPU, EU:C:2016:198.

CJEU judgment in *Palmisani v. INPS*, C-261/95, EU:C:1997:351.

CJEU judgment in *Pannon GSM Zrt. v. Erzsébet Sustikné Győrfi*, C-243/08, EU:C:2009:350.

CJEU judgment in *Pardini v. Ministero del commercio con l'estero*, 338/85, EU:C:1988:194.

CJEU judgment in *Pasquale Foglia v. Mariella Novello*, 244/80, EU:C:1981:302.

CJEU judgment in *Patrick Kelly v. National University of Ireland*, C-104/10, EU:C:2011:506.

CJEU judgment in *Peterbroeck, Van Campenhout & Cie v. Belgian State*, C-312/93, EU:C:1995:437.

CJEU judgment in *Pfeiffer and Others*, joined cases C-397/01 to C-403/01, EU:C:2004:584.

CJEU judgment in *Pierre Corbiau v. Administration des contributions*, C-24/92, EU:C:1993:118.

CJEU judgment in *Pohotovosť s.r.o. v. Miroslav Vašuta (II)*, C-470/12, EU:C:2014:101.

CJEU judgment in *Pohotovosť s.r.o. v. Iveta Korčkovská (I)*, C-76/10, EU:C:2010:685.

CJEU judgment in *Pretore di Salò v. X*, 14/86, EU:C:1987:275.

CJEU judgment in *Puligienica Facility Esco SpA (PFE) v. Airgest SpA*, C-689/13, EU:C:2016:199.

CJEU judgment in *Ramón Margarit Panicello*, C-503/15, EU:C:2017:126.

CJEU judgment in *Rampion and Godard*, C-429/05, EU:C:2007:575.

CJEU judgment in *Régie nationale des usines Renault SA v. Maxicar SpA and Orazio Formento*, C-38/98, EU:C:2000:225.

CJEU judgment in *Rendon Marín*, C-165/14, EU:C:2016:675.

CJEU judgment in *Republik Österreich v. Martin Huber*, C-336/00, EU:C:2002:509.

CJEU judgment in *Rewe v. Landwirtschaftskammer für das Saarland*, 33/76, EU:C:1976:188.

CJEU judgment in *Rewe-Handelsgesellschaft Nord mbH and Rewe-Markt Steffen v. Hauptzollamt Kiel*, 158/80, EU:C:1981:163.

CJEU judgment in *Rheinmühlen Düsseldorf v. Einfuhr- und Vorratsstelle für Getreide und Futtermittel*, 166/73, EU:C:1974:3.

CJEU judgment in *RO (Brexit/European arrest warrant)*, C-327/18 PPU, EU:C:2018:733.

CJEU judgment in *Sanchez Morcillo and Abril García (I)*, C-169/14, EU:C:2014:2099.

CJEU judgment in *Sanchez Morcillo and Abril García (II)*, C-539/14, EU:C:2015:508.

CJEU judgment in *SC Star Storage SA and Others v. Institutul Național de Cercetare-Dezvoltare în Informatică (ICI) and Others*, joined cases C-439/14 and C-488/14, EU:C:2016:688.

CJEU judgment in *Secretary State for the Home Department v. CS*, C-304/14, EU:C:2016:674.

CJEU judgment in *Seda Kücükdeveci v. Swedex GmbH & Co. KG*, C-555/07, EU:C:2010:21.

CJEU judgment in *Shirley Preston v. Wolverhampton Healthcare NHS Trust*, C-78/98, EU:C:2000:247.

CJEU judgment in *Silvia Georgiana Câmpean*, C-200/14, EU:C:2016:494.

CJEU judgment in *Simmenthal*, 106/77, EU:C:1978:49.

CJEU judgment in *Sky Österreich GmbH v. Österreichischer Rundfunk*, C-283/11, EU:C:2013:28.

CJEU judgment in *Soledad Duarte Heuros*, C-32/12, EU:C:2013:637.

CJEU judgment in *Soufiane El Hassani*, C-403/16, EU:C:2017:960.

CJEU judgment in *SpA Alois Lageder and others v. Amministrazione delle Finanze dello Stato*, joined cases C-31/91 to C-44/91, EU:C:1993:132.

CJEU judgment in *SpA Salgoil v. Italian Ministry of Foreign Trade*, 13/68, EU:C:1968:54.

CJEU judgment in *Specialarbejderforbundet i Danmark v. Dansk Industri (Royal Copenhagen)*, C-400/93 EU:C:1995:155.

CJEU judgment in *Stefano Melloni v. Ministerio Fiscal*, C-399/11, EU:C:2013:107.

CJEU judgment in *Steff-Houlberg Export and Others*, C-366/95, EU:C:1998:216.

CJEU judgment in *Stichting ROM-projecten v. Staatssecretaris van Economische Zaken*, C-158/06, EU:C:2007:370.

CJEU judgment in *TC*, C-492/18 PPU, EU:C:2019:108.

CJEU judgment in *TDC A/S v. Erhvervsstyrelsen*, C-222/13, EU:C:2014:2265.

CJEU judgment in *Texdata Software GmbH*, C-418/11, EU:C:2013:588.

CJEU judgment in *The Queen v. Secretary of State for Transport, ex parte Factortame*, C-213/89, EU:C:1990:257.

CJEU judgment in *Theresa Emmott v. Minister for Social Welfare and the Attorney General*, C-208/90, EU:C:1991:333.

CJEU judgment in *Trustees of the BT Pension Scheme*, C-628/15, EU:C:2017:687.

CJEU judgment in *Ufficio IVA di Piacenza v. Belvedere Costruzioni Srl*, C-500/10, EU:C:2012:186.

CJEU judgment in *Unibet (London) Ltd and Unibet (International) Ltd v. Justitiekanslern*, C-432/05, EU:C:2007:163.

CJEU judgment in *Unicaja Banco and Caixabank*, C-482/13, EU:C:2015:21.

CJEU judgment in *Unilever Italia SpA v. Central Food SpA*, C-443/98, EU:C:2000:496.

CJEU judgment in *Union royale belge des sociétés de football association and Others v. Bosman and Others*, C-415/93, EU:C:1995:463.

CJEU judgment in *United Kingdom of Great Britain and Northern Ireland v. Parliament and Council (ENISA)*, C-217/04, EU:C:2006:279.

CJEU judgment in *United Kingdom v. Parliament and Council (ESMA)*, C-270/12 EU:C:2014:18.

CJEU judgment in *United Kingdom v. Parliament and Council (Smoke flavourings)*, C-66/04, EU:C:2005:743.

CJEU judgment in *Vaassen-Goebbels v. Beambtenfonds voor het Mijnbedrijf*, 61/65, EU:C:1966:39.

CJEU judgment in *van der Weerd and Others v. Minister van Landbouw, Natuur en Voedselkwaliteit*, joined cases C-222/05 to C-225/05, EU:C:2007:318.

CJEU judgment in *van Gend en Loos v. Administratie der Belastingen*, 26/62, EU:C:1963:1.

CJEU judgment in *van Schijndel v. Stichting Pensioenfonds voor Fysiotherapeuten*, joined cases C-430/93 and C-431/93, EU:C:1995:441.

CJEU judgment in *Varec SA v. Belgian State*, C-450/06, EU:C:2008:91.

CJEU judgment in *VB Pénzügyi Lízing Zrt. v. Ferenc Schneider*, C-137/08, EU:C:2010:659.

CJEU judgment in *Vereniging Nationaal Overlegorgaan Sociale Werkvoorziening and Others (VNOSW)*, joined cases C-383/06 to C-385/06, EU:C:2008:165.

CJEU judgment in *Verholen and Others v. Sociale Verzekeringsbank Amsterdam*, joined cases C-87/90, C-88/90 and C-89/90, EU:C:1991:314.

CJEU judgment in *Vincenzo Manfredi v. Lloyd Adriatico Assicurazioni SpA*, joined cases C-295/04 to C-298/04, EU:C:2006:461.

CJEU judgment in *Virginie Pontin v. T-Comalux SA*, C-63/08, EU:C:2009:666.

CJEU judgment in *Vladimir Peftiev*, C-314/13, EU:C:2014:1645.

CJEU judgment in *Von Colson and Kamann v. Land Nordrhein-Westfalen*, 14/83, EU:C:1984:153.

CJEU judgment in *Willy Kempter KG v. Hauptzollamt Hamburg-Jonas*, C-2/06, EU:C:2008:78.

CJEU judgment in *Winner Wetten GmbH v. Bürgermeisterin der Stadt Bergheim*, C-409/06, EU:C:2010:503.

CJEU judgment in *Zlawomir Andrzej Zdziaszek*, C-271/17 PPU, EU:C:2017:629.

CJEU Opinion *delivered pursuant to Article 218(11) TFEU*, 1/09, EU:C:2011:123.

CJEU Opinion *delivered pursuant to Article 218(11) TFEU*, 2/13, EU:C:2014:2454.

Opinions of Advocates General of the CJEU

Opinion of Advocate General Bot in *ET-Agrokonsulting-04*, C-93/12, EU:C:2013:172.

Opinion of Advocate General Bot in *Heemskerk BV and Firma Schaap v. Productschap Vee en Vlees*, C-455/06, EU:C:2008:258.

Opinion of Advocate General Bot in *ZZ v. Secretary of State for the Home Department*, C-300/11, EU:C:2012:563.

Opinion of Advocate General Cruz Villalón in *Coty Germany GmbH*, C-580/13, EU:C:2015:243.

Opinion of Advocate General Cruz Villalón in *Société Landsbanki Islands HF*, C-85/12, EU:C:2013:352.

Opinion of Advocate General Darmon in *Verholen and Others v. Sociale Verzekeringsbank Amsterdam*, joined cases C-87/90, C-88/90 and C-89/90, EU:C:1991:223.

Opinion of Advocate General Elmer in *Aannemersbedrijf P.K. Kraaijeveld BV e.a. v. Gedeputeerde Staten van Zuid-Holland*, C-72/95, EU:C:1996:135.

Opinion of Advocate General Jääskinen in *Bundeswettbewerbsbehörde v. Donau Chemie AG and Others*, C-536/11, EU:C:2013:67.

Opinion of Advocate General Jääskinen in *Liivimaa Lihaveis*, C-562/12, EU:C:2014:155.

Opinion of Advocate General Jääskinen in *Orizzonte Salute – Studio Infermieristico Associato v. Azienda Pubblica di Servizi alla persona San Valentino – Città di Levico Terme and Others*, C-61/14, EU:C:2015:307.

Opinion of Advocate General Jacobs in *Peterbroeck, Van Campenhout & Cie v. Belgian State*, C-312/93, EU:C:1994:184.

Opinion of Advocate General Jacobs in *van Schijndel v. Stichting Pensioenfonds voor Fysiotherapeuten*, joined cases C-430/93 and C-431/93, EU:C:1995:185.

Opinion of Advocate General Léger in *Kühne & Heitz NV v. Produktschap voor Pluimvee en Eieren*, C-453/00, EU:C:2003:350.

Opinion of Advocate General Maduro in *van der Weerd and Others v. Minister van Landbouw, Natuur en Voedselkwaliteit*, joined cases C-222/05 to C-225/05, EU:C:2007:124.

Opinion of Advocate General Mazak in *Banca Antoniana Popolare Veneta*, C-427/10, EU:C:2011:595.

Opinion of Advocate General Mengozzi in *Abdelhafid Bensada Benallal v. État belge*, C-161/15, EU:C:2016:3.

Opinion of Advocate General Mengozzi in *Rampion and Godard*, C-429/05, EU:C:2007:199.

Opinion of Advocate General Mischo in *Theresa Emmott v. Minister for Social Welfare and the Attorney General*, C-208/90, EU:C:1991:164.

Opinion of Advocate General Saggio in *Eco Swiss China Time Ltd v. Benetton International NV*, C-126/97, EU:C:1999:97.

Opinion of Advocate General Saggio in *Océano Grupo Editorial and Salvat Editores*, joined cases C-240/98 to C-244/98, EU:C:1999:620.

Opinion of Advocate General Sharpston in *Online Games Handels GmbH*, C-685/15, EU:C:2017:201.

Opinion of Advocate General Sharpston in *SC Star Storage SA and Others v. Institutul Național de Cercetare-Dezvoltare în Informatică (ICI) and Others*, joined cases C-439/14 and C-488/14, EU:C:2016:307.

Opinion of Advocate General Szpunar in *Finanmadrid EFC SA v. Jesús Vicente Albán Zambrano and Others*, C-49/14, EU:C:2015:746.

Opinion of Advocate General Szpunar in *Silvia Georgiana Câmpean*, C-200/14, EU:C:2016:99.

Opinion of Advocate General Tizzano in *Cofidis SA v. Jean-Louis Fredout*, C-473/00, EU:C:2002:239.

Opinion of Advocate General Tizzano in *Elisa María Mostaza Claro v. Centro Móvil Milenium SL*, C-168/05, EU:C:2006:265.

Opinion of Advocate General Trstenjak in *Asturcom Telecomunicaciones SL v. Cristina Rodríguez Nogueira*, C-40/08, EU:C:2009:305.

Opinion of Advocate General Trstenjak in *Pénzügyi Lízing*, C-137/08, EU:C:2010:401.

Opinion of Advocate General Wahl in *Macinský and Macinská*, C-482/12, EU:C:2013:765.

Opinion of Advocate General Wahl in *Sanchez Morcillo and Abril García (I)*, C-169/14, EU:C:2014:2110.

Opinion of Advocate General Warner in *Rewe v. Landwirtschaftskammer für das Saarland*, 33/76, EU:C:1976:167.

Opinion of Advocate General Wathelet in *Puligienica Facility Esco SpA (PFE) v. Airgest SpA*, C-689/13, EU:C:2015:263.

Opinion of Advocate General Wathelet in *Test Claimants (III) in the Franked Investment Income Group Litigation*, C-362/12, EU:C:2013:538.

ECtHR case-law

ECtHR judgment in *Airey v. Ireland*, application no. 6289/73.

ECtHR judgment in *Andret et autres v. France*, application no. 1956/02.

ECtHR judgment in *Avotiņš v. Latvia*, application no. 17502/07.

ECtHR judgment in *Avotiņš v. Latvia*, application no. 17502/07, Joint concurring opinion of Judges Lemmens and Briede, 3.

ECtHR judgment in *Borgers v. Belgium*, application no. 12005/86.

ECtHR judgment in *Bulut v. Austria*, application no. 17358/90.

ECtHR judgment in *Burdov v. Russia*, application no. 59498/00.

ECtHR judgment in *Clinique des Acacias et autres v. France*, applications no. 65399/01, 65406/01, 65405/01 and 65407/01.

ECtHR judgment in *Engel and Others v. Netherlands*, application no. 5100/71; 5101/71; 5102/71; 5354/72; 5370/72.

ECtHR judgment in *Eskelinen and Others v. Finland*, application no. 63235/00.

ECtHR judgment in *Ferrazzini v. Italy*, application no. 44759/98.

ECtHR judgment in *Göç v. Turkey*, application no. 36590/97.

ECtHR judgment in *Golder v. the United Kingdom*, application no. 4451/70.

ECtHR judgment in *Janosevic v. Sweden* Case, application no. 34619/97.

ECtHR judgment in *Jussila v. Finland*, application no. 73053/01.

ECtHR judgment in *Kress v. France* application no. 39594/98.

ECtHR judgment in *Menarini v. Italy*, application no. 43509/08.

ECtHR judgment in *Prikyan and Angelova v. Bulgaria*, application no. 44624/98.

ECtHR judgment in *Société Stenuit v. France*, application no. 11598/85.

ECtHR judgment in *Stanford v. United Kingdom*, application no. 16757/90.

ECtHR judgment in *Steel and Morris v. the United Kingdom*, application no. 68416/01.

ECtHR judgment in *Vermeulen v. Belgium*, application no. 19075/91.

Order of the European Commission for Human Righs, *X. & Co. Ltd. V. the Federal Republic of Germany*, application no. 3147/67.

Case-law of national courts

Judgment of the Cour de Cassation (FR), Assemblée plénière, in *Pourvoi N° 06-11343*, Bull. civ. 2007, N° 10, 21 décembre 2007.

Judgment of the Court of Appeal (UK) in *Dresser UK Ltd v. Falcongate Ltd* (1992) QB 502 522 H, CA, per Bingham L.J.

Judgment of the Court of Appeal (UK) in *Goldsmith v. Sperrings*, (1977) 2 All E.R. 557.

Judgment of the Court of Appeal (UK) in *Letang v. Cooper*, (1965) 1 Q.B. 232, per Diplock L.J.

Judgment of the Court of Appeal (UK) in *Lever Bros Ltd. v. Bell*, (1931) 1 K.B. 557, per Scrutton L.J.

Judgment of the Court of Appeal (UK) in *Official receiver v. Stern*, (2000) 1 WLR 2230, per Sir Richard Scott.

Judgment of the Court of King's Bench (UK) in *Holman v. Johnson*, (1775) 1 Cowp 341, per Lord Mansfield.

US Supreme Court judgment in *Burton v. Wilmington Parking Authority*, 365 U.S. 715, 81 S. Ct. 856, 6 L. Ed. 2 d 45 (1961).

US Supreme Court judgment in *Mitsubishi Motors Corporation v. Soler Chrysler Plymouth, Inc.*, 473 U.S. 614, 628 (1985).

US Supreme Court judgment in *Shelley v. Kraemer*, 334 U.S. 1, 68 S. Ct. 836, 92 L. Ed. 1161 (1948).

International Treaties and other international legislation

Convention of 27 September 1968 on jurisdiction and the enforcement of judgments in civil and commercial matters (Brussels Convention), OJ L 299, 31/12/1972, 32.

Council of Europe, European Convention for the Protection of Human Rights and Fundamental Freedoms (ECHR), as amended by Protocols Nos. 11 and 14, 4 November 1950, ETS 5.

Council of Europe, Protocol 11 to the European Convention for the Protection of Human Rights and Fundamental Freedoms, Restructuring the Control Machinery Established Thereby, 11 May 1994, ETS 155.

United Nations Commission on International Trade Law Model Law on International Commercial Arbitration (1985) (UNCITRAL), United Nations document Al40117, annex I, as adopted by the United Nations Commission on International Trade Law on 21 June 1985.

National legislation and preparatory works

Arbitration Act of the Netherlands – Code of Civil Procedure [*Wetboek van Burgerlijke Rechtsvordering (Rv) – Boek IV. Arbitrage*], wet van 1 december 1986, herziening van 2011.

Belgian Income Tax Code [*Code des Impôts sur les Revenues*] CIR de 1992.

French Consumer Code [*Code de la Consommation*] Loi nº 95-125 du 8 février 1995 en vigueur le 1er août 1995.

French New Code of Civil Procedure [*Nouveau Code de Procédure Civile*], version consolidée au 1 octobre 2016.

General Administrative Law Act of the Netherlands [*Algemene Wet Bestuursrecht*], wet van 4 juni 1992, als gewijzigd.

German Basic Law [*Grundgesetz für die Bundesrepublik Deutschland*] vom 23. Mai 1949 (BGBl. S. 1).

Italian Civil Code [*Codice Civile*], Regio Decreto 16 marzo 1942, n. 262, aggiornato il 21 aprile 2015.

Napoleonic Code, French Civil Code [*Code Napoléon, le Code civil des Français*], ordonné le 21 mars 1804.

Preparatory works for Swedish New Law on Legal Aid [*Ny rättshjälpslag*], Regeringens proposition 1996/97:9.

Spanish Arbitration Act [*Ley de Arbitraje*], 36/1988 de 23 de diciembre.